PRAISE FOR EMILY K. HOBSON'S *LAVE*.

Emily Hobson's illuminating book, *Lavender and Red,* transforms our understanding of queer history. Focusing on gay and lesbian internationalism and left solidarity politics in late Cold War San Francisco, she provides a deeply researched, surprising, and compelling account of the ways a politics of affiliation can expand forms of organization, practices, vision, and impact. The stories she tells offer us new historical narratives as resources for imagining new possible futures.
—Lisa Duggan, author of *The Twilight of Equality?: Neoliberalism, Cultural Politics, and the Attack on Democracy*

Lavender and Red deftly tells the story of the other "L" word: liberation. LGBTQ activists erupted in the 1960s committed to ending U.S. imperialism, militarism, racism, and all forms of oppression and exploitation. They fought not to win acceptance by the mainstream, heteropatriarchal society but to overturn it. By recovering the forgotten story of gay liberation, Emily Hobson revises the history of the U.S. left and reveals a political and intellectual history of how queer radicals understood and re-fashioned anti-imperialist, nationalist, feminist, and Third World thought to imagine new meanings for sexuality, community, and emancipatory politics. After reading this astonishing book, the standard Stonewall-to-marriage-equality narrative suddenly rings hollow.
—Robin D. G. Kelley, author of *Thelonious Monk: The Life and Times of an American Original*

Lavender and Red shines light on two of the most important queer colors, reminding us that somewhere over the rainbow lie visionary dreams of radical sexual politics and transformational social justice. An inspiring account of the 1970s and 1980s, when a strong gay and lesbian left fought against racism, sexism, colonialism, and war.
—Marc Stein, author of *Rethinking the Gay and Lesbian Movement*

In this superb book, Hobson writes the political and intellectual history of the gay liberation and lesbian feminist movements that linked sexual liberation to radical solidarity—the mobilizations against imperialism, capitalism, and racism, demanding universal health care and "money for AIDS, not for war." For too long, gay and lesbian activism in the 70s and 80s has been remembered as single-issue and racially white-washed. *Lavender and Red* is the antidote we've been waiting for.
—Laura Briggs, author of *Reproducing Empire: Race, Sex, Science and U.S. Imperialism in Puerto Rico*

Over the past decade, we have witnessed the emergence of revisionist work on the Black Power, antiwar, women of color feminist, and gay liberation movements. Emily Hobson's *Lavender and Red* is a brilliant addition to this vital body of scholarship. She rewrites the history of political struggles of the 1970s, 1980s, and 1990s and, most impressively, intertwines them.
—Sherie M. Randolph, author of *Florynce "Flo" Kennedy: The Life of a Black Feminist Radical*

Lavender and Red is a page turner, not the case for most well-researched academic works; this story of liberation and solidarity in the gay and lesbian left, focused on the San Francisco Bay area in the 1970s and 1980s, is inspiring as well as cautionary, a primer for social justice activists today as well as a solid history in the field of social movement history and theory.
—Roxanne Dunbar-Ortiz, author of *An Indigenous Peoples' History of the United States*

The publisher gratefully acknowledges the generous support of the Anne G. Lipow Endowment Fund for Social Justice and Human Rights of the University of California Press Foundation, which was established by Stephen M. Silberstein.

COVER IMAGE

"Unite to Fight! June 28 / Day of Solidarity with Gay Struggles"

June 28, 1969 was the date of the Stonewall riots in New York City.

Poster designed by Donna Pillar, published and distributed by Inkworks Press, Oakland, Calif. (1974–2015), 1976.

The face, a coarse halftone dot image of a woman at a feminist demonstration, was taken from "Lucy Stone," an early second-wave feminism poster published in 1970 by Times Change Press, New York, NY (1970–1974). The text read: "In education, in marriage, in everything, disappointment is the lot of woman [. . .] Lucy Stone, 1855." A first edition of that poster credited Su Negrin as graphic artist, a second edition of the poster labeled it TCP poster #2 and did not.

Image courtesy Lincoln Cushing / Docs Populi.
Image description courtesy of Lincoln Cushing.

Lavender and Red

Lavender and Red

*Liberation and Solidarity in
the Gay and Lesbian Left*

Emily K. Hobson

UNIVERSITY OF CALIFORNIA PRESS

University of California Press, one of the most
distinguished university presses in the United States,
enriches lives around the world by advancing scholarship
in the humanities, social sciences, and natural sciences. Its
activities are supported by the UC Press Foundation and
by philanthropic contributions from individuals and
institutions. For more information, visit www.ucpress.edu.

University of California Press
Oakland, California

© 2016 by The Regents of the University of California

Library of Congress Cataloging-in-Publication Data

Names: Hobson, Emily K., author.
Title: Lavender and red : liberation and solidarity in the
   gay and lesbian left / Emily K. Hobson.
Other titles: American crossroads ; 44.
Description: Oakland, California : University of
   California Press, [2016] | Series: American crossroads;
   44 | Includes bibliographical references and index.
Identifiers: LCCN 2016017328 (print) | LCCN 2016018860
   (ebook) | ISBN 9780520279056 (cloth : alk. paper) |
   ISBN 9780520279063 (pbk. : alk. paper) | ISBN
   9780520965706 ()
Subjects: LCSH: Gay liberation movement—United
   States. | Sexual minorities—United States.
Classification: LCC HQ76.8.U5 H63 2016 (print) |
   LCC HQ76.8.U5 (ebook) | DDC 306.76/60973—dc23
LC record available at https://lccn.loc.gov/2016017328

Manufactured in the United States of America

25 24 23 22 21 20 19 18 17
10 9 8 7 6 5 4 3 2

In memory of
Armando
Bill and Branch
Callie and Carl
David and Don
Emmanuel
Hank and Howard
Jade, Jeff, and José
and Jim, times two
and John, times three
Keith
Larry
Margarita, Martin, and Marvin
Michael, times four, and Miguel
Phil and Phillip
Regina, Rodrigo, and Ron
Sam, Simeon, and Stephen
Tede, Terry, Tim, Timo, Tita, Tom

Eileen Hansen (1951–2016)
Horacio N. Roque Ramírez (1969–2015)

and the many unnamed

Contents

Illustrations

Acknowledgments

First and foremost, I offer my deep thanks to all the activists who made the histories I seek to narrate and understand in the pages that follow. Many are named and others are not, but I am deeply grateful to all who have dreamed, built, and struggled through the politics of sexual liberation and radical solidarity.

This book's dedication honors first the many activists who died before I could meet them, most gone years before I began my research and most, though not all, taken by AIDS. I list their first names to recognize the unknowability and intimacy of our collective losses. All these activists appear again in the book by full name or through organizations in which they participated. Two other people whom I was fortunate to know died just as I was completing the book. Eileen Hansen was a dedicated and generous activist central to the AIDS Action Pledge and the 1987 civil disobedience at the Supreme Court; I am indebted to her contributions to my research and share in her widely felt loss. Horacio N. Roque Ramírez was a treasured scholar-activist of queer and Latina/o histories, oral history, and Central American studies. I cherished him as a colleague and wish he were here to critique my work and to keep writing.

This is also a book about people still living, and I am deeply grateful to all the individuals I interviewed who gave generously of their time and reflections. I look forward to their responses to this book; of course, any flaws of fact or understanding are my own. I especially thank all those whose words appear in the pages that follow: Leonel Argüello,

Amy Bank, Lucrecia Bermudez, Bill Blackburn, Henry (Camo) Bortman, Catherine Cusic, John D'Emilio, Pam David, Linda Farthing, Carol Fields, Brian Freeman, Marcia Gallo, Ellen Gavin, Ruth Grabowski, Roberto Gurdián, Eileen Hansen, Rebecca Hensler, Charlie Hinton, Diane Jones, Julie Light, Ruth Mahaney, Ana Quirós, Kate Raphael, Michelle Roland, Martha Sacasa, Lupita Sequeira, Dora María Tellez, Dan Wohlfeiler, and Joel Zúñiga Traña. Joel and Amy gave especially generously of their time to help me contact others and discussed their experiences with great honesty. I also thank Amy, Sofia Bank Criquillion, Benjamin Bank Criquillion, Ana Criquillion, and Adriana Aguinaga for their warm hospitality in Nicaragua.

In addition to those named above, a good many other people provided research leads, helped me to understand the contexts that shaped gay, lesbian, and queer radicalism from the 1960s through 1990s, or provided me with archival materials. Chuck Barragán opened his home so that I could explore Tede Matthews's treasure trove of the gay, lesbian, and queer left. Adrianne Bank and Amanda Newstetter provided me invaluable access to Amy Bank's letters. Bill Blackburn, Ellen Gavin, Eileen Hansen, John Lindsay-Poland, Naomi Schapiro, and Dan Wohlfeiler added to their personal recollections with important materials from Nicaraguan solidarity and AIDS activism. Mrs. Lois White, Douglas White, Jane Lazarre, and Robert Levering offered moving insights into the committed activism of their son, brother, and friend Simeon White. My fellow radical historian Max Elbaum offered me crucial insights into the 1970s left. Bob Siedle-Khan was one of the first individuals I talked with for this project, and his ongoing interest encouraged me when I faltered. I also benefited from conversations with Jan Adams, Otto Aguilar, Tommi Avicolli Mecca, Jennifer Beach, Diana Block, Kasey Brenner, Cathy Cade, Leslie Cagan, Susan Colson, Penn Garvin, David Gilbert, Jeremy Grainger, Jim Green, Deeg Gold, Rebecca Gordon, Luz Guerra, Michael Hoffman, Ericka Huggins, Mary Isham, Lenn Keller, Don Kilhefner, William Maldonado, Julieta Martínez and Elena Hendrick, Silvia Martínez, Terri Massin, Marisa Monasterio, Holly Near, Michael Novick, Lisa Roth, Margaret Randall, Nora Roman, Ces Rosales, Estelle Schneider, Ann Schwartz, Mayra Sirias, Carmen Vázquez, and Ken Yale.

My research is rooted in archives and indebted to archivists. I thank especially Rebekah Kim, David Reichard, Jacob Richards, and Alex Barrows at the Gay, Lesbian, Bisexual, and Transgender Historical Society (GLBTHS); Loni Shibumaya at the ONE National Gay and Lesbian Archives; Claude Marks of the Freedom Archives; Rukshana Singh of the Southern California Library for Social Studies and Research; Lincoln Cushing; Alan Miller of the Canadian Lesbian and Gay Archives; and multiple staff and volunteers at the San Francisco Public Library, UC Berkeley Bancroft and Ethnic Studies Libraries, New York Public Library, and the Lesbian Herstory Archives.

This book has benefited tremendously from the incisive feedback of Laura Briggs, Roxanne Dunbar-Ortiz, and three anonymous reviewers, as well as the patient shepherding of Niels Hooper and the hard work of Bradley Depew, Ryan Furtkamp, Cindy Fulton, Steven Baker, and Laurie Prendergast. I am beholden to Niels for his ongoing enthusiasm and so grateful to Laura for her years of mentorship and her deep historical insights. Susie Woo read nearly every word of the manuscript, helped improve many passages, and kept me going with her infectious cheer. I look forward to more of her incisive scholarship on kinship in the aftermath of the Korean War.

Lavender and Red began as a dissertation in the Department of American Studies and Ethnicity at the University of Southern California, which has created a model for graduate education by dedicating itself to students of color and first-generation students. I am very proud to have been a student of my advisor, George J. Sánchez, and of my committee members Robin D. G. Kelley, David Román, Ruth Wilson Gilmore, and Bill Deverell. George's slow, attentive smile buoys me to know when I get it right; his network of students stretches far and wide, and at conferences we make the giddiest of family reunions. I appreciate Robin for so many things, not the least being his care to remember the differences between the academy, intellectual life, and the movement. David pushed me to see this book's conceptual archive from nearly our first meeting and is one of the most nurturing scholars I know; I hope to live up to his model as a mentor someday. I cannot imagine *Lavender and Red* without Ruthie Gilmore, who provoked my move from dissertation to book by asking at my defense: How does alliance become more than the sum of its parts?

While at USC I benefited from Provost's and Beaumont Fellowships, travel grants from the Center for Feminist Research, a Dissertation Fellowship and a Huntington Library Fellowship from the John R. Haynes & Dora Haynes Foundation, and a Dana & David Dornsife College Distinguished Postdoctoral Teaching Fellowship. Beyond my committee I am indebted to the teaching and guidance of the late Maria Elena Martínez, Roberto Lint Sagarena, Macarena Gomez-Barrís, Jack

Halberstam, Sarah Gualtieri, Viet Nguyen, Kara Keeling, Jane Iwamura, Lanita Jacobs-Huey, and John Carlos Rowe, and to the administrative expertise and community-building labor of Jujuana Preston, Sandra Hopwood, and Kitty Lai. Laura Pulido and Diana Williams provided especially important mentorship during my time as a postdoctoral fellow. While in the Department of Feminist Studies at the University of California, Santa Barbara, I benefited from a Dissertation Fellowship and employment as a lecturer; from the mentorship of Leila Rupp, Eileen Boris, and Mireille Miller-Young; and from the friendship of Monica López, Zakiyyah Iman Jackson, Lisa Slavid, and Nathaniel Burke.

It has been wonderful to make a home as an assistant professor in the Department of History and the Program in Gender, Race, and Identity at the University of Nevada, Reno. I completed the last of my research and much of the writing for this book at UNR, benefiting from a Scholarly and Creative Activities Grant and Junior Faculty Research from the university and a Joan Heller-Diane Bernard Fellowship from the Center for LGBTQ Studies (CLAGS, City University of New York). Among my colleagues at UNR I am especially grateful to Jen Hill and Debbie Boehm in the Program in Gender, Race, and Identity and, in the Department of History, to Chris Church, Linda Curcio-Nagy, Greta DeJong, Dennis Dworkin, Martha Hildreth, Jennifer LeZotte, Bruce Moran, Jennifer Ng, Meredith Oda, Elizabeth Raymond, Eleanor Rivera, Ned Schoolman, Cameron Strang, and Charles Tshimanga-Kashanga. None of us could function without Jennifer Baryol. I also thank my colleagues and friends Jane Detweiler, Katherine Fusco, Patrick Jackson, Bev Lassiter, Albert Lee, Eunkang Koh, Louis Niebur, Amy Pason, Daniel Enrique Pérez, Brett Van Hoesen, and Erica Westhoff. My students at UNR have pushed me to become a better scholar; I thank Ivón Padilla-Rodriguez and Alisse Ulrich for research assistance and Ivón, Escenthio Marigny Jr., Maddie Poore, Levi Rojas, Maggie Salas-Crespo, and Erica Wirthlin for doing so much to generate intellectual and political community on campus and in Reno.

I have benefited from the feedback of many audiences at conferences, workshops, and presentations in developing the arguments and analyses in *Lavender and Red,* and extend a particular appreciation to the Committee on Lesbian, Gay, Bisexual, and Transgender History for its intellectual and professional community. Among many wonderful colleagues, Christina Hanhardt, Priya Kandaswamy, and Aaron Lecklider have become among my favorite friends and big siblings in academic life. For intellectual exchange, ongoing generosity, and making conferences fun, I especially thank Laura Barraclough, Dan Berger, Kathleen Belew, Maylei Blackwell, Jennifer Brier, Margot Canaday, John D'Emilio, Rebecca Davis, Erin Durban-Albrecht, Gill Frank, Marcia Gallo, Victoria Gonzáles-Rivera and Karen Kampwirth, Lucy Grinnell, Eva Hageman, Nancy Hewitt, Tammy Ho, Kwame Holmes, Dan Martinez HoSang, Moon-Ho Jung, Ronak Kapadia, Regina Kunzel, Viet Le, Ian Lekus, Amanda Littauer, Alexis Lothian, Alejandra Marchevsky, Kevin Mumford, Clare Potter, Gautam Premnath, Sherie Randolph, Chandan Reddy, Renee Romano, Don Romesburg, Dan Royles, Anahi Russo Garrido, Josie Saldaña-Portillo, Nayan Shah, Stefanie Snider, Tamara Spira, Marc Stein, Tim Stewart-Winter, Emily Thuma, Judy Tzu-Chun Wu, Stephen Vider, and Greg Youmans.

Before I completed my PhD, I gained a critical education as a staff member of the Center for Third World Organizing and Californians for Justice, in Education for Action and UNITE at Harvard-Radcliffe, and in networks that produced the Catalyst Project. I learned a great deal from and with Gina Acebo, Faith Adiele, Frances Calpotura, Shash Yázhí Charley, Mike Chavez, Chris Crass, Nicole Davis, Nisrin Elamin, Mickey Ellinger, Mark Engler, Adam Hefty, Isaac Simon Hodes, Carmen Iñiguez, Yvonne Paul, Cathy Rion Starr, Rinku Sen, Abdi Soltani, and Rosslyn Wuchinich, and am grateful for our ongoing connections.

So many good friends have enriched my life over the past several years. I extend my love especially to my dear friends Wendy Cheng, Meredith Oda, Hannah Tashjian, and Blake Ulveling, and to Michelle Commander, Araceli Esparza, Chris Farrish, Laura Sachiko Fugikawa, Jason Goldman, Perla Guerrero, Jesus Hernández, Hillary Jenks, Imani Kai Johnson, Nisha Kunte, Rebecca Meyer, Mark Padoongpatt, Jen Scherba, Micaela Smith, Jared Stanley, and Jason Warriner. Eleanor, Frances, and Eloise are great joys. Ann and Dickran Tashjian have fed, housed, and encouraged me more times than I can count.

I treasure queer chosen family and am so glad to include my own and Felicia's roots within it. Erin O'Brien, Kimi Lee, and Sophie Fanelli are a dream team, and Janko, Berlin, Lucy, Deb, and Makua and Macaroni the best crew. I delight in the laughter and drama of Phyllis Perez, Lena Perez, and Michaela and Eva Marie and in our holiday parties. Bekki and Neil Bergeson and Patricia Decker and Jack Delay have nurtured my ties to the Pacific Northwest. My brother, Jeff Hobson, has inspired me for over forty years, and in the long course of researching this book he, Kim Seashore, and Benjamin and Nathan have sustained me with a home back home full of everyday joys.

My mother's and father's affection, intellectual curiosity, and support are stamped on every page of this book. I am so grateful to each of them for having guided me to see myself as well as others in the past. I cherish my dad Wayne's deep interest in his children and treasure the memories of our road trips, during which he taught me to think about historical memory, to pack snacks, and to read maps—good advice for archival research as well as for hours in the car. I thank him and Sharon for steadfast encouragement over the past several years. My mother, Nancy, is my savviest cheerleader and the person who taught me how to observe closely as well as to speak up; I appreciate her love and strength more than I can say. I channel her whenever I step into the garden as well as each time I sit down to edit, as in both places the joy comes from extending care.

Felicia Perez has seen this book from start to finish, helping me hash out my ideas over and over and providing great insights into the present as well as the past. Amidst her own work and illness, she has sustained me in more ways than I ever imagined another person might, and I cannot imagine this book without her influence as a teacher and organizer or without her honesty, passion, and creative mind. It is rare to meet someone who has such good comic timing that their funny stories never get old; rarer still to make inside jokes together. Felicia is my ring of keys and I love her beyond all telling.

Abbreviations

The following abbreviations are used frequently in the book. Not all are specifically gay and lesbian left organizations.

AAP	AIDS Action Pledge
AAWO	Alliance Against Women's Oppression
ACT NOW	AIDS Coalition to Network, Organize, and Win
ACT UP	AIDS Coalition to Unleash Power
AMNLAE	Asociación Mujeres Nicaragüenses Luisa Amanda Espinoza (Nicaragua)
BAGL	Bay Area Gay Liberation
BOWU	Berkeley-Oakland Women's Union
CEP-SIDA	Colectivo de Educación Popular contra el SIDA (Nicaragua)
CHF	Committee for Homosexual Freedom
CISAS	Centro de Información y Asesorías en Salud (Nicaragua)
CISPES	Committee in Solidarity with the People of El Salvador
CMJ	Citizens for Medical Justice
CNE	Casa Nicaragüense de Español (Nicaragua)

CHRICA/CHRIA	Committee for Health Rights in Central America/ Committee for Health Rights in the Americas
FORMICA FAG	Fags Organizing to Resist Militarism in Central America—Fight AIDS Group
FSLN	Frente Sandinista de Liberacíon Nacional (Nicaragua)
GALA	Gay Latino Alliance
GLF	Gay Liberation Front
GPNR	Gay People for the Nicaraguan Revolution
GSCR	Gays in Solidarity with the Chilean Resistance
GWL	Gay Women's Liberation
KDP	Katipunan ng ma Demokratikong Pilipino (Union of Democratic Filipinos)
LAG	Livermore Action Group
LAGAI	Lesbians and Gays Against Intervention
LAPV	Lesbians Against Police Violence
MINSA	Ministerio de Salud (Sandinista Ministry of Health, Nicaragua)
NAEP	Nicaragua AIDS Education Project
NIN	Non-Intervention in Nicaragua Committee
PFOC	Prairie Fire Organizing Committee
RGMU	Revolutionary Gay Men's Union
RPCC	Revolutionary People's Constitutional Convention (Black Panther Party)
RU	Revolutionary Union
SANOE	Stop AIDS Now Or Else
SDS	Students for a Democratic Society
SFPD	San Francisco Police Department
SFWAR	San Francisco Women Against Rape
SFWU	San Francisco Women's Union
SIR	Society for Individual Rights
SLA	Symbionese Liberation Army
TWGC	Third World Gay Caucus

Introduction

In March 1988, thousands of lesbian and gay activists took to the streets of San Francisco to protest war in Central America (figure 1). United States president Ronald Reagan, falsely claiming that the forces of Nicaragua's socialist government had crossed into Honduras, had sent 3,200 US soldiers to the region to prepare for a military assault. He turned back this intervention after significant protests around the United States, including ten days of demonstrations in San Francisco. Lesbian and gay radicals were key to organizing the San Francisco protests, and among other contributions they mobilized two specifically queer anti-intervention marches, the first numbering between 2,000 and 3,000 people and the second over 4,000.[1]

Participants in these protests claimed a long history of anti-militarist, anti-imperialist organizing as lesbians and gay men. As Kate Raphael stated at the week's closing rally, "Since 1980, gay men and especially lesbians have been in the leadership of the Central America solidarity movements. We have fought with you in meetings, we have worked with you in the fields of Nicaragua, and we have been with you in jail." Tede Matthews, reporting for the local gay and lesbian newspaper the *San Francisco Sentinel,* expanded the historical narrative further with a timeline that traced Bay Area lesbian and gay activism in solidarity with Latin America to the early 1970s. AIDS activist Guillermo Gonzalez spoke out about his frustration that despite their long-standing presence, "gay people of color are invisible to the left," and he defined

FIGURE 1. Lesbians and gay men lead a march against US intervention in Central America, San Francisco, March 18, 1988. Photograph by Rick Gerharter. Courtesy Rick Gerharter.

lesbian and gay solidarity with Central America as one way out of that invisibility and beyond a single-issue, racially limited gay politics. All three of these people described the Reagan administration as a common enemy, one that gay men and lesbians in the United States shared with Central Americans. They defined anti-war and anti-imperialist commitments as crucial to lesbian and gay movement building.[2]

Raphael, Matthews, and Gonzalez were three among many participants in the gay and lesbian left, a movement that stretched from the heights of the 1960s to the depths of the AIDS crisis and that defined sexual liberation and radical solidarity as interdependent. Gay and lesbian leftists saw heterosexism as interconnected with war, racism, and capitalism, each system using the other as a mechanism and support. They argued that full sexual freedom depended on anti-imperialist and anti-militarist change and that, by organizing as gay and lesbian radicals, they could achieve multiple and overlapping goals.

The gay and lesbian left did not simply pursue alliance between distinct political causes, but also, more aspirationally, worked to forge an integrated and nonbifurcated politics. Its participants saw sexual liberation and radical solidarity as constituted within each other rather than as wholly separate. They defined gay and lesbian identities not only as forms of desire but also as political affiliations that could create the

conditions of possibility to set desire free. And, by pursuing their politics across bodily, local, and global as well as national scales, gay and
lesbian leftists crafted a vision for change that moved beyond liberal
and neoliberal inclusion in the United States or other capitalist states.[3]

A history of the gay and lesbian left moves against narratives that
approach US lesbian, gay, bisexual, transgender, and queer activism only
through a domestic political frame, as well as those that assume that
when LGBT and queer activists do look globally, they do so only by
exporting their goals outward and imposing perceptions from the Global North onto the Global South. Certainly, domestic politics, national
agendas, and globalization have been major currents within sexual politics, and they have shaped gay and lesbian radicalism as well as other
aspects of queer life. But there has also been another story worth telling.
The gay and lesbian left drew inspiration for sexual as well as other
freedoms from anti-colonial, anti-imperialist, and anti-capitalist movements around the world. In addition, the gay and lesbian left was a
transnational phenomenon. It held strength not only in multiple US cities
but also in Britain, Canada, Mexico, Argentina, and Nicaragua, among
many other countries.[4] Gay and lesbian leftists communicated with one
another across disparate locations, and they shared investments in looking beyond national borders and pursuing internationalist radicalism.

Aware of this context, *Lavender and Red* addresses the gay and lesbian left from the perspective of one particular location in the United
States: the San Francisco Bay Area, especially the city of San Francisco
and to a lesser extent Berkeley and Oakland. The gay and lesbian left
flourished in the Bay Area, gaining strength from the converging currents
of queer life and radical politics that have long lent San Francisco special
meaning. In addition and more unexpectedly, the gay and lesbian left
was fueled and given direction by circuits of migration, exile, and travel
linking San Francisco to Central America. My focus on the San Francisco Bay Area draws on a tradition of local studies in LGBT and queer
history, but also expands the meaning of such local studies to larger
scales. By building queer life through radical internationalism, Bay Area
gay and lesbian leftists defined a politics typically conceived of as personal and domestic—that of sexuality—in relation to global concerns
shaped by the place of the United States in the world.

. . .

The history traced in this book moves across the second half of the Cold
War—the period from 1969 to 1991, which began, as a participant in

the 1970s gay and lesbian documentary *Word Is Out* put it, "on this other side of 1968."[5] In 1968, North Vietnam's Tet Offensive presented US military defeat in Southeast Asia as a serious possibility; Dr. Martin Luther King Jr. and Robert F. Kennedy were assassinated; the Democratic Party fielded a pro-war candidate; and uprisings around the world, especially in France, Mexico, and the United States, pushed many radicals to see themselves at the verge of global revolution. While gay politics had gained ground since the mid-1960s, a movement for "gay liberation" truly exploded following the Stonewall Riots in New York City in June 1969—a rebellion that mobilized a multiracial mix of "street kids" and "queens," trans of color activists Sylvia Rivera and Marsha P. Johnson prominent among them. New Yorkers formed the Gay Liberation Front immediately after Stonewall, naming themselves after the National Liberation Fronts of Algeria and Vietnam, while members of Berkeley's Gay Liberation Theater articulated anti-militarist gay identity by claiming that "No Vietnamese Ever Called Me a Queer."[6] As gay liberation and lesbian feminism grew, their participants pursued self-determination at intimate and gendered scales, as when Berkeley activist Konstantin Berlandt celebrated New Yorker Jim Fouratt "turning a militant macho fist into a queen's finger snap."[7] Activists remade sexuality and gender through their radical alliances: the members of Gay Women's Liberation, a major Bay Area lesbian feminist group, were inspired by their support for the Black Panther Party to develop a politics of collective self-defense that blended resistance to rape with support for the revolutionary underground.

While these beginnings laid a foundation, what truly defined the gay and lesbian left was not that it was born in the late 1960s but that it grew for years thereafter. Quite a lot happened after Stonewall. Over the course of the 1970s and 1980s, gay and lesbian leftists pursued an interconnected vision of liberation and solidarity, a combination they frequently represented through the metaphor "lavender and red"—the first color indicating gay and lesbian sexualities, the second an internationalist left.[8] They engaged socialist and women of color feminism and struggled against the US and global New Right. They organized as lesbians and gay men for peace and justice in Central America and drew on lessons from Central American solidarity to organize direct action against the political crisis of AIDS. Their efforts find legacies today in contemporary queer activism, including queer work against prisons, queer immigrant organizing, queer involvement in Palestinian solidarity, and the Black Lives Matter movement.

Despite such contributions, certain narratives that dominate queer studies, LGBT/queer history, and histories of post–World War II social movements have obscured the history of the gay and lesbian left. Queer studies has tended to assume that gay and lesbian politics of the 1970s and 1980s rested on static and essentialist conceptions of sexual identity. Tied to this assumption is the idea that, in the aftermath of Stonewall, gay and lesbian politics found only two forms of expression—separatist radicalism and liberal electoral politics—and that both of these modes were overwhelmingly white and inattentive to race and class. Such a narrow portrait of the 1970s and 1980s bolsters contrasts between the supposedly fixed categories of "gay" and "lesbian" and the slippages and contingencies that lend analytical power to "queer." Yet any dip into the archives of lesbian, gay, bisexual, transgender, and queer activism undermines this simple narrative, which papers over as much as it reveals. As is true today, many who marked themselves as gay or lesbian in the past conceived of sexuality, sexual identities, and sexual politics in dynamic, even fluid terms and understood sexuality as intersecting with gender, race, class, and nation. Further, many gay and lesbian radicals of the 1970s and 1980s rejected both separatism and liberalism in favor of multi-issue alliances and left movement building.

In 2004, Roderick Ferguson helped propel a crucial shift in queer studies when he observed that black lesbian feminists of the 1970s and 1980s, along with women of color feminists more broadly, approached identity as a flexible and changing "goal" and a space of contestation—something that must be "constantly contravened to address the variety of social contradictions that nationalism strives to conceal."[9] While scholars of queer studies had tended to imagine critiques of essentialism as original to the 1990s, Ferguson demonstrated their earlier genealogy in the Combahee River Collective and other groups that generated what has come to be known, following Kimberlé Crenshaw, as intersectional analysis.[10] As Ferguson points out, Combahee used identity not to reinforce boundaries of race, gender, or sexuality but rather to question them. The group organized as black women, and largely as black lesbians, to challenge the ways that "black" remained imagined as male and "women" and "lesbian" as white.

The gay and lesbian left was not the same as women of color feminism, though the two formations did overlap and shared common geographies. Much of the gay and lesbian left was white and included men; these activists learned from, rather than created, the intersectional feminism that Cherríe Moraga called "theory in the flesh."[11] More broadly, however, the gay and lesbian left and women of color feminism shared a willingness to see identity not as a rigid container of political claims but as a flexible medium with which to reimagine political possibility. Tracing the history of the gay and lesbian left thus helps to highlight the constructed meanings—and the transformative potential—of sexuality and sexual politics.

Building on these points, a history of the gay and lesbian left intervenes against dominant narratives that define the so-called Stonewall moment as foundational yet exceptional, initiating radical change yet out of step with the general character of LGBT activism over time. Aligned with broader patterns of US exceptionalism, such narratives contend that the neoliberal incorporation of sexual minority rights proves lesbian, gay, bisexual, transgender, and queer radicalism to be ineffectual, isolated, and rare.[12] But a fuller accounting of the past shows that an anti-imperialist, anti-militarist gay and lesbian left survived well past Stonewall and that this gay and lesbian left fostered alliances that redefined sexuality.

In other words, *Lavender and Red* challenges Stonewall exceptionalism, or the false narrative that gay and lesbian radicalism flared up spontaneously in 1969 but quickly disappeared.[13] One of the reasons that challenging such a narrative matters is that the framework of Stonewall exceptionalism leaves us few insights for analyzing or building activism and organizing today. It implies that those who seek radical change must simply lie in wait for opportunity and that radical transformations will always, inevitably, be short-lived. By contrast, a history of the gay and lesbian left traces the day-to-day, month-to-month, and year-to-year work of movement building, including not only activists' successes but also their frustrations and missteps.

Accounts of the rapid disappearance of gay and lesbian radicalism after Stonewall are linked to broader claims that 1960s movements disintegrated through violence, cultural nationalism, and sectarianism. Often summarized as the "good 1960s" versus "bad 1960s," such claims paper over the role of the US state in imprisoning and assassinating radicals and in repressing dissent.[14] They also typically center white men in the New Left at the expense of black and other radicals of color and participants in feminist and gay and lesbian activism (all categories that must be understood as overlapping). We can hear a curious echo between these claims about the 1960s and the assumptions in queer studies that obscure the gay and lesbian left.

The obsession with 1960s "failure" obscures a good deal, not least being the breadth of the influence that anti-imperialist politics held both across the globe and in the United States. Attention to anti-imperialism helps to explain the length of the "long 1960s," a period typically marked from 1955 through 1975 and whose history challenges the simple bifurcation of the era into good and bad. The year 1955 marks the Montgomery Bus Boycott and the Bandung Conference, a meeting of African and Asian decolonizing nations, while 1975 and signals the end of the Vietnam War (the "fall" or "liberation" of Saigon, depending on one's perspective). Across the long 1960s a wide assortment of radicals—ideologically diverse, working in conversation, and often aspiring to be a common "Movement"—came to reject the idea that the US nation-state set the horizon of equality and freedom. They created not just a "New Left" set apart from the Communist Party, but a "Third World Left" motivated by anticolonial struggle and Chinese, Cuban, and diasporic black revolutions. They pursued Chicano, Asian American, Native American, and black liberation, forged an antiwar movement and radical underground, and organized women of color, socialist, and other radical feminisms.[15] They brought anti-imperialism into new areas of struggle and expanded what anti-imperialism meant, including by naming the centrality of heterosexual norms and violence to colonial power. For the radicals in this book, anti-imperialism was a radical tradition that sutured together multiple movements. It gained meaning in three major phases: at the height of the late 1960s and early 1970s through Black Power and opposition to the Vietnam War; in the 1970s through socialist and women of color feminism and a growing attention to US intervention in Latin America; and across the 1980s through the Central American solidarity movement.

Gay and lesbian radicals drew on and contributed to anti-imperialist politics by analyzing how colonialism and capitalism restricted sexuality and gender and by arguing that anti-imperialist struggles might expand sexual and gender freedom. They not only pursued alliances between gay and other causes, but also worked to challenge norms of womanhood, manhood, and sexual behavior. They began to argue, for example, that military masculinity was oppressive to US soldiers as well as their targets, and that by claiming distance from such masculinity, gay liberation might help to end the US war in Vietnam. As another example, they formed practices of lesbian feminism through and in relation to the radical underground. The appeal of these arguments was made evident in their proliferation, in their utility for organizing, and in individuals' life stories. Multiple gay radicals became draft resisters or conscientious objectors and linked their gayness to their refusal to fight in the Vietnam War.[16] Multiple lesbian feminists came to see their collective households as sites of shelter for political fugitives as well as survivors of gendered violence.

An alternate form of the "good 1960s" and "bad 1960s" narrative describes gay liberation and lesbian feminism as facing only hostility, rather than support, from the straight left. Certainly such hostility existed, yet it was complex and contested, not monolithic or unchanging. As Aaron Lecklider and others have shown, the US left in the 1930s and 1940s included significant numbers of writers, artists, and activists who identified as homosexual or acted on same-sex desire.[17] These individuals' histories shaped the 1950s emergence of the gay and lesbian (then termed "homophile") movement. Across the bulk of the twentieth century, queer radicals faced proscriptions against homosexuality by the Communist Party, as well as perceptions of homosexuality as a decadent and bourgeois outgrowth of capitalism and empire. Although Lenin decriminalized homosexuality in 1917, Stalin recriminalized it in 1934, and other Communist and socialist nations and parties followed this lead.[18] Possibilities for radical sexual politics seemed to expand by the late 1950s as the New Left moved away from the Communist Party and toward critiques of cultural repression. But many anti-colonial and racial liberation projects mobilized heteronormative frameworks of gender and family, if in part to redress the sexual violence and insult of colonial and imperial regimes.[19] The Cuban Revolution imprisoned sexual dissidents in work camps throughout the 1960s and pushed many off the island in the 1980 Mariel boatlift; the US-based Venceremos Brigades to Cuba voiced formal opposition to gay liberation in 1970 and banned out gay and lesbian participants through the early 1980s.[20] Antigay attitudes were often blamed primarily on Black Power, yet gay and lesbian leftists often met their sharpest opposition from white radicals who sought to inhabit a masculinity they associated with black and white working-class men.[21]

Facing this context, gay and lesbian leftists built a way out of no way. One means by which this book tracks their politics is through the keywords "liberation" and "solidarity," which roughly mirror the metaphor of "lavender and red" to describe the goal of bridging sexual politics with an internationalist left. At the height of the late 1960s, gay and lesbian radicals adapted the concept of liberation from black and anti-colonial movements. In calling for "gay liberation" and "lesbian feminist liberation," they sought not just rights or inclusion but a fundamental transformation in the meanings of sexuality, a wholesale end to sexual limits and norms. They pursued liberation through political activism and through art and performance, by building a counterculture, and by rethinking sex itself.[22] Gay and lesbian leftists described themselves as the central proponents of a liberation agenda and often laid claim as its true inheritors, not just because they pursued it intensely but because they defined it as interconnected with "solidarity." They argued that sexual liberation could be won only through a broader social revolution and that, conversely, sexual liberation was a necessary part of revolutionary change. Further, they held that because gay and lesbian liberation challenged both material structures of oppression and leftist hostility, it could be won only through mutual support across difference. Solidarity described a day-to-day habit of activism: the work of showing up at protests, joining campaigns, and building a culture of political camaraderie. In simple terms, liberation was the theory and solidarity the practice. (My formulation remakes a phrase from New York lesbian feminist Ti-Grace Atkinson—"Feminism is the theory, lesbianism is the practice"—to recognize the provocations and pleasures activists found in their goals.[23])

Liberation and solidarity inspired gay and lesbian leftists in shifting ways, and became keywords around which viewpoints and ideas accrued, not fixed yardsticks to measure activists' work.[24] In tying together liberation and solidarity, gay and lesbian leftists drew models from socialist and women of color feminists, who described sexism as interwoven with racism, capitalism, and empire and who used Third Worldist and Marxist thought to critique both hegemonic and radical nationalisms.[25] Feminist influences proved central not only for lesbian radicals but also for radical gay men, who in addition to supporting women's organizing sought to remake masculinity and effeminacy. Thus, a history of the gay and lesbian left underscores the multigender power of feminisms and helps to explain how and why lesbians and gay men forged coalitions against right-wing attack.

By the late 1970s and 1980s, solidarity gained another crucial meaning due to the growth of the Central American solidarity movement opposing US intervention in Nicaragua, El Salvador, and Guatemala. This movement gained particular strength among Central and other Latin American immigrants, exiles, and refugees in San Francisco's Mission District. As Cary Cordova has explained, Central and other Latin Americans in San Francisco forged a barrio, or neighborhood, transnationalism that linked local organizing to networks across the Americas.[26] The Mission District was also important to lesbian and gay activism and communities, and so it grounded lesbian and gay engagements with Central American solidarity. Lesbian and gay radicals not only joined the broader solidarity movement but formed specifically lesbian and gay solidarity organizations. Through such work, they linked gay and lesbian liberation to socialist change and strengthened Latina/o and multiracial gay and lesbian community.

By the mid-1980s, civil disobedience against US intervention in Central America significantly influenced the AIDS activist movement. In detailing this, *Lavender and Red* challenges exceptionalism about both Stonewall and ACT UP. Standard narratives imagine New York City's AIDS Coalition to Unleash Power (ACT UP) as the first and only organization to pursue street protest against AIDS. These accounts tend to suggest that AIDS suddenly radicalized a generation and that ACT UP sprang up suddenly with little history behind it. Yet, in fact, AIDS direct action grew out of multiple radical genealogies. Lesbian and gay participation in Central American solidarity and in the antinuclear movement provided practical and conceptual tools to challenge the epidemic as a problem enabled by heterosexism, misogyny, racism, and capitalism. AIDS direct action stood as the culmination of two decades of gay and lesbian left organizing even as it marked the start of a new queer politics.

. . .

Lavender and Red integrates archival research and oral history interviews to analyze how gay and lesbian leftists practiced their political commitments, conceptualized their identities, and carried out their activist lives. The book's action moves across the latter half of the Cold War from 1969 to 1991. The epilogue considers the gay and lesbian left's resonances in queer radicalism since that time.

As my description up to this point hints, I use the terms "gay" and "lesbian" as activists did. This means that I encourage readers to consider that these terms were at times less stable or rigidly bounded descriptors of sexuality and gender than they have come to be assumed. Scattered dimensions of the efforts I study connect to transgender expression, and where those links exist, I seek to make them clear. Some people whose lives are reflected in these pages saw or came to see their desires as bisexual, though most did not describe themselves with this term until the 1980s or later, if at all, and bisexual organizations did not define themselves centrally through left solidarity.[27] Nonetheless, my later chapters hint at a shifting politics by gradually expanding the language of "lesbian and gay" to "lesbian, gay, and bisexual," though not the more recent formulation of "lesbian, gay, bisexual, and transgender." I use "queer" only rarely before the late 1980s but increasingly from that point on.

Readers new to analyzing radical movements should keep in mind the distinctions between "left" and "liberal" agendas, which are important differences both within and beyond this book. *Lavender and Red* does not draw a strict or partisan boundary around the left, but approaches it broadly as a set of anti-imperialist, anti-capitalist, and internationalist commitments shaped by the context of the Cold War. As detailed in chapter 1, the gay and lesbian left developed as a product of the New Left—which grew out of a mid-1950s break with the Communist Party—as well as the Third World Left—a network of organizations led by people of color invested in anti-colonial struggle both beyond and within the United States. The left can be broadly distinguished from "liberal" politics by its pursuit of radical and internationalist, rather than reformist and domestic, goals and by the centrality of street protest and direct action versus electoral or legal change. Yet leftists and liberals have at times collaborated, and some chapters of the book explore the tensions of left-liberal coalitions in gay and lesbian politics. To avoid repetition and to reflect my archives' own terms, I use the terms "leftists" and "radicals" more or less equally, setting both of these apart from liberalism.

Another boundary in this book is that of race. The Bay Area gay and lesbian left was predominately white, though it included important involvement by gay and lesbian radicals of color. Its demographics lagged behind broader population trends. San Francisco was majority white in 1970 but by 1990 about half people of color, and while the city lost black residents over the 1970s and 1980s, it gained growing numbers of Asian, Pacific Islander, and Latina/o people. Over this same period, Oakland became majority people of color and especially more black.[28] The Bay Area gay and lesbian left did not reflect local demographics entirely and was not a simple microcosm of society. Rather, it was a historically contingent product of interconnecting movements and countercultures and of the constrained discourses of sexuality and race. Its emergence against US intervention in Latin America and its strong networks in San Francisco's Mission District meant that its largest cohort of people of color were Latina and Latino, with scattered numbers of black, Native, and Asian activists. Queer of color activism overlapped with the gay and lesbian left but also held meanings, logics, and histories well beyond it, as by seeking to challenge racist objectification within gay life; to trace black, Latina/o, Asian and Pacific Islander, and

Native genealogies of sexuality; and to sustain queer of color communities.[29] Gay and lesbian people of color held different relationships to the discourse that imagined homosexuality as bourgeois and white, and at times found that the energy white gay and lesbian radicals expended in countering such discourse recentered whiteness to the exclusion of other leadership, experiences, and concerns. *Lavender and Red* seeks to illuminate these dynamics as well as efforts toward alternatives.

The book begins with two chapters that analyze the emergence of gay liberation and lesbian feminism in relation to black liberation, the Vietnam War, and state repression. Chapter 1 centers on how, between 1969 and 1973, radical gay men in the Bay Area came to see radical alliances as central to their sexual liberation. Gay liberationists drew on black and other radical analyses of racism as "internal colonialism" to analyze the so-called gay ghetto, a concept they used to critique existing gay oppression and to draw analogies between sexuality and race. They built on their critiques of the gay ghetto by pursuing solidarity with the Black Panther Party and by defining gayness as a means to resist the Vietnam War and militarism. Moreover, they drew on their critiques of the "gay ghetto" to distinguish leftist gay liberation from a different strand emerging within the movement, one termed "gay nationalism." In 1970 and 1971 gay nationalists prompted a major schism in the gay liberation movement when they represented gay people as colonizers in the US West who could take over California's rural, remote Alpine County. Although this "colonization" project was never carried out, it had a lasting effect because it prompted gay leftists to argue that such colonization would replicate structures of capitalism, imperialism, and the "gay ghetto" itself. By rejecting the Alpine project, Bay Area gay radicals aligned the gay left with a multiracial and socialist agenda.

While gay men remade their sexualities in part by resisting the draft, many lesbian feminists posed a different remaking of violence. Chapter 2 traces a lesbian feminist politics that I term collective defense and that stretched from personal self-protection to armed resistance and the revolutionary underground. This chapter moves from 1969 through 1975 and shows how women used collective defense to build lesbian community and to refuse alignment with the US state. It begins with an analysis of Gay Women's Liberation (GWL), a Bay Area lesbian feminist organization that drew concepts of collective defense from the Black Panther Party. A racially mixed but largely white effort, GWL operated alongside the Bay Area lesbian of color group Gente. These groups help to illustrate how collective defense mobilized anti-racist commitments yet contributed to the isolation of lesbian of color identities. A similar divergence appeared as lesbian feminists defined collective defense in relation to armed radical groups and political trials—namely, the cases of the Symbionese Liberation Army (SLA), an armed group with lesbian participants; Susan Saxe, a white radical and lesbian feminist arrested after five years in the revolutionary underground; and Inez Garcia and Joan Little, women of color who killed their rapists. Coupled with the growth of both lesbian feminist community and state repression, these cases pushed lesbian radicals to define their politics through support for the underground and the anti-imperialist left.

If the first third of the book destabilizes Stonewall exceptionalism, the following third seeks to knock it to the ground by recounting gay and lesbian radicalism across the second half of the 1970s. Most histories describe this period as a time when gay liberation was abandoned in favor of more liberal agendas, as by electing San Francisco supervisor Harvey Milk and organizing against the New Right. Yet while gay liberalism grew in this period, the gay and lesbian left did as well. Gay and lesbian leftists articulated their politics through socialist and feminist organizing and by building lesbian and gay of color community, and they solidified their internationalist commitments by starting to fight the right not only domestically but also through solidarity with Chile and Nicaragua.

Chapter 3 begins with a focus on radical gay men, analyzing mid-1970s efforts to organize multi-issue alliances, to theorize anti-gay oppression, and to challenge constructions of gay identity as white and male. It traces such small but influential organizations as Gays in Solidarity with the Chilean Resistance, which reflected a new attention to US imperialism in Latin America, and the Third World Gay Caucus, which marked a rapidly expanding network of activism among gay and lesbian people of color. These groups helped to seed and set the context for Bay Area Gay Liberation (BAGL), a hundreds-strong organization that fought against police harassment, opposed racism in gay bars, worked for the rights of gay and lesbian teachers, and supported many nongay radical campaigns. BAGL tensely balanced anti-imperialist solidarity with more liberal reform and ultimately split apart over debates about military inclusion. Building on BAGL's story, this chapter considers the opportunities and challenges both gay and lesbian radicals faced in joining left-liberal coalitions against the New Right. It discusses leftists' impact on the campaign to defeat Proposition 6, a ballot-box attack on gay and lesbian teachers and workers' rights, as well as describing those who opposed both Proposition 6 and the death penalty initiative Proposition 7. The chapter closes with a consideration of the White Night Riots, the 1979 uprising against the light sentence meted out for the assassinations of Harvey Milk and San Francisco mayor George Moscone.

Chapter 4 turns to lesbian and gay solidarity with Central America, tracing this politics from its first expressions in 1978 through its expansion in 1983. Having defined themselves as among US conservatives' primary targets, gay and lesbian leftists began to critique alliances between the US, Nicaraguan, and Salvadoran right wings, and they looked to Nicaragua's Sandinista Revolution as a venue for lesbian and gay incorporation in socialist change. Gay and lesbian solidarity with Nicaragua found its first expression through efforts by BAGL and the Gay Latino Alliance. It won a greater platform through Gay People for the Nicaraguan Revolution, which collaborated directly with Nicaraguan exiles in the Mission District and with the Nicaraguan Revolution's Frente Sandinista de Liberación Nacional (FSLN). Along with organizing situated in the San Francisco Women's Building, these groups countered the ideas that socialism moved at odds with gay and lesbian freedom and that people of color and lesbian and gay identities stood in conflict. Thus, lesbian and gay solidarity reenergized and expanded the anti-militarist and anti-imperialist sexual politics formulated during the Vietnam War. By 1983, lesbian and gay solidarity gained another foothold through involvement in the campaign to pass Proposition N, which declared the city of San Francisco's opposition to US military aid to El Salvador. Lesbian and gay participation in that campaign generated Lesbians and Gays Against Intervention (LAGAI), a group that would have a significant impact on lesbian, gay, and queer radicalism across the 1980s and beyond.

The last two chapters of *Lavender and Red* analyze lesbian and gay solidarity with Central America in relation to two other political formations: first, women of color and transnational feminism, and second, the growth of direct action against AIDS. Chapter 5 recounts exchanges between Bay Area and Nicaraguan lesbian and gay activists from 1984 to 1990. It begins by considering activist travel to Nicaragua, in particular Somos Hermanas and the Victoria Mercado Brigade, two majority women of color groups that traveled from San Francisco and helped to make Nicaraguan solidarity a venue for constructing lesbian of color and antiracist lesbian feminism. It then turns to examine how Nicaraguan lesbian and gay activists interacted with both Bay Area activists and the Sandinista government in order to win recognition from that government and to organize their own work against AIDS. The chapter considers the formation of Nicaragua's first lesbian and gay organization; the Sandinista State Security's crackdown on that group; and the creation of Nicaragua's Colectivo de Educación Popular contra el SIDA (CEP-SIDA, or Collective for Popular Education Against AIDS), which won support from the Sandinista Ministry of Health. US radicals saw CEP-SIDA in direct contrast to the Reagan administration's inaction on AIDS, but Nicaraguan lesbian and gay activists had a different relationship to the effort: they achieved it in part by ensuring that solidarity activists did not know about Sandinista State Security repression. Nicaraguan gay and lesbian activists managed Bay Area lesbian and gay solidarity in order to stake their claims both within the Sandinista Revolution and within a transnational gay and lesbian left.

In addition to organizing transnational exchanges and brigades, the Central American solidarity movement worked to stop intervention from inside the United States, using civil disobedience and protests in the streets. Chapter 6 traces how lesbian and gay leftists drew on these anti-militarist politics and tactics to organize the AIDS direct action movement. Telling this story expands the history of AIDS activism beyond ACT UP, revealing that gay and lesbian leftists drew on their histories in 1970s radicalism, in the anti-nuclear movement, and in Central American solidarity to initiate and guide the development of street protest to confront AIDS. These influences first appeared in San Francisco in 1984, took on force from 1986 through 1988, and shaped national networks of AIDS activism. The chapter details this history through the formation of Citizens for Medical Justice and the AIDS Action Pledge as well as the transition into ACT UP San Francisco and the work of Stop AIDS Now Or Else. Along the way, it returns to the March 1988 anti-intervention protests cited at the beginning of this introduction. But the chapter concludes with loss: the influences of anti-militarism and anti-imperialism waned in AIDS direct action as more and more activists died, taking their political mentorship with them.

The gay and lesbian left diminished as the Cold War ended, a transition that fractured the meanings of radical change even as millions died of AIDS worldwide. In the aftermath of these shifts, a significant strand of gay and lesbian activism turned toward inclusion in the military. Although this goal stood at odds with past histories, the gay and lesbian left held powerful legacies in other queer politics. *Lavender and Red* concludes by considering the lessons that the gay and lesbian left offers for understanding queer radicalism from the 1990s until today.

CHAPTER I

Beyond the Gay Ghetto

Founding Debates in Gay Liberation

In October 1969, a group called Gay Liberation Theater staged a street performance entitled "No Vietnamese Ever Called Me a Queer." These activists brought their claims to two distinct audiences: fellow students at the University of California, Berkeley's Sproul Plaza and fellow gay men at a meeting of the San Francisco–based Society for Individual Rights (SIR). The student audience was anti-war but largely straight, while SIR backed gay inclusion in the military and exemplified the moderate center of the "homophile" movement—homophile being the name for an existing and older network of gay and lesbian activism. Gay Liberation Theater adapted Muhammad Ali's statement when refusing the draft that "no Viet Cong ever called me nigger," and, through this, indicted a society that demanded men kill rather than desire one another. They opposed the Vietnam War and spoke to the self-interest of gay men by declaring: "We're not going to fight in an army that discriminates against us. . . . Nor are we going to fight for a country that will not hire us and fires us. . . . We are going to fight for ourselves and our lovers in places like Berkeley where the Berkeley police last April murdered homosexual brother Frank Bartley (never heard of him?) while cruising in Aquatic Park." Frank Bartley was a thirty-three-year-old white man who had recently been killed by a plainclothes officer who claimed that Bartley "resisted arrest" and "reached for his groin."[1] In highlighting Bartley's case, Gay Liberation Theater pushed back against the demands of assimilation and respectability and linked opposition to the Vietnam War with support for sexual expression. The group termed it "queer, unnatural and perverse" to "send men half way around the world to kill their brothers while we torment, rape, jail and murder men for loving their brothers here."[2]

"No Vietnamese Ever Called Me Queer" encapsulated three founding elements of gay liberation: a break with existing homophile groups, a demand for sexual freedom, and a claim that such freedom would be won only through radical alliance against militarism, racism, and police violence. This chapter details how these tenets structured Bay Area gay liberation and laid the groundwork for the gay left. It contextualizes this history by tracking the shifting meanings of the "gay ghetto" in the homophile movement and gay liberation. In the mid-1960s, homophiles used the concept of the gay ghetto to describe the urban geography of antigay oppression and to theorize sexuality as analogous to race. By 1969, gay liberationists altered the meanings of the gay ghetto by using the concept to criticize homophile activism, to defend everyday gender and sexual transgression, and to link sexual liberation to the anti-war movement and black liberation. When self-declared "gay nationalists" schemed to take over California's rural Alpine County, more radical gay men rejected that project on the grounds that it would replicate the exclusions of the gay ghetto. They used that break to align themselves instead with a more multiracial and socialist agenda. Through these responses, gay leftists began to theorize radical solidarity as central to sexual liberation and to organize accordingly.

. . .

Gay liberation emerged both against and in debt to the homophile movement, which stretched from 1950 through 1970 and worked to normalize the status of homosexuality in psychiatry and medicine and to curtail legal and police persecution. Homophile activists formed local and national organizations (the two best-known being the Mattachine Society and Daughters of Bilitis, though these were joined by many others) and circulated national and international publications. Harry Hay, until that point a member of the Communist Party in Los Angeles, founded the Mattachine Society in 1950, and while Mattachine soon turned away from Hay's leadership, members around the country remained bold and militant against state persecution.[3] Homophile groups and publications varied in their politics and approaches, and historian Marc Stein questions a "canonization of homophile sexual respectability" that emphasizes the influence of the publications *Mattachine Review, The Ladder,* and *One* over the more openly erotic and widely circulated *Drum*.[4] But divisions did appear between many homophile groups and the working-class, gender-transgressive, and racially diverse queer life of gay bars, house parties, and cruising grounds. Nan Alamilla Boyd has found these divisions to be significant in San Francisco, and other scholars have made similar observations for other sites.[5] Differences also emerged between local and national agendas. By the later 1960s, homophile activists in San Francisco, Chicago, and other cities posed strong challenges to police abuse, but the national homophile movement's pursuit of military inclusion and liberal civil rights fell out of step with growing anti-war and black liberation struggles.[6] Further, by this point many homophile activists' efforts toward gender and class norms—at protests, men wore suits and ties, women dresses—stood in contrast to androgynous and casual styles among radical youth.

Although many gay radicals came to perceive homophile activists as out of touch, the earlier movement influenced gay liberation in multiple ways. One of these was through the concept of the "gay ghetto." The term was frequently used in homophile publications and activism and by the mid-1960s held two principal meanings. First, the concept of the gay ghetto was used to communicate the idea that gay people and people of color, especially black people, shared parallel experiences in urban life. This highlighted the segregation of queer life in heavily policed, working-class, multiracial "vice" districts, yet imagined race and sexuality as parallel or analogous rather than intersecting—making it difficult for queer people of color to place themselves within gay politics. A second definition of the gay ghetto argued that gay people were isolated and exploited by collusions between police, organized crime, and the owners of gay bars. Across the 1950s and 1960s, many gay and lesbian bars upheld rather than challenged antigay laws. They enforced bans on same-sex dancing and affection, made police payoffs to minimize raids, charged high prices, and hired few gay staff.[7] The concept of the gay ghetto thus also became a way to name queer people's confinement within a narrow and abusive geography of public life.

San Francisco's queer life held unique characteristics that shaped the ways activists understood and used the concept of the gay ghetto locally. On the one hand, an unusually high number of the city's gay and lesbian bars were gay or lesbian owned—by 1964, as many as a third.[8] These owners formed the Tavern Guild and built the organization into an influential and comparatively conservative force in the homophile movement. At the same time, the exploitation of queer life remained widely apparent, most especially in the Tenderloin—a "red-light" neighborhood near downtown known for its cheap housing, sex economy, and high concentration of gay youth and transgender women. Those who lived in and visited the Tenderloin were frequently arrested or harassed by police on charges of prostitution, cruising, gender transgression, vagrancy, and drug activity, and as Susan Stryker observes, police frequently left transgender women there following arrests elsewhere in the city. Some residents were homeless or precariously housed "street kids." By the mid-1960s, daily existence in the Tenderloin became ever more difficult as urban redevelopment displaced residents from the surrounding neighborhoods of the Fillmore, Western Addition, and South of Market and made the area's housing more crowded.[9]

Although some homophile activists rejected Tenderloin dwellers as embarrassments, others organized with and for gay and transgender people against poverty and harassment. By 1965 homophile activists worked in the Tenderloin through two key groups: the Council on Religion and the Homosexual, an alliance of left-liberal clergy drawn from across the city; and Glide Memorial United Methodist Church, located in the heart of the Tenderloin and headed by the African American preacher Reverend Cecil Williams. As Christina Hanhardt has detailed, homophile activists drew on these networks to win funding for a project they termed the Central City Anti-Poverty Program. They wrote a report detailing the discrimination and poverty experienced by gay and transgender residents, giving their document the official title "The Tenderloin Ghetto" and the unofficial name "The White Ghetto." As the terms "Tenderloin" and "white" served as placeholders for "gay," the label of whiteness both described the Tenderloin's dominant demographics and set up a parallel between sexuality and race. Homophile activists in San Francisco also drew parallels between sexuality and race through their responses to police, forging alliances in which they defined their interests alongside those of communities of color. In 1966 Reverend Williams founded Citizens Alert, a police accountability organization that homophile activists helped to staff and that brought homophile efforts into coalition with black, Latina/o, Chinese, Japanese, and other civil rights groups.[10]

By spring 1966 another organization had formed in the Tenderloin. Called Vanguard, it sought to mobilize gay and transgender youth and in July helped to stage a protest in front of Compton's Cafeteria, a Tenderloin diner that had begun to call the police on its queer patrons. On a weekend night in August 1966, officers attempted to arrest a transgender woman inside Compton's. She fought back, and a multiracial mix of queens joined in by throwing dishes, smashing the windows of the cafeteria, and then moving into the streets of the Tenderloin where they fought back physically against police and damaged a police car. Susan Stryker estimates that fifty to sixty Compton's customers, plus police and passersby, joined in the riot, which she terms the "the first collective, organized" queer resistance to police harassment in US history.[11]

The Compton's riot preceded the Stonewall Riots by nearly three years but failed to prompt activism on the scale that followed the 1969 protest in New York. Indeed, Compton's remained little known until Stryker resuscitated it in 2005 as a foundational account in queer history. The riot's principal outcome was to accelerate the creation of transgender-affirming programs in San Francisco, including access to job training, the selection of a liaison within the San Francisco Police Department, the first known transsexual support group in the United States, and a public health program (the Center for Special Problems) that provided counseling, hormone prescriptions, surgery referrals, and accurate ID cards.[12] Nonetheless, many gay and lesbian activists—both liberal and more radical—formulated sexual identities and politics in ways that marked boundaries between themselves and transgender people.[13]

Moreover, even as Tenderloin organizing grew, San Francisco's queer life expanded beyond that neighborhood. Gay men and lesbians also found each other in the motorcycle scene of South of Market, the bohemian spaces of North Beach and the Haight, and residential communities of the Castro and Polk.[14] The Castro emerged as the most middle-class and gender-normatively masculine of all of these areas, and by 1971 nearly a third of all Castro businesses (not only its gay bars) were gay-owned.[15] By the late 1960s San Francisco's gay scene was second only to that of New York City, and the Bay Area was increasingly seen as a queer haven. Although the concept of the gay ghetto still resonated with many, it seemed less tenable as a description of San Francisco's geography because queer life was increasingly widespread. In addition, black liberation and Third World radicalism began to inspire activists to use the concept of the gay ghetto to analyze sexual identity at scales beyond the urban neighborhood.

Black liberation held a central place in the 1960s Bay Area because of three interwoven factors: the Oakland formation of the Black Panther Party, the Party's rootedness in local black community, and the strength of the student left. Huey Newton and Bobby Seale founded the Black Panther Party on October 15, 1966, initially naming it the Black Panther

Party for Self-Defense, and the organization grew by mobilizing southern black migrants to Oakland, Richmond, South Berkeley, and San Francisco's Fillmore and Hunters Point neighborhoods. Donna Murch argues that Newton, Seale, and other early Party leaders and members bridged "campuses and streets" in a "convergence . . . inseparable from the vast increase in educational access among poor youth" in 1960s California: by the end of the decade the Bay Area and Los Angeles claimed higher rates of college attendance among youth of color than anywhere else in the United States.[16] In addition, the internal diversity of Bay Area Latino and Asian communities fostered pan-ethnic internationalism and contributed to the linking of student activism and urban protest. These trends inspired activists around the country and heightened both the local and the national significance of the Panthers along with other Bay Area groups.

While the Black Panther Party was born in the Bay Area, its political imagination stretched much farther. As Murch states, "The Oakland Party drew its inspiration from a rural movement in Lowndes County, Alabama [the first to use the black panther as symbol] while internationally it embraced the Cuban, Vietnamese, and Chinese revolutions as its own."[17] Moreover, the Party's early police patrols "translated" a key idea becoming widespread across Black Power: that black people were an "internal colony" within the United States.[18] Other uses of the internal colonialism thesis defined US police violence as interconnected with the war in Vietnam and named the exploitation of US communities of color as a facet of US imperialism. Through these and other aspects of its thought, the Black Panther Party contributed to an ongoing redefinition of blackness as not only a racial category but also a source of political power and a transnational ideological formation.

In May 1967 a contingent of Black Panther Party leaders and members traveled to Sacramento to protest the Mulford Bill, a measure that expressly targeted Panther police patrols by banning the open display of loaded weapons. Entering the state capitol bearing their legally owned, registered, and loaded rifles, the Panthers won substantial media attention and cemented their public image of armed black radicalism. The California legislature's passage of the Mulford Act in July 1967 compelled the Party to end its police patrols and, combined with the growth of new Black Panther Party chapters in Richmond, San Francisco, and East Oakland, led to a sharp uptick in police harassment.[19] On October 28, 1967, Oakland police officer John Frey pulled over Huey Newton and another Panther member. A series of disputed events left Frey dead, another officer and Newton wounded, and Newton painfully shackled in a local emergency room. When Newton was charged with three felonies and faced the death penalty, the Party responded with a campaign to "Free Huey." As Donna Murch observes, the campaign's "most striking claim was not [only] that Newton was innocent but that a fair trial was impossible."[20] During 1968, the Black Panther Party grew nationally through the Free Huey campaign and its newspaper the *Black Panther,* which reached a weekly circulation as high as 139,000. This campaign continued through August 1970, when Newton's conviction was reversed and he was released.

Amidst the Free Huey campaign, students at San Francisco State College (now San Francisco State University) launched the Third World Strike. Extending from November 6, 1968, through March 21, 1969, the strike was born as a coalition between the campus Black Student Union and Latino and Asian American organizations, which collectively adopted the name the Third World Liberation Front and forged an alliance with the local, white-led Students for a Democratic Society (SDS). Among the Third World Strike's key demands were the admission of four hundred new first-year students of color, the creation of nine positions to be filled by faculty of color, and the elimination of campus ROTC training. Following extended protests and record mass arrests, the college president, conservative S.I. Hayakawa, partially conceded to the Strike by creating the School of Ethnic Studies.[21]

As Daryl Maeda argues, the Third World Strike aligned with black radicalism by redefining race as an ideological identity and a basis for coalition. Asian American radicals played a central role in the Strike and, by countering the conservative Japanese American president of the college, constructed a new pan-Asian identity that oriented itself through alliance with black radicalism rather than assimilation into whiteness.[22] Latina/o radicalism was fostered by the convergence between the Strike and the case of Los Siete de la Raza, seven young men who, following their activism in favor of ethnic studies at the College of San Mateo, found themselves charged in a fatal police shooting (casting suspicion on the charges, four of the men were not present at the shooting itself). The Black Panther Party gave prominent support to the Third World Strike, to the Asian American radicalism that grew from it, and to the Los Siete case.

The growth of black liberation and Third World radicalism influenced gay politics in multiple ways. Shifts within the black freedom struggle were echoed in the transition from homophile to gay liberation politics, while the Black Panther Party's openness to nonblack allies and the development of the Third World Strike offered evidence of ways people might redefine their identities through radical commitment. Adding a new layer to the concept of the gay ghetto, the Panthers' use of the internal colonialism thesis encouraged gay radicals to see links between their exclusion by the military and their exploitation by police. Gay activists thus drew inspiration from the solidarities multiplying around them. At least two Third World Strike supporters became important in local gay activism: San Francisco State student Charles Thorpe and faculty member Morgan Pinney, who was fired in retaliation for his backing of the Strike. As activists began to declare gay liberation, they defined it as a vehicle for and expression of the alliances summoned in the Free Huey campaign, the Third World Strike, and the anti-war movement.

Gay liberation emerged definitively in spring and summer 1969, as marked by a set of key events in San Francisco and New York. In San Francisco in March 1969, Leo Laurence, a young white man who served as editor of the homophile SIR's publication *Vector* and worked with Reverend Williams's Glide Church, held an interview with the countercultural newspaper the *Berkeley Barb*. In an article entitled "Homo Revolt: Don't Hide It!" Laurence challenged SIR to join the broader left movement, especially by abandoning gay inclusion in the military in favor of opposition to the Vietnam War. He urged gay and lesbian radicals to see links between sexual liberation and support for the Black Panthers, and he lambasted SIR and the Tavern Guild for "middle class bigotry and racism," in part because of the Guild's refusal to work with Citizens Alert against police abuse.[23]

The *Barb* illustrated its article with a front-cover photo of Laurence embracing a shirtless Gale Whittington, Laurence's boyfriend and a clerical worker for San Francisco's Steamship Lines Company. A copy of the *Barb* made its way to the Steamship Lines office in the Financial District and Whittington was promptly fired. Meanwhile, SIR pushed Laurence out of *Vector* and declared itself a resolutely "one-issue" organization addressing only "those issues that pertain to the homosexual as a homosexual."[24] Laurence and his comrades responded by creating a new and more multi-issue group, the Committee for Homosexual Freedom (CHF), which began lunchtime pickets of antigay discrimination at Steamship Lines, Tower Records, Safeway, Macy's, and the Federal Building. These protests lasted throughout April and much of May and received wide, though generally mocking, coverage in local media.[25] CHF issued calls for multisector alliance, with one broadside urging supporters to attend an upcoming Free Huey rally and stating that the "CHF is in the vanguard of homosexuals who know they must form coalitions with the Movement."[26] Laurence termed gay freedom "the same as 'Black is Beautiful,'" while the CHF's fliers held that "our condition is a part of the oppression which blacks, chicanos, and—yes—the Vietnamese have known."[27]

Meanwhile, another local gay radical, Carl Wittman, began to write and circulate an essay, "Refugees from Amerika: A Gay Manifesto," that furthered calls for alliance and comparisons between sexuality and race. Wittman had been an important leader in the era's leading anti-war organization, SDS, first as a student at Swarthmore College and then as a member of SDS's national council. He left SDS in 1966 after experiencing sharp antigay hostility, then married Mimi Feingold the same year; they moved to San Francisco and continued to lead anti-war work.[28] Wittman came out as gay in 1968, wrote and circulated drafts of his "Gay Manifesto" throughout spring 1969, and finalized it in May. The essay began, "San Francisco is a refugee camp for homosexuals."[29] This proclamation marked gay geography through both oppression and escape. In naming all of San Francisco rather than just one neighborhood, Wittman acknowledged the distinctiveness of gay life in the city, but also held that San Francisco was "a ghetto rather than a free territory because it is still theirs." Rather than simply proposing a takeover of property, he argued that gay liberation required deep transformation in structures of power, including "police, city hall, capitalism." He echoed Leo Laurence's call for gay activists to join with other radicals and stated Laurence's analogies in cruder terms: "Chick equals nigger equals queer. Think it over."[30] From summer 1969 forward, Wittman's essay circulated as a stand-alone broadside and was published across the radical and gay press. His ideas met both acclaim and critique, with some holding that his analogies between race and sexuality undermined goals of alliance. As one lesbian activist noted in December 1970, "Naming revolutionary groups—blacks, chicanos, Indians, women, gays—in this linear fashion" made it difficult to discuss overlapping agendas or to understand "gay" as inclusive of anyone other than white men.[31]

Gay liberation expanded dramatically following the Stonewall Riots in New York's Greenwich Village. This uprising began on June 28, 1969, when a multiracial mix of queens, gay men, and lesbians, most of them people of color and many of them "street kids," fought back against a routine police raid at the gay bar the Stonewall Inn. Conflict continued on the streets for two full nights and grew through the support of other radicals, including some who were straight. By July 31 a group of gay, lesbian, and transgender radicals—some of them riot participants, others not—formed the first Gay Liberation Front, or GLF.[32] News of the Stonewall rebellion and of the GLF spread through the radical and underground press, and within months other Gay Liberation Fronts formed around the country. Significantly, although New York's GLF began as a mixed-gender group including lesbians and transgender people along with gay men, it was soon fractured by tensions over gender, race, and political viewpoints. Multiple New York groups began as GLF caucuses and then became independent; for example, white lesbian feminists formed the Radicalesbians and Sylvia Rivera, Marsha P. Johnson, and other trans radicals founded the Street Transvestite Action Revolutionaries. But in contrast to New York, GLFs in the Bay Area formed directly out of previous gay men's organizing, and both began and remained composed primarily of white men. Transgender organizing linked to Glide Church and the Center for Special Problems remained largely separate from gay liberation, though some forms of gender transgression overlapped, as through the countercultural performance group the Cockettes.[33]

By August 1969 San Francisco's Committee for Homosexual Freedom changed its name to the Gay Liberation Front, and in October the group began to picket the *San Francisco Examiner* for using antigay language to report on earlier protests against the Steamship Lines.[34] One of the group's fliers layered the words "Gay Liberation Front" against an outline of three figures standing with raised fists, two wearing Afros, who symbolically evoked Black Power (figure 2).[35] On the left side of the flier, a heavyset, balding white man held a bayonet and a weapon that combined a fountain pen and a spiked club. This figure of military violence and media power threatened two younger, racially ambiguous men, standing on the genitals of one while the other— gagged by a cloth—shielded his crotch with his hand. Here, as in other statements, the San Francisco GLF represented gay masculinity and sexual autonomy as threatened by establishment authority yet recuperable through alignment with the black freedom struggle.[36]

Amidst this rhetoric, gay liberationists also shifted their view of the gay ghetto. Increasingly, rather than naming any specific location, they used the concept of the gay ghetto to describe a wide-ranging social system that constrained sexuality and gender. Activists especially developed this analysis through their critiques of sex and gender norms. For example, radicals attacked homophile groups for demanding normative gender presentation in everyday life while limiting drag to special occasions.[37] They held that SIR sought "total integration within the establishment" through suits and ties and that "passing for straight is SIR's

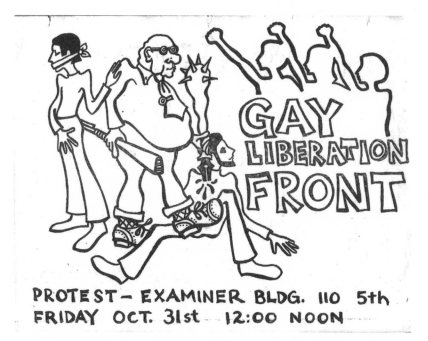

FIGURE 2. Committee for Homosexual Freedom/Gay Liberation Front flier, San Francisco, 1969. Courtesy of Ephemera Collection—LGBT Groups, Gay, Lesbian, Bisexual, Transgender Historical Society (GLBTHS).

ideal."[38] Further, in fall 1969 the San Francisco GLF called for a picket of the Halloween and New Year's drag balls organized by SIR and the Tavern Guild. Far from welcoming the "street queens" of the Tenderloin, these balls required tickets, occurred behind closed doors, and demanded formal gowns and tuxedos. The GLF held that "these balls are being promoted by the same Gay Establishment who promote the 'Gay Bars' and other Ghettos," and argued that true freedom would be won not through privacy but rather by enabling gender transgression and same-sex affection "*in the road, in the streets.*"[39] As Betty Luther Hillman has shown, many gay liberationists preferred "political drag," or undermining gender by mixing its norms—for example, wearing a beard with a dress or feminine jewelry over a masculine shirt. Within a few years this style would be termed genderfuck.[40] Yet political drag did not necessarily entail a full recognition of transgender expression, as some gay radicals who praised political drag held that transsexuals and "street queens" replicated stereotypes.

Broadly, the San Francisco GLF linked a remaking of gender expression with anti-capitalist and anti-racist goals. By terming gay bars "ghettos," activists suggested that gay bars exploited their customers by enforcing antigay laws. They also continued parallels made by earlier homophile activists by comparing "homosexuals in the Tenderloin . . . [to] Black children in the Hunters Point Ghetto."[41] Their statements illustrated a view of the gay ghetto as simultaneously localized and ever present. They named isolation, poverty, and policing in the Tenderloin not as neighborhood problems that could be swept away in a cleanup, but as the consequences of imperatives that sexuality be either private or commercial and that gender transgression only be enacted on stage. Increasingly, gay radicals used the concept of the gay ghetto to distinguish a minoritarian, assimilationist view of homosexuality from an expansive, universalizing vision of sexual and gender liberation.[42]

Anti-war politics were central to this universalizing vision because the draft compelled young men of all sexualities to declare themselves straight. This pressure grew with the Vietnam War itself. The military expanded the draft multiple times, easing its standards in 1968 and then opening a draft lottery from December 1969 through 1972. Draft boards demanded that men acknowledge any "homosexual tendencies," and those who were discovered to be homosexual in the service risked the denial of veterans' benefits and up to five years' imprisonment. Working-class men and men of color, who were drafted and faced combat at disproportionately higher rates, often found their indications of homosexuality overlooked.[43] Meanwhile, men recorded as homosexual at induction were excluded both from the military and from civil service jobs and were placed on file with the FBI. They also risked public stigma, and revelations of their homosexuality could place others in danger, especially in smaller communities where members of draft boards might know their lovers as well as their relatives, employers, and friends.[44]

Nonetheless, as draft resistance grew, a small but growing number of men began to choose the risks of sexual stigma over participation in the war. The Los Angeles GLF produced brochures with advice on "revolutionary homosexual draft resistance," marking a decisive break with the homophile goal of military inclusion.[45] In turn, the military demanded stricter proof in the form of letters from lovers and psychiatrists and stereotypically effeminate behavior.[46] Public awareness of these phenomena became evident in *The Gay Deceivers* (1969), a Hollywood comedy about two straight men pretending to be gay to evade the draft. The vast majority of those who declared themselves homosexual before draft boards were indeed gay or bisexual, so *The Gay Deceivers* misrepresented "homosexual draft resistance" to play it for laughs. Nonetheless, the film hinted at mainstream awareness of a more radical truth: activists were remaking gay identity by "coming out against the war."[47]

In reframing their sexuality in anti-war terms, gay liberationists resisted antigay hostility from both the government and the straight left. As Ian Lekus has shown, by the late 1960s the US state used "tactical gay-baiting," particularly against men, to discredit and divide radical groups. The FBI worked to foster homophobia in the Venceremos Brigades, the Black Panther Party, and anti-war organizations, and during the Chicago Seven trial—which targeted leaders of protests at the 1968 Democratic National Convention—US Attorney Thomas Foran characterized witness Allen Ginsberg and the defendants as part of the "freaking fag revolution."[48] Many straight radicals reversed the charges, describing politicians as closeted "fags" or homosexuality as bourgeois.[49]

Gay liberationists pushed back against both the US state and their fellow radicals by politicizing homosexuality and effeminacy as means to resist the war. At their campiest, they riffed on the call to "make love, not war" with slogans such as "send the troops to bed together" and "suck cock to beat the draft"; more earnestly, they reframed gayness not only as a sexuality but also as a politics of opposition to US militarism and empire. In summer 1969 the San Francisco GLF set up shop in an office shared with the War Resisters League; that fall, the Gay Liberation Theater performed its play "No Vietnamese Ever Called Me a Queer." On October 15, 1969, gay men formed a contingent in the San Francisco march for the Vietnam Moratorium, and one of the arguments they presented was that repressed homoerotic desire led to military violence and that sexual liberation would allow peace.[50]

By early 1970 the Gay Liberation Theater became the Berkeley Gay Liberation Front. The group held its meetings at a house rented by activist Konstantin Berlandt, and this site also became home to the commune that launched the influential newspaper *Gay Sunshine*.[51] UC Berkeley students and alumni were well represented in the Berkeley GLF and *Gay Sunshine*, and Berlandt brought journalism experience as the previous editor of the university's student newspaper, the *Daily Californian*. Gay liberationists built another home base a few miles away in North Oakland through the "People's Alternative," a recurring dance party hosted at the apartment of activist Nick Benton.[52] Echoing rhetoric from the San Francisco GLF, Benton and others termed the People's

Alternative a direct substitute for the "gay ghetto"—especially the nearby gay bar the White Horse Inn, which refused to distribute *Gay Sunshine* and barred same-sex couples from kissing or holding hands.[53] In September 1970 GLF members picketed the White Horse and the San Francisco bar Leonardo's for these restrictions, and their comrades in Los Angeles and other cities engaged in similar battles.

Activists won changes in bar policies over the next several months and in the meantime built a counterculture that challenged social marginalization instead of profiting from it. Their collective households offered emotional support, fostered sexual discovery and the gender transgressions of "political drag," and became venues for political dialogue including consciousness-raising practices modeled on women's liberation.[54] At the same time, as participant Hal Tarr later noted, the gay counterculture produced "a huge gap between GLF men and the much larger number of guys who socialized in gay bars."[55] Against the stated intentions of gay liberation, such a gap furthered racial and class divides.

Aware of such segregation, though rarely questioning the dominant construction of gayness as white, many gay liberationists sought to act in solidarity with the Black Panther Party. These efforts met controversy within the broader gay movement, in part because of the antigay rhetoric of Eldridge Cleaver, who had served as the Party's de facto leader during much of 1968 while Huey Newton and Bobby Seale were imprisoned or jailed. (Newton and Seale regained more prominent leadership after their charges were overturned and they were released in 1970 and 1972, respectively.) Cleaver's prison writings, published in the radical magazine *Ramparts* and in book form as *Soul on Ice,* had won wide circulation and admiration, but his avowed hostility to homosexuality and his views of rape as "insurrection" incurred criticism.[56] Cleaver's influence in the Black Panther Party began to be contested after he and Kathleen Neal Cleaver, his wife and a fellow Panther leader, went into exile following the police murder of Oakland Party member Bobby Hutton. The Black Panther Party dropped the term "Self-Defense" from its name and turned greater attention to "survival programs" such as free breakfasts for children; these shifts drew more women into Party chapters and fostered greater discussion of women's liberation both within the Party and among its allies.[57]

In November 1969, the New York GLF's declaration of support for the Black Panther Party prompted the more moderate Gay Activist Alliance to split off and become an independent organization.[58] New York's GLF continued as a radical network with multiple offshoots, including two socialist groups formed by summer 1970, Third World Gay Revolution and Red Butterfly. The first of these was a people of color group and the second primarily white; both actively supported the Panthers and held that the "bourgeois nuclear family as the basic unit of capitalism creates oppressive roles of homosexuality and heterosexuality."[59] Yet as these groups coalesced in New York, another radical group became infamous for its antigay policy. The Venceremos Brigades, formed in 1969 as a project of SDS, organized activist trips to Cuba in violation of the US travel embargo. When a multiracial gay and lesbian caucus formed on the second brigade in August 1970, the group opposed it and termed homosexuality a capitalist and white phenomenon.[60] The Brigades justified these exclusions through Cuban antigay policy, including the imprisonment of homosexuals in work camps, and stated that gay liberation was part of "a cultural imperialist offensive against the Cuban Revolution."[61]

Against this backdrop, gay radicals sat up and took notice when Huey Newton praised women's and gay liberation. Newton was released from prison on August 5, 1970, after a California appellate court reversed his conviction for voluntary manslaughter in the death of Oakland police officer John Frey. On August 11, in an interview on the Berkeley leftist radio station KPFA, Newton stated that the Panthers "would like to have unity with the homosexual groups who are also politically conscious" and that gay people were "oppressed because of the bourgeois mentality and the bourgeois treachery that exists in this country that tries to legislate sexual activity."[62] Four days later he gave a speech to Black Panther Party members that was published in the *Black Panther* and by late August began to circulate across the gay and radical press.[63] In this statement, titled "A Letter from Huey Newton to the Revolutionary Brothers and Sisters about the Women's Liberation and Gay Liberation Movements," Newton called on his fellow Panthers to confront their "insecurities" about women and gay men, to reject sexist and homophobic language, and to include gay and women's groups in events. He questioned the idea that homosexuality was the result of the "decadence of capitalism" and most famously stated: "There is nothing to say that a homosexual cannot also be a revolutionary. And maybe I'm now injecting some of my prejudice by saying 'even a homosexual can be a revolutionary.' Quite the contrary; maybe a homosexual could be the most revolutionary."[64] As Joshua Bloom and Waldo Martin Jr. observe, Newton's statement made the Black Panther Party "the first major national black organization to embrace gay rights."[65]

Gay liberationists around the country responded enthusiastically to Newton's letter, with the Los Angeles GLF calling it a "vanguard revolutionary action."[66] In New York, Panther leader Afeni Shakur contacted the GLF to request a meeting, and three GLF members journeyed to a gathering at Jane Fonda's penthouse on the Upper East Side. Newton told them that "while in prison he had become acquainted with gay brothers who talked to him at length and were largely responsible for a change in his thinking about gay people," and he proposed that the GLF and the Black Panther Party organize "joint demonstrations . . . in the months ahead."[67] The meeting heightened support for the Panthers in the New York and other GLFs. When Philadelphia police raided Panther offices, arresting fifteen members and conducting a public, naked strip-search, local gay newspapers and gay liberation groups issued sharp protests.[68] The FBI took note.

With their relationship to the Panthers shifting, many gay and lesbian radicals looked to the Black Panther Party's Revolutionary People's Constitutional Convention (RPCC) as a means to imagine a new society. Through the RPCC, the Party called for "all progressive forces" to join in crafting "a true people's constitution . . . that takes into account the ethnic and pluralistic nature of this society, and that guarantees proportional representation to all of its people in a society free of the exploitation of man by man."[69] To fulfill this goal, the Panthers held a "plenary session" over Labor Day weekend (September 5–7, 1970) in Philadelphia that drew an estimated ten to fifteen thousand people. The conference drew activists from around the country; it was approximately two-thirds black, with a significant number of white allies and a handful of international representatives from African, Latin American, and Palestinian liberation movements and the German left.[70] The Party planned to follow the Philadelphia conference with a second that would finalize the new constitution in Washington, DC. Ultimately, however, the Philadelphia conference turned out to be the largest and best-known RPCC event. The RPCC's disappointments reflected a rising factionalism splitting the Black Panther Party apart even as allies placed heightened hope in its leadership.

Self-declared gay and lesbian activists constituted a small percentage of participants at the Philadelphia RPCC, just a few hundred among thousands, with gay men most prominent. But, with large GLF contingents from Philadelphia and New York joined by others from "cities across the nation, including many from Boston, Milwaukee, San Francisco, Chicago, Lawrence [Kansas], Tallahassee, and other places in between," the conference was "in effect the first national gay liberation gathering."[71] The gay men's contingent, a few-hundred strong, made a grand entrance at the RPCC by marching into the opening session chanting, "Gay, gay power to the gay, gay people! Black, black power to the black, black people! Power to the people!" The thousands of others in the hall rose to their feet and joined in, adding "Red, Brown, Women, Youth, and Student" groups to the chant.[72] The gay men's contingent was further noted for its racial diversity. It held a meeting at the RPCC on Saturday, picketed against racism at local gay bars on Saturday night, and on Sunday finalized a collective statement that received strong applause—though also some giggles—at the conference's closing event. The *Black Panther* included a note on gay participation in its reports on the RPCC, and a number of the conference's nongay workshops—especially those on women, on children, and on health—listed sexual freedom and respect for gay and lesbian people as elements of their platforms for change.[73]

Gay men's experiences at the Philadelphia RPCC stood in contrast, however, to those of lesbian feminists, whose contingent was overwhelmingly white and led by the New York Radicalesbians. The women in this contingent had sought to contribute to RPCC planning, but on arriving at the conference, found one of their workshops canceled, and ultimately met independently and left early.[74] Although a women's workshop termed homosexuality and bisexuality to be basic "rights," the conference report ignored the Radicalesbians' demands for the "abolition of the nuclear family" and a "women's militia."[75] The Radicalesbians issued sharp critiques of their experiences at the Philadelphia RPCC, and gay men's otherwise positive reports on the conference called for greater inclusion of lesbian feminism in upcoming RPCC meetings.[76]

Further RPCC plans were hampered by broader tensions fracturing the Black Panther Party's work. A "Regional RPCC" held in Berkeley in early November drew only a few hundred participants, almost all of them white; local gay and lesbian radicals attended but termed it unsuccessful and came away without concrete plans.[77] The final RPCC gathering was held over Thanksgiving weekend in Washington, DC, and drew nearly five thousand people, but was seriously weakened by disorganization as Party leaders faced a new onslaught of state repression and internal disputes. The conference was left in real disarray when the location where it was to be held, Howard University, suddenly canceled its venues. Some workshops and events were nonetheless held, and notably, the women's meeting issued a critique of lesbian feminists' exclusions in Philadelphia while also holding that the

Radicalesbians' demand to "abolish" the family "invalidat[ed]" black women.[78] Gay men's participation, again multiracial, numbered about 150 men, and activists adapted Panther style to gay terms with "brightly colored, hand-crocheted berets" and the chant "Homo, homo, homo-sexual, the ruling class is ineffectual."[79] Yet, more broadly, participants experienced the conference as markedly disorganized and left with little to no follow-up.[80]

Although the RPCCs sparked excitement within gay liberation, they did little to ground formal gay alliance with the Black Panther Party. Nonetheless, the visions sparked by the conferences informed Bay Area gay radicals' responses to a separate project that fall: a so-called gay nationalist project to take over California's Alpine County. In debating the Alpine project, gay radicals re-energized their critique of the gay ghetto and affirmed the centrality of radical alliance to sexual freedom.

In June 1970 Los Angeles activist Don Jackson had issued a proposal in the *Los Angeles Free Press:* "I imagine a place where gay people can be free. . . . A place where a gay government can build the base for a flourishing gay counter-culture and city. . . . The colony could become the gay symbol of liberty, a world center for the gay counter-culture, and a shining symbol of hope to all gay people in the world."[81] Jackson proposed that this "colony" occupy California's sparsely populated Alpine County, located in the Sierra Nevada south of Lake Tahoe. He called for gay men and lesbians to move by the hundreds to Alpine and build a "Gay homeland" or "Stonewall Nation."[82] Only about 500 people lived in Alpine County in 1970, including some 150 in Mar-kleeville, the county seat and largest town.[83] Roads into the area traversed 7,000- to 8,000-foot mountain passes frequently snowbound in winter. But, because the California Supreme Court had recently cut the residency requirement for voter registration to ninety days, a few hundred newcomers could quickly constitute the majority of voters, hold a recall, and take political power.[84] Jackson stated that Alpine promised a "gay territory . . . a gay government, a gay civil service, a county welfare department which made public assistance payments to the refugees from persecution and injustice."[85]

Jackson's proposal remained just an idea until October, when a *Los Angeles Times* reporter who had noticed the *Free Press* article phoned the Los Angeles GLF. Activist Don Kilhefner answered the call and told the journalist he was in luck: the GLF would be holding a press conference about the Alpine project. Kilhefner was bluffing, but he and others sprang into action; when the reporter arrived at the "press conference" on October 18, Kilhefner and two other GLF members described Alpine project plans and declared that three hundred people had signed up. The *Los Angeles Times* ran an article on the project the next day.[86] Both the alternative and mainstream press took note of the Alpine story, and throughout late October and November coverage expanded to the *San Francisco Chronicle,* the *Wall Street Journal, Time* magazine, and radical newspapers. Bay Area radicals began to discuss the project, with some declaring an "Alpine Liberation Front" independent of the San Francisco and Berkeley GLFs. Charles Thorpe, who had been a white student supporter in the Third World Strike, declared the formation of another Alpine support group: Bay Area Gays for Unification and Nationalism, or BAGFUN. By late November the *London Observer* reported that Alpine was attracting hundreds of potential migrants, verifying 479 from Los Angeles and as many as 1,179 overall.[87] Los Angeles activists claimed 128 financial backers offering more than $250,000 in capital, sought consultations from architectural and financial firms, and planned a trip to Alpine over the Thanksgiving weekend.[88] Meanwhile, Dr. Carl McIntire, a radio evangelist and pro-war organizer, called for "missionaries" to stop the takeover.[89] *Time* reported that members of the Alpine County Board of Supervisors traveled to Sacramento to meet with an advisor to Governor Ronald Reagan but came away "despondent and empty-handed" and were told "there was nothing they could do to stem the gay tide as long as the G.L.F. complied with the law."[90]

As the bravado of the press conference suggested, the Alpine County project was mostly a stunt, a bit of political theater used to define gay and lesbian identity as a question of oppression and power rather than pathology or deviance. Some of Don Jackson's earliest proposals neglected to name Alpine County at all, promoting only the general idea of a gay county takeover.[91] A publicity photo taken in Los Angeles featured a long-haired, barefooted young white man with a guitar case and small dog, hitching a ride at a freeway entrance with a sign reading "Alpine County—or other appropriate destination."[92] Measured in media terms, Alpine was massively successful: articles about the project said nothing about psychiatry and instead quoted activists speaking about legal recalls, voter registration, and police repression.

The centrality of media helps to explain the Alpine project's shallow treatment of race. Although project leaders made frequent reference to alliance with the Panthers, they did not take part in the RPCC and had no working relationship with any chapters of the Black Panther Party. Don Jackson spoke out about antigay oppression in prisons, jails, and mental institutions, yet, even when addressing this topic, failed to draw links to black or other Third World liberation movements.[93] Charles Thorpe, echoing his earlier claim that his gayness made him a "white Negro," compared the Alpine project to Native American activism: "It's like the Indians, if they take Alcatraz and stay, it's theirs."[94] This ignored the point that the occupation of Alcatraz Island, which had been launched by the group Indians of All Tribes in November 1969 and was ongoing, reclaimed already stolen land.[95]

Indeed, Alpine project leaders aimed to supersede racial liberation. Don Jackson claimed that while slavery had ended for black people, "gay people are still slaves today. . . . Huey Newton spoke truth when he said that Gay People are the most oppressed minority of all."[96] In implicit and explicit ways, Jackson and other project leaders described gay people as the Panthers and others were describing people of color: a colonized group inside the United States whose liberation could overthrow the establishment from within. The analogy implied building gay power through global alliance, but it marginalized people of color in order to claim a vanguard status for white gay men. Thorpe's San Francisco State group proposed an "ambassador of Stonewall Nation to Algeria," where Eldridge Cleaver lived in exile.[97] Don Kilhefner posited gay liberation as the model for radicals of color, calling the Alpine project "a scheme every oppressed minority could latch on to—there's an Alpine County in every state in the union."[98]

Blending the rhetoric of settler colonialism, global decolonization, and radical masculinity, Alpine project spokespeople described gay migrants as "pioneers" and the mountain county as "open land."[99] A *Berkeley Tribe* article promoting the project stated: "There will be hostile natives. Chopping wood, drawing water from a stream, severe Alpine winters, living in tents and Quonset huts. . . . A Gay city will rise from the huts and tents . . . [with] camaraderie and brotherhood."[100] Kilhefner compared it to a TV Western and described project participants enthusiastically as "a new breed of hardy, outdoor homosexuals."[101] Ostensibly this new "breed" could include people of color and white women; a project flier depicted three white men, one black man, and two white women over the headline "WANTED: FOR SEEKING REFUGE AND FREEDOM. 'THE ALPIONEERS'" (figure 3). Yet Alpine signups were almost entirely men, the leadership was entirely white men, and the language of "pioneer" was all but explicit in its racial and gender meaning.

Alpine was "open" only in project leaders' imaginations: it was home both to Anglo residents and to a few hundred members of the Washoe

FIGURE 3. Alpine County poster, 1970. Courtesy of Gay Liberation Front/Los Angeles Records, ONE Archives, University of Southern California Libraries.

tribe, whose land straddles eastern California and northern Nevada. Alpine leaders declared themselves friends of Washoe people even as they sought to conquer Washoe land. From October through December 1970, articles in the gay and radical press proclaimed "AlpLib for Washos Too" and "Gay Radical Says Alpine Indian Turf."[102] When the project sent an "Alpine County Penetration Committee" over Thanksgiving, the *San Francisco Examiner* quoted Los Angeles GLF member Morris Kight as saying, "The Washoe Indians have a private alliance with us."[103] This claim was false. In an internal project letter, Don Jackson proposed a meeting with Washoe people and wrote that "they are a primitive tribe . . . we can make no presumptions until we study them. It would be an immense asset if we could find a couple of Gay Indians to take along, but caution must be used that they are not from a tribe that is an ancient enemy. . . . The underground press will eat up a story of peace talks between Gays and Indians with photos of gift exchange etc."[104] Jackson's comments revealed his anti-Native racism, his ignorance of both Washoe history and pan-Indian radicalism, and his orientation toward media spectacle. Alpine project leaders never met with Washoe leaders and, in attempting to cull information on Washoe culture, emphasized peyote and traditional pine nut harvesting because "health food people and hippies dig" both.[105]

By November 1970, the Berkeley GLF formally opposed the Alpine project, rejecting it in a two-thirds vote that the national gay magazine *The Advocate* termed "the first major split . . . of the West Coast Gay Liberation Movement."[106] The split was both ideological and regional, dividing the largest Bay Area gay liberation group from the one in Los Angeles. A Berkeley GLF representative argued that Jackson's proposal for a gay-Native gift exchange and treaty was nothing more than "buying people. And I think it would be a much better approach if someone asked the Indians how they felt about our coming up there."[107] Activist Nick Benton termed the project "racist, sexist, impractical and counterrevolutionary nationalist."[108] He and others argued that Alpine threatened to reproduce the "gay ghetto," establishing another site of isolation and exploitation rather than a transformed society. As one article stated, "Even if we seize the county, we cannot outlaw private property or keep out the Tavern Guild or the money of organized crime."[109] *Gay Sunshine* added, "Among Gay people there is resentment and fear of . . . [Alpine project leaders], who somehow have the Gay world by the balls, who somehow understand the Establishment 'mysteries' of County government, mass media manipulation, and land financing and development."[110]

Alpine leaders responded with a shallow vision of diversity: Alpine would be for "gays and straights, men and women, black and white and red and brown and yellow, young and old alike in a spirit of peace and fellowship. It is, indeed, a gay project for spreading freedom all over the world and to all kinds of people."[111] The Bay Area Alpine Liberation Front issued a resolution of support for Washoe people and called for the majority of the Alpine County Board of Supervisors to be gay and lesbian people of color.[112] Yet these responses ignored the substance of critics' opposition, which held that gay nationalism co-opted gay liberation by making gay people colonizers in the US West.[113] Assailed by critics, the Alpine project lost steam by March 1971, and no gay group ever moved in.[114]

Alpine did, however, have at least one lasting effect: it prompted clarification of the differences between gay nationalism and a gay left. The radicals who rejected the Alpine project held that gay nationalism stood in conflict with Third World solidarity and that it replicated the gay ghetto. By contrast, they argued that sexual liberation could be achieved only through anti-capitalist, anti-imperialist revolution. Thus, in opposing the Alpine project, gay leftists crystallized their own goals.

In January 1971 a group of gay men of color, Third World Gay People, formed out of the Berkeley GLF. The group was prompted in large part by a police assault at the Stud, a gay bar in San Francisco's South of Market neighborhood that was popular with both white and black men.[115] Police surrounded the bar at closing time on December 11, 1970, and fired on a young white man trying to drive away.[116] Third World Gay People member Michael Robinson described the Stud shooting as an example of police violence against gay men and argued that only a multiracial alliance against the police could end such violence. Robinson asserted that most white men who frequented the Stud "have failed to deal with their racism" and urged white gay readers of *Gay Sunshine* not only to rally against the Stud shooting but also to support "Bobby Seale, [the] Seattle 7 . . . John Cluchette, or any of the powerful Indians of Alcatraz," since white gay people needed "the people of the world fighting with them" to achieve liberation.[117] Indeed, *Gay Sunshine* reported in February 1971 that members of the San Francisco and Berkeley GLFs had attended "solidarity days" for Panther and prison activists Bobby Seale, Ericka Huggins, Angela Y. Davis, and Ruchell (Cinque) Magee.[118]

Gay liberation also continued to make significant inroads in anti-war work, particularly the veterans' and GI movement, in which activists defined sexism as a tool of military control.[119] By 1971 GI newspapers gave positive coverage to gay sailors' and soldiers' concerns, GI bookstores stocked gay liberationist newspapers, and GI organizing centers hosted gay discussion groups.[120] Some leaders of Vietnam Veterans Against the War, most prominently Vince Muscari, came out as gay, and in fall 1971 Muscari took a Vietnam Veterans Against the War contingent to a national gay conference in Madison, Wisconsin.[121] Gay radicals organized large contingents in anti-war marches held nationally on April 24, 1971, and in a protest in the US capital on May Day. In such efforts, activists identified military masculinism as a gendered "role" that held deadly consequences.[122] Similarly, a reflection in *Gay Sunshine* held that the anti-war movement allowed gay people to come out in broad daylight rather than only in stigmatized "gay ghettos." In this article, activists contrasted the freedoms of a march with the alienation they observed in San Francisco's Tenderloin and stated that "this bright Saturday afternoon, marching under the many banners and a transformed lavender and purple Viet Cong flag . . . we demonstrated to ourselves and everyone else that we are no longer hiding and apart."[123]

Adding to these efforts, by 1973 gay radicals produced a new organization in Oakland, the Gay Men's Political Action Group. Rooted in a collective household, the Political Action Group drew a mix of white and black gay radicals who focused on supporting the campaign of Black Panthers Bobby Seale and Elaine Brown for Oakland mayor and city council.[124] Seale and Brown had announced their candidacies on May 13, 1972, nearly a year before municipal elections. Their campaign confronted the city's Republican- and white-dominated political machine and reflected a national push for black candidates to elected office as well as the contraction of the Black Panther Party's work to the Bay Area. During spring and summer 1972 the Oakland Party promoted electoral power through food giveaways that combined voter registration with the distribution of groceries to thousands of people. While both Seale and Brown ultimately lost, Seale forced the incumbent mayor into a runoff, drew over a third of the total vote, and galvanized unprecedented voter turnout that laid groundwork for the 1977 mayoral election of black moderate Lionel Wilson.[125]

As Donna Murch notes, Seale and Brown's campaign "cultivated a broad range of alliances" that included gay groups.[126] Members of the Gay Men's Political Action Group conducted voter registration and outreach in gay bars and community sites and met with Seale, Brown, and other Black Panther Party leaders, while the *Black Panther* reprinted the Political Action Group's flier. This piece of publicity stated, "Gay men and women, who reject the definition of homosexuals as mentally ill, are another part of the population who have been oppressed by and invisible to the Readings, the Kaisers, and the Oakland Tribune," and noted that as "an inter-racial group, [the Political Action Group] is aware of the connection between racism and sexism."[127] Seale and Brown opposed antigay discrimination in employment, housing, and by the police and backed a city measure to end such bias; supported city funding of a gay community center and clinic; and called for the reform of laws affecting gay and lesbian people in child custody and adoption, mental hospitals and prisons, and taxation and inheritance. At one Political Action Group event, one hundred gay men and lesbians met with Ericka Huggins and other Black Panther Party leaders to discuss "prison oppression of gay people, women and Third World peoples, and the stand of the Black Panther Party on prostitution and transvestism."[128] Although the Gay Men's Political Action Group faded after Seale and Brown's electoral defeat, its members remained active in forging ties with the labor movement for the next several years.[129]

Thus, far from representing only a brief upsurge of gay liberation, the early 1970s marked the start of a new political current: a gay left. Over the next few years gay leftists began to seek alliances with lesbian feminists, and by the end of the decade, activists built a gay and lesbian left that pursued multiracial and anti-imperialist solidarity. The path toward this future would run through lesbian feminists' autonomous organizing—a form of activism that developed simultaneously with gay men's politics but that responded specifically to women's experiences of sexual repression, gendered violence, and radical struggle.

CHAPTER 2

A More Powerful Weapon

Lesbian Feminism and Collective Defense

On March 27, 1975, police arrested Susan Saxe, a white lesbian and radical, in Philadelphia. Saxe had spent almost five years underground, pursued by the FBI following her participation in two actions in 1970: the theft of National Guard documents that revealed government plans for suppressing dissent against the Vietnam War, and a bank robbery that was intended to direct funds to the Black Panther Party and in which a member of Saxe's group unexpectedly shot and killed Walter Schroeder, a Boston police officer. Following her capture in 1975, Saxe made a public statement in which she affirmed her anti-imperialism and refused to testify against her fellow radicals. She also linked her lesbian identity and feminism to her refusal to collaborate with the federal government, closing her statement by declaring: "A greeting of love and strength to all my sisters—courage for our warriors, hope for our people and especially for all my sisters and brothers underground in Amerika. Keep on fighting, stay free, stay strong. I promise you a courage to match your own. I intend to fight on in every way as a Lesbian, a feminist, and an Amazon. The love that I share with my sisters, my people, is a far more powerful weapon than any the police state can bring to bear against us."[1]

It was not incidental or exceptional that Saxe described her "love" for her comrades as a "weapon." Nor was it insignificant that she named this love as simultaneously erotic and political, her lesbian identity overlapping with solidarity with both "sisters and brothers" evading the US state.

Saxe's statement reflected a politics well established by 1975, one that defined lesbian feminism as a strategy of opposition to US state violence. Guided by support for the Black Panther Party, prison radicalism, and the anti-war movement, as well as by opposition to gendered violence, lesbian radicals argued that their safety, survival, and self-determination demanded they refuse to collaborate with the US government.

Lesbian feminists linked the goals of community protection and radical alliance in a politics I term *collective defense*. They drew the politics of collective defense from the black liberation movement, adapted it through their support for armed resistance and the underground, and used it to counter the intersection of gendered violence and racial criminalization. They also lived collective defense through their shared households, which sheltered both political fugitives such as Saxe and more ordinary women escaping domestic violence. Collective defense describes the means by which women constructed lesbian feminism as interdependent with anti-imperialism from the early through the mid-1970s.

For older women, collective defense resonated with decades of struggle against state harassment; as activist Joan Nestle reflected on the passage of time from the 1950s through 1970s, "The police that I had grown accustomed to confronting in the Village bars became the state troopers of Baltimore and Alabama; the mounted troops of Washington, D.C. became the carefully dressed undercover FBI agents snapping our photographs at every demonstration."[2] Police brutality, politically motivated trials of black liberation and anti-war radicals, and prison organizing deepened alliances across race and social movement sectors and made noncooperation with the US state central to multiple forms of radical identity just as lesbian feminism was emerging.[3] Moreover, shaped by the longtime policing of queer life, sensationalist media defined even straight women's radicalism as deviant, and state surveillance placed lesbian and feminist communities on high alert.

The links that lesbian leftists drew between gendered militancy, armed resistance, and the underground were influenced by years of experiences and alliances, but they were not automatic nor did everyone share them. Rather, collective defense emerged in contrast to other lesbian and feminist responses that separated themselves from a male-dominated left and that turned toward alliances with the police and courts to address rape and battering. Because collective defense describes only some aspects of lesbian feminism, it helps to trace debates within that broader movement. In addition, it helps to counter historical narratives that have misrepresented lesbian feminism as essentially or monolithically white and separatist. As a growing number of scholars show, women of color were key actors in lesbian feminism, and intersectional, anti-statist, and anti-carceral politics were central aspects of the movement.[4] Likewise, the rhetoric, theory, and practice of collective defense fueled the growth of a lesbian feminist left dedicated to anti-imperialist solidarity. At the same time, collective defense proved contradictory in its politics of race: it defined lesbian feminist politics as anti-racist but furthered the representation of lesbian identity as white.

Collective defense gained early expression in Gay Women's Liberation, or GWL, the first lesbian feminist organization in the Bay Area to form independent of the homophile movement.[5] Active from 1969 to 1972, GWL adapted ideas and tactics from the Black Panther Party and embedded these politics into its approaches to collective living and its creation of new community institutions. Following on GWL, lesbian feminists developed collective defense through their responses to three other major issues between 1973 and 1976. These were the Symbionese Liberation Army (SLA), an armed radical group whose notoriety centered on its women members, both lesbian and straight; the case of Susan Saxe, whose defense gained meaning in part through Saxe's contrast to another feminist radical, Jane Alpert; and the cases of Inez Garcia and Joan Little, two women of color charged with murder for acts taken to protect themselves against rape.

This chapter uses the term "collective defense" rather than a phrase activists used more often, "self-defense," so as to avoid confusion over the latter term's varying meanings. In the southern civil rights movement, self-defense stood as practical accompaniment to nonviolence, as pursued by the Deacons for Defense; with the turn to Black Power it grounded self-determination in opposition to state assault, as exemplified by the Panthers' original full name, the Black Panther Party for Self-Defense.[6] A related term, "mass defense," described campaigns to support radicals who were imprisoned or charged in political trials, such as Huey Newton and Angela Davis. Lesbian and radical feminists shifted the meanings of self-defense by working against the interpersonal threats of rape, battering, and street harassment, and they expanded mass defense by backing Inez Garcia, Joan Little, and other women who killed their rapists. Feminists also responded to the proliferation of radical images of armed women. Many on the left celebrated images of Vietnamese and other "Third World" women cradling babies and guns, although as scholar Judy Tzu-Chun Wu observes, these images furthered heteronormativity by suggesting "that in order to fulfill her role as a mother, the female peasant must take up arms."[7] In partial reaction to such constraints, some expressions of lesbian separatism placed men in the gunsights; Martha Shelley of New York's Radicalesbians responded to images of armed motherhood by stating that women "must pick up the gun and turn it on the men who are issuing all these orders."[8] The concept of collective defense brings together varying expressions of counterviolence, but somewhat against Shelley, it highlights how lesbian feminists tied women's autonomy to left solidarity against the US state.

As the above discussion suggests, collective defense held ties to "armed resistance" and "armed struggle," or violence, sabotage, and theft for radical and revolutionary aims—for example, obtaining government documents, destroying military equipment, funding radical groups, or compelling negotiation inside prisons for changes in conditions or for prisoners' release. Those who took up such actions inside the United States aligned themselves with struggles for anti-colonial liberation and hoped to provoke broader rebellion. Most limited their efforts to property destruction and robbery and worked to avoid human casualties; the Weather Underground adopted this limitation after its 1970 Townhouse explosion, in which a bomb under construction detonated prematurely, killing three group members rather than their intended targets.[9] By the mid-1970s, however, some armed groups employed kidnapping or assassination, and some acts intended not to cause personal harm did so either because of the response of government forces or because of mistakes or disagreements among activists.

Lesbian feminist collective defense was not the same as armed resistance, and indeed, many who engaged in a rhetoric or practice of collective defense opposed or were critical of armed groups. But collective defense did align with the "radical underground," a set of strategies and networks used to organize clandestinely and to evade arrest or prosecution for political activity, including but not limited to armed struggle. Going underground included living in hiding, operating under an alias, and moving from place to place. Defense of the underground gained significantly more adherents than did armed activity itself, in part because some underground tactics were initiated in draft resistance and tied to the pacifist movement, and also because even those innocent of criminal charges might feel compelled to evade the state.[10] For example, in August 1970 Angela Davis was accused of supplying guns to Jonathan Jackson, the seventeen-year-old brother of prison radical George Jackson. Jonathan staged a raid on the Marin County Courthouse in hopes of freeing three prisoners collectively known as the Soledad Brothers: his brother George,

Fleeta Drumgo, and John Clutchette. Facing conspiracy charges, Davis fled underground until she was arrested in October, and a broad movement sprang up in her defense. As activist and historian Bettina Aptheker notes, the "Free Angela Davis" movement mobilized support simply by demanding that Davis be released on bail; this was an effective demand because while many people believed Davis innocent, others felt that she could be guilty but nonetheless backed her right to fair treatment before trial. Amidst police murders of Black Panther Party leaders and other radicals, Davis's supporters understood her time underground not necessarily as evidence of her guilt, but rather as reflecting her reasonable fear of state persecution and assassination.[11]

Similar dynamics played out in the Susan Saxe, Joan Little, and Inez Garcia campaigns. Both Saxe and Little spent time evading arrest, and all three women's supporters defined them as political prisoners who would not get fair trials without public pressure.[12] Little and Garcia acknowledged they had committed murder in self-defense and argued that the courts must respect these acts in order to support their and all women's rights to bodily autonomy. Saxe's defense campaign described her as innocent of the murder of police officer Walter Schroeder and held that she was now targeted for her other, expressly political acts. Moreover, lesbian feminist community itself became a resource to the underground: Saxe sustained herself through the early 1970s in lesbian feminist communities around the United States, and her supporters praised her refusal to inform on those who had sheltered her during this time.

Lesbian support for the underground drew on feminist critiques of policing and imprisonment, which understood the criminalization of radical dissent—particularly by women—as interwoven with the criminalization of gender transgression and of homosexuality. In June 1970, when gay, lesbian, trans, and other people in New York City commemorated the first anniversary of the Stonewall Riots, they took their march past the Women's House of Detention in Greenwich Village (commonly known as the House of D). The jail was notorious among those arrested for gender and sexual nonconformity as well as political activism. On the day of the Stonewall commemoration it held Afeni Shakur and Joan Bird, two members of the "Panther 21" who had been arrested on bomb conspiracy charges and were later revealed to have been framed by the FBI. Members of the Gay Liberation Front chanted "Free Our Sisters! Free Ourselves!" in front of the jail, and the next month they held a gay and lesbian march against police harassment that ended at the House of D.[13] Critiques of criminalization continued across the 1970s as the FBI sought Saxe and other fugitive radicals within lesbian feminist communities. Government agents threatened to out women to families and employers if they did not collaborate, and these tactics fueled lesbian feminist resistance to cooperation with the state. This resistance also shaped lesbian and gay prisoner activism, including the gay men's collective Join Hands and the prisoner project of Boston's *Gay Community News,* which provided the newspaper free to prisoners and maintained correspondence with them.[14]

Finally, collective defense was shaped by a broader cultural slippage between "lesbian" and "feminist." For some, this link was simply negative association—an image used to keep women in line, or the "lavender menace" that Betty Friedan and other anti-lesbian feminists defined as a threat to women's chances for rights, power, and respectability. But many radical women actively embraced the slippage between "lesbian" and "feminist" in order to emphasize the argument that all women, regardless of their desires, were oppressed by compulsory heterosexuality. An extension of this argument posed lesbianism as a "vanguard" strategy of women's liberation, inspiring the claim that "feminism is the theory, lesbianism the practice" (a popular misstatement of Ti-Grace Atkinson's original, less prescriptive contention that "feminism is a theory, lesbianism is a practice").[15] The related label "political lesbian" described someone who chose to center her political, emotional, and sexual loyalties with other women even if she had not previously understood or experienced her sexual desire in these terms.[16]

Collective defense tied "lesbian" to "feminist" in terms that echoed depictions of women in armed resistance and the underground. In 1970 Angela Davis, Weather Underground member Bernadine Dohrn, and Susan Saxe and her associate Kathy Power all made the FBI's Ten Most Wanted list. Women linked to radical violence aroused public fascination, and the mass media focused especially on educated, middle-class white women who seemed to demonstrate that black radicalism "turned" or "seduced" them toward criminality.[17] (Angela Davis did not fit this narrative so neatly, but her prosecution also described her as controlled by her love for George Jackson.[18]) White lesbian radicals, such as Saxe and those in the SLA, added a twist to this narrative that linked racialized seduction to homosexual deviance, underscoring the view that white women who claimed solidarity with black men broke sexual as well as racial norms. Although black lesbians had long been represented as criminal, mainstream responses to the underground merged with the concept of the "political lesbian" in ways that pushed black and other lesbians of color out of view: the trope of white girls gone wrong left little space for anyone else.[19] This phenomenon partly explained why, despite its multiracial origins and anti-racist commitments, lesbian feminism during the early to mid-1970s seemed to further rather than challenge the construction of lesbian identity as white.

. . .

The organization Gay Women's Liberation, which formed in 1969, has received a rich recounting through the memoir of Judy Grahn, one of the premier poets of lesbian feminism and one of GWL's founders. Born in 1940, Grahn grew up white and working class in New Mexico and in 1960 joined the army, where she trained as a medic and was soon dishonorably discharged for homosexuality. She went on to earn a BA from Howard University, where she was introduced to the homophile movement by the black sociologist Nathan Hare, later the first chair of Black Studies at San Francisco State.[20] Prior to GWL, Grahn joined the Mattachine Society in Washington, DC, and participated in the first gay rights picket at the Capitol, held in front of the White House in spring 1965. In late spring 1968 she and her lover Wendy Cadden moved to San Francisco, where the two dove deeply into radical community and activism. They participated in the Third World Strike at San Francisco State as "nonstudent organizers," did publicity work with and for the Black Panther Party, joined the radical film collective Newsreel, and took part in Berkeley protests for People's Park. Grahn also joined a writing group of gay men who congregated around the poet Robert Duncan; one of its participants, Henry Noyes, owned a communist bookstore in San Francisco called China Books and later featured Grahn's first book of poems, *Edward the Dyke,* in the window. By 1969, anti-lesbian attitudes in a group of straight women pushed Grahn toward organizing with other lesbians and gay men, and in November she, Cadden, their friend Linda Wilson, and Wilson's girlfriend attended the North American Conference of Homophile Organizations (NACHO) in Berkeley.[21]

While at NACHO, Grahn gave a speech, "On the Development of a Purple Fist," that pushed her audience to consider how corporations, the government, and militarism benefited from maintaining divisions along lines of sexuality as well as gender, race, and class. Grahn insisted that the only effective response to established power was for lesbians and gay men to unite with their "natural allies": women's liberation, the student left, the environmental movement, and black, Chicano, and poor white radicals. By expressing these ideas, Grahn echoed similar statements circulating both in gay men's liberation and in feminist groups. Historian Sherie Randolph observes that in New York, black feminist Flo Kennedy had long been pushing younger white women to see Black Power as "a potential model for organizing both in their own interest and as part of broad-based progressive coalitions"; Grahn adapted such an approach for lesbians and gay men, and she drew on socialist feminist thought by identifying antigay hostility as an outgrowth of capitalism.[22] Most centrally, Grahn argued against single-issue politics by concluding:

> If heterosexuals hated us just for the hell of it, massive love potions would be the answer. But if they are taught to hate us in order to protect the nuclear family structure—which also cuts people off from each other, and forces them to buy more products than, say, communal living would; or if they are taught to hate us because it puts a sharper edge to job competition; or if they are taught to hate us because we function as a social control and scapegoat that ultimately works to keep the money and power and resources of this country in the hands of only a very few people—then we have to be doubly armed against that hatred, and ready to fight it at many different levels.[23]

Although this speech eventually became widely distributed among lesbian and gay radicals, it initially produced little response because the NACHO audience was composed of politically moderate, noncountercultural gay men. As a result, Grahn and her friends turned to each other to form their own organization and, in December 1969, created GWL.

The women who formed GWL began from the "agreement that we wanted revolutionary changes for everyone, but that separate lesbian political meetings—separate from straight people, separate from gay men, separate from everyone—needed to happen."[24] Here "separate" meant autonomous more than separatist, as Grahn and Cadden at the time lived in a mixed-gender household that included straight men interested in feminism, and GWL participated in activist campaigns alongside men. GWL's weekly meetings numbered upward of sixty women—largely white, though with several people of color, principally black women. Linda Wilson and the poet Pat Parker were two black lesbians involved from the outset; another black lesbian, Pat Norman, joined in 1970; and Red Jordan Arobateau, a mixed-race person who today lives as a trans man, also played a central role. The group's most active white members were Grahn, Cadden, Alice Molloy, Carol Wilson, Natalie Lando, Naomi Greschel, Patricia Jackson, and Louise Merrill. Merrill was the oldest in the group and in the 1950s had lived in

New York, where she was married, ran for state senator on the Socialist Workers Party ticket, and helped found a chapter of the Workers World Party. Yet while Merrill and Grahn had histories in the Old Left and the homophile movement, GWL belonged decisively to its own time. The group was active from the end of 1969 through mid-1972, and its work included consciousness-raising, protests, participation in political coalitions, and dances and poetry readings. Straight feminists were drawn politically if not sexually to this scene, since as Grahn puts it, "Overnight, 'dyke' had gone from the status of a Category 5 hurricane to the only possible site of rescue from harm."[25]

Collective households were central to GWL and to lesbian feminism and gay liberation generally, serving as bases of activism, hubs to germinate regional and national networks, and venues for developing a multi-issue sexual politics. As historian Stephen Vider observes, they were a form of prefigurative politics—that is, a way to enact goals of social transformation in the here and now. These households became a means to "redefine lesbianism as a form of political resistance," and liberationist gay men followed lesbians' lead in using collective households to create alternative family and to challenge sex and gender roles.[26] Bars were not irrelevant; the San Francisco bar Maud's, located in the Haight, was seen as especially open to activism because it drew black as well as white women. Though women of color remained distinctly in the minority at Maud's, Pat Parker and Linda Wilson both became regulars there, and black lesbian Mandy Carter (a prominent leader in the War Resisters' League) tended the bar for a number of years.[27] But as compared to bars, households became venues for meetings, for hosting visiting activists from out of town, and for binding activist groups together through day-to-day living. They provided locations from which to challenge gendered domestic labor, to destabilize the centrality of couples to domestic life, to pursue anti-capitalist and cooperative economics, and to create new intimate bonds that blurred sexual relationships, comradeship, and other bonds of family. Lesbian and gay collective living queered the household form itself and helped activists ground multi-issue politics in sexual community.[28]

From late 1969 to early 1971, GWL revolved around an apartment on Lexington Street in San Francisco's Mission District and a rented house on Benvenue Street in Berkeley; residents were eventually evicted from the latter after too many loud parties that included women sitting topless on the porch.[29] In late spring 1971, two other GWL members purchased a home on Terrace Street in North Oakland and those from

Lexington Street, including Judy Grahn and Wendy Cadden, moved in. The Terrace Street property housed several women at a time and a total of about forty over five years. A policy that every woman have her own room diminished the centrality of couples, and the house also served as an organizing base for the Women's Press Collective, the Lesbian Mothers' Union, and the bookstore ICI: A Woman's Place, which was located nearby and had opened in 1970 (the initials stood for Information Center Incorporated).[30] Terrace Street and other collective houses grounded GWL in a distinct politics of place, affirming central Berkeley, North Oakland, and San Francisco's Mission District as key sites of lesbian feminist community from at least 1970 onward. All of these were working- to middle-class neighborhoods near multiple venues of activist organizing and community, and were racially and ethnically mixed yet set apart from the majority-black areas of West and East Oakland. In the following decades lesbian and gay people both challenged and participated in gentrification in these areas.[31]

Taken together, lesbian feminist households aided efforts toward autonomy from both the market and the state. Some GWL homes sheltered women who were fugitives underground or helped to broadcast messages issued by underground groups. One informally housed battered women; GWL member Louise Merrill lived here with her lover and their two children. Another functioned as the Oakland Feminist Women's Health Center by day and a regular household by night, with women storing bedclothes, dishes, and other items each morning to make way for clinic space. Lesbian feminist households helped to both launch and support new institutions such as bookstores and cafés, a function that black lesbian Lenn Keller recalls as key to attracting newcomers to the Bay Area seeking out political and social resources. Even as collective households tended to reflect the racial and class segregation of the broader society, lesbians of color used them to counter isolation. Many Bay Area lesbians of color formed households together, and their house parties proved more central to lesbian of color community than did the predominately white dance clubs and bars. Pat Parker shepherded households in Oakland and in the San Francisco neighborhoods of Haight-Ashbury and Potrero Hill that supported activism and cultural work among black women, and another cluster of black lesbians lived adjacent to Berkeley and West Oakland in the city of Emeryville.[32]

From its outset, GWL worked in solidarity with the Black Panther Party. Pat Parker played an important role in that she participated as a member in both the Party and GWL, while white lesbian Louise Merrill was deeply involved in Panther support work. In December 1969 Merrill, Grahn, and Cadden joined a "living wall of defense" or "white buffer" against law enforcement called by the San Francisco Black Panther Party after the Chicago police assassinated Fred Hampton and the police waged a four-hour assault on the Panther office in Los Angeles.[33] In early fall 1970, the Panthers held their Revolutionary People's Constitutional Convention (RPCC) in Philadelphia; gay men's experiences here were largely positive, but the lesbian caucus felt tension and exclusion and reported their responses widely in the gay, feminist, and radical press (see chapter 1). However, while New York's Radicalesbians found themselves in conflict with Panther leadership, GWL forged a much stronger relationship with the Party and, in November 1970, participated in two follow-up gatherings for the RPCC. At the Bay Area regional RPCC held in Berkeley, GWL crafted a list of demands to be implemented in the city of Berkeley and its public schools: free twenty-four-hour-a-day bus transportation for women, free self-defense classes for all women and girls, women's right to bear both concealed and unconcealed loaded weapons, and diversion of a portion of the Berkeley police budget to women's liberation groups.[34] These concrete, tangible goals reflected the influence of the Panthers' Ten Point Plan, free breakfast, and other "survival programs" alongside women's day-to-day experiences of sexual harassment and gendered violence. Soon after the Bay Area gathering, GWL members Patricia Jackson, Naomi Greschel, and Carol Wilson traveled across the country to attend the final RPCC conference in Washington, DC.[35] Although the RPCCs were hindered by internal fractures within the Party and produced few, if any, follow-up plans, the process of attending RPCC gatherings helped GWL define and declare its politics.

As GWL developed, it reworked the Panthers' early tactics of police patrols to confront gendered violence. The group leafleted a neighborhood to shame a man who had raped a dancer at a bachelor party, staged interventions to interrupt domestic violence, held vigils outside the homes of batterers, and on at least one occasion called itself the Women's Defense League of Oakland to intimidate an alleged batterer. GWL also engaged in verbal and even physical confrontations with men who harassed or assaulted women on the street or in lesbian bars. Red Jordan Arobateau taught self-defense skills to GWL members, and some in the group owned guns or visited shooting ranges. By 1972, aspects of these efforts informed one of the first rape crisis centers in the

United States, San Francisco Women Against Rape (SFWAR), which ran a rape hotline from a Mission District apartment.[36]

Collective defense also fueled lesbian feminist erotics. Grahn recalls that GWL members "considered ourselves a guerilla army and dressed that way" and that displays of militant strength held sexual charge: "We found each other sexy in fatigues, boots, and colored, tight-fitting under-shirts with no bras."[37] This "uniform" was consciously adapted from a Panther aesthetic and, like much of radical and feminist fashion, enabled a kind of guerrilla street performance.[38] It also aligned with the desire some felt toward Panther women, controversially made evident in lesbian feminism when Lois Hart, a member of the Radicalesbians in New York, praised Panther leader Afeni Shakur as a "beautiful Black woman, virile, revolutionary, nickname 'Power.'"[39] Hart's rhetoric reflected long-standing cultural depictions of black women as masculine and evidenced white people's privilege to define black people as objects of desire.

Associations like Hart's could easily be posed in negative terms to define women of color as aggressive or imposing. By 1974 this problem helped to spur the creation of Gente, a Bay Area group of lesbians of color that numbered as many as forty people and that first formed as a softball team. Gente's members observed that when they entered bars as individuals, they found themselves racially "invisible," yet when they entered as a group "somehow, we cause a threat." These receptions inspired black and Latina women to form Gente to claim and remake their identities as lesbians of color. Tellingly, Gente engaged in much of the same alliance work as white-dominated lesbian feminist groups, but it was not nearly so invested in support for the underground or other dimensions of collective defense. Rather, Gente used softball to generate multiracial bonds among women of color and to redirect energy away from responding to white women's perceptions and expectations.[40]

Gente's experiences suggest that collective defense encouraged white lesbians to define their politics by emulating a black militancy that was popularly perceived as masculine or androgynous, but not feminine. In some ways, this representation echoed what Judy Tzu-Chun Wu has termed a "radical orientalism" in the anti-war movement, a representa-tion through which North American radicals "romanticized and identi-fied with revolutionary Asian nations and political figures" in order to define their own liberation.[41] After GWL dissolved in mid-1972, lesbian feminists in the Bay Area and beyond continued to enact collective defense through their responses to the SLA and the cases of Susan Saxe, Joan Lit-tle, and Inez Garcia. Activism around these cases continued both to propel anti-racist solidarities and to draw racialized boundaries around lesbian identity.

. . .

The Symbionese Liberation Army (SLA) sprang into public view in November 1973 when it assassinated Marcus Foster, the first black superintendent of the Oakland Unified School District. The SLA justified this murder by claiming, mistakenly, that Foster supported a strict identification card policy and the introduction of police into the city's schools. Three months later, in February 1974, the SLA kidnapped Patty Hearst, heir to the family that controlled San Francisco's media establishment. The group initially sought to free the SLA members charged with Foster's murder, then used Hearst's kidnaping to demand a massive food giveaway. The SLA was part of a new wave of armed resistance in the United States, West Germany, Italy, and Japan that moved beyond property destruction to include tactics of assassination and bombings that risked human life.[42] Although some radicals believed this new stage of violence to be warranted, many prominent leftists disassociated themselves from the SLA. Some felt the group's members "spoke like agents provocateurs" or accused its leader, black radical Cinque Mtume (earlier known as Donald DeFreeze), of collaborating with the federal government; others saw Mtume's leadership as sincere but cultish.[43] However, the SLA generated somewhat more support in spring 1974 when the Los Angeles Police Department firebombed the group's safe house and killed six of its core leaders. The May 1974 attack was fully televised and widely broadcast. In addition, it occurred in a working-class black neighborhood, involved a SWAT team, and directly recalled the department's December 1969 assault on the Los Angeles Black Panther Party. Following the safe house bombing, the SLA's remaining members moved back to the Bay Area, from which base they gained some new adherents, carried out a fatal bank robbery near Sacramento, and attempted to bomb members of the LAPD. The group disbanded when Hearst and others were captured in fall 1975, and its aboveground support dissolved soon after.

Radical feminists and lesbians were especially affected by the SLA because of women's highly visible participation in the group and media fascination with these women's roles. Patty Hearst provided a spectacular example of links between women and violence, as narratives of her time in the SLA frequently conflated her use of guns with a heterosexual seduction by Cinque Mtume.[44] Such accounts adapted the long-standing trope of black men as raping white women into a new image: black radical men using sex to unleash white women's own capacity for violence. Besides Hearst, two other white women in the SLA—Camilla Hall and Mizmoon (Patricia Soltysik)—were significant because they were lovers. Media reports typically characterized these women's participation as a natural outgrowth of their deviant, masculine, and criminal sexuality; they also described Mizmoon as sexually and politically more assertive than Hall, implying that she "awakened" Hall much as Cinque Mtume was assumed to have moved Hearst. In response, SLA supporters held that mass media distorted the SLA's actions as evidence not of political commitment but sexual "psychopathology"; they paraphrased media coverage as claiming that "the women are lesbians and therefore are sick to start with" and that "the white women are all sexual slaves to one black stud."[45] In highlighting such sexual and racial anxieties, SLA supporters sought to undercut the authority of those who deemed the group a threat.

The FBI conducted several raids of lesbian feminist households and community spaces during the height of its hunt for Camilla Hall, Mizmoon, and other members of the SLA. These raids were concentrated in the Bay Area because of the group's local roots, and as activist Ruth Mahaney recalls, they were amplified by "plainclothes [agents] in the bars and everywhere lesbians went." Indeed, Mahaney was once detained by undercover agents who claimed she looked like Camilla Hall. The agents were conducting surveillance outside a San Francisco concert by Malvina Reynolds, a folksinger with a large women's audience, and though Mahaney and Hall share little resemblance, both fit the image of "lesbians" in being white and semiandrogynous. Mahaney was highly critical of the SLA, but her experience with the agents—who surrounded her, blocked her way, and flashed their badges when she stepped outside the concert to buy chewing gum—bolstered her opposition to state surveillance.[46]

Beyond profiling and raids, the FBI pushed activists to inform on one another, a pressure that grew over the early 1970s owing both to the growth of lesbian feminist communities and to changes in federal law. In 1970 the Organized Crime Control Act enabled grand juries to more easily compel testimony from witnesses, and by 1973 grand juries had questioned more than two thousand people in over eighty cities about their activities in the anti-war movement. Emboldened by the grand jury system, FBI agents used antigay hostility to pressure radicals to speak. Susan Saxe's associate Kathy Power later recalled that "the feds would threaten our lesbian friends with exposing them to their families and employers, and then they would carry out their threats."[47] This climate of intimidation held serious material effects for many women and motivated support for the underground.

For all these reasons, an influential number of lesbian feminists communicated with fugitive radicals, opposed state crackdowns, and argued for collective protection of those underground. Former GWL member Louise Merrill received publications from the SLA's front group, the Bay Area Research Collective, and paid enough attention to the group to keep its missives in her archives.[48] Judy Grahn met clandestinely for several years with women in the Weather Underground, and in 1975 the Oakland Women's Press Collective—an offshoot of GWL networks—published *Sing a Battle Song*, a book of poems by women in the Weather Underground, as well as *The Women's Gun Pamphlet: A Primer on Handguns*. The second publication focused on personal self-protection, but also strongly critiqued police and advised readers that "you wouldn't want to carry your gun when you expect to be in a place where police search is likely, like at a lesbian bar or at a political demonstration, or if you think you may be suspected of shoplifting."[49]

Support for underground activity became a means by which lesbian feminists declared their solidarity with other radical formations and causes. In summer 1974 a group of lesbian and radical feminists in Los Angeles held a protest against the LAPD's assault on the SLA's safe house, noting that "all of the women who burned [in the firebombing] were feminists; two were lesbians." Connecting sexism to racism, war, and the recent CIA-backed coup against Chilean president Salvador Allende, the SLA supporter argued that Camilla Hall, Mizmoon, and other SLA women had chosen to "fight" alongside—and, importantly, not against—men "because they saw that the oppression they experienced as women and as lesbians is not an isolated phenomenon. That the oppression of all people—black sisters and brothers, Chicanas and Chicanos, Native American people, workers, children, older people, etc.—are all linked. And that the linkage extends to the continuing war in Indochina . . . as well as the killing and jailing of thousands of Democracy-loving Chilean people by a Junta paid for by the CIA."[50] In naming the recent coup in Chile, this activist showed how radicals were beginning to turn their focus from US intervention in Southeast Asia to that in Latin America.

These expressions of support gained even greater meaning with the cases of Susan Saxe and Jane Alpert, each of whom drew major attention from both radical feminists and the national media. Alpert's case began first. She was a straight white woman who in 1969 had participated in a series of bombings linked to the Weather Underground and then fled. In August 1973 she wrote an essay, "Mother Right," that she sent to feminist media and published in *Ms.* magazine. The essay, directed to "sisters in the Weather Underground," posed a biological explanation for women's "nurturing" roles. Further, in "Mother Right" Alpert recanted her association with the left and stated that she had been manipulated into violence by her lover Sam Melville, who had been killed with other prisoners in the Attica Rebellion of September 9, 1971. In this uprising, men imprisoned in New York protested the murder of George Jackson by California prison guards, and New York officials responded with a brutal, days-long military assault. Attica left a long shadow across the 1970s and prompted black feminist Flo Kennedy to coin the term "Attica Amerika" to describe the United States.[51] Many feminists criticized Alpert's essentialist views of motherhood, but they were far more shocked when Alpert pronounced in reference to the men killed in the rebellion: "I will mourn the deaths of 42 male supremacists no longer."[52] Alpert implied that those killed at Attica were "male supremacists" simply by being men and were therefore not worth grieving. Her statement struck many as a betrayal of prisoners' basic humanity and led a significant number to believe she had become an informant for the federal government.

Many feminists rejected Alpert's view of radical violence as "male" and viewed her account of her manipulation by her lover Sam Melville as a self-serving accommodation to a common and already sexist media trope. After Alpert surrendered to authorities in November 1974, criticism of her statements and her possible collusion with the state grew. A quartet of prominent feminist leaders—Flo Kennedy, Susan Sherman, Joan Hamilton, and Ti-Grace Atkinson—signed a public statement condemning her, identifying racially and class-divided systems of justice, and arguing that feminism must define itself as interconnected with a broader left. These four women had collaborated for years and worked under Kennedy's mentorship to bridge black liberation and white feminism.[53] In their statement, "The Crisis in Feminism," they contrasted the state's relatively gentle treatment of Alpert to attacks on black liberationist Assata Shakur and argued that the government might use Alpert's brand of feminism to divide and destroy radical unity, especially support for the underground. Most famously, they stated: "We are what we identify with. And our identification must be with all oppressed people. We do not 'support' or 'not support' the brothers of Attica. We *are* Attica. We are Attica or we are nothing. . . . This is true feminism." When another, more liberal set of feminist leaders—NOW president Karen DeGrow, Kate Millet, Robin Morgan, and Gloria Steinem—signed a counterstatement defending Alpert, they held simply that they believed Alpert had not been an informant, not that her disavowal of Attica was valid. The limited nature of their claim underscored the impact of the politics of collective defense.

As the Alpert debate brewed, federal authorities heightened their pursuit of Susan Saxe, her associate Kathy (Katherine Ann) Power, and individuals tied to other armed resistance groups, including the Chicano Liberation Front, New World Liberation Front, and Red Guerrilla Family. Saxe's story had begun in 1970 when she and Kathy Power were students at Brandeis University, active in organizing the national "Student Strike" that brought at least a hundred US campuses to a full halt. The Student Strike was sparked by Nixon's invasion of Cambodia and the murders of students protesting that action at Kent State and Jackson State, and it voiced three demands: freedom for political prisoners, particularly Black Panthers; an end to the US war in Southeast Asia and a full withdrawal of US troops; and an end to universities' backing of the war and of political repression. The campaign stoked the fires of a volatile spring, and May 1970 brought sixty-nine bombings and acts of arson against campus offices and corporate and military installations inside the United States.[54] By summer 1970, Saxe and Power formed a small group with three men recently released from prison through parole programs sponsored by Boston-area universities—Stephen Bond, Robert Valeri, and William Gilday. The group of five sought to expropriate funds to arm the Panthers and to sabotage military trains, and in August they initiated a series of bank robberies in Los Angeles, Evanston (Illinois), and Philadelphia.

In September 1970 Susan Saxe's group returned to Boston, where they broke into a National Guard armory, stole weapons and classified documents that revealed the Guard's plans for suppressing protests in the United States, and released the documents to the press. On September 23 they conducted another bank robbery in which Saxe's associate William Gilday unexpectedly shot and killed Boston police officer Walter Schroeder. Gilday, Bond, and Valeri were soon arrested, and Saxe and Power went underground, which prompted the FBI to add them to the "Ten Most Wanted" list. Over the first half of the 1970s Saxe and Power sustained themselves in lesbian feminist communities in New

Haven, Hartford (Connecticut), Lexington (Kentucky), and Philadelphia. FBI surveillance and investigation infiltrated those communities, and in 1975, seeking in part to protect others, Saxe surrendered for arrest and pled guilty to charges related to the theft of documents from the National Guard. In 1977 she entered a plea to resolve the Boston robbery and Schroeder's murder; she served a total of seven years for all charges. Power remained underground for twenty-three years before turning herself over to the government in 1993 and serving a six-year sentence.[55]

Lesbian communities came under closer scrutiny as federal authorities searched for Saxe and Power. Those on the East Coast were especially hard hit, and lesbian and feminist radicals participated in national networks of resistance through the Grand Jury Project and the Committee to End Grand Jury Abuse.[56] Federal authorities charged several lesbians and one gay man in New Haven, Hartford, and Lexington for refusing to provide information about Saxe and Power, and in March 1975 events came to a head: the "Lexington 6" were sentenced, officers in Vermont captured Alpert's former comrade Patricia Swinton, and police in Philadelphia seized Saxe.[57] Although the Philadelphia lesbian feminist community remained divided over Saxe, opposition to collaboration grew. In April 1975 lesbian feminists in the city urged women not to tell federal or local police even the most innocent information, arguing that any cooperation could be used to out women as lesbian or to harass others into collaborating; they concluded, "By not talking to them we'll be protecting ourselves and each other."[58] The Los Angeles periodical *The Lesbian Tide* affirmed its strong support of the Lexington 6 and noted that two liberal gay organizations, the National Coalition of Gay Activists and National Gay Task Force, had taken stands against FBI surveillance and for grand jury resistance.[59] In Eugene, a small radical press printed posters of Saxe with quotes from her arrest statement (figure 4).

This context was central to Saxe's case, her ongoing statements of defiance, and the ways she linked her lesbian identity with her refusal to collaborate with the state. On June 9, 1975, Saxe pled guilty to a first set of charges on the condition that this would end FBI and grand jury investigation in Philadelphia. Two days later, she issued a statement affirming the belief that had driven her in 1970: "that armed struggle against the Amerikan state was a valid and necessary escalation of the politics of the '60's." At the same time, Saxe reflected on how her politics had changed: whereas in the past she had believed that women could be liberated through

FIGURE 4. Jackrabbit Press poster (Susan Saxe), 1975. Courtesy
Lincoln Cushing/Docs Populi.

involvement in a broader revolution, she now believed women's liberation
required autonomous feminist struggle. This was not a replacement of her
previous commitments but an extension of them, one that Saxe emphasized she shared with "many other women who came to politics through
socialist, anti-racist, and anti-imperialist causes." Crucially, she insisted
that feminist autonomy and left commitments could be intertwined. Saxe
identified a struggle for the heart of feminism between, on the one hand,
women such as Alpert who believed "that the Amerikan system can
peacefully accommodate their feminist demands and that women as
women have no obligation to support or protect any peoples' struggle
that is not explicitly feminist" and, on the other hand, "we women whose
growth into feminism has made us even more determined not to give in,

not to accommodate ourselves to Amerika, not to collaborate against sisters and brothers who are our natural allies in revolution. . . . My feminism does not drive me into the arms of the state, but even further from it."[60]

Saxe further explained that while she had recently agreed to plead guilty for some of her actions, she had steadfastly refused to give up information on anyone else, and could not have won an end to investigation in Philadelphia if local activists had not done the same.[61] Thus, her defense committee held that "what began as an unasked-for confrontation [with the government] has . . . become an important victory for her and for us."[62] Saxe called for support of the Lexington 6 and radicals in New Haven, and she affirmed the slippage between left feminism, lesbian identity, and collective defense by reiterating the idea that "the love I share with my sisters" was a "weapon" against the US state. Along with the Lexington 6, Saxe self-consciously represented an interconnection between lesbian feminism and the underground.

Through Saxe's case, lesbian and radical feminists reminded one another of their political pasts. Saxe offered an origin story for lesbian feminism rooted in support for anti-war and black radicalism, and her defense helped lesbian leftists affirm the idea that their sexual autonomy and their anti-imperialism were interdependent and that their sexual communities offered means to evade the US state.[63] The Susan Saxe Defense Committee held that "Susan has . . . raised issues many of us had conveniently forgotten, and she has forced us to take our own politics, our own hystery [herstory] seriously."[64] Elsewhere, her defense committee stated that state repression affirmed the political meanings of "lesbian": "If not by our own identification, then by the actions of the FBI, the Department of Justice, and the news media, we have all become identified as 'dangerous women' because of our lifestyles, our private lives, our own politics."[65] The committee also argued that these meanings attached to lesbian feminist community as a whole; Saxe's actions stood on a continuum with a "political alternative . . . that we are all a part of creating" through "a feminist perspective that includes women's centers, food co-ops, bookstores, restaurants—alternatives which center around our lives and not capital."[66] From 1975 through 1976, lesbian and feminist newspapers around the country reported on Saxe's defense, and lesbian feminists formed the center of Saxe's defense campaign.[67] Saxe's supporters continued to work on behalf of her case until her final plea deal in January 1977, when they filled the courtroom with seventy-five supporters and circulated news of her sentencing across both the mainstream and the radical press.[68]

The meanings of the SLA, Jane Alpert, and Susan Saxe carried over across the mid-1970s as lesbian and other feminists joined campaigns to defend women charged with murder for self-defense against rape. The two most important of these campaigns were those of Joan Little, a black woman in North Carolina, and Inez Garcia, a Latina from Monterey County, California. Through Little, Garcia, and the similar but lesser-known cases of Yvonne Wanrow and Dessie Woods, activists defined women charged with murder against rape as political prisoners. They viewed "mass defense" of Garcia and Little as parallel to that of Saxe, the Lexington 6, Patricia Swinton, and Assata Shakur, and they cited these connections to solidify their view of lesbian feminism as interdependent with a multi-issue left.[69] Further, they used these comparisons to highlight the limited recognition of women's rights to self-defense and to under-score the lax prosecution and even state enactment of gendered violence.[70] Garcia's and Little's cases highlighted these problems because the judge and jury initially denied Garcia's claims of self-defense and a white jail guard had raped Little. While both Little and Garcia were straight, lesbi-ans were actively involved in their defense campaigns; Garcia's defense gained special importance in the Bay Area but proved to be dominated by white lesbian feminists who generally did not organize in collaboration with people of color.

Garcia was a Cuban and Puerto Rican woman who had been living in Soledad, California so that she could visit her husband, who was incarcerated in the local prison. Significantly for activists, this prison was the same institution in which the Soledad Brothers—George Jackson, Fleeta Drumgo, and John Clutchette—had been held. In March 1974 two acquaintances of Garcia, Miguel Jimenez and Luis Castillo, came to her house to speak with her housemate. They then attacked Garcia, dragging her outside into an alley, where Jimenez held her down while Castillo raped her. Minutes after their attack the men phoned Garcia, mocking her and threatening her life if she did not leave Soledad. Garcia immediately went looking for them, carrying a gun, and when Jimenez threw a knife at her, she fired, killing him. She was arrested and charged with first-degree murder, her narrative of rape and self-defense ignored.[71]

Garcia's case quickly won significant attention from feminists and other radicals in the Bay Area. Former GWL member Louise Merrill worked with other lesbian and radical feminists in the East Bay to form the Inez Garcia Defense Committee, coordinating its fundraising and correspondence as well as its short-lived publication, *The Feminist*.[72] The Inez Garcia Defense Committee adopted the slogan "Inez Garcia Fights Back for All Women" and celebrated Garcia as "Guilty of Self Defense." Meanwhile, activists in San Francisco formed the Free Inez Garcia Committee. Garcia won the backing of Charles Garry, a radical lawyer who had earlier argued the cases of Huey Newton, Bobby Seale, and the anti-war radicals known as the "Oakland 7."

As her case moved toward trial, Garcia's campaign was accelerated by the case of Joan (also known as Joanne or Jo Ann) Little. In August 1974 Little was serving a short sentence in a North Carolina jail for a breaking-and-entering conviction when guard Clarence Alligood repeatedly harassed her, then entered her cell and initiated a sexual assault. Little seized the icepick Alligood held to her throat and killed him to protect herself. She then escaped from the jail and eight days later turned herself in. Much as with Garcia's case, Little's supporters assembled a team of lawyers who had defended members of the Panthers, the American Indian Movement, and the Attica Rebellion. They also won the backing of the National Alliance Against Racist and Political Repression, which Angela Davis had formed after her own acquittal in June 1972.[73]

Activists drew links between Garcia's and Little's cases through their rhetoric, protests, and material support. They expanded the category of political prisoner not only by describing Garcia's and Little's actions as valid but also by arguing that Garcia's and Little's rights to self-defense and self-determination must be won through popular support. In the Bay Area, Elaine Brown declared the Black Panther Party's support of Garcia. In North Carolina, Joan Little's supporters identified her as the target of state violence, and her lawyers placed histories of white men's state-sanctioned violation of black women at the center of the trial. Their efforts proved successful: in July 1975 the jury acquitted Little of murder after less than ninety minutes of deliberation. Yet in Garcia's case, the judge ordered the jury to not consider Garcia's allegations of rape, and lawyer Charles Garry rejected a self-defense claim in favor of arguing that Garcia had acted under diminished capacity because of emotional shock. This argument ignored Garcia's own statements and failed to win her freedom: in October 1974 the jury convicted Garcia of second-degree murder and sentenced her to five years to life.

For many, Garcia's conviction showed that the state saw women as "fair game" for rape—one man on the jury openly celebrated this as the case's message.[74] The loss galvanized Garcia's supporters to push harder and to reach a broader radical community. As Victoria Law records, they publicized Garcia's case at "rock concerts, Chilean solidarity meetings, services at San Francisco's progressive Glide Memorial Church, the weekly women's night at the [radical Irish bar] Starry Plough," and other venues.[75] Bay Area activists drew on the success of Joan Little's acquittal to demand Garcia's release, and sought to hire a feminist lawyer who would pursue Garcia's self-defense claim. A high point of this effort came on February 7, 1975, when more than three hundred people, nearly all of them women, marched through a pouring rain to San Francisco's State Building to deliver fifteen hundred signatures to Governor Jerry Brown demanding Garcia be freed. All of the protesters were involved in radical feminist, lesbian, or gay groups; the handful of men there were gay, and most of the women identified as lesbian. The activists occupied the building's lobby, refusing to leave until the governor appeared. San Francisco police arrested thirty-two women and six men, with photographer Cathy Cade documenting their rough treatment by officers (figure 5). Lesbian feminist Christa Donaldson suffered a wrist injury, was charged with battery on an officer and resisting arrest, and then was beaten at the county jail. A small group of activists marched on the jail to demand their comrades' release, while others marched to confront the governor at the Hilton. Garcia won an appeal hearing set for April 1975, and her supporters hired feminist lawyer Susan Jordan to challenge her conviction. They also defined Christa Donaldson's case as an adjunct to Garcia's, and at Garcia's appeal Donaldson was found not guilty.[76]

Significantly, the campaign to defend Inez Garcia sparked conflict within SFWAR (San Francisco Women Against Rape), which was then beginning to shift away from its radical origins toward tactics of police reform. Indeed, more and more feminists at this time were beginning to revise their work against violence by seeking stricter policing and the incarceration of men who assaulted women. These shifts were motivated in large part by the desire to make the criminal legal system treat rape as a serious problem and an act of assault, rather than a minor offense to be blamed on women's dress or behavior. Yet they also represented a dramatic turn away from critiques of state violence, and they divided those willing to collaborate with authorities from those working to challenge prison and police violence or to back radicals underground. In San Francisco, some members of SFWAR feared that backing Garcia would compromise their emerging relationship with the police,

FIGURE 5. Inez Garcia demonstration and arrests (Christa Donaldson at center), San Francisco, 1975. Photograph by Cathy Cade. Courtesy of Cathy Cade photograph archive (BANC PIC 2012.054), The Bancroft Library, University of California, Berkeley.

and so the group ultimately played only a supporting role in the Garcia campaign.[77]

For other activists, however, Garcia's case prompted a keener articulation of refusals of state collaboration—an approach sharpened by the concurrent case of Susan Saxe. By April 1975, the Inez Garcia Defense Committee and *The Feminist* enunciated a critique of the "protection racket," a term they used to describe how the government and media used gender paternalism to defend racist repression. It defined this "racket" as a means of "racist sexism," something that entailed an intersection of oppressions—for example, views of Latina women as hotheaded and therefore lacking self-control. Further, *The Feminist* described politicians and the courts as not only blaming women for their own rapes but "beefing up [the] forces of law and order . . . [to] decide who's guilty and who isn't, and who gets punished—and how much." Against "law and order," *The Feminist* argued:

> Any "protection" which robs us of our autonomy . . . [and] uses white women as pawns in racist frame-ups is no protection at all. It is a deadly poison designed not only to undermine the struggles of Third World men, but to render women of all colors immobile, powerless, and terrorized. We want no more of the protection racket. We want self-determination. Crimes

against women will not cease until they are dealt with by WOMEN, whether they are in the street, in the bedroom, in the kitchen, in the jail, in the court, in the welfare building, in the plant, in the office, in the bank, in the governor's office, or in the White House.[78]

Garcia's supporters sought to draw attention to the ways that the expectations of "ladyhood" served racist control. Through this analysis, they worked to warn women of divisions within feminism and to steer feminist rage toward a critique of state power.

While generating these analyses, however, Garcia's defense campaign remained dominated by white lesbians and radical feminists, with only small numbers of people of color appearing at protests and even fewer in leadership. For example, though the members of Gente joined campaign events, the Inez Garcia Defense Committee and Free Inez Garcia Committee remained virtually all white. This stood in contrast to the Joan Little campaign, which centered black radical leadership, including that of black feminists. The cases were also set apart by the nature of the assaults: Garcia was attacked by Latino men, so for some her case fit a view of rape as only about gender, in contrast to Joan Little, who was a black woman raped by a white jail guard. Organizational and regional differences held further sway. Little's defense forged an alliance of black feminist, civil rights, and Black Power groups in the South and on the East Coast; Garcia's remained grounded in a largely white network of lesbian and other radical feminists at a time when Bay Area Latina feminists and gay Latinos had just begun to build political power.

These factors converged with white women's relationship to the category "lesbian" to limit Garcia's defense. In a 1975 interview, Pat Parker commented with frustration that while "the lesbian community does seem to think that they're taking care of racism in the Inez Garcia case . . . it's futile," as white activists had done little to bring women of color into campaign leadership or to reach out to lesbian of color networks or groups.[79] She followed this comment by relating the many times that white lesbians had mistaken her for other black women at bars and parties; in one case, a white woman who had slept with Linda Wilson angrily confronted Parker, thinking that Parker was Wilson and thus should have come up to her to say hello. Parker shared bitter laughter over this event with another black woman who came into the room during her interview—someone unnamed by the white women filming the conversation but who chimed in with her own accounts of mistaken identity. Although Parker and her friend did not explicitly state that Garcia's supporters could not tell black lesbians apart, the

FIGURE 6. Inez Garcia and supporters at San Francisco Gay Freedom Day, 1976. Photograph by Cathy Cade. Courtesy of Cathy Cade photograph archive (BANC PIC 2012.054), The Bancroft Library, University of California, Berkeley.

incidents they experienced helped to explain why Parker might separate herself from the "lesbian community" with the pronoun "they" rather than "we." The conversation also underscored another obvious point: for white lesbians to organize in support of Inez Garcia was not the same as organizing in collaboration with Latina or black lesbians.

Garcia's new lawyer, Susan Jordan, made rape the central issue in her retrial, and Garcia was finally acquitted on March 5, 1977.[80] Organizing by lesbian and gay people of color expanded significantly as Garcia won her freedom, but by this time the energy of her case had shifted from the streets to the courtroom, so demonstrations were less central to her campaign.[81] Still, calls to "Free Inez" did gain new meaning as activists rallied around Garcia as a figure of Latina resistance. While out on appeal in June 1976, Garcia acknowledged these shifts and thanked her gay and lesbian supporters by marching in San Francisco's Gay Freedom Day alongside the recently formed Gay Latino Alliance (figure 6). Her choice to march with this group rather than other formations suggested a growing set of efforts to counter divides that had not been addressed in her campaign.[82]

The politics of collective defense established a lasting lesbian feminist commitment to radical solidarity even as it solidified tensions over the racial boundaries of lesbian feminist identity.[83] These tensions propelled the expansion of organizing by lesbian and gay people of color and, by the end of the 1970s, held a central influence on the Central American solidarity movement, in which Latina and other women of color moved front and center.

CHAPTER 3

Limp Wrists and Clenched Fists

Defining a Politics and Hitting the Streets

By the mid-1970s, while the broadest wave of gay liberation had received, in its wake radicals were building a gay and lesbian left. Radical gay men in this period pursued grassroots power and moved toward collaborations with lesbian feminists. Three phases of activism propelled these shifts. First, a small but active network of radical gay men began to bring socialist-feminist analysis into their anti-imperialist commitments. Rejecting the dismissals of straight leftists, they built alliances against problems as varied as rape, bias against effeminate men, and the US-backed Pinochet regime in Chile. They emphasized the personal meanings of gay liberation by proclaiming themselves "faggots" and by celebrating their juxtapositions of "limp wrists and clenched fists."[1] Second, radical gay men enlarged the scale of their activism by mobilizing with the broader gay men's community on issues including police harassment, racism in gay baths and bars, and the right to be gay on the job. A series of highly visible, influential campaigns on these issues won concrete changes in San Francisco and, at the same time, generated a productive tension between leftists' visions for sexual liberation and the more liberal agenda of gay and lesbian rights. This tension structured the largest gay left group of the mid-1970s, Bay Area Gay Liberation, whose agenda overlapped with and was shaped by rising activism by gay and lesbian people of color and greater alliances across gender and race. A third phase came as the political terrain shifted and the New Right launched a broad assault on the hard-won gains of gay and lesbian, feminist, racial justice, and anti-poverty activists. Facing this threat, radical gay men and lesbian feminists increasingly worked together, and they drew on alliances they had built with organized labor to defeat Proposition 6—the California ballot measure that sought to bar people who were gay, lesbian, or supported gay and lesbian rights from teaching in the state's public schools. The coalitions of the late 1970s did not mark a victory of left over liberal gay and lesbian agendas, as evident in the very small number of activists who confronted both Proposition 6 and the death penalty initiative Proposition 7. But, by the end of the decade, the gay and lesbian left had coalesced and claimed a sharp analysis of sexual politics, a radical critique of state violence, and a know-how for hitting the streets.

. . .

The gay men's left planted its roots amidst the waning of Black Power and of the Vietnam War. Most gay radical men of the early 1970s had experience working to support the Black Panther Party and the anti–Vietnam War movement, and as these movements diminished, they began to reorient their anti-imperialism to new sites of struggle and to deepen their analyses of how capitalism and empire structured antigay oppression. Yet gay leftists stood in the minority of two movements: they faced persistent antigay attitudes in the broader left, and they saw a lessening of radicalism in gay life. Thus, amidst multiple discourses framing gay issues as nonpolitical, bourgeois, or individualistic, radical gay men—especially white gay men, assumed to be otherwise privileged—invested renewed energy in explaining their own oppression.

At the outset of the 1970s, gay activists faced resistance from straight radicals that ranged from outright hostility to passive dismissal. One source of opposition lay in the Cuban Revolution, which in the latter 1960s targeted homosexual men and gender transgressors for imprisonment in agricultural work camps.[2] The US-based Venceremos Brigades to Cuba argued that gay liberation was part of "a cultural imperialist offensive against the Cuban Revolution," as well as "a social pathology which reflects left-over bourgeois decadence," and it banned gay and lesbian participants from 1970 through the early 1980s.[3] Cuban policy and that of the Brigades fueled intense debates among gay and lesbian activists and prompted some of these activists to leave the left. Radical gay men and lesbians, however, tended to argue that antigay exclusions misinterpreted socialism and that capitalism offered no meaningful alternative.[4]

Both gay and lesbian radicals were influenced by the New Communist Movement, which was active throughout the 1970s and held particular strength in the Bay Area. Participants in the New Communist Movement rejected the Soviet Union and Communist Party–USA as "revisionist," or state-capitalist, and sought to build an alternative communist party that would be rooted in Marxist-Leninist and Maoist thought. Fueled by support for Cuba, China, and anti-colonial liberation movements, the New Communist Movement was about a third people of color and overlapped with the Third World Left.[5] New Communist groups held both positive and negative influences on gay and lesbian radicalism; on the one hand, they modeled unorthodox adaptations of Marxism, but on the other, they often expressed hostility to gay and lesbian issues.[6] One notorious example of exclusion came through the Revolutionary Union, or RU, a largely white organization in the Bay Area.[7] RU was neutral on sexual politics when it formed in 1968 but, as gay liberation emerged, defined it as bourgeois and individualistic. By 1974 the group barred lesbian and gay members.[8] One of RU's founders, Steve Hamilton, later came out as gay and described the group's hostility to gay liberation as driven by "impatience with all but pure 'class' issues."[9] Similar impatience led RU to downplay racism in the crisis over the use of busing to integrate Boston public schools, a failing that brought sharp criticism of the group and pushed other radicals to think more seriously about the relationships between class and race. In the long run, disputes like these fostered openness to the gay and lesbian left, but change was hard-won and slow going.

In March 1974 a small group of gay and lesbian leftists in Los Angeles responded to the New Communist Movement by forming the Lavender & Red Union. The group described itself as "a group of dyke and faggot communists" and encapsulated its politics in the slogan "Gay Liberation is Impossible Without Socialist Revolution—Socialist Revolution is Incomplete Without Gay Liberation." Active for three years, the Lavender & Red Union organized study groups, hosted conferences, and published the magazine *Come Out Fighting* and the anthology *The Lavender and Red Book*. It positioned itself at the nexus of gay and New Communist activism, protesting antigay policies within RU, the Venceremos Brigades, and other left groups while also critiquing non-Marxist gay and lesbian activists.[10] However, though gay radicals around the country cited and reprinted the group's publications, the effectiveness of the Lavender & Red Union was limited by dogmatism—a problem it shared with the New Communist groups it sought to change.

Gay radicals drew somewhat greater inspiration from socialist feminism, which also gained strength during the early 1970s and made sexuality central to its analyses of class and gender. Speaking broadly, socialist feminists understand racialized reproductive labor as central to capitalist production and count collectivized housework, socialized child care, and welfare among their strategies for change. The two largest socialist-feminist groups in the Bay Area in the 1970s were the Berkeley-Oakland Women's Union (BOWU), which formed in January 1973 and claimed up to 250 members, and the San Francisco Women's Union (SFWU), which was somewhat smaller and formed in 1974.[11] Although in other parts of the United States women of color, including lesbians of color, were key to socialist feminism, BOWU and SFWU were overwhelmingly white. This shaped the networks in which their members participated and the ways they analyzed the intersections of gender and class.[12] BOWU and SFWU included many lesbian and bisexual women and viewed compulsory heterosexuality as a tool for containing workers' exploitation in the nuclear family.

Gay leftists drew on socialist feminism to analyze their own gendered oppression and to enact a politics of radical alliance.[13] For example, radical gay men began to provide child care at activist meetings, a contribution that recognized the necessity of reproductive labor, acknowledged that men as well as women should perform it, and undermined stereotypes of gay men as abusers of children. Other efforts included forming new organizations. In 1974 a small group of gay white men in the Bay Area formed the Revolutionary Gay Men's Union, or RGMU; they modeled their group explicitly on the BOWU and SFWU and took their slogan from the Lavender & Red Union. In explaining how capitalism, sexism, and racism oppressed gay men, RGMU cited "monopoly corporations that refuse to hire us, the family, bars that exploit our sociability and sexuality, sex roles, internalized oppression, alienation and racial and sexual divisions that prevent us from uniting in our common interests."[14] They called on gay men to organize as both subjects and allies of socialist feminism, using this politics to explain why the feminized jobs in which gay men were often concentrated (for example as waiters, hairdressers, and clerks) were low paid and offered little advancement.[15] Further, gay radicals adopted socialist-feminist strategies of consciousness-raising and study groups. In February 1974, San Francisco activist Tede (pronounced "Teddy") Matthews called on his fellow gay men to join a reading and discussion group on "the political, emotional realities of our oppression." The workshop, titled "Faggots,

Sissies, and Queens," aimed to address "how and why we've been kept in our ghettoes and closets by such institutions and ideals of society as the nuclear family, private property, economic class, the bars, beauty standards, the psychiatric and religious powers that be." Matthews held that "sexism . . . divides and conquers us, trying to make us into selfish, unfeeling blobs of butch masculinity," and "keeps us from discovering the ways we oppress each other and the women of the world."[16]

Tede Matthews had arrived in San Francisco one year earlier and quickly become a central figure in the gay left. Originally from West Palm Beach, Florida, he had moved to Boston in 1970 to evade the draft and became active in anti-war, gay, and other radical causes.[17] FBI surveillance of anti-war groups led to his door, and the military summoned him for induction. He showed up in high femme attire and camped his way through the army physical, declaring at one point, "Dahling, I AM a homosexual fantasy!" and convincing doctors he was unsuitable. The performance was no act, as Matthews had begun to live in drag and sometimes made ends meet through sex work. Matthews's gender presentation over this time was fluid, and for a period she lived a feminine identity; by the time Matthews moved to San Francisco in 1973, he defined himself primarily as an effeminate gay man and dressed in the style coming to be known as genderfuck.[18] One outfit might combine masculine pants and a feminine blouse cut low to reveal chest hair, all accessorized by makeup, earrings, and political buttons.[19] Later known for his statement "We're all born naked and anything anyone wears . . . is drag," Matthews criticized other gay men for their bias against effeminate men and drag queens.[20] He joined the Modern Times Bookstore Collective, a leftist bookstore founded a few years earlier in San Francisco's Mission District, and together with lesbian feminist Ruth Mahaney and others, built it into an important resource for gay and lesbian radicalism as well as activism more generally. Through Matthews, the "Faggots, Sissies, Queens" workshop met at Modern Times.[21]

Matthews also organized other gay men to work against rape. He had experienced rape, partner violence, and street harassment, and Ruth Mahaney and other lesbian feminists approved when their self-defense teacher decided to teach Matthews and other effeminate men skills for protecting themselves from violence.[22] In fall 1974 Matthews organized another gay men's study group, "Combating Sexism," which joined the campaign to support Inez Garcia's self-defense against rape (chapter 2).[23] The "Combating Sexism" group organized carpools to Garcia's sentencing hearing, coordinated child care for her courtroom supporters, and

FIGURE 7. Tede Matthews, San Francisco Gay Freedom Day, 1975. Photographer unknown. Courtesy Ruth Mahaney.

participated in the February 1975 protest for Garcia at City Hall. On a flier emblazoned "Faggots Against Rape," the group asserted that because gay men were also "victims of straight brutality . . . we must defend the right of women to fight back against our common oppressor."[24] Matthews was one of the six men, joined by thirty-two women, who were arrested at the City Hall protest for Garcia. In June 1975 he echoed the lesbian feminist rhetoric of collective defense by carrying a fake rifle and bearing a button that read "Lesbians Unite" at Gay Freedom Day (figure 7).[25] When interviewed in 1977 for the gay and lesbian documentary *Word Is Out*, he wore a button proclaiming "Free Inez" and compared rape to the earlier US war in Vietnam—thereby solidifying an anti-imperialist argument that posed a continuum of violence from bodily to global scales.[26]

Matthews and other gay leftists used the language of "faggotry" to bridge effeminate gender with radical politics. They politicized the word "faggot" much as later activists would reclaim "queer," using it in such venues as the 1975 publication *Gay Sparks*, the Faggots and Class Struggle conference held in Oregon in 1976, and the 1977 volume *The*

Faggots and Their Friends between Revolutions.[27] Boston activists published *Fag Rag,* while the magazine *RFD* termed itself "a journal for country faggots."[28] At San Francisco's Gay Freedom Day in 1977, a white man in a caftan held up a limp wrist, a clenched fist, and a sign proclaiming that "a gay landlord is still a landlord," while a comrade wore a shirt reading "Faggot Revolution." Self-defined faggots saw themselves as "androgynous, non-consumerist," as well as dedicated to revolutionary change, and their politics expanded arguments that had earlier been made under the label of "effeminism."[29] Building on Vietnam War draft resistance, they believed that normative constructions of masculinity underlay violence and imperialism and that gender must be transformed to allow nonoppressive self-expression.[30] They also critiqued the rise of hypermasculinity, consumerism, and assimilation in gay life—shifts marked through the so-called clone style. Typified by muscular, fit white men in tight jeans, work boots, and flannel shirts, the "clone" helped to commodify San Francisco's Castro neighborhood as a "mecca" for middle-class, largely white gay residents and businesses.[31] Men who embodied this look could more easily move between gay and straight worlds because of their normative presentations of male gender and because they lived their gayness through leisure and entertainment more than collective households or activism. "Faggotry," by contrast, fused countercultural identity and radical politics.

The politics of faggotry found concrete application not only through work against rape but also through the organization Gays in Solidarity with the Chilean Resistance, or GSCR. This group responded to the CIA-sponsored coup against Salvador Allende. Elected president of Chile in 1970, Allende had initiated a "Chilean path to socialism" that included nationalizing the copper industry and banks and expanding health care, education, and other social welfare programs. In 1973, Allende's government came under growing attack from the Chilean right and the military, and on September 11, 1973, Allende was assassinated in a coup led by General Augusto Pinochet, who instituted a brutal military dictatorship. The current Chilean government acknowledges at least 3,065 killed and 40,000 imprisoned and tortured by the regime, while other authorities place the figures much higher.[32] Pinochet ruled Chile as president of its military junta until 1990, was arrested on human rights violations in London in 1998, and died in 2006 with those charges still pending.

Pinochet's dictatorship provoked an international resistance movement fueled by tens of thousands of Chilean exiles, by admiration of the "Chilean path to socialism," and by opposition to US intervention in

Latin America following the wars in Southeast Asia. Notably, US activists' attention to Chile had first been sparked in 1972 when news broke that International Telephone and Telegraph, or ITT—a company that President Nixon protected from antitrust prosecution in exchange for campaign funds—had plotted with the CIA to block Allende's 1970 election.[33] ITT's goal was to preserve its shareholdings in Chile's telephone company, while the CIA was motivated to halt the growth of Latin American socialism. When journalist Jack Anderson exposed the plot against Allende's election, Nixon's operatives targeted Anderson for assassination; this plan was foiled when the agents were arrested in June 1972 for the Watergate break-ins.[34] From spring 1972 through 1975, while the Watergate scandal unfolded, Senate investigations uncovered damning proof of multinational corporations' power in Chile and elsewhere, as well as evidence of invasive counterintelligence by the CIA, FBI, and National Security Administration, including COINTELPRO.[35] US activists found their attention drawn to Chile by ever expanding reports of government repression and corporate greed and by their frustration that—in gay radical Charlie Hinton's words—"the U.S. was saying be peaceful and [make change] through the ballot box, and the Chilean people did that, elected a socialist government, and it gets destabilized and attacked."[36] Solidarity with Chile grew further as Chilean exiles began to settle in the Bay Area, proving especially active during the bloodiest years of the Pinochet regime—1974 through 1976.[37]

Through Chilean solidarity, gay radicals highlighted their own experiences as targets of repression against the left. The Chilean right wing had used antigay rumors to undermine Allende before the coup, and Pinochet enacted a ban on men wearing long hair and women wearing trousers, terming both to be "unlawful . . . 'Marxist' fashions."[38] The Homosexual Liberation Front of Argentina reported these policies and circulated the news across the Americas in gay periodicals ranging from the Toronto *Body Politic* to the San Francisco *Vector*. Gay leftists especially noted the murder of Lola Puñales, a drag queen whom the Chilean military subjected to public rape, torture, and castration, and the *Body Politic* quoted Argentinian activists as saying that "scores of homosexuals have suffered the same fate."[39]

Members of GSCR were active in many other groups, including straight Chilean solidarity organizations and gay left activism. Most of the members were Anglo and born in the United States, including Tede Matthews, Michael Bumblebee, and James Green (later a participant in and scholar of the Brazilian gay movement). Another member, Alejandro

Stuart, was a Chilean man who was also active in the La Peña Cultural Center, an arts and political venue in Berkeley founded by Chilean exiles.[40] GSCR was most active during the seasons of protest that marked the first and second anniversaries of the Pinochet coup, in September 1974 and 1975. It held a "gay picket" on September 11, 1974, at the Chilean consulate and continued a vigil there for ten days, lasting until a broader solidarity march. The group presented a film and discussions on Chile at gay meetings in San Francisco and Berkeley and forged an alliance with the sex workers' organization COYOTE (Call Off Your Old Tired Ethics), which organized sex workers to refuse service to sailors on the *Esmerelda,* a Chilean shipping vessel docked in San Francisco that had housed the murder or torture of Allende's supporters.[41] In September 1975, when several thousand San Franciscans marched to commemorate the second anniversary of the coup, GSCR contributed a large contingent and held a political and cultural event in the Haight-Ashbury district featuring films, music, and poetry. Pat Parker headlined the event, and Tede Matthews read a poem that he dedicated to Inez Garcia, jailed members of the Symbionese Liberation Army, and recently murdered prisoner activist Wilbert "Popeye" Jackson.[42] Three hundred and fifty people packed this gathering, which brought gay men and lesbian women together in ways that foreshadowed coalitions to come.[43]

Though relatively short-lived, Chilean solidarity proved a key marker in the growth of San Francisco's gay and lesbian left. It offered a highly visible demonstration of gay and lesbian anti-imperialism that was informed by, but moved beyond, the Vietnam War context. Activists framed their anti-imperialism against the sexual politics of the Pinochet regime, highlighting Pinochet's repression of drag queens and gay men and identifying links between local and hemispheric structures of sexual control. For example, the radical publication *Gay Sparks* argued that "the same forces that took control in Chile, threaten us here" in San Francisco through police assault against gay men.[44] Activists' point here was not to universalize all forms of violence, but rather to bring sexuality into an analysis of San Francisco's economic and political links with Chile. *Gay Sparks* noted that San Francisco's Financial District served as a "headquarters" in a system of resource extraction led by "B-of-A [Bank of America] and Standard Oil" that connected the "Pacific Rim area, including our coast, Alaskan oil, Chilean copper and stretching to Hawaii, the Philippines, S.E. Asia & Japan." Whereas Salvador Allende had sought to nationalize and socialize Chile's copper industry, Pinochet placed it back in the hands of global capital, so that San Francisco investors were now tied to his regime. *Gay Sparks* also saw links with Chile in San Francisco's recent surge of police harassment of gay men, which it argued was driven by the city's effort to "clean up" downtown in the interests of the tourism and global finance industries.[45]

Although discussions of Chile may have struck some gay men as distant, the rising incidence of police harassment that *Gay Sparks* cited was close to home. Over Labor Day weekend, 1974, San Francisco police officers conducted an unprovoked sweep of the Castro. They harassed dozens of gay men and arrested fourteen for loitering and "obstructing a sidewalk."[46] Harvey Milk, who had gained local prominence the previous year through his first and unsuccessful campaign for San Francisco supervisor, established a defense fund for the arrested men in his camera store. Gay men with politics ranging from liberal to radical crowded meetings of the local police community relations board, but found their demands stalled when the SFPD prepared to select a conservative gay Republican as community liaison. The crisis fueled a transformative expansion, and the second major phase, of the gay left.[47]

Noting the SFPD's resistance to protesters' demands, activists from the Revolutionary Gay Men's Union called for a meeting in the heart of the Castro at Trinity Methodist Church. They situated the Labor Day arrests in larger patterns of police brutality, racism, and repression, with one flier declaring: "We understand the police all too well—BY THEIR DEEDS! From the racist Zebra dragnet to the Chinatown payoffs to the failure to investigate widespread reports of brutality against Chicanos and Latinos in the Mission to police infiltration of progressive organizations to the 'cleanup' of pornography and prostitution in the Tenderloin to the crackdown on gays and shakedown of gay businesses—BEHAVIOR, NOT WORDS, TELLS THE STORY!"[48] Organizers posted this statement widely across the Castro, reaching many people with no prior contact with leftist groups.[49] On January 22, 1975, their hopes were far exceeded when more than two hundred men and a handful of women showed up to discuss police abuse. As a step toward change, they formed a new organization: Bay Area Gay Liberation, or BAGL.

Though incubated in earlier gay left groups, BAGL was a much larger and different organization, developing concrete, local campaigns that blended radical potential with populist appeal. The group's founding efforts centered on ending police abuse, protecting gay and lesbian schoolteachers, and confronting racism in gay baths and bars. In February 1975 BAGL staged a demonstration against Mayor Joseph Alioto's "complicity in police harassment," and in March it protested the beating and arrest of five women at a Mission District lesbian bar.[50] Each action drew about 150 participants, including some straight supporters, and attracted more energy to the organization. BAGL's political pressure helped to push George Moscone to install a somewhat more liberal chief of police at the end of that year, after he was elected mayor.

In spring 1975, BAGL became active in building gay-labor alliances. BAGL member Howard Wallace, an active member of the Teamsters Union (he worked at the Oakland factory of Planters Peanuts), brought the Coors boycott before BAGL and won enthusiastic support from the organization. Coors had a long history of anti-union policies and of discrimination against Latino, black, and gay workers, and Chinese American, Arab American, and black grocery store owners in the Bay Area were joining the boycott. BAGL activists hoped gay-owned businesses might do the same, and they won that support through militant organizing: as historian Miriam Frank records, "BAGL's packed weekly meetings regularly concluded with direct action in the bars where Coors was still available."[51] BAGL also built alliances with public sector unions when it joined a campaign against proposed cuts in salaries and pensions for San Francisco city workers.

In April 1975, BAGL joined the Gay Teachers Campaign, an effort led by Tom Ammiano, the first teacher in San Francisco Unified School District to be public about being gay. By June 1975 this campaign mobilized hundreds and compelled the school board to add sexual orientation to the district's anti-discrimination policy.[52] This victory framed lesbians and gay men as workers, union members, and caregivers of children— three representations central to gay socialist feminism—and fueled gay alliances with organized labor. BAGL formed a Labor Committee, and when the AFL-CIO held its annual convention in San Francisco in October 1975, the committee challenged the national labor federation to take stronger stands for school integration, equal pay for women, and abortion, as well as to recognize gay and lesbian people who were "teachers, office workers, public employees, hospital workers, truck drivers . . . sisters and brothers, employed and unemployed."[53] The Labor Committee also worked to win support for gay and lesbian issues in Bay Area union locals, which responded fairly quickly, though the national AFL-CIO did not adopt a gay rights resolution until 1983. By fall 1976, when BAGL promoted the Coors beer and Gallo wine boycotts among gay and lesbian consumers, it argued from a presumption of alliance already won: "Labor Supports *Our* Rights—Do We Support *Labor's*?"[54]

Following the teachers campaign, BAGL sought to address discriminatory and exploitative conditions in gay baths and bars. Several Castro businesses had become notorious for barring men of color, effeminate men, and drag queens, and many featured dangerous lighting, poor ventilation, and overcrowding. Bouncers often asked for two or three separate forms of identification from patrons who were black, Latino, Asian, or effeminate (let alone those who were queens of color), and many clubs would admit a few men of color early in the night but tighten the door after they hit an undeclared tipping point of undesirables. While BAGL's membership was largely white, it included several influential people of color who helped to make the larger membership aware of discrimination. The group initiated pickets outside the Mineshaft, a large and notoriously racist club, and by September 1975 threatened a boycott. Under this pressure, the Mineshaft agreed to BAGL's "Bill of Rights" for employees and patrons of gay bars, baths, and other businesses. This included asking only for one "valid ID," agreeing to consider people of color and women for jobs, and banning discrimination on the basis of "race, sex, lifestyle, or style of dress." Although bias was by no means eradicated, the campaign set bar owners on notice and defined BAGL as invested in the well-being of gay people of color.[55]

BAGL was dynamic, energetic, and enormously meaningful to many. Activist Charlie Hinton was drawn to BAGL by its first flier in January 1975 and remained active till its end. The organization gave him a "joy and happiness and sense of family" that "I can never describe."[56] The group's many committees and caucuses enabled participants to organize from shared experiences; for example, its Gay Parents' Support Group became active in work for lesbian mothers' custody rights.[57] BAGL also gained a reputation among activists nationally. Future historian John D'Emilio attended meetings while visiting San Francisco from his home in New York and was "really blown away" by BAGL's size and dynamism, recalling "a vibrancy and a passion . . . that was completely thrilling."[58]

Early on, BAGL members noted a divide within the group between the politics of "democratic rights/mass action" and that of anti-imperialism.[59] The "rights" framework centered on legal inclusion and public policy that explicitly focused on sexual orientation, as in the teachers campaign. It was associated with the practice of "mass action," which produced meetings of one hundred to two hundred participants led by a coordinating committee that designated a rotating set of meeting chairs. Anyone attending meetings was considered a member of BAGL, which allowed them to vote on decisions and to participate in topical caucuses or campaign committees. The anti-imperialist tendency was decisively leftist, linking gay liberation to socialist, feminist, anti-racist, and internationalist change and arguing that only radical unity would win sexual freedom. Anti-imperialists saw the goal of rights as valuable but argued that full sexual liberation required a transformation beyond existing structures of government. This tendency's organizing practices were mixed; some anti-imperialists advocated for a more structured organization with tighter political unity, while others hoped to merge anti-imperialist principles with mass action methods.

The coexistence of rights and anti-imperialist politics lent vibrancy to BAGL's first year, drawing in new participants alongside longtime activists and especially shaping BAGL's police and bar campaigns. This mix could be glimpsed in materials such as a June 1975 flier that, on the one hand, reminded readers of the link between gay liberation and the anti–Vietnam War movement and, on the other, broadcast the pragmatic goals of the legalization of sodomy and a federal ban on discrimination against lesbian and gay workers.[60] Anti-imperialism gained its greatest influence through BAGL's Solidarity Committee, which mobilized BAGL contingents to join pickets, marches, and protests in support of the Coors beer boycott, the defense of Inez Garcia, Chilean solidarity, United Farmworkers organizing, and the campaign to defend housing for elderly Filipino men at San Francisco's International Hotel. The Solidarity Committee exposed many BAGL members to anti-racist and internationalist causes for the first time and thereby expanded the base of the gay left.

At times, straight radicals resisted BAGL's solidarity work; for example, organizers of a May Day celebration in Oakland denied BAGL a booth, upsetting more than a hundred BAGL members who had traveled from San Francisco to have a presence at the event.[61] Yet BAGL slowly broke down such resistance, particularly through involvement in the International Hotel (I-Hotel) campaign. Located in San Francisco's Manilatown, the I-Hotel housed Filipino elders, or *manongs,* whose family lives had been limited by the United States's combination of restrictive migration policies and laws against "miscegenation." The building was slated for demolition and urban renewal in the late 1960s, prompting a fierce struggle against displacement that ended with its residents being violently removed in 1977. The I-Hotel campaign galvanized an intergenerational Asian American movement led by KDP, a transnational organization that also opposed the Marcos regime in the Philippines (the initials KDP stood for Katipunan ng mga Demokratikong Pilipino, or the Union

FIGURE 8. Third World Gay Caucus, San Francisco Gay Freedom Day, 1977.
Photograph by Marie Ueda. Courtesy of Marie Ueda Photographs Collection, GLBTHS.

of Democratic Filipinos). BAGL members participated in KDP's support
committee, volunteered in its security detail, and attended protests with
banners bearing the BAGL name. Within KDP, homosexuality was a
"known secret": three of its leaders were lesbian or gay but remained
closeted in an effort to protect the organization both publicly and in the
left. Combined with this silence, BAGL's presence affirmed an uneasy pattern in which gay people were most visibly white and people of color
were most visibly straight. Yet, at the same time, the collaboration
between BAGL and KDP helped to bring that binary into question,
because KDP challenged other radicals who rejected gay support.[62]

The Third World Gay Caucus, or TWGC, was a group of gay and
lesbian people of color that formed in fall 1975 and explicitly challenged the divide between gay and people of color identities (figure 8).
At its formation, the TWGC sought to bring together "Raza, Black,
Native American, Asian, Oceanic, Near and Middle Eastern and all
other Non-white Gay and Bi-sexual Women and Men."[63] In practice it
consisted largely of black gay men, but it collaborated with other
groups, including the Gay Latino Alliance (or GALA, also formed in

1975) and the lesbian of color group Gente.[64] Some of the notable participants of the TWGC included Simeon White, who came of age in the
North Carolina civil rights movement and had challenged the Vietnam
War as a conscientious objector; Bill Beasley, who had been a member
of the Los Angeles Gay Liberation Front; the folksinger Blackberri; and,
after 1977, Brian Freeman, who in 1990 cofounded the performance
group Pomo Afro Homos. All of these men were migrants to San Francisco—White from North Carolina and Philadelphia, Beasley from Los
Angeles, Blackberri from Buffalo (New York), and Freeman from Boston. Their experiences tracked a difference that Freeman observed
among both white gay men and gay men of color: "locals" to the Bay
Area were often less political, while "newcomers"—who had gained
privacy and mobility apart from their families of origin—were more
likely to be activists. By challenging issues of bar racism and gentrification and by building opportunities for socializing, the Third World Gay
Caucus sought to affirm the coexistence of gay and people of color identities as well as those of locals and newcomers. Freeman first encountered the TWGC by attending a dance it sponsored—a room "full of
Black and Latino people" that he likened to "discovering paradise."[65]
The group was initially part of BAGL but soon made itself autonomous,
a separation that underscored BAGL's whiteness.

As the Third World Gay Caucus formed, BAGL's rights and anti-
imperialist tendencies split from each other over the question of military
inclusion. This divide began with a debate over whether to support air
force sergeant Leonard Matlovich, a Vietnam veteran who sought to
remain in the US military after coming out as gay. Featured on the cover
of *Time* magazine in September 1975, Matlovich had embarked on a
speaking tour across the country. On December 4, 1975, Howard Wallace brought Matlovich's case before BAGL's general meeting, asking
the group to adopt Matlovich's cause as its next campaign. Controversy
was immediate. While pro-Matlovich activists agreed to an amendment
"opposing US militarism," opponents saw that as a token gesture.
Meanwhile, members of the TWGC grew frustrated that the Matlovich
debate delayed a discussion of the campaign against discrimination in
baths and bars, and they ultimately walked out of the meeting and
accused Matlovich supporters of "blatant racism." Third World Gay
Caucus members aligned themselves with BAGL's anti-imperialist
"tendency" yet were less interested in debating that direction than in
the concrete work of the bar campaign, which directly challenged racism among gay men. Other BAGL members remained at the meeting,

arguing in favor of the Matlovich campaign until the organization dropped the question. Soon after, Howard Wallace and another leader, Claude Wynne, created a group separate from BAGL called the Coalition to Defend Gays in the Military.[66]

The Matlovich debate reflected both ideological and personal tensions. Wallace and Wynne, prominent leaders of the "rights" framework since BAGL's beginning, held longtime experience in the Socialist Workers Party.[67] While the SWP was clearly part of the left, many radicals criticized it as "incorrect," "opportunistic," and "reformist" because it had opposed the Vietnamese national liberation movement and efforts to link the anti-war and civil rights movements in the United States.[68] Wallace and Wynne were respected for their success in building gay-labor alliances, but a significant number of BAGL members were suspicious of their histories in the SWP. Some also cast doubt on Wynne because, though he was black, he did not join the Third World Gay Caucus.

While Wallace and Wynne met criticism, so did the anti-imperialist group the June 28 Union.[69] Formed in May 1975, the June 28 Union was composed of twelve white men who were central to BAGL's Solidarity Committee and whose experience ranged from Students for a Democratic Society and the Berkeley Gay Liberation Front to the more recent Gay Men's Political Action Group of Oakland, the Revolutionary Gay Men's Union, and Gays in Solidarity with the Chilean Resistance.[70] The leaders of the June 28 Union were respected for their expertise and networks but also seen by many as arrogant and insular; in BAGL member Charlie Hinton's view, they "kept themselves separate."[71] Further, June 28 Union members sought to join the Prairie Fire Organizing Committee (PFOC), a white anti-racist group that had formed in 1974 as the aboveground offshoot of the Weather Underground Organization.[72] Echoing critiques of the SWP's influence on Howard Wallace and Claude Wynne, some BAGL members feared that the language of anti-imperialism might be code for PFOC controlling BAGL. The twinned critiques of Wallace and Wynne on the one hand and of June 28 Union on the other threatened to put BAGL at an impasse.

In the short term, BAGL's rejection of military inclusion revealed a grassroots radicalism that won out over sectarian or personality disputes. The rejection of the Matlovich campaign also showed that, while rights and anti-imperialist tendencies had converged in activism for workers' power and protection from police, they moved apart over the question of military citizenship. It was one thing to claim the "right" to organize as workers, to be gay on the job, or to be protected from state abuse, but quite another to seek the "right" to participate in the US Army, Navy, Air Force, or Marines. The distinction between these causes defined the gay left both in and beyond BAGL.

Beyond the Matlovich debate, another catalyst for defining gay anti-imperialism developed through participation in the "Counter-Bicentennial" protests held July 4, 1976. These protests were led by Puerto Rican independence activists, resisted the nationalism of the official US Bicentennial, and drew more than 30,000 in Philadelphia and 10,000 in San Francisco.[73] Notably, the Prairie Fire Organizing Committee had made organizing for the Counter-Bicentennial central to its Hard Times Conference, which it held in Chicago in January 1976. Yet, at Hard Times, many different activists criticized PFOC for posing a narrow class analysis that neglected race, nationality, gender, and sexuality.[74] Because of this critique, PFOC held less influence in the Counter-Bicentennial than it had hoped, and the June 28 Union's influence in BAGL diminished further. Instead, a more autonomous cluster of gay men and lesbian feminists forged collaborations while working for the Counter-Bicentennial, and they persuaded Counter-Bicentennial leaders to include gay and lesbian issues in the protest's platform.[75]

The proximity in time between the Counter-Bicentennial and the year's commemoration of the Stonewall Riots, then termed Gay Freedom Day, further encouraged the expansion of gay and lesbian radicalism. The poster "Unite to Fight!"—created in 1976 and adapted for this book's cover—incorporated an image from a women's liberation flier into the leftist iconography of a red and lavender star and cited June 28 as a "Day of Unity With Gay Struggles." The Women's Motorcycle Contingent, commonly known as Dykes on Bikes, joined Gay Freedom Day for the first time in 1976, and the demonstration included prominent participation by the Gay Latino Alliance and by the recently formed Black Gay Caucus, the Gay American Indians, and BAGL. The magazine *Magnus* commemorated the day's contingents of people of color with photographs taken by Gay Latino Alliance members Daniel Arcos and Efren Ramírez.[76] In addition, leading up to and following Gay Freedom Day, BAGL hosted a performance by black gay folksinger Blackberri and a skit by Tede Matthews that illustrated gay experiences of poverty through a theatrical "consciousness-raising tour of a welfare hotel . . . & through the hustle scene."[77] The Stonewall Contingent, a loose network of groups that migrated between gay and other protests, marked 1976 as a year of "rebirth" for gay and lesbian radicalism that "deepened our commitment to political action against the system that oppresses all people."[78] Its "Stonewall Gay Funnies" reflected growing collaboration between gay, lesbian, and straight radicals by calling on activists to oppose grand jury harassment as well as rising rents, social service cutbacks, police violence, and denials of lesbian mothers' custody rights.[79]

In October 1976, BAGL formally adopted "Principles of Unity" that affirmed anti-imperialist commitments rather than military inclusion.[80] The anti-imperialist agenda won decisively among the membership, passing by a vote of 69 to 21 with eight abstentions. Members of BAGL's dissenting minority, including those who had backed the Matlovich campaign, split off from the group and launched the Richard Heakin Memorial Butterfly Brigade, an effort to patrol against anti-gay violence that soon collaborated with San Francisco police.[81] Meanwhile, the Principles of Unity focused on six goals: fighting economic crisis, racism, sexism, and state repression; solidarity with anti-imperialist struggles, including those in southern Africa and Chile; and gay and lesbian community building.

Significantly, rather than defining their agenda as a combination of "gay" and "nongay" causes, radicals in BAGL defined all their goals as key to sexual freedom. Reflecting the lasting influence of socialist feminism, they viewed "gay oppression" as intertwined with capitalism, sexism, and imperialism both historically and in the present.[82] Drawing on such ideas, BAGL's new Principles of Unity declared:

> We cannot separate our struggle from that of other oppressed peoples for two reasons. First, because THE OPPRESSION OF GAY PEOPLE IS TIED TO ALL THE OTHER FORMS OF OPPRESSION UNDER IMPERIALISM . . . Second, AMONG GAY PEOPLE ALL THE FORMS OF IMPERIALIST OPPRESSION ARE FOUND . . . all gay people of all sexes, races, and classes can only be united by a movement that commits itself to fighting racism, sexism, and class oppression as well as gay oppression. Furthermore, to unite all gay people such a movement must also commit itself to struggling against the special oppression of effeminate men and transsexuals. This is the movement we commit ourselves to building: one that struggles against gay oppression at its roots, one that struggles against all other forms of oppression as part of the world-wide struggle against imperialism, and one that carries on this struggle within the gay community and among ourselves.[83]

In citing "effeminate men and transsexuals," BAGL underscored the significance of "faggotry" in countering norms of masculinity and reflected awareness of the economic and social exploitation faced by those who broke gender and sexual rules.

Although radicals acclaimed the October 1976 vote, BAGL soon lost steam, diminishing over the course of 1977 and going into a final decline after mid-1978.[84] A number of factors brought the group to its end. Although a majority of BAGL members affirmed the anti-imperialist agenda, fewer had been compelled by the theoretical debate that agenda seemed to demand. Those most comfortable with theoretical discussion were termed "heavies" for their influence, intensity, and aptitude for dealing with difficult ideas; not everyone could be a "heavy," and as BAGL prioritized such leadership, other members drifted away. In addition, some members of the June 28 Union left BAGL after the October 1976 vote. Thus, the Principles of Unity cohered only some of the radical strands in BAGL, and the path toward them produced both ideological and personal fractures. BAGL also met new challenges because, while anti-imperialism fired the imaginations of many, the growing power of the New Right raised questions about how to put this radicalism into practice.

The New Right's attacks on gay and lesbian freedom captured national attention in spring 1977 when Anita Bryant, a Christian singer turned representative of the Florida Citrus Commission, led "Save Our Children"—a successful campaign to repeal a gay and lesbian rights ordinance in Dade County (Miami), Florida. Throughout the next year Bryant backed similar repeals of gay and lesbian rights ordinances in St. Paul (Minnesota), Wichita (Kansas), and Eugene (Oregon). Gay and lesbian activists mobilized from around the country to face these attacks. Hank Wilson, a gay San Francisco schoolteacher who had led the Gay Teachers Campaign with Tom Ammiano in 1975, traveled to Miami seeking to replicate California's gay-labor alliances through a boycott of Florida orange juice. Once Bryant's repeal passed, Wilson returned home to more bad news: California state senator John Briggs was launching an attack on public schoolteachers who were gay, lesbian, or supported gay and lesbian rights, an initiative soon known as Proposition 6. Modeled after a law passed in Oklahoma, California's Proposition 6 sought to allow discrimination on the job and to undermine collective bargaining and the contractual process for all workers.[85]

The threats posed by Bryant and Briggs realigned gay and lesbian activism by shifting the context that defined left-liberal coalitions. As BAGL had shown, gay leftists differentiated the rights they would fight to defend, such as those of workers and in housing, from assimilatory rights they did not seek, including military inclusion and collaboration with the police. When conservatives assailed the former kind of rights, many radicals were again willing to collaborate with liberals and to shift their language to reach wider audiences.

At the same time, many radicals saw new potential for building political power through Harvey Milk, whose local career rose as the threats of Bryant and Briggs grew. In 1977 Milk mobilized his final, successful run for San Francisco supervisor while Tom Ammiano made a successful run for the school board. Both Milk and Ammiano were left-leaning liberals who counted radicals among their volunteers and whose campaigns relied on the local gay and lesbian left as both fuel and counterweight. Indeed, many of the stances that won Milk broad support—including his backing of the Coors boycott and his opposition to police harassment—drew on energy and networks that had been tapped or even organized by gay and lesbian radicals.[86] Thus, as BAGL member Charlie Hinton puts it, although Milk "was not a socialist," his "campaigning made a big impact, and made us less relevant as BAGL."[87]

The Bryant and Briggs attacks further transformed gay and lesbian activism by grabbing the attention of straight activists. As the New Right rocketed to power through the rhetoric of preserving the "traditional family," it helped to move gay and lesbian concerns from the margins toward the center of national debate. Straight leftists who had previously dismissed gay and lesbian claims as "bourgeois" or insignificant were compelled to take another look. Straight liberals began to take more seriously the radical gay and lesbian arguments that sexual politics were interconnected with other structures of power. In addition, labor activists of all sexualities took notice because Proposition 6 attacked sexual freedom, workers' rights, and unions simultaneously: it sought to require local school boards to fire or refuse to hire any teacher, teacher's aide, counselor, or administrator known to have "engaged in public homosexual activity or homosexual conduct" that "renders the person unfit for service." The measure defined "activity" and "conduct" as including "advocating, soliciting, imposing, encouraging or promoting of private or public homosexual activity directed at, or likely to come to the attention of, schoolchildren and/or other employees," meaning that teachers and staff might be fired not only for sexual behavior but also for voicing a political opinion in support of gay and lesbian people.[88] Briggs linked fears of child sexual abuse to alarm over social movement activism and termed gay and lesbian visibility the excess of a "permissive society"—a problem that must be curtailed by limiting workers' private lives and political expression.[89]

California state senator John Briggs drew political inspiration from the political careers of former California governor Ronald Reagan and then-US senator S.I. Hayakawa, the former president of San Francisco

State College who in 1968 and 1969 had opposed the Third World Strike. When Briggs failed to move antigay measures through the state legislature in summer 1977, he turned to the initiative process, gathering enough petitions to place the measure on the June 1978 ballot.[90] Challenges to the constitutionality of Proposition 6 pushed it to the November 1978 election, but Briggs used the delay to develop Proposition 7, a measure to expand California's death penalty.[91] This initiative posed a new problem, but the delay also gave gay and lesbian activists more time to organize and shifted the vote from a primary to a general election—one that would draw a larger and more progressive electorate. Ultimately, although early polls gave Proposition 6 a strong lead, voters rejected it by a 58 percent "no" vote.

Grassroots organizing lay at the heart of Proposition 6's defeat, and activists framed the initiative as an assault on gay and lesbian dignity, one that served broader attacks from the New Right. Cesar Chávez, Angela Davis, and Lieutenant Governor Mervyn Dymally (an important black politician) spoke out early on to define Proposition 6 as part of the broader conservative movement. Harvey Milk, who had been elected San Francisco supervisor in November 1977, was prominent in leading the "No on 6" campaign, along with his campaign leader Gwenn Craig (a black lesbian), new school board member Tom Ammiano (a white gay man), and hundreds of lesser-known activists. Further, Milk and others wrested control of "No on 6" from *Advocate* magazine owner David Goodstein, who had proposed a "low profile" campaign that would keep gay and lesbian people out of public view.[92] This shift enabled a decentralization of leadership and undermined the myths linking homosexuality to child sexual abuse. In the last days of the campaign, moderates and even former governor Ronald Reagan spoke out against Proposition 6; though these politicians voiced concern primarily about the costs of the measure, their actions revealed the broader base of opposition that had been built. "No on 6" prompted a public conversation of nearly unprecedented scale about sexuality, with liberals and radicals working together in speaking engagements and door-to-door outreach.[93] Decentralization also allowed for activists to build on regional interests and strengths. The Sonoma County campaign network, "SCRAP 6," proved noticeably feminist, while that in San Jose was "headed by Libertarians and gay church members."[94] Mobilizations by gay and lesbian people of color against Proposition 6 were strongest in East Los Angeles, Oakland, and San Francisco, led by the groups Lesbians of Color, Latina/os Unidos, and the Third World Gay

Caucus, respectively. Bay Area activists also established the California Outreach Group, a statewide speakers' bureau.

Gay and lesbian activists built coalitions against Briggs that reflected the influences of left groups and that strengthened coalitions across lines of gender. Harvey Milk made campaign appearances with lesbian feminist professor Sally Gearhart, while the Sonoma County campaign group held a firm rule that all door-to-door outreach be done in co-gender pairs.[95] One goal of such strategies was to undermine fears of child sexual abuse, but other aims were to equalize campaign leadership between men and women and to mobilize women voters, who polls showed to be more likely to oppose Proposition 6. Radical Amber Hollibaugh participated in the statewide speakers bureau and later noted that, while speaking to audiences of straight women, she drew sympathy to the "sexual outlaw" by naming "what it meant to be female and try to discover my own sexuality in a society that refused to acknowledge me as having rights of my own as a sexual person."[96]

In the campaign's final push, labor unions provided the key infrastructure—phone-banking offices, direct voter outreach, and publicity—that brought Proposition 6 to defeat. Leftists and left-liberals had been key to forging gay-labor alliances since 1975, and they framed Proposition 6 as an issue of workers' power along with gay and lesbian freedom. They won support first inside Bay Area locals' racial and ethnic caucuses, then the local Labor Council, and finally the California AFL-CIO.[97] As Hollibaugh noted, activists defined the initiative in the media as both an antigay and antilabor measure and won strong opposition from public employees and black voters.[98] Radicals also organized the Workers Conference Against the Briggs Initiative, held in San Francisco in September 1978. This conference drew twenty-one different organizations from around the state, including union locals, black and gay union caucuses, and women's labor groups, and it linked Proposition 6's assault on union solidarity with other conservative attacks.[99] Its logo, later reprinted as the cover of the national magazine *Radical America* and captioned "An Attack on One Will Be Answered by All," pictured labor solidarity through a lineup of flexed arms that included women, people of color, and lesbians (indicated by a tattoo of two female symbols on a bicep).[100]

These declarations of coalition threw into relief the relative absence of efforts against the death penalty measure, Proposition 7. Despite the critiques of state violence circulated through lesbian feminist collective defense, "No on 6" activists were far more prepared to build coalitions around workers' rights than around policing or incarceration. The largest "No on 6" groups refused to take a stand on Proposition 7 out of fear of alienating swing voters, and there was no developed campaign against Proposition 7 led by other groups. Even the "L.A. 5," an offshoot of the Weather Underground that plotted to bomb the office of Senator Briggs, focused only on Proposition 6, though those arrested for the plot chose to forgo trial because they regretted not having also worked against the death penalty measure.[101] In the absence of broadly organized opposition, Proposition 7 passed by a landslide of 72 percent in favor.

The two Bay Area organizations that did take up grassroots organizing against both Proposition 6 and 7, the Third World Gay Caucus and Lesbian Schoolworkers, were small in scale but demonstrated possibilities for radical mobilization. The TWGC centered its efforts on voter registration and outreach among communities of color in San Francisco and Oakland. It defined gay and lesbian people as everyday members of black and Latino families and countered the "No on 6" campaign's tendency to treat people of color solely as allies to a white gay and lesbian community.[102] Its "No on 6 and 7" poster, carrying the bilingual caption "It'll hurt us all! ¡Nos hace daño a todos!" depicted black, Latino, and Latina members of the group standing with their arms around one another, the photo framed as if in a family album (figure 9).[103] One of the activists depicted, Brian Freeman, recalls that most voters they spoke with already knew about Proposition 6, which made the group's outreach especially useful for conversations about Proposition 7. He adds that "people were thrilled to see [us]" doing outreach in San Francisco's Mission District, and that the poster captured the "lovely charm" of the warm reception they received from Latino and black communities during the campaign.[104] His recollections suggest the potential that might have been developed if other and larger groups had collaborated with the Third World Gay Caucus to oppose Propositions 6 and 7 across the state.

The other group to work against Proposition 7, Lesbian Schoolworkers, was a small but active network of socialist-feminist women, mostly white, who had spun off from the broader group Gay Teachers and School Workers.[105] It developed a campaign slideshow that contrasted Senator Briggs's ideal family—"white, upwardly mobile, politically conservative, and highly traditionalist"—with family diversity both past and present, including "single-parent households, families hit by unemployment, families without children, extended families, Gay families, and many other arrangements."[106] But while the Lesbian Schoolworkers discussed both Proposition 6 and Proposition 7 in relative depth, it failed to draw many

FIGURE 9. Rodrigo Reyes/Third World Gay Caucus, "It'll hurt us all! ¡Nos hace daño a todos! Vote No on 6 & 7," 1978. Courtesy Lincoln Cushing/Docs Populi.

connections between them. For example, it termed Proposition 7 a racist measure against prisoner activism but did not detail the history of prisoner organizing, name the experiences of gay and lesbian prisoners, or note that teachers of color might be framed as sexual threats.[107] The group thus failed to note that antigay repression and state violence might operate through one another. The group's activists would begin to articulate such connections, however, after a series of events that underscored the links between sexual politics and police assault.

Three weeks after voters defeated Proposition 6 and passed Proposition 7, former San Francisco supervisor Dan White assassinated Mayor

George Moscone and Supervisor Harvey Milk. White was a former officer in the San Francisco Police Department who had been elected supervisor alongside Milk and had recently resigned from that post. On November 27, 1978, he murdered Moscone and Milk in their offices at City Hall. He soon turned himself in, confessed, and was arrested. As he awaited trial, SFPD officers rallied to his defense with T-shirts and bumper stickers reading "Free Dan White." Lesbians and gay men began to report an increase in police harassment, and in February 1979 two officers of the SFPD assaulted and arrested two women, Sue Davis and Shirley Wilson, as they left the well-known lesbian bar Amelia's.[108]

Within days of the Amelia's attack, more than one hundred lesbian and bisexual women—mostly white, many Jewish, and many working class—came together to address the incident. As Christina Hanhardt notes, those present debated a range of responses, including demanding that the SFPD create an accountability department or that it hire more lesbian officers. Those who rejected these goals and sought more systemic, radical change formed Lesbians Against Police Violence (LAPV). The group's founding leaders, who included members of Lesbian Schoolworkers, were self-identified Marxists who openly challenged state violence and state repression. Hanhardt argues that LAPV identified "police violence, as it affected lesbians . . . [as] the issue that . . . might place their political struggles within the context of a broad-based antiracist left."[109] The group's "Principles of Unity," formalized in March 1979, began simply: "We do not work with the police."[110]

Throughout spring 1979, LAPV organized meetings and demonstrations to protest the assault at Amelia's, an attack by off-duty officers at the lesbian bar Peg's Place, the Oakland Police Department's murder of a black teenager named Melvin Black, and recent police killings of black men in Los Angeles and elsewhere. The group held that Dan White's assassinations of Milk and Moscone "encouraged attacks on gay men, Lesbians, prostitutes and Third World people," and it sounded the alarm on a new wave of "ANTI-GAY, ANTI-THIRD WORLD, ULTRA RIGHT WING POLITICS," including the recently passed Proposition 7.[111] LAPV also worked with an East Bay group of lesbians and gay men of color, the Third World Gay Coalition (separate from the Third World Gay Caucus), to challenge perceptions of gentrification as a vehicle for lesbian and gay freedom.[112]

Dan White was acquitted of first-degree murder on May 21, 1979. The jury backed his claim that he had suffered diminished mental capacity because of depression and a junk food diet, an argument that would become known as the "Twinkie defense." He was found guilty of man-slaughter, sentenced to seven years and eight months, and ultimately served five years. Within hours of hearing his light sentence, several thousand people took to the streets, marching from across the city to City Hall. Drag queens living in marginal Tenderloin housing joined middle- and working-class gay men and lesbians from the Castro, Mission, and other neighborhoods.[113] When some in the crowd began tactics of nonviolent resistance, the police marched in a wedge formation, beginning to push protesters back and to swing their batons. As Ruth Mahaney recounts, when some in the crowd attempted to sit down, others moved in to funnel the police out, "like a dance," and it became clear how many gay and lesbian people had been "fighting with the police for years."[114] Protesters began breaking the glass of City Hall's front doors, ripping parking meters from the sidewalk, setting fire to police cruisers, and chanting "Dan White, hitman for the New Right."[115] SFPD officers continued to beat protesters and, later that night in the Castro, raided and assaulted patrons at the bar the Elephant Walk.[116] In total, twenty-eight people were arrested that night at City Hall and in the Castro, beaten in jail, and charged with crimes including assault and battery on police, incitement to riot, and burning police cars.[117] The events became known as the White Night riots.

While the responses of May 21 were unorganized and unplanned, radicals sprang into action to define the night through multi-issue left politics and to protect participants from further police abuse. An anonymous flier posted on May 22 showed a burning police car captioned with the words "No Apologies! May 21, 1979 San Francisco" (figure 10). This image was soon remade as a color-by-numbers outline whose creators instructed that it be filled in with shades such as "Sissy Chartreuse," "Pig Blue," and "Off White." Here the image was accompanied by revised lyrics to "America the Beautiful": "Oh beautiful, for sissy power that cannot be contained / We fought at Stonewall decked in drag, we want more fruited plains."[118] The authors of these anonymous broadsides included members of LAPV and other groups who pasted their missives around the city. They recommended that people form affinity groups to protect one another in case of further police reprisal, offered tips for minimizing injury from police clubs and tear gas (multiple layers of clothing, a wet bandanna for the face), and pointed to White's sentence as proof that the death penalty reinstated through Proposition 7 would be used only against people of color and the working class.[119] Another flier held that "Dan White got off

FIGURE 10. White Night Riot flier, 1979. Courtesy of Ephemera Collection—LGBT General Subjects, GLBTHS.

because he's white, a family man, an ex-cop, an ally of big business. Are you? What sentence would you get?" and urged, "Don't let the right wing use this riot as an excuse for stepped-up law and order." Radicals also answered condemnations of property destruction by redefining violence:

REAL VIOLENCE IS: Cops singling out women for special beatings Monday night. Cops marching storm-trooper file, yelling, "Danny's free!" Broken ribs, punctured lungs, multiple skull wounds, tear gas, billy clubbing, and no cops in the hospital. Dan White getting special treatment while prisons are filled with Third World people whose only crime is trying to survive. Cops murdering unarmed Black youths like Melvin Black. Going to robot jobs every day for shit pay just to make some fucker rich. The daily threat of being hassled or beat up for being queer. Cops beating up prostitutes.[120]

Activists demanded an end to police assaults on gay, lesbian, and people of color and insisted that the city not prosecute those arrested in the riots. Further, they urged that there be no grand jury investigation and that the riots must not allow any expansion of police funding, equipment, or personnel. LAPV advised people not to cooperate with police or to pin responsibility for the May 21 events on anyone, even unwittingly, as through casual conversations on the street or in a bar.[121]

Irrespective of LAPV's goals, authorities did pursue grand jury investigations and prosecutions of activists, and by fall 1981 they focused charges on two men, David Waddle and tenants' rights organizer Peter Plate.[122] By the end of that year Waddle and Plate were convicted on reduced charges and sentenced to several years' probation.[123] But memories of the White Night riots remained alive in San Francisco for years after 1979, and May 21 became a key date for marking gay and lesbian radicalism. In the late 1980s, AIDS activists bore the "No Apologies" logo during a march on the Bay Area office of the drug manufacturer Burroughs-Wellcome and organized a radical commemoration of the riots' tenth anniversary. Such commemorations claimed a history of radical queer resistance against narratives that would frame gay and lesbian politics solely through liberal reform or electoral change.

A night of limp wrists and clenched fists, the White Night riots reflected not only the potential for gay and lesbian anger but also the political analyses and mobilizing capacity of gay and lesbian radicalism. In the next few years, as the New Right's threats proved ever more hemispheric, gay and lesbian leftists would organize more sustained and more multiracial challenges to conservatism and state violence through an unexpected venue: the Central American solidarity movement.

CHAPTER 4

24th and Mission

Building Lesbian and Gay Solidarity with
Nicaragua

The intersection of 24th and Mission Streets in San Francisco is a major gathering point that, since the early 1970s, has stood as a crossroads of many overlapping communities: Chicana/o, Central American, working class, radical, and queer. In 1978, the Third World Gay Caucus conducted outreach at the plaza above the 24th and Mission BART (Bay Area Rapid Transit) station to combat the antigay initiative Proposition 6 and the death penalty measure Proposition 7. Organizing here reflected the group's investment in working across identities and its slogan that Propositions 6 and 7 would "hurt us all."[1] Moreover, by organizing at 24th and Mission, the Third World Gay Caucus followed the lead of Central American exiles, migrants, and refugees who were establishing the site as a central hub of the Nicaraguan solidarity movement. By 1977 and 1978, activists supporting Nicaragua's Sandinista Revolution held frequent marches along 24th and rallied so frequently at 24th and Mission that they named the site "Plaza Sandino." Informed by a broader Third World radicalism, the intersection came to represent Nicaraguan and Central American solidarity as causes that were both international and close to home. Cary Cordova argues that the Mission District built a barrio, or neighborhood, transnationalism that situated local struggles in a context beyond US borders.[2] As an area of high unemployment and low wages that was home to Chilean, Puerto Rican, Cuban, Salvadoran, Nicaraguan, Mexican, and Chicana/o migrants and exiles, the Mission District became a place where global and local struggles intertwined. To undertake international solidarity at 24th and Mission was to enter a hemispheric activist community grounded just around the corner, one that could be joined through neighborhood protests and a politically charged, multiracial arts scene.

Lesbian and gay radicals were inspired by the Mission District's barrio transnationalism to embed sexual liberation in broader radical change. While these meanings became attached to the neighborhood in general, 24th Street stood in contrast to the gentrifying Valencia Street corridor, particularly closer to 16th Street, where the Mission was becoming known for a cluster of lesbian and feminist bookstores, music venues, cafés, and bars.[3] The feminist metaphor of "intersections" fit quite literally in the Mission, as many politics and identities overlapped in ways that reflected both stark inequalities and opportunities for multi-issue mobilization and change. Given this context, gay and lesbian activists looked to Central American solidarity as means to resolve potential conflicts through a radical, multiracial agenda. As the Central American solidarity movement grew across the late 1970s and 1980s, gay and lesbian leftists not only joined that movement but also constructed it as their own cause.

This chapter and those that follow use the term *lesbian and gay solidarity* to describe specifically gay and lesbian organizing for liberation, justice, and peace in Central America, particularly Nicaragua. This term denotes something more than simply the presence of lesbian and gay people in the broader, ostensibly straight Central American solidarity movement. Although hundreds, even thousands, of queer people took part in Central American solidarity, lesbian and gay solidarity describes something more precise: a network of explicitly gay and lesbian solidarity groups, and a politics by which activists adapted barrio transnationalism to further radical sexual politics and to build multiracial lesbian and gay community. Lesbian and gay solidarity began in 1978 through the Gay Latino Alliance and Bay Area Gay Liberation, expanded in 1979 through the group Gay People for the Nicaraguan Revolution, and by the early 1980s became a defining concern of the gay and lesbian left.

Historians of conservatism in the United States have observed that during the late 1970s the New Right shifted its focus from "external" to "internal" enemies, from anti-communism to the rhetoric of the "traditional family."[4] Yet three decades into the Cold War, foreign and domestic threats remained tightly linked in the conservative imagination. Gay and lesbian leftists named those links by identifying themselves and Central Americans as fellow targets of the New Right. By confronting the links between social conservatism and anti-communist intervention, activists expanded their anti-militarist and anti-imperialist sexual politics as well as their grassroots power.

. . .

Since lesbian and gay solidarity developed most strongly in relation to the Nicaraguan Revolution, it is important to review at least a capsule history of Nicaragua, especially as understood by the participants in the Central American solidarity movement themselves.

Nicaragua has faced United States intervention since the mid-nineteenth century and became a target of US empire building after the Civil War.[5] Capitalists were drawn to Nicaragua as a possible location for an interoceanic canal and an ongoing site of agricultural production (notably coffee, sugar, and cotton). The US Marines occupied Nicaragua beginning in 1910 and remained until 1933, when peasant forces led by revolutionary Augusto Sandino ejected them. Immediately after Sandino's victory, the Nicaraguan National Guard—which had been established and trained by US forces—stepped in as the proxy for North American interests. Nicaraguan general Anastasio Somoza García ordered Sandino assassinated, took the presidency by coup, and began a repressive regime that kept the bulk of the population poor, illiterate, and landless for four decades.[6] At the outset of the Cold War, the United States created the School of the Americas, a training institute that taught counterinsurgency tactics and antiradical containment to military personnel. Throughout the 1960s, Nicaragua—whose population represented less than 1 percent of the hemisphere—boasted more graduates of the School of the Americas than any other country in Latin America.[7] Somoza's regime became a family dynasty; the dictator's second son, Anastasio Somoza Debayle, took the presidency in 1967 after a bloody campaign in which the Nicaraguan National Guard fired directly into a crowd of protesters. By the early 1970s the National Guard had assassinated more than 30,000 opponents and driven more into exile. As Walter LaFeber observes, "No regime in the world cooperated more fully with the United States than did the Somozas between 1930 and the late seventies, and no Central American nation . . . more directly challenged U.S. policies in the area than the post-1979 Nicaraguan government."[8]

The Frente Sandinista de Liberación Nacional (FSLN), or Sandinista National Liberation Front, named in honor of Sandino, became the central vehicle of opposition to the Somoza dictatorship. Radicals founded the FSLN in 1961 and built strong bases among urban radicals, students, and peasants. Guided by Marxist-Leninism and nationalism, they forged ties to guerrilla vanguardist movements across Latin America and built footholds in revolutionary Cuba, within the Mexican left, and in San Francisco's Mission District.[9] The FSLN drew growing popular support after Somoza broadcast National Guard brutalities on television in 1969, but saw its biggest growth after December 1972, when a massive earthquake decimated Managua—killing some 20,000 people—and the dictatorship stockpiled and sold international aid.[10] As Somoza's abuses accelerated, the Sandinistas built an ever larger base of support with factions pursuing both armed struggle and pragmatic political coalition. Nicaraguan moderates and conservatives increasingly voiced protests, expanding opposition and producing alliances across political lines. Over the 1970s the FSLN brought together multiple "tendencies" of opposition, including students, women, liberal, nationalist, social-democratic, Leninist, Guevarist, and radical Christian groups.[11] It also gained growing international support from radicals who embraced the FSLN's flexible relationship with mass movements and the strong role that poets, artists, and journalists played in the movement and its leadership.[12] Most aspirationally, as Cary Cordova observes, "if the Sandinistas succeeded, Nicaragua promised to become a new and better Cuba, an amends for the loss of Chile in the 1973 coup, and a model for freedom and equality around the world, including within the United States."[13]

By 1977, a group of Nicaraguan professionals known as "the twelve" demanded that Somoza resign, and the FSLN began an all-out attack on the Somoza regime. US president Jimmy Carter called for human rights reform in Nicaragua but appealed to the hemispheric agency the Organization of American States to support Somoza's hold on power until elections scheduled for 1981. That agency refused, marking the first time it had ever rejected United States directives so forcefully. Opposition to Carter's proposal revealed the extent of international support for the Sandinistas as well as frustration with both Somoza's and the United States's hegemony.[14] In 1978 Somoza's forces assassinated the moderate journalist Pedro Joaquin Chamorro and carried out mass killings, while twenty-five FSLN leaders seized the National Palace and Managuans carried out a general strike. The Sandinistas' guerilla army grew tenfold; gained material aid from Mexico, Venezuela, Costa Rica, and Panama; and began to take key cities. Dora María Tellez—a woman who had been "Comandante Dos" (second in command) in the seizure of the National Palace—led the capture of the first city, León. In May 1979 the FSLN began a final military offensive while Somoza's National Guard rocket-bombed Managua and murdered an ABC newsman at point blank. On July 17, Somoza resigned and fled to Paraguay while the FSLN entered Managua and claimed its "Triumph."[15]

On taking power, the Sandinistas instituted a broadly socialist program that brought massive gains in workers' and women's rights and the nationalization and redistribution of land. Their health and literacy brigades dramatically improved the lives of everyday Nicaraguans and won international acclaim. Yet Nicaragua now faced violent attacks—on schools, health centers, rural villages, and other targets—by counterrevolutionary forces, or *contras*, whom the United States funded and trained in collaboration with Somoza loyalists. CIA and contra opposition began immediately after the Triumph and accelerated after President Reagan's inauguration in January 1981. The Sandinistas responded both by fighting the contras and by instituting a "state of emergency," which not only allowed them to hold contras without trial but also restricted broader civil liberties; the state of emergency lasted from March 1982 through January 1988. By 1983 the United States was mining Nicaraguan harbors and guiding air bombings of Managua, even as US public opinion polls through the 1980s registered consistent and strong opposition to military assault.[16] US intervention in Nicaragua ran alongside US backing of the Salvadoran and Guatemalan governments in their wars against leftists and indigenous people. In addition, US immigration policy and officials worked to exclude Salvadoran refugees while welcoming Nicaraguan supporters of Somoza. Although Congress moved to limit contra funding and training in 1982 and 1984, it approved $100 million in aid in 1986, and—outside of public view—the Reagan administration funded the contras through secret arms sales to Iran (exposed as the "Iran-contra scandal") and collaboration with cocaine traffickers (as documented by journalist Gary Webb and by a Senate subcommittee).[17] The Sandinistas agreed to peace plans in 1983 and 1987, and in 1984 they fulfilled a major international demand by holding national elections; FSLN leader Daniel Ortega won the presidency in a vote closely scrutinized by outside observers, who deemed it free and fair. But US economic sanctions fueled hunger and rising inflation, and ultimately these challenges defeated the revolution.

The FSLN lost national elections in 1990, and US ally Violeta Chamorro, the widow of the slain journalist, won the presidential vote.

Although the election was again declared clean, Chamorro and other opposition forces had benefited from $9 million from the US-based National Endowment for Democracy.[18] Nicaragua was left with 30,000 dead from the contra war and a bankrupted treasury and remains one of the poorest countries in the Western Hemisphere today.

Meanwhile, activists around the world had worked in support of the region's liberation movements, against US intervention, and in defense of Central American immigrants and refugees. Broadly—beyond lesbian and gay solidarity—the solidarity movement grew out of the Central American diaspora, the secular left, and liberation theologians in the Catholic Church.[19] It met repression both inside the United States and internationally, as the FBI broke into and stole files from the offices of the Committee in Solidarity with the People of El Salvador (CISPES) and the CIA monitored phone calls between Sandinistas and members of Congress.[20] The San Francisco Women's Building, which became a key hub of feminist and lesbian and gay solidarity work, saw a suspicious and still-unsolved break-in in March 1987.[21] Such pressure aimed to intimidate activists and echoed past red scares by linking ethnicity to radicalism as "foreign" threats. Although Anglo activists sometimes countered such links by defining their dissent as homegrown, it was indeed Central Americans—many of them temporary exiles, as well as others who would become citizens—who initiated Central American solidarity writ large. Hector Perla Jr., Maria Cristina García, and other scholars emphasize that Central Americans founded the first solidarity organizations in San Francisco, Washington, DC, New York City, Chicago, Los Angeles, and Houston, exercising leadership to define the movement and to craft the collaborations that sustained it. Many white radicals took part in the Central American solidarity movement, and whiteness became evident in various ways, including activists' tendency to overlook Sandinista exclusions of black and indigenous Nicaraguans as well as the state of emergency that limited organizing outside the FSLN.[22] But, without discounting these dynamics, any full accounting of solidarity must acknowledge the leadership of Central Americans and consider the varying knowledge that both Central Americans and non–Central Americans brought to the table.

The Bay Area became a key site of Central American solidarity both because of the region's broader radical history and because of its large Nicaraguan and Salvadoran populations. A Nicaraguan community grew in San Francisco from the late nineteenth through mid-twentieth century, initially propelled via trade routes and then by the violence and poverty of Somoza's regime.[23] More Nicaraguans, and other Central Americans, migrated after US immigration policy expanded in 1965 and as regional conflicts grew. By the 1970s as many as 50,000 Nicaraguans lived in the Bay Area, primarily in the Mission District.[24] While Somocistas (supporters of Somoza) built a base with Cuban anti-communists in Miami, opponents of Somoza were more likely to head to San Francisco, where they built links with other Chicana/o and Latina/o radicals. Within a week of the Nicaraguan earthquake in 1972, a Latino news show on the Bay Area radio station KPFA publicized a benefit concert in the Mission District and offered listeners the names of San Francisco and San Jose churches where they could donate aid.[25] The same radio show became one of the first Bay Area outlets to report on Somoza's expropriation of assistance for earthquake recovery. By 1973, activists were plastering "Wanted" posters of Somoza around the Mission and beginning to form pro-Sandinista groups.

Nicaraguan-born poet Roberto Vargas was one of the most important founders of Central American solidarity in San Francisco. He had immigrated to San Francisco as a young child in the wave that fled after Sandino's assassination, then graduated from Mission High School in 1958, attended San Francisco State College, and became active in the 1968–69 Third World Strike. By the early 1970s he had considerable experience in local Latina/o arts and activism and had performed in Jane Fonda and Donald Sutherland's anti–Vietnam War troupe FTA (Free the Army/Fuck the Army). After the 1972 earthquake, Vargas helped found El Comité Cívico Pro Liberación de Nicaragua, commonly known as El Comité, among Nicaraguan exiles in San Francisco, and cofounded and led distribution of a Spanish-language newspaper, *La Gaceta Sandinista*. In December 1974 Vargas helped organize a march in the Mission District that was the first pro-Sandinista demonstration in the United States. The FSLN established an office in the Mission on Valencia Street, using its relative safety from Somoza's forces both to plan actions inside Nicaragua and to organize transnational cooperation. Seeking to expand its support among US-born activists, El Comité worked with Colombian American activist and poet Nina Serrano to form the Non-Intervention in Nicaragua Committee (NIN), which pressured Congress to halt military aid to Somoza and to hold hearings on National Guard abuse. Joined by Chicano activist and writer Alejandro Murguía, Vargas and others began regular demonstrations in support of the Sandinistas at 24th and Mission and along 24th Street, and in 1977 carried out a nonviolent takeover of San Francisco's Nicaraguan consulate.[26]

Vargas, Murguía, and Serrano also developed the Mission Cultural Center as a key site for solidarity activism. Located on Mission Street between 24th and 25th, the center was the product of activist struggles for city funding of arts programming; it opened in summer 1977 with an inauguration led by Nicaraguan poet and priest Ernesto Cardenal, who symbolically baptized children present with the wish that they remain free of the spirit of Somoza.[27] In Juan Felipe Herrera's words, the institution developed as an effort of poets, artists, and activists "intent on reconnecting strong international histories and social movements throughout the Americas into the Mission *conciencia* (consciousness)."[28] The Mission Cultural Center represented a localized and Latina/o iteration of Third World left politics, and Alejandro Murguía served as director, while Vargas and Nina Serrano worked as its community organizers. In addition, Vargas, Murguía, and others trained for guerrilla struggle in the Bay Area hills, and in June 1979 they traveled to Nicaragua to fight in the Sandinistas' final military offensive. In their absence, a new director, who claimed Central American solidarity to be "divisive," took the helm of the Mission Cultural Center. Nicaraguan radicals responded by forming a new venue for organizing, Casa Nicaragua, located on Mission at 26th and covered with a mural that illustrated the interplay of the Chilean and Nicaraguan struggles. In the aftermath of the Sandinista victory, Ernesto Cardenal returned to Nicaragua and became its minister of culture, while Vargas moved to Washington, DC, to serve as the Sandinistas' cultural attaché.[29]

Both Central American solidarity writ large and lesbian and gay solidarity specifically found another home base at the San Francisco Women's Building, located about ten blocks northwest of 24th and Mission at 18th Street and Valencia. The roots of the San Francisco Women's Building began within the San Francisco Women's Centers, which had been initiated as a nonprofit in 1969 and through the 1970s initiated or sponsored efforts including a feminist credit union, San Francisco Women Against Rape, and La Casa de Las Madres women's shelter.[30] The Centers were led by a network of white lesbians who, by 1977, sought a larger office space and to strengthen their base amidst the pressures of the New Right and the economic recession. After a challenging fundraising process, activists purchased the Women's Building and in June 1979 moved in. At this point the white-led Centers owned the property and a network of lesbians of color, Latina and black, managed it. In 1980 activists began to merge the two entities under the auspices of the Women's Building to solidify the leadership of women of color and to bridge racial and political divides.[31] One group that influenced this shift was the women of color organization the Third World Women's Alliance, which had recently aligned itself with the socialist network Line of March and was opening itself to a small number of white women. Renamed as the Alliance Against Women's Oppression, or AAWO, this group helped to guide socialist-feminist and anti-racist political education amidst the Women's Centers–Women's Building merger. Meanwhile, Central American and other Latin American women advanced the Women's Building's ties to solidarity work.[32] These links were highlighted in the early 1990s when a collective of seven women muralists—at least two of whom, Juana Alicia and Miranda Bergman, had traveled to Nicaragua—wrapped the building in the "MaestraPeace" mural.[33] Thus, the Women's Building came to illustrate Maylei Blackwell's point that Third World internationalism "bound together the political category women of color."[34] The fact that such politics grew through the leadership of lesbian and bisexual women greatly advanced lesbian and gay solidarity.

Bolstered by the Mission Cultural Center, Casa Nicaragua, and the Women's Building, Central American solidarity knit together a wide range of political communities and transformed each strand in the process. Many of the activists who initiated and led solidarity were not Nicaraguan or Salvadoran, but rather situated other Chicana/o and Latina/o identities in relation to the Mission District's barrio transnationalism. This pattern could be seen in both Central American solidarity writ large and lesbian and gay solidarity in particular. For example, the Chicano activist Alejandro Murguía and the Colombian American Nina Serrano were paralleled in lesbian and gay solidarity by Carmen Vázquez and Lucrecia Bermudez, who were Puerto Rican and Peruvian lesbians and active leaders in the Women's Building. Activists, especially people of color and more especially Latinas and Latinos, constructed a pan-ethnic and multiracial radicalism that spoke to their own localized needs as well as their hope for the Sandinista Revolution. Slogans linking Nicaragua to Vietnam, Chile, El Salvador, Puerto Rico, and the campaign to free Angela Davis all became common, written into protest signs, political posters, and Mission District murals.[35]

Central American solidarity also proved open—albeit unevenly—to gay and lesbian politics. Among early solidarity leaders, Roberto Vargas was one of the friendliest to gay and lesbian participation, later terming the Mission District "our village within a village," a site "where we fought for human rights, voting and union rights/women's, gay, and national liberation struggles with one hand on the Bible and the other on my gun."[36]

Alejandro Stuart, a Chilean exile who had earlier been part of Gays in Solidarity with the Chilean Resistance, worked in El Comité with Vargas and Murguía. Paul Albert, a white gay lawyer, took part in early protests and pushed a federal magistrate for activists' release when a protest at the Salvadoran consulate drew FBI harassment. Albert further joined Roberto Vargas at an FSLN solidarity conference held in Panama in October 1978 and recalls that he found it "moving" to be "welcomed . . . and accepted" as a gay man engaging in solidarity with Nicaragua.[37]

Nicaraguan activists Roberto Gurdián and Rita Arauz also played important roles. Gurdián was born in Nicaragua to a privileged family and left the country in the mid-1970s; once in San Francisco, he participated in the Non-Intervention in Nicaragua Committee (NIN), the Gay Latino Alliance, and the first gay and lesbian solidarity group, Gay People for the Nicaraguan Revolution. He continued to foster gay and lesbian solidarity in the 1980s, first after taking a job back in Nicaragua with the Sandinista tourism bureau, and later while working in the New York City office of the Casa Nicaragüense de Español, a school in Managua that welcomed solidarity activists and that combined language study with political education.[38] Meanwhile, Arauz was the daughter of a Somocista diplomat who left Nicaragua in the mid-1960s when her father took a job in the San Francisco consulate. By the early 1970s she became active with the United Farm Workers and the Puerto Rican Socialist Party, then came out as a lesbian feminist, and in 1977 was recruited into the FSLN's international solidarity network.[39] In the mid-1980s she moved back to Nicaragua and became a key figure in gay, lesbian, and AIDS organizing there. Arauz, Gurdián, and other immigrants took risks by being out as gay or lesbian in the United States, since the United States excluded homosexual immigrants from 1952 to 1990 under the McCarran-Walter Act and the Supreme Court's 1967 *Boutilier* ruling.[40]

As solidarity grew, gay and lesbian radicals began not only to join existing groups but also to formulate their own responses—that is, to form a specifically lesbian and gay solidarity. In June 1978 Roberto Gurdián, Charlie Hinton, and other activists from the Gay Latino Alliance and Bay Area Gay Liberation collaborated to produce "Strange Bedfellows," an evening of political theater and discussion that linked the fight for gay and lesbian freedom in the United States to self-determination in Zimbabwe and Nicaragua. Organizers highlighted political alliances between Somoza, Ian Smith (a white supremacist controlling Zimbabwe under the banner of Rhodesia, which took its name from the

British imperialist Cecil Rhodes), and California state senator John Briggs (author of the anti-gay Proposition 6 and the death penalty measure Proposition 7). They termed Somoza, Smith, and Briggs "fascists" who expressed "the last gasp of empire" and were a "COMMON ENEMY" to multiple communities—gay, lesbian, and straight, white and of color, globally and inside the United States.[41]

As the first lesbian and gay response to the Nicaraguan Revolution, "Strange Bedfellows" affirmed the challenges of bringing radical sexual politics into left internationalism. The event energized the faithful but drew only a small audience and met resistance from straight solidarity activists. NIN had initially granted Roberto Gurdián sponsorship but withdrew it as the event approached, arguing that the fight against Briggs should not be placed "on the same level" as those against Smith or Somoza. As Gurdián recalled in 1983, this rejection compelled organizers to print new publicity and left him and other gay radicals feeling "really burned." He maintained that while it was "true that the fighting in Zimbabwe and Nicaragua meant death, whereas the Briggs initiative meant teachers' jobs," the goal of "Strange Bedfellows" was not to rank issues but rather to build coalition; after all, if the global right drew strength from alliances across scales and locations of struggle, radicals must as well.[42] "Strange Bedfellows" revealed two parallel needs: one, to mobilize greater gay and lesbian involvement in solidarity, and two, to win backing for lesbian and gay solidarity from straight groups.

By late spring 1979, as the Sandinistas made increasing gains against the Somoza regime, the Central American solidarity movement grew. Demonstrations became ever more common in San Francisco and nationally. Lesbian and gay radicals who had been active in BAGL, GALA, and work against Proposition 6 joined in these protests. The year's Gay Freedom Day occurred just a month after the White Night Riots and weeks before the Sandinistas took power in Managua; Paul Albert and Roberto Gurdián along with others from GALA met applause along the march route as they carried the FSLN flag and other signs of support. While Albert and Gurdián had not previously worked together, they knew one another and now discussed the possibility of forming a gay solidarity group. Within the next several days they organized a meeting at the Women's Building that kicked off a new organization, Gay People for the Nicaraguan Revolution. The group took its first action by joining a solidarity march on July 14, 1979, carrying a banner with its name and marching through the Mission alongside contingents from GALA and Lesbians Against Police Violence.[43]

Gay People for the Nicaraguan Revolution (GPNR, sometimes also called Gays for Nicaragua) coalesced a number of the political currents that had sustained gay and lesbian radicalism over the previous decade, including socialist feminism, unity against the right, opposition to US militarism, and lesbian feminist collective defense. Paul Albert notes that many participants brought experiences from the anti–Vietnam War movement, while member Linda Farthing recalls the group being spurred by experiences of the Cuban Revolution. A Canadian who had moved to San Francisco by way of Boston, Farthing traveled to Cuba in May 1979 and met lesbian and gay Cubans as well as lesbians from the United States participating in the Venceremos Brigades.[44] This trip informed her perspective on GPNR, which she describes as motivated by a desire to back socialist change while "increasing the space for gay people to live reasonable lives." Aware of Cuba's history of antigay policies, GPNR sought "to avoid similar outcomes in Nicaragua" and at the same time to "educate the gay community about why they should support" the Nicaraguan Revolution.[45] These motivations would only become heightened by the Mariel crisis, a period of mass emigration from Cuba that lasted from April to October 1980 and during which the Cuban government encouraged the departure of homosexuals among others it deemed "scum," lumpen proletariat, or criminals.[46] Cuban policy threw the Sandinistas' lack of an antigay policy into relief, and the contrast suggested that the Nicaraguan Revolution might resolve conflicts between socialism and sexual freedom.

While Roberto Gurdián played a key role in GPNR, he proved to be the only Nicaraguan in the group. It was almost entirely white and mostly women, with key leaders including Gurdián, Albert, and Farthing as well as Carrie Cianchetti, Kasey Brenner, and Liz Jacobs. Most of these activists were recent migrants to the Bay Area who had gained their greatest exposure to Latina/o, Latin American, and Third World politics in the Mission District. In this context, the ties that Gurdián and Albert held to solidarity networks were crucial, and GPNR made strong use of them. Gurdián's brother was one of Casa Nicaragua's founders, and this helped GPNR establish a strong relationship with that group.[47] GPNR received its mail at the Casa Nicaragua office and organized child care for Casa Nicaragua meetings and events, a contribution that reflected socialist-feminist commitments and helped to shift Casa Nicaragua's gender politics by allowing mothers as well as fathers to participate fully.[48] GPNR also deepened its relationship with Casa Nicaragua by holding a "gay education 101" session to explain gay and lesbian identities and politics. Linda Farthing recalls that although Casa Nicaragua members had initially seemed "baffled" by GPNR, the workshop undid misconceptions, "released a whole lot of tension," and helped Casa Nicaragua activists to empathize with "who we were as people and why we were doing" solidarity work.[49]

Beyond Casa Nicaragua, GPNR sought direct ties to Sandinista leadership and broadcast these links as evidence of the possibilities for gay and lesbian inclusion in the Nicaraguan Revolution. Paul Albert helped Aura Lila Beteta, the FSLN's new consul in San Francisco, set up a meeting with Mayor Dianne Feinstein, and afterward Beteta attended a GPNR meeting and issued statements of support for gay and lesbian freedom.[50] GPNR also raised over $12,000 from presentations, dances, and garage sales and sent this directly to the FSLN.[51] In January 1981 GPNR sent member Carrie Cianchetti to Nicaragua's First International Solidarity Conference, where she met with the Sandinista women's organization AMNLAE (Asociación de Mujeres Nicaragüenses Luisa Amanda Espinoza) and discussed the possibility of a US-Nicaraguan women's network as well as the question of lesbian and gay rights inside the Sandinista Revolution.[52]

GPNR's materials focused on building coalition against the right by calling on lesbian and gay activists to "Stand for Nicaragua—Support the Revolution—Anti-Gay Leaders Support Somoza." They highlighted one political opponent in Georgia senator Larry McDonald, a staunch anti-communist and conservative Democrat who introduced antigay legislation in Congress, met with Somoza in Nicaragua, and voted to send arms to his regime. GPNR also observed that citrus companies operating in Latin America backed Somoza alongside Anita Bryant; in this, it echoed and expanded the Mission District transnationalism that had helped activists link Nicaragua to Chile. The group warned that the United States might build on its support for Chile's Pinochet by unseating the Sandinistas, and it reiterated arguments that Gays in Solidarity with the Chilean Resistance had used in the mid-1970s to relate Latin American oppression to Bay Area residents' lives. For example, addressing the question, "Why should I care about Nicaragua when I'm struggling to get my own life together?" GPNR responded: "We are forced to work unsatisfying jobs that make Somoza and his buddies rich (e.g. PG&E [Pacific Gas & Electric], Exxon, Del Monte, Coca Cola). While they make their millions, we are faced with rising gas prices, escalating rents and outrageous food costs. The corporations that support Somoza are the same ones that have the ultimate control over our basic survival needs. When they lose control over a nation, it weakens their ability to rip us off." GPNR also specifically addressed gay and lesbian self-interest. In response to the query, "But aren't gay people oppressed in socialist countries?" a GPNR brochure stated:

> Gay people are oppressed everywhere in the world. How much differs greatly based on our economic and racial position in a particular country. We must realize that gay liberation is not a main struggle in countries where people are starving, even for gay people themselves. The [Nicaraguan] revolution is a beginning for *all* people. . . . At the same time, we must always be clear that we are fighting as openly gay people, that we demand recognition of our struggle and an end to gay oppression wherever it exists.

Backing this up, GPNR emphasized that it had been "welcomed" into solidarity work by Nicaraguan activists in San Francisco as well as by the Sandinista consul, and it held that solidarity activism offered a chance to build a gay and lesbian politics that would be both anti-imperialist and multiracial: "White people in the gay community must begin to make connections to Third World struggles or we all remain divided and isolated."[53]

GPNR also developed its political vocabulary by drawing on the rhetoric of lesbian feminist collective defense. It illustrated its brochures with a photograph of an androgynous woman soldier poised for battle with her eyes cast toward the distance and an assault rifle in her hand (figure 11). Although not a portrait of Dora María Tellez, who had been "Comandante Dos" in the Sandinistas' seizure of the National Palace and who had led the capture of León, the image struck a chord for those aware of Tellez and other Sandinista women in combat. The timing of GPNR's emergence shaped its imagery. Linda Farthing, who did the typesetting and layout for the brochures, argues that "we were very much caught up in . . . a revolutionary romanticism of fighting against imperialism," because up to that point Nicaraguan solidarity had centered on "supporting insurrection, a revolutionary war."[54] While this romanticism was apparent in the solidarity movement at large, it held a distinctly feminist meaning for gay and lesbian radicals. Farthing speculates that had GPNR formed a few years later, once solidarity had shifted toward aiding Nicaraguan reconstruction and delegitimizing US attack, the group might have represented itself through "women in a construction brigade, or women doctors," rather than a "woman as warrior."[55] In addition to suggesting change over time, Farthing's comments underscore that GPNR consistently saw itself in the Sandinista Revolution through the roles of women, who advanced the group's view

Lesbians & Gay Men:

Stand for Nicaragua
Support the Revolution

**Do you know that anti-gay leaders support-
ed Somoza and also oppose sending aid?**

FIGURE 11. Gay People for the Nicaraguan Revolution
brochure, c. 1979. Courtesy Vertical Files—United States
organizations and individuals (Gay People for the
Nicaraguan Revolution), Canadian Lesbian and Gay
Archives.

of the revolution providing "inspiration to all oppressed peoples that
we CAN win."[56] GPNR's imagery also hinted at how militancy, self-
sacrifice, and radicalism might be read through a lesbian aesthetic that
merged identification and desire. Lesbian and gay leftists looked to Nicaragua as the site of a revolution they must defend, as an inspirational
model for their own struggles, and as a vehicle for sexual liberation
whose meaning could be glimpsed in women seizing arms.[57]

GPNR absorbed the transnationalism that surrounded it in the Mission and rearticulated that politics to a gay and lesbian community that
it approached as predominately white but potentially multiracial. The
group made frequent presentations to gay and lesbian organizations
around the Bay Area, including some on college campuses. It further
organized and spoke at events that might draw a large lesbian and gay

audience, such as presentations on women in Nicaragua at the Women's Building and the La Peña Cultural Center (a political and arts venue founded by Chilean exiles, located in Berkeley close to the BART line that connected the East Bay to the Mission District). GPNR's brochures, which provided a map of Nicaragua and a short history of US intervention and the Sandinista Revolution, were designed in a pedagogically oriented question-and-answer format. The group sought and gained recognition in the broadest venues of gay and lesbian politics. In 1981 Carrie Cianchetti reported on her trip to Nicaragua as an official speaker at San Francisco's Lesbian and Gay Freedom Day, and Roberto Gurdián served as an official speaker in 1983.[58]

As a mostly white group, GPNR posed a different politics than GALA, which articulated Nicaraguan solidarity as an expression of Latina/o and Third World gay and lesbian identities. In October 1979 hundreds of Bay Area activists traveled to Washington, DC, for the first National March on Washington for Lesbian and Gay Rights and the first national Third World Lesbian and Gay Conference; the latter was organized by the National Coalition of Black Gays and featured a keynote speech by Audre Lorde.[59] GALA leader Rodrigo Reyes attended the conference and received loud, sustained applause when he read a statement of support from Sandinista consul Aura Lila Beteta: "To the first national conference of Third World lesbians and gay men, revolutionary Sandinista greetings. May from your conference be born a movement that identifies, that unites and struggles with the liberation movements of all oppressed people."[60] Notably, while Beteta had also offered a statement of support to GPNR, the one that Reyes read was directed specifically to the Third World Lesbian and Gay Conference and showed Beteta's awareness of both groups. Latina/os from the United States, Mexico, and Costa Rica met and forged ties at the Third World Lesbian and Gay Conference, initiating a transnational network that fueled an international gay and lesbian meeting held in Mexico in 1980, as well as a succession of feminist conferences among Latin American and Caribbean women.[61] Rodrigo Reyes continued to address the intersections of gay, Latina/o, Central American, and HIV/AIDS politics in his work throughout the 1980s as a playwright and actor, staging multiple performances in the Mission District that spoke to these concerns.[62]

The expansion of US intervention in Central America placed pressure on the solidarity movement's racial politics. Once President Ronald Reagan took office in January 1981, the US military presence in Central America accelerated rapidly, and the focus of solidarity expanded from backing the Sandinistas to opposing a US-led war. As the movement grew, more white people joined, and solidarity organizations both proliferated and professionalized by moving into policy advocacy and legal aid. Streams of refugees fled El Salvador and Guatemala, and US media began to represent Central Americans less as agents of revolution and more as martyrs and labor migrants.[63]

As the stakes of leadership in the solidarity movement became ever more heightened, lesbian and gay newspapers such as the *San Francisco Sentinel,* the Oakland-based *Plexus,* and *Coming Up!* increasingly juxtaposed coverage of Central American solidarity with articles about local Latina/o gay and lesbian organizing, debates over racism in lesbian and feminist communities, and articles on gay and lesbian politics in Mexico, Argentina, Cuba, and elsewhere in Latin America.[64] The placement of all these articles in the same issues of newspapers, often on adjacent pages or side by side, encouraged readers to see Central American solidarity as linked to the goals of anti-racist community and cultural understanding. Some articles drew these connections directly, as when Rodrigo Reyes, riffing on Frederick Douglass in an article titled "On the Fourth of July: What America Means to Me," discussed the shifting meaning of his Chicano gay identity amidst US intervention in Central America.[65] Carmen Vázquez, by then a well-known leader in the Women's Building, and writer Aurora Levins Morales contributed frequent articles in gay and lesbian newspapers that linked their identities as Latinas, as lesbians, and as feminists to their participation in Central American solidarity (Vázquez is Puerto Rican; Levins Morales is Puerto Rican and Jewish). Meanwhile, John Kyper, a white gay leftist, wrote articles in both San Francisco– and Boston-based gay newspapers that linked gay involvement in Central American solidarity to the history of gay draft resistance against the Vietnam War.[66]

The potential for building anti-racist and multiracial gay and lesbian community through Central American solidarity came into focus through solidarity's differences with antinuclear activism. The Bay Area provided a home base for the Abalone Alliance and the Livermore Action Group, two of the most important antinuclear organizations in the country and arguably the most important on the West Coast. The Abalone Alliance formed in 1977 to protest the Diablo Canyon Nuclear Power Plant, located 250 miles south of San Francisco in San Luis Obispo. The Livermore Action Group, or LAG, formed in 1981 as Abalone's successor; it shifted focus from nuclear power to nuclear war and targeted the Lawrence Livermore National Labs, a nuclear weapons design facility located 35 miles east of Oakland.[67] LAG grew swiftly: at its first major blockade in June 1982, more than five thousand people mobilized and more than thirteen hundred were arrested.[68] It organized somewhat smaller blockades in 1983 and 1984. Amidst this growth LAG was shaped by the confluence of feminism and antinuclear activism, a politics visible nationally in the Seneca Women's Peace Encampment and the Women's Pentagon Actions.

The antinuclear movement played a key role in challenging US militarism, in linking anti-militarism with environmentalism, and advancing tactics of nonviolent direct action. It did not, however, strongly foster anti-imperialism, nor did it draw on the same transnational networks as Central American solidarity. Antinuclear activists were overwhelmingly white and middle class and generally did not analyze the links between militarism and racism. Lesbian and gay radicals, including some white activists, often noted these racial limits; for example, a December 1981 report in *Coming Up!* criticized LAG for failing to foster any affinity groups among people of color.[69] These demographics shaped political practices.[70] For example, antinuclear groups' "nonviolence code" called for "openness, friendliness and respect" toward all people, including police.[71] A cluster of LAG members proposed changing this code from "openness, friendliness and respect" to "openness and nonviolence," arguing that the movement needed to "open" itself more fully to those "millions of people . . . [who] do not feel 'open, friendly, and respectful' toward people they rightly perceive as their oppressors"—implicitly, people of color, working-class people, and queer people frequently abused by police.[72] But the change was rejected and the original code stood.[73] The LAG handbook further held that, when interacting with police, "you are less likely to get hurt by someone who sees you as a calm, sensible human being," and it offered an object lesson in a woman who stopped a police officer from beating her by turning to him and saying, "I'm your daughter!"[74] These statements failed to acknowledge the routine nature of police violence. They ignored the ways that race, class, sexuality, and gender shaped perceptions of "calm" or "sensible" behavior and the fact that only some people could imagine police as benevolent fathers.

The antinuclear movement did draw in significant numbers of lesbians and gay men, most of them white and middle class. An estimated third to half of the women arrested in LAG's 1982 blockade—potentially two hundred of the women jailed—identified as lesbians, and as activist Kate Raphael recalls, these women were "generally pretty prominent and accepted."[75] Gay men were also present, joining in smaller numbers but organizing affinity groups that included Body Electric, Oz, Queens United in Efforts to End Repressive Society (QUEERS), and Enola Gay (this group named itself ironically after the plane that dropped the atomic bomb on Hiroshima, Japan, and used the unforgettable slogan "Gomorrah for a tomorrah").[76] But these activists were not immune from bias or marginalization; for example, during LAG's 1982 blockade, some straight women claimed that lesbians violated principles of nonviolence when they had sex with each other in jail.[77] More broadly, as Raphael notes, tensions arose over the priority granted to lesbian and gay concerns. Straight activists often defined sexual politics as a "side issue" rather than as interwoven with problems of militarism or capitalism, and in 1982 and 1983, straight leaders ignored objections to scheduling blockades at the same time as Lesbian and Gay Freedom Day.[78] Similarly, activists recalled that the 1978 Diablo Canyon blockade had rejected a plea for a speaker to address Proposition 6.[79]

Lesbian and gay leftists drew important skills from antinuclear organizing but found Central American solidarity a richer site for advancing multiracial radical community and mobilizing unity against the New Right. More generally, many networks of antinuclear activism simply morphed into Central American solidarity work, which by the early 1980s was shifting attention to opposing US intervention in El Salvador. In 1982 the Livermore Action Group began to collaborate with CISPES to coordinate civil disobedience at the Concord Naval Weapons Station, which was located near Livermore Labs and shipped weapons to the right-wing Salvadoran government. By 1984 many LAG participants—across all categories of sexuality—were moving into two new Central American solidarity organizations, Witness for Peace and Pledge of Resistance.[80]

In November 1983 San Francisco voters overwhelmingly approved Proposition N, which called on the federal government to end its support for El Salvador. Many lesbian and gay activists were involved in the Proposition N campaign and created a Lesbian and Gay Task Force—an effort that produced an impact felt for years thereafter. Ruth Grabowski was an organizer in both the general Proposition N campaign and its Lesbian and Gay Task Force. A young white woman, she had first become involved in Central American solidarity in 1981 while a student at Washington State University, where she minored in women's studies; was exposed to left, gay, and women of color feminist scholarship; and became active in a campus group that protested at the nearby University of Idaho when the leader of El Salvador's military junta, José Duarte, came to speak. Grabowski spent the summer before her senior year doing grassroots canvassing in San Francisco and, after graduating, decided to return to the Bay Area to continue solidarity work. She moved immediately into the Proposition N campaign, which already had "a very explicit gay focus," she recalled, "and it was almost all women doing that work. It made it easy to get involved right away."[81]

The Proposition N campaign's Lesbian and Gay Task Force linked the Gay Latino Alliance, the city's Democratic Clubs, and other groups, and it brought speakers from the Salvadoran women's organization to San Francisco women's bookstores and community organizations. Liz Jacobs, earlier a member of Gay People for the Nicaraguan Revolution, helped to create the task force, which like GPNR sought to "educate and organize" lesbians and gay men. It coordinated contingents in the June 1983 Lesbian and Gay Freedom Day parade, mobilized within an anti-intervention march at Concord Naval Weapons Station, and participated in a peace march held in August.[82]

Grabowski and two other activists reported on Proposition N for *Coming Up!* and drew on "fight the right" rhetoric by emphasizing the harm of social welfare cuts justified by defense spending in Central America. They argued that "lesbians and gay men are realizing the necessity of joining these issues together in order to fight both our oppression and that of the Central American peoples," and they held that conservative "economic cut-backs have struck lesbians and gays hard, particularly those of us who are Third World and in the working class."[83] The women also cited San Francisco's "impressive history of lesbian/gay solidarity work" through, among other groups, Gay Solidarity with the Chilean Resistance, GALA, and GPNR. Their awareness of past organizing solidified the growing association between gay and lesbian radicalism and Central American solidarity.

After the Proposition N victory, the task force seeded a new effort: Lesbians and Gays Against Intervention, or LAGAI (pronounced "la gay"; the group sometimes appended "Central America" to its name, but eventually dropped that in favor of a simpler pronunciation). Founded by several members of Proposition N's Lesbian and Gay Task Force, LAGAI defined itself as an "anti-imperialist, gay liberation, feminist, internationalist, and left" group committed to Latin American, left, and anti-racist struggles and to gay and lesbian struggles across the hemisphere.[84] An early LAGAI poster used a Lesbian and Gay Task Force symbol, an inverted pink triangle surrounded by multicolored and interlocking hands (figure 12). The Proposition N version of this

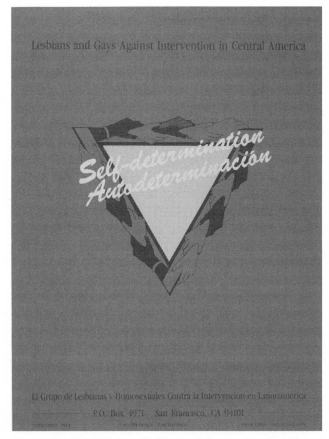

FIGURE 12. Tede Matthews/Lesbians and Gays against Intervention, "Self-determination/auto-determinación," c. 1983. Courtesy Lincoln Cushing/Docs Populi.

image had used the slogan "Money for AIDS, not war," while the LAGAI poster used the bilingual slogan "Self-determination/Auto-determinación."

For longtime member Kate Raphael, LAGAI offered an alternative to straight solidarity groups such as CISPES, which included many lesbian women yet did not vocally recognize them.[85] Continuing past efforts, LAGAI's earliest activities included building relationships with Casa Nicaragua, the Salvadoran women's organization, and Casa El Salvador (which printed the "Self-determination" poster). In February 1984 LAGAI coordinated an educational event, "Alliances: Lesbians and Gay Men in Solidarity," that was held at the Mission Cultural Center, drew an audience of some three hundred people, and addressed sexual politics across Latin America.[86] Suggesting the relatively taken-for-granted place of Nicaragua, speakers addressed gay and lesbian solidarity with, and gay and lesbian issues within, El Salvador, Guatemala, Peru, Grenada, Colombia, and Puerto Rico. That June, Lesbian and Gay Freedom Day paid substantial attention to Central American solidarity as the Sandinista consul, a Salvadoran representative, and Roberto Gurdián all spoke on the rally platform.[87]

Like GPNR and the Lesbian and Gay Task Force, LAGAI was predominately white, but proved more purposeful in organizing with people of color than other groups had been, often creating bilingual materials and later working with Amaranto, a group of lesbian and gay Latin American immigrants. Further, as gay and lesbian solidarity expanded, people of color increasingly challenged its white face. When LAGAI proposed a travel project, lesbians of color took control of the planning and by 1985 remade it as the Victoria Mercado Brigade—the first gay and lesbian brigade to Nicaragua and a majority–people of color group. Chapter 5 explores the Victoria Mercado Brigade in detail.

In reflecting on the emergence of lesbian and gay solidarity, Ruth Mahaney recalled that "the connections to Central America felt very personal and there all the time for us."[88] The substance of those connections varied just as the "us" did. Many distinct characteristics made San Francisco a vibrant site for a queer solidarity: the presence of Central American immigrants alongside other Latinas and Latinos; the long-intertwined influences of anti-war and anti-imperialist politics; the presence of gay and lesbian people within and alongside all these histories. When Mahaney termed the connections to Central America "personal" and "there," she spoke to her own physical, emotional, and political embeddedness in the Mission District. "All the time" could be tracked in an activist's datebook with events including not only meetings and protests but also cultural events. The Bay Area women's musical group Swingshift sang for visiting Central American labor activists and was then invited to perform in Nicaragua; the San Francisco Mime Troupe, in which former Third World Gay Caucus member Brian Freeman was active, produced multiple shows about Central America and in 1986 was welcomed to the Nicaraguan National Theater Festival; gay activist Tede Matthews organized numerous poetry readings and other cultural events related to solidarity, hosting some of them at Modern Times Bookstore, where he and Ruth Mahaney worked.[89] As in any movement, comrades became friends and lovers, lovers became comrades and friends, and activists brought one another to meetings, protests, and events.

Yet while activists shared a common calendar and geography, they entered Central American solidarity with distinct interests and networks shaped by race, nationality, and ethnicity as well as sexuality and gender. Fully understanding lesbian and gay solidarity requires considering how its participants theorized women of color feminism and how Nicaraguan lesbian and gay activists directed the work of North Americans. The following chapter takes up these concerns.

CHAPTER 5

Talk About Loving in the War Years

Nicaragua, Transnational Feminism, and AIDS

In September 1984, a delegation of eighteen women called Somos Hermanas ("we are sisters") traveled from San Francisco to Nicaragua to learn about women's experiences in the Sandinista Revolution and to link feminist organizing in the two countries. Somos Hermanas was a project of the Alliance Against Women's Oppression, an offshoot of the 1970s Third World Women's Alliance that now housed itself in the San Francisco Women's Building. Reflecting those networks, a strong majority of Somos Hermanas delegates were women of color (principally Latina and Chicana but also black and Asian) and half were lesbian or bisexual.[1] The group's members cited their racial, gender, and sexual identities to explain their support for revolutionary Nicaragua, defining themselves not only as opponents of US intervention but also as fellow victims of President Reagan. More informally, they declared their sexual diversity when their Nicaraguan hosts threw a party for them and a delegation of Cuban musicians. As Somos Hermanas member Carmen Vázquez recalls, she and her fellow delegate Lucrecia Bermudez began to dance together, and the Cuban men—motivated seemingly by anxiety as much as chivalry—"came to help us out" by offering to dance. Faced with this offer, "Lucrecia and I looked at each other. I mean, Lucrecia's a butch, too, but whatever. And said, 'No, thank you,' . . . so, then it was clear women were going to dance."[2] Although Vázquez and Bermudez were not interested in each other, their pairing and their gender expressions challenged heterosexual norms. Their "No, thank you" opened the door for other members of Somos Hermanas to dance together that night, whether as friends, in flirtation, or as potential lovers. Indeed, the evening sparked a new relationship by emboldening Vázquez to ask another Somos Hermanas participant, Marcia Gallo, "'Would you dance?' and she did and we danced right off the floor into the woods and had wild, you know, making out sessions that didn't stop for twelve years . . . talk about loving in the war years."[3]

In recalling that night, Vázquez self-consciously echoed the title of Cherríe Moraga's *Loving in the War Years* (1983), in which Moraga continued the theorizations that she had begun in the anthology she coedited with Gloria Anzaldúa, *This Bridge Called My Back: Writings by Radical Women of Color* (1981).[4] *Loving* and *Bridge* were central in theorizing "women of color" as an identity of multiracial solidarity grounded in anti-imperialist liberation.[5] *Loving* also tied lesbian feminism to Central American solidarity in multiple ways, among them by describing romance born in wartime. In the book's title poem, two women fall in love against the sound of "bombs," as if in a scene from the film *Casablanca*: "I *do* think of Bogart & Bergman / not clear who's who."[6] Similarly, Vázquez's relationship with Gallo began amidst contra attacks on Sandinista forces. At moments on the Somos Hermanas trip when she and Gallo began to be intimate, they either heard gunshots or were warned that, by going outside to find privacy, they risked meeting violence. In Vázquez's words, "It just doesn't get more intense than that."[7]

Vázquez's reference to Moraga hints at tensions that structured lesbian and gay solidarity with Central America. At points, Moraga's *Loving* suggests that lesbian identity is itself a "front" in a war, and her title poem contends that "being queer / and female / is as warrior / as we can get."[8] In this line, she risks collapsing highly distinct struggles into one metaphor. Yet later in *Loving* Moraga doubles back to resist such slippages, arguing both that "the danger lies in ranking the oppressions" and that *"the danger lies in failing to acknowledge the specificity of the oppressions."*[9] Moraga's claims raise questions about how lesbian and gay radicals understood the differences among the forms of violence and injustice that inspired their solidarity with Central America. What did sexual politics and sexual identities mean amidst the Sandinista Revolution and the contra war? More pointedly, how might the answers have varied between the United States and Nicaragua?

Transnational feminist analysis recognizes that colonialism, imperialism, and anti-colonial and anti-imperialist movements have constructed multiple, often divergent experiences of gender and sexuality around the world. Patriarchy and desire do not operate in the same ways across time and space. Similarly, while solidarity brings together multiple forms of self-interest, it arises out of contexts in which these interests carry uneven risk and unequal clout. Despite their stated goals, solidarity movements risk homogenizing their participants' interests in ways that marginalize those with less power. Transnational feminism seeks a bulwark against these risks by pushing us to recognize our sharp, even unknowable differences. Sara Ahmed clarifies this when she describes feminist solidarity as "a way of facing the world, which includes facing what we might not recognise, with others we do not yet know," while insisting upon "the recognition that even if we do not have the same feelings, or the same lives, or the same bodies, we do live on common ground."[10] In Maylei Blackwell's words, "We do not have to be each other (or labor under the fiction of sameness) to work together politically."[11] Viewed in these terms, solidarity stands at its most powerful when we imagine its goals as continually elusive, reached only in moments—when, as Araceli Esparza suggests, we approach it as "risky, temporary, conditional, and without guarantees."[12]

This chapter draws on these insights of transnational feminism to analyze lesbian and gay solidarity and exchanges between Bay Area and Nicaraguan lesbian and gay activists from 1984 to 1990. The chapter is broken into three major sections. The first considers how the dynamics of activist brigades, feminist views of the Sandinista Revolution, and North American views of sexual diversity in Nicaragua shaped lesbian and gay solidarity in the Bay Area. The second section details the Somos Hermanas delegation and the Victoria Mercado Brigade, two groups that traveled from San Francisco to Nicaragua in 1984 and 1985. The chapter's third section examines organizing by Nicaraguan lesbian, gay, and HIV/AIDS activists and their interaction with both US activists and the Sandinista government. It analyzes the formation of Nicaragua's first lesbian and gay organization; a crackdown against that group by Sandinista State Security; the group's interaction with Bay Area activists; and the formation of Nicaragua's Colectivo de Educación Popular contra el SIDA (CEP-SIDA, or Collective for Popular Education Against AIDS).[13] CEP-SIDA received approval from the Sandinista Ministry of Health (MINSA), furthered lesbian and gay recognition in the Nicaraguan Revolution, and stood at the heart of Nicaragua's AIDS prevention until the Sandinistas' 1990 defeat.

US and Nicaraguan activists exchanged a good deal—ideas, support, and resources—but their collaborations were also structured by silences.

They sought but only partially achieved what Maylei Blackwell terms "translenguaje," or a practice of "translating, reworking, and contesting meaning" in transnational organizing. Blackwell holds that translenguaje occurs when marginalized people in one site adapt the political strategies of similarly marginalized people in another site to meet the needs of their local contexts, structures of oppression, and formulations of identity.[14] More than a simple practice of interpretation, translenguaje seeks an extended remaking of political discourse, and it may be necessary even among people who speak the same language. For example, the 1988 Spanish-language edition of *This Bridge Called My Back* (*Esta puente, mi espalda*) sought to extend US women of color feminism to Latin America, but because it did not reformulate the concept of women of color to address anti-black, anti-indigenous, or anti-Asian racism outside the United States, it failed to achieve a full translenguaje of its own politics.[15] Blackwell's concept of translenguaje helps to name the challenges lesbian and gay solidarity activists faced.

Lesbian and gay solidarity with Nicaragua—meaning, to repeat the previous chapter's formulation, explicitly lesbian and gay activism in support of the Sandinista Revolution and against US intervention—developed out of transnational currents of political exchange. Debate about how to incorporate gender and sexual freedom into socialist programs of national liberation circulated across the Americas and more globally.[16] Radicals both outside and inside Nicaragua invested hope in the Sandinista Revolution's positive recognition of women's rights, its lack of antigay policy, and its multiple contrasts with the Reagan-era United States. Ideas and strategies flowed from Nicaragua to the United States and vice versa; for Somos Hermanas member Diane Jones, Nicaragua mattered first because "they *won*" and second because of "the elements of feminism, the dedication to health care and education, the images of women with guns, and the ways AIDS was treated—here was Nicaragua, so poor, and prioritizing AIDS work and literacy while the U.S. isn't acting."[17] To support Nicaragua was both to stand against US attack and to back socialist-feminist possibility. By looking to and following the lead of Nicaraguans, lesbian and gay solidarity activists adapted the ideals of the Sandinista Revolution to transform and further their organizing within the United States.

Yet amidst their exchanges with Nicaraguans, US-based activists often failed to understand the full contexts shaping both solidarity and sexual politics. From 1982 through early 1988, the Nicaraguan government responded to the contra war with a state of emergency that restricted organizing outside the Frente Sandinista de Liberación Nacional, or FSLN. Although Nicaraguan lesbian and gay activists identified strongly as Sandinistas, their lesbian and gay organizing was not party affiliated or approved, and this was one of the factors that enabled its repression by Sandinista State Security. Nicaraguan lesbian and gay activists carefully controlled international news of their experiences, keeping silent about government harassment while enthusiastically laying claim to evidence of Sandinista support. They followed this practice because many of their US allies supported the Sandinista Revolution only if they were kept ignorant of its flaws. From a US perspective, lesbian, gay, and AIDS solidarity fit the call to fund feminist social programs instead of interventionist war. From a Nicaraguan point of view, solidarity offered a means to reverse State Security harassment and open doors within the Sandinista government—but only if news of such harassment was kept under wraps. As a result, Nicaraguans managed what US activists knew, using silence and miscommunication strategically to triangulate US activists' support and to define their own sexual politics.

. . .

By the early 1980s, transnational circuits of travel were key to the Central American solidarity movement, guiding its communication networks and political culture and encouraging its growth. Activists from the United States, Europe, and elsewhere in Latin America traveled frequently to Nicaragua (less often to El Salvador or Guatemala) to forge direct activist ties and to serve as witnesses to US intervention. Representatives of the Sandinista government and of Nicaraguan organizations traveled on speaking tours to the Bay Area and elsewhere, and helped to coordinate solidarity groups' visits inside Nicaragua. Nicaraguans who had returned from exile and foreigners who moved to the country played significant roles in solidarity because of their transnational connections and language skills. Traveling activists often carried correspondence and material aid in order to circumvent a slow postal system and the US blockade.

Circuits of travel accelerated in 1983 and 1984 in response to several factors, including regional peace plans, Nicaraguan national elections, and the founding of Witness for Peace, which took US activists to war zones to record action by contra soldiers and US forces. In November 1983, when Nicaraguan groups issued a call for international assistance with the coffee harvest, activists around the world responded by forming coffee brigades; these soon expanded to include harvesting cotton, constructing buildings, and other projects.[18] Many foreigners believed that brigades offered them a way to experience the revolution directly, as these projects opened opportunities to participate in Nicaragua's reconstruction and echoed the Sandinistas' celebrated literacy and health campaigns. (In 1980 thousands of young urban Nicaraguans had mobilized across the countryside in the Ejército Popular de Alfabetización, or People's Literacy Army, and through the early 1980s Nicaraguans continued similar efforts through vaccination programs.)

Activists who traveled to Nicaragua could face dangers; in April 1987 Ben Linder, a young engineer from Oregon, was killed by contras while in the town of El Cúa to help build a hydroelectric dam. But activist travel was also an exercise of privilege: it demanded time away from paid work or family responsibilities, funds for travel and daily living, and passports and visas that could assure transit and return. Because of these facts, as well as the histories that marked Nicaragua, Central America, and the Caribbean as sites of tropical escape, the boundary between politics and tourism could be an unstable one. Some solidarity activists sought to shore up that boundary by mocking dilettantes as "sandalistas," rather than Sandinistas, but in many ways the distinction was a continuum rather than a stark binary. The Sandinista government ran a tourism ministry and encouraged visitors to bring goods and spend money. Nicaraguans also knew that even when activists brought few skills to assist in reconstruction, their trips helped strengthen their willingness and ability to organize against intervention from within the United States. Activist travel thus reinforced a dynamic in which Nicaraguans, having greater knowledge and understanding of their own country, worked to manage foreign activists' knowledge, perceptions, and actions.

Unlike the Venceremos Brigades to Cuba, no delegations to Nicaragua formally excluded lesbians or gay men; however, straight US activists often told their lesbian and gay counterparts on brigades not to come out to Nicaraguans or pushed them to conform to gender norms.[19] These problems made some lesbian and gay activists want to address sexuality and gender more explicitly, and many looked to feminism inside the Sandinista Revolution as evidence of opportunities for more open dialogue. The revolution did suggest opportunities for sexual freedom. Women formed 30 percent of the Sandinistas' insurrectionary militia in the 1970s and about a quarter of the army in the 1980s. Sandinista laws guaranteed women's right to equal wages and paid maternity leave, banned sexually exploitative advertising, ended distinctions between "legitimate" and "illegitimate" children, and recognized common-law marriage.[20] The Sandinista women's organization, AMNLAE, portrayed women as militant mothers, as depicted in a famous poster that showed a smiling young woman with an AK-47 on her shoulder, an infant at her breast, above the words "Nicaragua debe sobrevivir/Nicaragua must survive."[21] But like radicals across the hemisphere, Sandinistas also employed the discourse of the "New Man," a concept formulated in the Cuban Revolution that defined political commitment through a self-sacrificing and heterosexual masculinity—and thereby seemed to exclude women from revolutionary leadership.[22]

Lesbian and gay Nicaraguans moved both within and against dominant gendered frameworks to approach the revolution as a vehicle for sexual liberation. While networks of same-sex culture existed under Somoza, they were strongly associated with prostitution and not defined as radical; by contrast, Nicaraguan lesbian and gay activism that arose in the Sandinista context was distinctly leftist.[23] Many lesbians came out in the militia, the army, or the vaccination and literacy brigades.[24] According to one gay Sandinista, many "cochónes were very active in the Sandinista movement from the very beginning" because "naturally we identified with the vanguard of the oppressed" (cochón is a Nicaraguan term indicating the receptive partner in anal sex as well as effeminacy or the "passive").[25] These experiences and forms of identification resonated with currents in US, European, and Latin American gay liberation. But, while the Sandinista state did not develop institutionalized antigay policies, the army did eject some gay and lesbian militants, and in the early years of the revolution the government closed some heterosexual brothels and gay bars.[26] Conservatives in Nicaragua faulted the FSLN for upsetting gender and family norms, and several women who rose to FSLN leadership were rumored to be lesbians—gossip that was in some cases true but that was circulated to discredit them and the revolution.[27] Further, as this chapter details, Sandinista State Security harassed and sought to shut down lesbian and gay activism in 1987. The revolution's freedoms converged with its limits to fuel Nicaraguan lesbian and gay activism in the 1980s.[28]

The vast majority of outsiders, however, learned little about the Sandinista government's antigay practices until after the revolution's end in 1990. Instead, lesbian and gay solidarity activists consistently argued that the feminist potential of the revolution could enable sexual freedom, particularly for women. In 1979, San Francisco's Gay People for the Nicaraguan Revolution hinted at this potential by centering the image of an androgynous woman soldier on their brochures (figure 11, chapter 4).

Another of the group's fliers showed uniformed young women in a Sandinista literacy brigade, smiling and with arms draped around one another, representing the blending of militancy and affection that US activists had already linked to lesbian feminist collective defense.[29]

Images like these gained a wider audience through Margaret Randall's widely read volume *Sandino's Daughters: Testimonies of Nicaraguan Women in Struggle* (1981).[30] Randall's interview of Dora María Tellez drew particular attention. Tellez was "Comandante Dos" in the FSLN's assault on the National Palace in 1978, led the Sandinistas' capture of Léon in 1979, and in the 1980s served as minister of health. *Sandino's Daughters* implicitly compared her to Che Guevara, citing Tellez's training as a doctor and including a photograph that showed her in military uniform, slouched in a chair and holding a cigarette—an image strongly reminiscent of portraits of Che.

Tellez inspired many women in the solidarity movement. Somos Hermanas met with Tellez on the group's 1984 trip to Nicaragua, and as Carmen Vázquez later noted, Tellez "did not come out to us as a lesbian, but several of the women came out of the meeting wanting her baby, I'll tell you that."[31] Another Somos Hermanas delegate, Pam David, recalled that "we all had crushes" on Tellez not only because she was "gorgeous" but also because she had become a doctor, led a revolution, and rebuilt a nation.[32] Marcia Gallo remembered that women who met Tellez fell "madly in love. Because she was smart and hot and strong and funny and incredibly human," and because she revealed the Revolution's potential to "deal with capitalism, and . . . feminism or sexism at the same time . . . that was the other reason to get excited."[33] Gay men in solidarity occasionally celebrated Sandinista militants as well, typically in ways that reflected their histories in the anti–Vietnam War movement. Gay leftist John Kyper held that Nicaraguan soldiers were "the first men in uniform I have found sexually attractive since the Vietnam Veterans Against the War a decade ago—and for similar reasons."[34] As in so much activism, including that coded as straight, erotic attraction and political commitment coexisted and reinforced each other.[35] The presence of desire did not discount activists' dedication but served as one more thing that gave it life. Moreover, naming such desire could valorize and politicize lesbian and gay sexualities.

Yet desire never exists innocent of its context. Outsiders who found potential for lesbian and gay freedom through the Sandinista Revolution or solidarity risked imposing perceptions of sexuality and gender that Nicaraguans did not claim or want. Anglo-European discourses of sexuality have long ascribed hypersexuality and sexual perversion to people of African and Latin American descent, and these histories lingered as an undercurrent in both queer and straight US activists' identification with and desire for Sandinista militants. Another dimension of these discourses fixed gay identity in the "modern" Northern Hemisphere and defined homosexuality as "foreign" to Latin America.[36] The potential for exploitative transnational desire was matched by the pull of a developmentalism that assumed Nicaragua was too backward for lesbian and gay life. Many lesbian and gay radicals from the Global North, and indeed from Latin America, struggled with the assumptions that same-sex desire was alien to Nicaragua; some adopted the view that it was "foreign," while others questioned and challenged that notion.

Lesbian and gay solidarity activists—indeed, even casual readers of the Bay Area gay and lesbian press—could find reasons to reject the idea that homosexuality was non-Nicaraguan. In July 1983 Aurora Levins Morales, a Puerto Rican and Jewish writer who had contributed to *This Bridge Called My Back,* published an interview with the Nicaraguan activist Roberto Gurdián in the San Francisco gay and lesbian newspaper *Coming Up!*. Gurdián had identified as gay in Nicaragua, then lived in San Francisco from 1978 to 1980 and, during that time, helped organize the first lesbian and gay solidarity event, "Strange Bedfellows," as well as the first lesbian and gay solidarity group, Gay People for the Nicaraguan Revolution. Speaking to Levins Morales, he described gay and lesbian people as part of everyday life in Nicaragua and described Dora María Tellez as "butch, butch, butch to the nth degree . . . everyone *says* she's a lesbian." As he also noted, he had returned to Nicaragua after the revolution took power and, together with a gay friend who had never left the country, applied for a job at the Sandinista tourism bureau. The supervisor apparently felt that both men could not be hired because "they'll say 'Inturismo is full of queers. So let's just hire one of them.' So I was hired. But, you know, it's true . . . Inturismo *is* full of queers, and the Ministry of Culture, and the airline."[37] Gurdián's gossip challenged readers to abandon the assumption that sexual diversity was unique to the United States.

Still, many activists feared that they would violate principles of respectful solidarity if they expressed lesbian and gay identities inside Nicaragua. Activist Rebecca Gordon offered one example of this concern. A white lesbian from San Francisco, Gordon worked in Nicaragua from May through December 1984 with Witness for Peace, during which time she sent many letters home to her partner, Jan Adams, and their wide network of activist friends. Gordon published her correspondence in 1986 as *Letters from Nicaragua,* an important document of lesbian feminist participation in solidarity.[38] As her correspondence showed, throughout her time in Nicaragua Gordon sought to express solidarity by staying in the closet. Rigidly distinguishing sexual behavior from identity, she argued that gay and lesbian identities could not exist in Nicaragua because it was not a site of advanced capitalism, and she cited homosexuality as part of a "genuinely mixed bag of other cultural imports—from tractors to dictatorships—to which Latin Americans understandably have mixed reactions."[39] She was apparently unaware of the long track record of gay and lesbian politics and culture in Mexico, Argentina, Chile, and Brazil or of the lesbian and gay activism that was emerging in Nicaragua itself. After returning to the United States Gordon noted that other solidarity activists had met lesbian and gay Nicaraguans, and by 1998 she published work critiquing her earlier claims.[40] However, during her time in the country and in the text of *Letters,* she defined staying closeted as a self-sacrificial act of "cultural sensitivity."[41]

Reactions to claims like these varied and, notably, did not divide out neatly between white women and women of color. In a laudatory introduction to *Letters from Nicaragua,* black lesbian feminist Barbara Smith read Gordon's views as evidence of her "humility, not to pass judgment on the Nicaraguan people, especially in regard to gay and women's issues, but to try to find out how a totally different history affects a people's relationship to everything, including sexual politics."[42] But others responded to the idea of the respectful closet with frustration. Somos Hermanas member Lucrecia Bermudez argued that rather than a mark of cultural respect, "I think it's the opposite—to assume . . . that what you have in front of you is underdeveloped, uncivilized . . . that their minds are so small they can't conceive of it."[43] Bermudez was a Peruvian immigrant who, before moving to the United States, had been active in a leftist lesbian and gay group in Lima and frequented that city's gay bars. She talked with lesbian, gay, and straight Nicaraguans about sexuality both on the Somos Hermanas delegation in 1984 and on an individual trip she made to Nicaragua with a girlfriend in 1985.[44] Bermudez's fellow delegate Carmen Vázquez reported a similar ease in talking with Nicaraguan feminists about lesbian identity, facilitated by a context of "deep respect and . . . lots of rum and dancing."[45]

Thus, gender expression, language, cultural expression, and racial and ethnic identities all played roles in inhibiting or sparking dialogue about sexuality. Gordon was a white woman and a fluent but not native Spanish speaker, and as recorded in *Letters,* assumed she was invisible as a lesbian unless she stated it outright. Meanwhile, Bermudez and Vázquez were native Spanish speakers and Peruvian and Puerto Rican, respectively. Both also identified as butch and found themselves fairly easily recognized as lesbian across multiple social contexts. Further, both of them rejected lesbian feminist critiques that termed butch-femme expression to be merely imitating heterosexual norms, and they viewed these critiques of butch-femme identities as the province of white and middle-class women.[46] The debates among Gordon, Vázquez, and Bermudez reflected many overlapping binaries—mind versus body, verbal declaration versus physical performance, authentic versus imitative—that had long been mapped onto a geography of developed versus underdeveloped sexualities.

. . .

Activist travel to Nicaragua presented freighted opportunities for dialogue about sexuality and lesbian and gay recognition. Two Bay Area projects, the Somos Hermanas delegation and the Victoria Mercado Brigade, became particularly important vehicles for this exchange. Planning for these projects began almost simultaneously in summer 1984, but the Somos Hermanas delegation occurred first, in September; about half of its participants were lesbian or bisexual women. The Victoria Mercado Brigade traveled in May 1985 and was composed entirely of activists identifying as lesbian and gay. Both projects were majority women of color and seeded further trips, including two "AIDS brigades" organized in 1986 and 1987. Both had profound effects on their participants both personally and politically. For Carmen Vázquez, Somos Hermanas "finally brought the . . . Latina activist part of me, the socialist, communist part of me and the lesbian part of me all together."[47]

The history of Somos Hermanas reflected the intertwined links between women of color feminism and barrio transnationalism in the San Francisco Mission District. The group grew out of the Alliance Against Women's Oppression (AAWO), which a few years earlier had formed out of the Third World Women's Alliance; AAWO headquartered itself in the San Francisco Women's Building and helped to push that institution to become more anti-racist and multiracial.[48] Somos Hermanas traveled to Nicaragua for ten days in September 1984 and, on its return, launched itself as an ongoing project, remaining active until the Sandinistas' 1990 defeat.[49] In March 1985 Somos Hermanas held a five-hundred-person conference in the Mission District with presenters including women from the Nicaraguan and Salvadoran women's organizations (AMNLAE and AMES); that July it organized a delegation to the United Nations Women's Conference in Nairobi, Kenya.[50] At the group's height in the mid-1980s, about seventy-five women were core members, and beyond its San Francisco headquarters Somos Hermanas included small chapters in Watsonville–Santa Cruz (California), New York, Boston, and Louisville (Kentucky). Elsa Granados, a Chicana member in Watsonville–Santa Cruz, contributed an essay to the Spanish-language edition of *This Bridge Called My Back* about her trip to Nicaragua with Somos Hermanas in 1986.[51]

Somos Hermanas defined itself as a "national, multi-racial organization of women, lesbian and straight, who are committed to organizing ourselves and others to promote peace and stop US intervention in Central America and the Caribbean."[52] It argued that conservatives used intervention in Central America to justify cuts in US domestic spending—cuts it held were aimed at limiting women's autonomy, curtailing sexual freedom, and criminalizing people of color.[53] Intriguingly, Somos Hermanas was at times mistakenly described as a Latina lesbian organization, even though it was about evenly split between straight and lesbian, Latina and non-Latina (about a third of its members were white and a fifth were other women of color, notably black and Filipina). Those who mischaracterized the group seemed to assume leaders such as Carmen Vázquez represented a monolithic whole or to imagine that only lesbians would bring sexual politics into transnational feminism. The group consistently asked about the status of lesbian and gay people in Nicaragua and, along with many Nicaraguan feminists and lesbian and gay people, expressed hope that nondiscrimination on the basis of sexuality might become incorporated into the Nicaraguan constitution. On Somos Hermanas's 1984 trip, AMNLAE representatives treated their questions about lesbian and gay issues seriously but associated homosexuality with drug addiction and prostitution; by 1987 Somos Hermanas representatives noted that such associations had faded.[54]

Somos Hermanas's imagery reflected the fluid status of sexual politics within the group, which occupied neither the center nor the periphery of its political imagination. When the group returned from its 1984 delegation to Nicaragua, it adapted a photograph from the trip to represent solidarity through an image of two embracing women. Juan Fuentes, the husband of a fellow activist and a well-known artist in the Mission District, remade the image as a full-color silkscreen poster for Somos Hermanas's March 1985 conference (figure 13).[55] He also adapted the image as a black-and-white logo that Somos Hermanas

FIGURE 13. Somos Hermanas poster; artwork by Juan R. Fuentes, 1985. Courtesy Lincoln Cushing/Docs Populi.

printed on T-shirts, buttons, and calendars sold to raise funds. The image depicted a Somos Hermanas member and a Nicaraguan woman who mirrored one another physically in their wavy black hair, overlapping arms and heads, rounded bodies, and light-brown skin tone. Accompanied by the slogan "embracing our sisters in solidarity," the portrait became well loved by Somos Hermanas members.[56] It also reflected a tension between universalism and difference within transnational feminist solidarity.[57] Should the viewer see these two women as basically the same or as different? How might the answer alter the meanings of their embrace?

While Somos Hermanas linked lesbian and gay solidarity to women of color feminism, the Victoria Mercado Brigade more directly interacted with lesbian and gay activism in Nicaragua. The idea for this second project was raised in summer 1984 at a meeting of LAGAI (Lesbians and Gays Against Intervention), which organized lesbian and gay contingents at Central America protests and worked to raise consciousness about solidarity among lesbian, gay, and feminist audiences. For several reasons, however, LAGAI members were split in their views of organizing a brigade. Some participants, arguing that the main focus of solidarity activism should be to change US policy, felt that a brigade might distract from this goal or that it would center inappropriately on changing Nicaraguan society. These debates helped divide the brigade from LAGAI by September 1984.[58]

Another debate emerged around the project's racial dynamics. The initial planning network for the brigade was almost completely white, and while it proposed a trip that would "raise the issue of gay liberation as an essential element in national liberation struggles" and "reflect the diversity of gay people: in nationality, race, religion, education, income, social background, and 'lifestyle,'" a number of women of color were concerned by the prospect of a white-led group representing the US lesbian and gay movement in Nicaragua.[59] Thus, by the end of 1984 about a dozen lesbians of color—African American, Cuban, Puerto Rican, and Chicana—took over the planning of the project.[60] The collective was grounded in a women of color writing group at the bookstore Old Wives' Tales, and the name they adopted, the Victoria Mercado Brigade, honored someone many had counted as a close friend—a Chicana lesbian and radical labor activist who had been murdered in Oakland in 1982.[61] Ultimately thirteen people participated in the trip, including four Latina women (Chicana, Cuban, and Puerto Rican), four black women (one who was both black and Filipina), two men (one of whom was Native American, the other Chicano), and three white people (two women and one man). A number of other people from San Francisco helped to organize the trip but did not go for various reasons, including precarious immigration status.[62]

Like Somos Hermanas, the Victoria Mercado Brigade was fueled in part by events and organizing at the San Francisco Women's Building, but it differed from Somos Hermanas in holding a stronger presence of artists, writers, and musicians. Its ties to Old Wives' Tales were also significant, as that bookstore, located in the Mission District on Valencia Street, had developed a multiracial leadership collective and become known as a site for lesbian and feminist antiracism.[63] Another central organizer of the Victoria Mercado Brigade was Ellen Gavin, a white woman who was strongly connected to organizing with women of color and who had

FIGURE 14. Victoria Mercado Brigade members in Managua, 1985. *Left to right:* Margaret Benson Thompson, Ellen Gavin, and an unnamed person. Photographer unknown. Courtesy Ellen Gavin.

previously organized women's dance parties called Us Girls. Gavin helped set up fundraisers for the Brigade at clubs and theaters, including a benefit called Salsa Picante that featured Blackberri, the black gay singer; Swingshift, a women's musical group; the Afro-Cuban music group Conjunto Cespedes; and Sistah Boom, a multiracial women's drumming ensemble in which Brigade member Carol Fields and another important lesbian solidarity activist, Amy Bank, both participated. This event and others raised $17,000.[64] Members of the Victoria Mercado Brigade were proud of their racially diverse artistic and political culture and brought Salsa Picante posters to Nicaragua to give as gifts; in a snapshot from the trip Ellen Gavin, Margaret Benson Thompson, and another member posed with the poster on a Managua street (figure 14).

Ruth Grabowski remained involved in the Victoria Mercado Brigade as it transitioned beyond the LAGAI network and recalls that as the project developed its organizers received "freaked out" warnings about how to express cultural sensitivity in Nicaragua, including cautions to avoid being too aggressive about defining themselves as lesbian and gay.

At this time various straight-dominated solidarity groups imposed gender and clothing requirements on trips in order to meet Central American cultural norms, both real and perceived. For example, a CISPES trip to El Salvador in which Grabowski participated required women to wear modest skirts, dresses, or tailored and feminine slacks; Grabowski, who had to borrow the appropriate clothing, felt herself to be more or less "in drag."[65] Warnings about not being too overt about gayness reflected the assumptions that homosexuality was foreign to Nicaragua and that solidarity activists traveled without cultural sensitivity or cultural rapport. As a group dominated by lesbians of color, the Victoria Mercado Brigade seemed to undermine the logic of these views. Nonetheless, one theme of its political education sessions before the trip was "that we weren't there to scream at people that they were patriarchal" and that conversations with Nicaraguans about "deeper, harder, uncomfortable things," including sexuality and gender, might be possible once trust was built.[66] The group traveled to Managua in May and June 1985, with part of the group staying two weeks and others a month.[67] Participants installed the concrete foundation for a neighborhood community center (paying for materials with the $17,000 they had raised), lived with host families, attended meetings with groups including the Nicaraguan women's organization AMNLAE, and met informally with Nicaraguan lesbians and gay men.

Day-to-day experiences in Nicaragua pushed Victoria Mercado Brigade participants to think about both their own identities and their identification with Nicaraguans. As member Carol Fields recalls, "Nicaraguans would often assume that we were Cuban" because the group was multiracial. The response echoed those Somos Hermanas had encountered (some Nicaraguans had misperceived that group as one of "international mothers" because of their racial diversity, rather than women of color from the United States) and underscored the widespread perception of the United States as white.[68] Indeed, Fields had joined the Brigade with the goal of analyzing her blackness in global terms; she describes one of her motivations as "diasporic . . . I was interested in how blackness and race played out in Nicaragua." Since the group did not travel to the Atlantic Coast where Nicaragua's black community is concentrated, Fields found that she was unable to seriously explore this interest—one that might have introduced her to sharp critiques of Sandinista policy, which generally excluded people of indigenous and African descent.[69] Instead and somewhat unexpectedly, her attention was drawn toward the combination of her national privileges and her alienation from the

United States. She found herself deeply affected by seeing Nicaraguans' poverty and hunger, and she was often at a loss because of her limited Spanish. One evening, while she sat with her host family watching televised coverage of the Philadelphia police department firebombing the black radical organization MOVE, she felt "embarrass[ed]. . . . I had to really think about my own relationship to the U.S.—what's my alliance? What's my country doing?"[70] The Brigade made her sharply aware of her status and location as a US citizen even as it solidified her opposition to US state violence and her identification as a black feminist.

In addition to compelling complex reflections on racial and national identities, the Victoria Mercado Brigade fostered dialogue with Nicaraguans about sexual politics. The group encountered varying views of sexuality among straight Nicaraguans, and they observed the women's group AMNLAE, the teachers' association, Sandinista Defense Committees, and even clergy to be "polite and concerned" about gay and lesbian issues. They also met, talked, and socialized with some two dozen Nicaraguan lesbians and gay men. They reported these experiences to a broader Bay Area audience through an article about their trip in the gay and lesbian newspaper the *San Francisco Sentinel*. Ellen Gavin noted that while the Sandinista government had closed gay sites "associated with criminality," people continued to find one another in the cruising grounds of the ruined National Palace and in men's gay bars. Women in the Victoria Mercado Brigade went to one of these bars, and after asking one of their new Nicaraguan friends for clearance, danced together; they found, however, that since the only other women there were sex workers, they were assumed to be prostitutes as well.[71]

Once back in the Bay Area, the Victoria Mercado Brigade presented a series of report-backs—events at which they discussed their trip and showed photographs, a frequently used strategy in the solidarity movement for generating interest and sharing knowledge. The presenters contrasted the welcome they received in Nicaragua to US policies excluding gay and lesbian immigrants to North America, and they suggested that the Nicaraguan Revolution offered greater freedom than the Reagan-era United States.[72] The group also formed a contingent in the June 1985 Lesbian and Gay Freedom Day, with participant Regina Gabrielle and organizer Maria Cora speaking at the day's events. The group's example helped to inspire at least two other gay and lesbian travel projects from the United States, including one from Philadelphia a few months later.[73] By 1986, it also held reverberations in transnational AIDS activism—yet to understand these effects, it is necessary to shift direction and consider the experiences and perspectives of Nicaraguan lesbian and gay activists.

. . .

Nicaragua's first recorded lesbian and gay organization began with a group of friends from two Managua neighborhoods. Joel Zúñiga, Martha Sacasa, and two other women were from Máximo Jerez, a working-class area that had played a strong role in the final "Insurrection" that brought the FSLN to power in 1979. Lupita Sequeira lived nearby in a slightly better-off neighborhood called Centroamérica. This cluster of friends were in their early to mid-20s, lived with their families, and were active in FSLN-related organizations, including the neighborhood committees through which the party organized in Managua. Sequeira held a more prominent position in that she worked for the Ministry of the Interior (this agency, known as the MINT, governed Sandinista State Security). By early 1985, the group began to gather purposefully as lesbian and gay people, generally meeting in or near a park in Máximo Jerez.[74]

In part because of its history in the revolution, Máximo Jerez was home to the Casa Nicaragüense de Español (CNE), a language school that drew hundreds of foreign students each year, mostly from the United States and Canada. CNE students attended sessions ranging in length from two weeks to two months; in addition to studying Spanish, they attended presentations about Nicaraguan politics and lived in homestays with neighborhood families. Roberto Gurdián, the Nicaraguan gay man who had cofounded Gay People for the Nicaraguan Revolution and later held a job in the Sandinista tourism ministry, worked in CNE's New York City office by the mid-1980s.[75] The school consistently included one foreigner on staff, generally a US or Canadian citizen. For a time Nicaraguan Joel Zúñiga worked as a CNE housekeeper, and he often talked politics with visitors.[76] Zúñiga recalls that while it was obvious to him that CNE students included lesbian and gay people, many of these visitors thought they should not speak about their sexualities in Nicaragua, and some assumed gayness did not exist in the country. He slowly learned to distinguish not only who was gay or lesbian but also who was, in his words, "militante" (politicized or out) enough to talk about it.[77] In other words, while some US activists assumed they should express their radical political commitments by being silent about homosexuality in Nicaragua, Zúñiga felt the opposite.

Zúñiga, Sequeira, and Sacasa place the origins of Nicaraguan gay and lesbian activism squarely in the Sandinista struggle, but they valued evidence of lesbian and gay participation in solidarity and enjoyed opportunities to compare notes about sexual politics with visitors from around the world.[78] When the Victoria Mercado Brigade visited Managua in spring 1985, a US activist who served as coordinator at the CNE invited Lupita Sequeira and Martha Sacasa to be the people who would speak to them about the history of the Nicaraguan Revolution. Although the coordinator purposefully arranged the connection among lesbian and gay activists, she did not state that motivation explicitly to Sequeira, Sacasa, or any of the Brigade members. The activists quickly saw their points of commonality, however, and socialized together as well as discussing lesbian and gay politics during the Brigade members' stay in Managua.

Connections like these expanded after activist Amy Bank moved to Nicaragua and took the job of neighborhood and program coordinator at the CNE. A white and Jewish lesbian, Bank had grown up in Los Angeles, graduated from UC Santa Cruz, been part of the Bay Area women's drumming group Sistah Boom, and worked for Redwood Records, a women's music label founded by progressive singer-songwriter Holly Near. Bank moved to Nicaragua in November 1985 at the encouragement of the same CNE coordinator who had introduced Sequeira and Sacasa to the Victoria Mercado Brigade and whom she directly replaced. Although she initially planned to stay in Nicaragua just a year, Bank ended up living in Nicaragua for nearly three decades. Over the latter half of the 1980s she sent letters home that were circulated to more than sixty U.S.-based activists and friends, including many in the Redwood Records network.[79] Her role at the CNE resembled that of another white lesbian from the Bay Area, Callie Williams, who coordinated a different language school in the Nicaraguan city of Estelí. Another woman in this network was Julieta Martínez, a Nicaraguan woman who had spent her early childhood and college in Ohio, then returned to Nicaragua in 1985 to work for Witness for Peace; in the later 1980s Martínez and Williams formed a romantic relationship that tied their lesbian, gay, and feminist networks together.[80]

When Bank moved to Managua, she carried a letter from her predecessor at the CNE to introduce her to Joel Zúñiga, Lupita Sequeira, Martha Sacasa, and other friends. Sequeira recalls being given strong hints about Bank and was asked to welcome her warmly.[81] Bank recalls being told that these friends were gay and lesbian, but was warned, "Don't [tell them] that I told you that they're gay because they're not really 'out' and could be interpreted as being indiscreet."[82] The day after Bank arrived, Zúñiga, Sequeira, Sacasa, and another woman came by the house where she was staying to invite her out for a beer. Bank's host mother was immediately suspicious, and as soon as Bank returned from the evening, an FSLN representative arrived to warn her to be cautious about who she socialized with and that she was being watched. Meanwhile, another US activist, a white woman named Julie Light, moved to Managua to work as a journalist. She too lived with a family in Máximo Jerez and joined the social circle around the neighborhood and the CNE. Light briefly dated Sacasa—this was Light's first relationship with a woman and sparked her coming out—while Bank began a longer-term relationship with one of the Nicaraguan women among their friends. Although heterosexual romances between Nicaraguans and solidarity activists were fairly common, these women's relationships were constrained by lack of privacy, and Light's host family "essentially kicked [her] out" when they discovered her relationship with Sacasa.[83]

By summer 1986 Light and Bank pooled funds with two other US citizens to purchase a house in the Centroamérica neighborhood, where Sequeira lived.[84] In a letter to friends, Bank noted that buying the house allowed her and Light to avoid the rapid escalation in rent occurring because of the hyperinflation spurred by the US blockade.[85] The house cost $11,000, and though it was cheap compared to homes in the United States, the purchase threw national privileges into sharp relief. As Light later noted, she and Bank wanted privacy and independence but also to live in everyday Nicaraguan society instead of with "journalists in an upper class neighborhood" or "a bunch of expats." These goals stood in tension, and they knew that they were "doing something in someone else's country that our [Nicaraguan] friends couldn't afford and couldn't even dream of ever affording. . . . And it was because we had access to dollars; it was because [families with property] . . . were leaving the country. We were excruciatingly aware of all the contradictions, the paradoxes involved in that."[86] They also soon became aware of the dilemmas of living in a house where Nicaraguan gay and lesbian life began to flourish.

The Centroamérica house had a generous living room and patio and quickly drew dozens for parties with dancing, drinks, and political conversation; Nicaraguan artists, dancers, and visiting solidarity activists joined the scene.[87] Some of the Nicaraguans, especially Zúñiga, lived in the house. The home's importance was underscored by Nicaraguans' cramped housing, the state of emergency that constrained organizing outside the FSLN, and the limits on supplies of food and other goods imposed by the US-backed economic blockade. Zúñiga, Sequeira, and Sacasa began to hold meetings at the house that drew sixty or more people, and by fall they established Nicaragua's first gay and lesbian organization—called simply "the lesbian and gay group" or the "Nicaraguan gay movement." They held elections that made Zúñiga and Sequeira directors, Sacasa secretary, and Rita Arauz—a Nicaraguan psychologist who had lived in San Francisco and returned in 1985—the group's "advisor."[88] Their central activities revolved around holding meetings and consciousness-raising. Yet while invested in forming lesbian and gay political community writ large, the organizers established a prerequisite that all members had to be formally involved in a Sandinista council, the militia, or some other government entity. Light and Bank sat out the group's meetings out of concern that perceptions of foreign influence might bring state repression, but both she and Bank served as the group's liaisons with visiting US activists.[89] When Light and Bank traveled to the United States for winter holidays, Nicaraguan activists continued to live, meet, and hold parties in the house. By early 1987 neighbors were beginning to realize the house was—as Sequeira reported at the time—"frequented by lesbians and gays."[90]

Sandinista State Security (a division of the Ministry of the Interior, or MINT) had begun to take notice as well. By January, group members learned the house was under surveillance, and by February they began to be individually called in to meet with State Security officials.[91] While not formally arrested, they were questioned and verbally intimidated, particularly about the risk that the group could be infiltrated by opponents of the Sandinista Revolution. Lupita Sequeira believes she was the first target; following the death of her mother, she had spent all of 1986 on paid leave from her job with the MINT, and she had devoted much of her spare energy during that time to the gay and lesbian group. Just before she was due to return to work in February, her supervisor visited to warn her that the Centroamérica house was frequented by "suspicious people with suspicious reputations," that "wild parties" had been observed, and that Amy Bank and Julie Light might be working for the CIA. He concluded by implying she had lost her job. As Sequeira tells it, she paused in shock, then pushed back against the pressure by saying, "They are my friends and I'm a lesbian." Sequeira was fired and required to give up her uniform, badge, and FSLN membership, but insisted that "with or without the party, I am a Sandinista." Although her discharge papers required her to stop meeting with foreigners, she handwrote an addendum refusing this directive, as she fully intended to keep working with solidarity activists and to communicate with an uncle in the United States.[92]

Other members of the group were questioned as well. State Security detained Arauz overnight and asked Bank's girlfriend about the couple's sex life.[93] Zúñiga was expelled from the army and, while being questioned, was asked to report on others and their organizing, a demand he refused.[94] On March 13, 1987—a day that activists refer to as the *quiebre* (break-up) and that remains commemorated as an important anniversary among LGBTI activists in Nicaragua today—the members of the Nicaraguan group received a collective subpoena and were told to stop their activism, as well as being warned that State Security would not be so "lenient next time."[95] Soon after the quiebre, State Security also pressured Bank and Light to inform on others, including by demanding that Light pass along information about the international press corps; both refused.[96]

"After the quiebre, [we felt] a mix of frustration and anger," Zúñiga recalls. "This was a dangerous mix, and it was smart to calm down."[97] The Nicaraguan lesbian and gay group stopped meeting formally, and although the treatment they received had profoundly shaken their faith in the FSLN, they decided to keep silent about the quiebre both within Nicaragua and internationally. They asked Bank, Light, and the few other solidarity activists aware of the events to maintain the same silence, and all held to this commitment until after the FSLN's fall from power. The quiebre did not become widely known until 1991 in Nicaragua and 1993 in the United States. When first reported, it was most widely circulated through an interview with Rita Arauz in Margaret Randall's *Sandino's Daughters Revisited,* a volume that took a more critical look at gender and sexuality in the revolution than Randall's earlier, more celebratory *Sandino's Daughters.*[98]

The goal of keeping the quiebre a secret was to prevent an outcry from lesbian and gay participants in the Central American solidarity movement. Such an outcry might bring further repression from State Security, and it also might undermine solidarity efforts by revealing the fact of repression to foreigners who wanted to believe such repression did not exist. In addition, the quiebre occurred just as the FSLN was debating how to end Nicaragua's state of emergency and its limits on autonomous organizing; that debate had already led some in the party to push the most outspokenly feminist leaders out of the Sandinista women's group AMNLAE. Conflicts over autonomous organizing both helped to allow the quiebre, since the gay and lesbian group was independent, and may have kept it from become worse, since some in the FSLN were pushing for more independent organizing to be permitted.[99] Amidst this debate, the outside perceptions mobilized through solidarity operated as a double-edged sword. A carefully maintained silence about the quiebre might maintain space through which Nicara-guan lesbians and gay men could renew their work informally as well as maintain support from the solidarity movement.

A month before the quiebre, as people began to sense that State Secu-rity investigation was imminent, Bank wrote a letter asking US friends "not to talk with others" about the existence of the gay and lesbian group because "they basically just feel that since it's so new, it's very fragile, and they need time, so discretion is important, and publicity in the exterior could do them damage if rumors get started that get dis-torted, etc. . . . I'll let you know if and when that changes. Thanks, comrades."[100] Bank's message reflected the harassment that the group was already experiencing, her effort to contain any crackdown, and her desire to preserve US activists' faith in the revolution. By concealing existing harassment, she asked her US friends to respect the fact that in the context of the war and the state of emergency, Nicaraguan gay and lesbian organizing needed more discretion than publicity. Bank's state-ment offered her readers a way to express their solidarity through silence and, without knowing it, to protect the Sandinista state from criticism by others in the Central American solidarity movement.

US activists' idealized views became reinforced in May 1987 when Bank offered more promising news: the Sandinista Ministry of Health was developing an AIDS program, and groups in the United States were invited to raise money, resources, and materials to support it.[101] This opportunity represented a dramatic shift in gay and lesbian activists' relationship to the Sandinista state, but it was a change that held two competing meanings. For Nicaraguan activists, AIDS work offered a chance to reverse the quiebre; for US activists unaware of the quiebre, the AIDS program was just one more revolutionary success.

Nicaragua's responses to AIDS were shaped by the revolution's broader commitment to popular education and health. After gaining power in 1979, the Sandinista government had carried out extensive vaccination brigades and won praise from the World Health Organization as a "model" for primary health care.[102] A powerful strand of solidarity devel-oped around health, and health professionals traveled to Nicaragua to both receive and provide training. Leonel Argüello, then vice-minister and head of epidemiology for the Ministry of Health (MINSA), received solidarity groups every week and met frequently with foreign public health experts; Ana Quirós, then codirector of an independent non-governmental organization called the Centro de Información y Asesorías en Salud (CISAS), recalls twice as many contacts.[103] Both Argüello and

Quirós are bilingual, and the combination of their language abilities, political viewpoints, and personal commitments made them key players in the networks that produced AIDS solidarity.[104]

A number of lesbian and gay solidarity activists from the Bay Area both worked in health and became involved in AIDS solidarity. Catherine Cusic was a medic, respiratory therapist, and physician's assistant who had been part of creating some of the first widely distributed safer sex brochures ("Can We Talk?" produced by the Harvey Milk Democratic Club). Miguel Ramírez was a psychologist who worked at the San Francisco AIDS Foundation and volunteered with the Latino AIDS Project. Dan Wohlfeiler had been active in grassroots safer sex education and was preparing to enter a master's program in public health. Naomi Schapiro, a nurse, had first traveled to Nicaragua in 1984 as part of the women's music group Swingshift and was active in People's Medics, which provided emergency aid at protests when police turned violent. (Schapiro had herself been beaten by San Francisco police in 1984 during protests against the Moral Majority, clubbed so severely by a mounted officer than she required six stitches, while her fellow activist Lucrecia Bermudez was knocked unconscious and charged with "lynching" for her attempt to escape police.)[105] Cusic, Schapiro, and Somos Hermanas member Diane Jones all worked at varying times in Ward 5B/5A, the inpatient HIV/AIDS ward at San Francisco General Hospital. They and others were attuned to the Sandinista government's use of popular health education and community organizing and believed that the US government's recalcitrance in supporting such work reflected a profit-driven and discriminatory health care system. Schapiro stated that Nicaragua's approaches to health made nursing more "valued," in contrast to the United States, where she feared she could offer only a "band-aid."[106]

Several US lesbian and gay activists entered AIDS solidarity through the Committee for Health Rights in Central America (CHRICA; now Committee for Health Rights in the Americas, or CHRIA).[107] Based in San Francisco, this was a broad-based organization, not lesbian or gay, that starting in November 1983 sent North American health workers to Managua for the US-Nicaragua Colloquia on Health—events organized by CISAS and endorsed by the Pan American Health Organization, American Medical Student Association, and American Public Health Organization. Scheduled alongside a larger Nicaraguan health conference, the colloquia served as vehicles for training and material aid. While Nicaraguans taught visitors about the Sandinista health system, foreign attendees presented workshops, led teaching rounds, and built relationships with Nicaraguan health workers that they later expanded by hosting mini-residences in Canada or the United States.[108] Catherine Cusic attended the first colloquium through CHRICA in November 1983 and while there met Ana Quirós, one of the codirectors of CISAS. By 1986 the women's friendship as fellow lesbians helped foster AIDS solidarity work.[109]

MINSA epidemiologist Leonel Argüello, with the support of Minister of Health Dora María Tellez, was the first person in the Sandinista government to address AIDS. He attempted to travel to Atlanta for the first international AIDS conference in April 1985, but was denied a visa by the United States. His Cuban counterparts were able to attend and passed him information distributed there. Although no cases of AIDS had yet been found in Nicaragua, Argüello was concerned about transmission because "we had . . . something like 40,000 [blood] transfusions a year because of the war," most of them administered in combat hospitals with no chance of screening.[110] Condoms were hard to find because of the economic blockade, and Nicaragua received an estimated 100,000 foreign visitors each year, primarily from countries with significant rates of HIV/AIDS. The first cases of AIDS in Central America had appeared among sex workers in Honduras whose clients included US soldiers, and Nicaragua's border with Honduras was porous.[111] Well before MINSA had the necessary materials to test for HIV, Argüello observed through the Red Cross that rates of hepatitis B—epidemiologically linked to HIV—were rising, and together with Red Cross personnel he decided that Nicaragua would not use blood from foreigners: "Because it was solidarity [to donate], we collected it, but we threw it away."[112] As this story underscores, the Sandinista government managed solidarity efforts rather than receiving them passively.

Outside the Sandinista government, staff of the nongovernmental organization CISAS began to discuss how to address AIDS after late 1985, while actor Rock Hudson's AIDS diagnosis occupied international news and AIDS fearmongering became common. In 1986 Ana Quirós asked Catherine Cusic to gather San Francisco activists in an "AIDS brigade," and Cusic recruited Naomi Schapiro, psychologist Miguel Ramírez, and Victoria Mercado Brigade participant Ellen Gavin. The group soon expanded to include Luisa Blue, a Filipina nurse and labor activist; social workers from the AIDS Healthcare Project; and a doctor at the San Francisco General Hospital AIDS Clinic.[113] In November 1986 this group traveled to the international health colloquium to make a presentation on AIDS. Their trip was sponsored by the Victoria Mercado Brigade and the Harvey Milk Democratic Club and dedicated to the memory of Bill Kraus, an activist who had died of AIDS that January.[114]

Cusic recalls that the leadership of CHRICA initially hesitated to host an AIDS presentation at the colloquium and that they told Cusic and others that "you can't talk about sex in a Latin American Catholic country." Cusic was taken aback, having felt that Nicaraguans "were in the sexual revolution as much as they were in the political revolution" and wondering, "Have they been to the same Nicaragua we've been to?"[115] Because of CHRICA's anxiety, the session was initially scheduled in a small venue, but it was relocated to a bigger one when a major speaker canceled and Nicaraguan health workers realized that there was a group ready to speak about AIDS. The AIDS brigade's talk was received with great enthusiasm, and activists' supply of Spanish-language information material was quickly exhausted. From there, brigade members spoke at a medical university in the city of León, and Miguel Ramírez presented a safer sex workshop to a Managua gathering of gay and bisexual men. Some in his audience were members of the gay and lesbian group that had recently begun meeting in the Centroamérica house; the quiebre had not yet occurred.[116]

By the end of 1986, drawing on the energy evidenced by the colloquium, Argüello initiated a national AIDS commission composed of MINSA staff, a Red Cross representative, and Nicaraguan doctors. The commission began to craft a national plan focused on testing and prevention, laying political groundwork and helping Argüello initiate contacts with Nicaraguan media. Nicaraguan gay and lesbian activists felt confident that MINSA's interest would open a path to nondiscrimination based on sexuality within the Sandinista government. Back in San Francisco, "AIDS brigade" members founded the Nicaragua AIDS Education Project (NAEP), which aimed "to send technical and financial assistance to MINSA and to our contacts in the [Nicaraguan] gay community" and to publicize contrasts between Sandinista and US policies on AIDS.[117]

Although the connections built around AIDS work were shaken by the State Security crackdown in March 1987, this disruption was minimized by the fact that most US activists did not know about the quiebre and by the fact that, within Nicaragua, State Security and MINSA did not coordinate their work—indeed, the two arms of the government were associated with distinct factions of the FSLN. The activists who had been targeted by the crackdown knew of all the events, but were careful to keep quiet lest news of the quiebre create international protest against the Sandinistas and risk giving State Security or any other part of the government an excuse to shut down AIDS prevention work in the gay community. State Security harassment did not reflect a widespread FSLN directive, and Argüello and Dora María Tellez (Argüello's supervisor as head of the Ministry of Health) maintain that they did not learn of the quiebre until fall 1987.[118] Instead, Argüello invited Catherine Cusic to return to Nicaragua to assist in developing the AIDS program, and she did so in April 1987. Dan Wohlfeiler joined her, carrying luggage packed with $2,000 raised by the NAEP and one thousand Trojan-Enz condoms.[119] Cusic and Wohlfeiler stayed in Managua for a month and met with Argüello, other members of the AIDS Commission, and gay and lesbian activists, seeking to strengthen gay and lesbian activists' contacts with MINSA and to help develop educational materials and programs on AIDS.

By their own accounts, neither Cusic nor Wohlfeiler were aware of the quiebre when they visited Nicaragua in April 1987.[120] For Cusic, this lack of knowledge stood in contrast to her generally strong familiarity with Nicaraguan politics. For example, she had worked with Casa Nicaragua in San Francisco; had visited Nicaragua multiple times and presented on AIDS at the fall 1986 health colloquium; had met with the head of Nicaragua's Human Rights Commission to discuss gay and lesbian rights and repression; and had attended parties at the Centroamérica house.[121] Wohlfeiler also brought expertise, as he had worked as associate producer on the film *Faces of War,* which profiled solidarity workers and others in Nicaragua and El Salvador confronting US intervention.[122] Soon after his and Cusic's trip to Nicaragua, Wohlfeiler wrote a report that revealed how Nicaraguan gay and lesbian activists worked to manage his and Cusic's roles. He believed the narrative Nicaraguan activists needed him to believe: that he and Cusic were initiating HIV/AIDS prevention in Nicaragua and MINSA's ties to it. He perceived gay and lesbian Nicaraguans as disinterested in HIV/AIDS work, failing to understand that expressions of indifference could have been their self-protective façade, given that the quiebre had occurred just a month before. When his contacts seemed to stall, he wondered "if I should cut my losses, abandon the project and fly home. . . . I felt that we'd erred in trying to get everything done so fast, especially when enthusiasm from the people we'd decided to 'help' (albeit, to a great extent, on our own initiative) seemed so tenuous."[123] He did not know that "enthusiasm" had been generated earlier by Nicaraguans themselves but then purposefully contained. Despite his qualms, Wohlfeiler stayed, working with Cusic to make a presentation to health workers, to draft a comic book about HIV transmission and prevention, to accompany a contact to hand out condoms at a cruising site, and finally to hold a safer sex workshop attended by Argüello, two other MINSA staff, and seven gay men. At the close of the workshop, Argüello asked the gay men to help initiate a government-sponsored AIDS prevention campaign, and they enthusiastically agreed. Wohlfeiler was stunned: "Somehow, despite resistance from gay men, and what I'd interpreted as insensitivity from the government, something had happened here that was, well, revolutionary."[124] Neither he nor Cusic nor Argüello were aware of the behind-the-scenes organizing that had laid groundwork for the new campaign.

MINSA used the $2,000 that the NAEP had donated, and Wohlfeiler had transported, to print the country's first educational materials on AIDS and to purchase reagents for the ELISA test, an early means of identifying HIV antibodies in blood.[125] In July 1987 Argüello was invited to attend a summer course in Minnesota on the epidemiology of AIDS, and although he was again denied a visa, he was granted one after Minnesota governor Rudy Perpich—a major opponent of US policy in Central America—intervened.[126] The permission came so late that Argüello missed the most useful parts of the conference, but he made use of the trip by overstaying his visa to visit San Francisco and New York. In San Francisco he met people with AIDS, members of AIDS organizations, and members of lesbian and gay solidarity groups, and he gave a public interview in which he urged safer sex and termed the use of condoms "a beautiful way to express . . . solidarity," particularly by HIV-positive visitors to Nicaragua. He expressed relief that MINSA's full-page poster about AIDS—which was printed in Nicaraguan newspapers and which discussed anal sex, oral sex, and homosexuality—had not provoked a backlash from Nicaragua's conservative cardinal. Further, he argued that gay and lesbian rights were consistent with the revolution and—optimistic by nature—declared that he looked forward to franker discussions of sexuality inside Nicaragua: "People are always more ready than we think."[127]

In the wake of the November 1986 US-Nicaragua Colloquium on Health, MINSA staff had attempted to hold workshops on AIDS at public health centers, but had been unsuccessful because potential participants were afraid of being stigmatized as gay.[128] By early fall 1987, Argüello—who states he did not yet know of the quiebre—approached earlier members of the Nicaraguan gay and lesbian group about the possibility that they might lead AIDS education themselves. The activists insisted on first meeting with Dora María Tellez, so she telephoned Zúñiga at the

Centroamérica house and asked to meet with him about AIDS outreach; Zúñiga asked to bring the whole group, and Tellez agreed.[129] After hanging up the phone, he recalls, he and others were screaming with excitement, "going crazy . . . we couldn't believe it," because now they had an opportunity to directly address their experience of repression by the MINT and their desire for incorporation in the revolution.[130] Some twenty-five lesbian and gay activists met with Tellez, telling her about the quiebre and detailing their expulsions from the military and government jobs.[131] They asked for and received formal letters from MINSA to carry as protection if approached by police, and they signed up to work as AIDS educators who carried these guarantees in hand. Granted this safeguard, they established the Colectivo de Educación Popular contra el SIDA (CEP-SIDA, or Popular Education Collective Against AIDS), a project independent of the government but supported and protected by MINSA.[132]

CEP-SIDA renewed and expanded activism that had been initiated by the gay and lesbian group. The collective began conducting outreach in cruising areas and leading safer sex workshops at universities, in high schools, and among groups of gay men. In November 1987 the international health colloquium dedicated a full morning to AIDS, and Naomi Schapiro and other Bay Area health workers returned and presented a workshop on HIV/AIDS prevention. The Nicaraguan newspaper *Nuevo Diario* reported on these events in matter-of-fact terms that emphasized condoms as a means to reduce HIV risk.[133] CEP-SIDA recruited as many as two hundred outreach workers, and word of mouth sent many men to the Centroámerica house to ask for condoms that were in flush supply because visiting activists brought boxes of them.[134] In some workshops CEP-SIDA workers screened *Ojos que no ven,* an hour-long film about AIDS that had been created by San Francisco's Latino AIDS Project; one night, trying to play the film at Managua's biggest cruising ground, they plugged Amy Bank's television into an outdoor outlet and exploded the set.[135]

Notably, *Ojos que no ven* was used for different audiences in Nicaragua than it was created for in the United States. The Latino AIDS Project had been founded in early 1987 when the Instituto Familiar de la Raza, a Latino community health organization in San Francisco, won a grant from the California Department of Public Health to carry out AIDS education in communities of color.[136] Miguel Ramírez, a member of the Nicaragua AIDS Education Project, participated in the

Latino AIDS Project, as did Rodrigo Reyes, earlier a founder of the Gay Latino Alliance and now a playwright and actor. Reyes wrote the screenplay and conducted the casting for *Ojos que no ven*—whose title, meaning "eyes that cannot see," held a connotation similar to "out of sight, out of mind." He set the film in the Mission District with overlapping story lines and a primarily Latina and Latino cast. As the film's story lines and characters made evident, *Ojos que no ven* was created as a tool whereby Latina/o gay and lesbian activists in San Francisco might teach straight members of the Latina/o community about HIV/AIDS, safer sex, and safer intravenous drug practices. The film portrayed gay Latino men as experts on AIDS and showed two other characters, a married man who slept with men and the mother of a gay son, gradually becoming compelled to recognize their connections to the gay community and to the epidemic. The characters of an IV drug user, a sex worker, and her client demonstrated other circuits of risk.

In Nicaragua, CEP-SIDA used *Ojos que no ven*—which was filmed entirely in Spanish and so did not require translation—to reach self-identified gay and bisexual men and anyone who frequented men's cruising grounds. They likely drew particular value from the film's exposition of HIV transmission and disease and its emphasis on behavior over identity. At the film's conclusion, a gay man reminded the married man who has slept with men that "what we do and what we are are very different things." The film's portrayal of community health activism also resonated with the Sandinistas' public health methods and consciousness-raising ethos. In one scene, a counselor at San Francisco's Instituto Familiar de la Raza encourages her client to let go of her prejudices toward "sexual freedom," and she terms AIDS a "double-edged sword" because, while life-threatening, it compels people to unite against attitudes that would keep them divided and ignorant. At the end of the film the actors and filmmakers face the camera directly and state that an "extraordinary response" to AIDS is in reach because "our history has been a history of struggle" and because, "united, we can create a community that is healthy, strong, and free from prejudices." Although these lines were written by and intended to reach Latina/o people in the Bay Area, their rhetoric overlapped with the Sandinista Revolution—which after all held long influences within the Mission District.

While the film's messages could be adapted, a difference did appear between Bay Area and Nicaraguan activists' responses to AIDS. This difference had to do with whether to push more for governmental or nongovernmental responses. The San Francisco groups that created the Latino AIDS Project hoped that the California Department of Public Health would take over the task of outreach to communities of color rather than continuing to "subcontract" it to nonprofits. However, reflecting a rising use of nonprofits to outsource responsibilities that might otherwise have been addressed by a state-sponsored safety net, the Latino AIDS Project remained a nongovernmental effort.[137] Elsewhere, Naomi Schapiro proclaimed that while "our government is spending millions of dollars, which could be spent on AIDS, to create refugees in Central America," Nicaragua's AIDS program "puts our government's . . . to shame."[138] The contrast underscored US activists' demand that their government, and in particular the Reagan administration, take responsibility for addressing the AIDS epidemic.

Yet if Bay Area activists sought a stronger state response, gay and lesbian activists in Nicaragua—both because they had been burned by the quiebre and because they faced the rapid defunding of the Sandinista state—moved in the opposite direction.[139] CEP-SIDA hoped to establish a nongovernmental "Center for Sexual Information and Education" in Managua and to use this center to create educational materials, organize conferences, and staff a hotline. They sought to raise $10,000 to initiate the project and asked the Nicaragua AIDS Education Project to hold fundraising events in San Francisco to help them meet their goal.[140] NAEP indeed did so, with one reception featuring Nicaraguan artist Otto Aguilar and musician Holly Near as guests. Aguilar had been invited to the United States by gay activist Tede Matthews, while Near was brought in by her friend and former Redwood Records staffer Amy Bank, who herself made a trip to the Bay Area to promote CEP-SIDA.[141] The Latino AIDS Project and Amaranto, an organization of lesbian and gay Latin American immigrants, cosponsored the event.[142] Praising "Nicaragua's matter-of-fact and honest response to AIDS," the fundraiser invitation reflected US activists' ongoing admiration of the Sandinista government as well as their lack of knowledge of Nicaraguan state repression (figure 15).

The Bay Area gay and lesbian press continued to praise Nicaraguan AIDS policy through the late 1980s. An article in *Coming Up!* contrasted Nicaraguan policy to both US and Cuban approaches, emphasizing that the Sandinista government had formed a national AIDS commission before the Reagan administration did, and terming Nicaragua's national safer sex information more explicit than what the US surgeon general had recently mailed to the nation's households.[143] While cases of

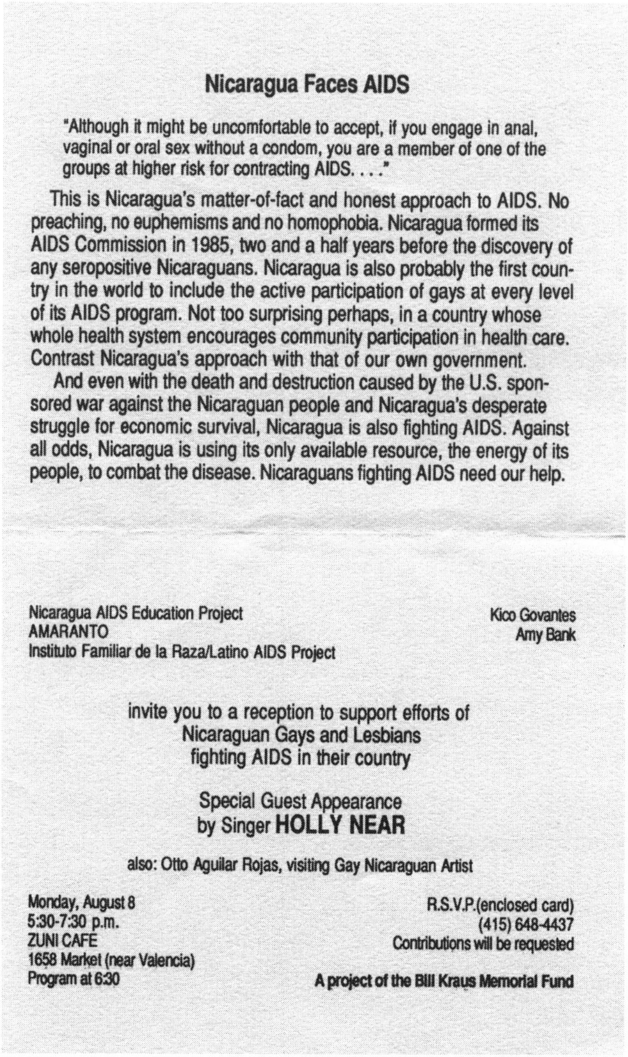

Nicaragua Faces AIDS

"Although it might be uncomfortable to accept, if you engage in anal, vaginal or oral sex without a condom, you are a member of one of the groups at higher risk for contracting AIDS. . . ."

This is Nicaragua's matter-of-fact and honest approach to AIDS. No preaching, no euphemisms and no homophobia. Nicaragua formed its AIDS Commission in 1985, two and a half years before the discovery of any seropositive Nicaraguans. Nicaragua is also probably the first country in the world to include the active participation of gays at every level of its AIDS program. Not too surprising perhaps, in a country whose whole health system encourages community participation in health care. Contrast Nicaragua's approach with that of our own government.

And even with the death and destruction caused by the U.S. sponsored war against the Nicaraguan people and Nicaragua's desperate struggle for economic survival, Nicaragua is also fighting AIDS. Against all odds, Nicaragua is using its only available resource, the energy of its people, to combat the disease. Nicaraguans fighting AIDS need our help.

Nicaragua AIDS Education Project
AMARANTO
Instituto Familiar de la Raza/Latino AIDS Project

Kico Govantes
Amy Bank

invite you to a reception to support efforts of
Nicaraguan Gays and Lesbians
fighting AIDS in their country

Special Guest Appearance
by Singer **HOLLY NEAR**

also: Otto Aguilar Rojas, visiting Gay Nicaraguan Artist

Monday, August 8
5:30-7:30 p.m.
ZUNI CAFE
1658 Market (near Valencia)
Program at 6:30

R.S.V.P.(enclosed card)
(415) 648-4437
Contributions will be requested

A project of the Bill Kraus Memorial Fund

FIGURE 15. Nicaragua AIDS Education Project fundraiser invitation, 1988. Courtesy of Ephemera Collection–LGBT Groups (Instituto Familiar de la Raza), GLBTHS.

Nicaraguans living with AIDS had earlier been mere speculation, by July 1988 five Nicaraguans and twenty-one foreigners living in the country had tested positive.[144] Leonel Argüello and Dora María Tellez resisted pressure from others in the Sandinista government to disclose these patients' names, and both made strong public statements against proposals for practices of mandatory testing and quarantine.[145] The first two Nicaraguans known to die from AIDS inside the country passed away in August and September 1988. One of them, a man named Marvin, had been a friend of Victoria Mercado Brigade members and other US activists. Tede Matthews made a commemorative altar for him in the window of the Mission District's Modern Times Bookstore and read a poem for him at a Mexico City memorial for AIDS.[146]

Yet, even as the need for Nicaragua's AIDS program became more evident, both solidarity activism and the Sandinistas' hold on power were beginning to slide. US lesbian and gay radicals were increasingly focused on their own experiences of AIDS, shifting energy to confront US policy on the epidemic and moving into periods of intense personal loss if they were not dying themselves. As attention to CEP-SIDA waned in the Bay Area, NAEP raised far short of its $10,000 goal. Zúñiga and other activists made plans to visit the United States and publicize CEP-SIDA but were denied visas, as Argüello had been earlier; this time, no one with power to challenge the denial stepped in.[147] By 1989 MINSA sought to expand its testing and prevention efforts, but it and CEP-SIDA were hamstrung as the FSLN grappled with new peace negotiations, planned for new elections, and faced mounting popular frustration at the war and blockade. Internal conflicts also emerged in CEP-SIDA that withered US activists' support.[148]

In July 1989, the Sandinista government invited CEP-SIDA to participate in celebrations of the revolution's tenth anniversary, and the group mobilized a contingent. Some thirty-five gay and lesbian Nicaraguans marched in Managua's anniversary events, wearing black shirts with pink triangles—symbolism popularized by US-based activists but that also played on the Sandinista red and black. They chanted slogans that revolution was impossible without lesbian and gay participation.[149] But seven months later, in February 1990, the Sandinistas lost the national elections. CEP-SIDA dissolved soon after that as a result of its internal divisions.

. . .

The Nicaraguan solidarity movement would not have existed had the Sandinista Revolution not inspired the left worldwide. As evidenced by murals and commemorations that persist around the country, Nicaraguans view the solidarity movement as a source of pride, evidence of their nation's global impact. Similarly, Joel Zúñiga, Lupita Sequeira,

Rita Arauz, and other Nicaraguan activists define their lesbian and gay activism both as extensions of the revolution and as a means by which they have shaped transnational sexual politics. In making these claims, they assert a Sandinismo that exceeds the FSLN as a party. In 1995, Dora María Tellez cofounded the Movimiento Renovador Sandinista (MRS, or Sandinista Renovation Movement), a leftist political party that is closely tied to the feminist movement, is critical of the turn to neoliberalism by the contemporary FSLN, and serves as an important hub for Nicaraguan LGBTI activism today.

As Arauz stated soon after the Sandinistas' defeat, the Nicaraguan Revolution was "the seed, the source" of local lesbian and gay activism, and Nicaraguans sought "a gay and lesbian movement of the Left."[150] Sequeira insisted that homosexuality was "not imported from San Francisco, from England, from any other country"; in comments at the time, she described sexual freedom as flowing from South to North, and she painted a mural portraying lesbian and gay activism in Nicaragua through a pre-colonial "goddess of the revolution"—a figure who could represent "all the people in the world who feel identified with us."[151] She and other Nicaraguan lesbian and gay activists noted that their conversations with US activists helped them sharpen their critiques of consumerism and individualism in sexual politics; in other words, they did not admire everything about the US lesbian and gay movement. As Zúñiga now states, "I'm not afraid to tell you that US gay and lesbian organizing contributed to what was here; the exchange was powerful. . . . I'm not afraid to tell you that there was influence, but there's a difference between what the influence was and what we took from it."[152]

Nicaraguan activists used their relationships with US activists to triangulate a relationship to the Sandinista state and to push forward their own goals within the revolution. US activists could test uncertain waters with MINSA and other government officials, assessing the attitudes of those in authority and initiating contacts that Nicaraguans such as Zúñiga or Sequeira might pursue more deeply. Even if they generated hostile reaction, outsiders from the United States had no government jobs or party memberships to lose, and were too valued by the Sandinista state to be deported or detained. Further, Nicaraguan lesbian and gay activists could control the information that visiting activists knew about and were able to repeat, allowing visitors to exhibit solidarity even if—or sometimes precisely because—they did not know every detail. Although US activists who did not understand these dynamics might have operated with an inflated sense of their own importance, Nicaraguan activists were able to manipulate that fiction to their advantage. The history of lesbian, gay, and AIDS solidarity with Nicaragua is thus in part a history of the gaps of communication that structured it. Both through these gaps and in the substance of ideas exchanged, Nicaraguans actively directed lesbian and gay solidarity and shaped a transnational gay and lesbian left.

CHAPTER 6

Money for AIDS, Not War

*Anti-militarism, Direct Action against
the Epidemic, and Movement History*

In September 1984, several gay men poured fake blood at the entrance
of a nuclear weapons laboratory to protest the funding of the arms race
rather than research on AIDS. Blocking the road to Lawrence Livermore
National Laboratory, roughly thirty-five miles from Oakland, they
added a new layer of meaning to the symbolism of death that marked
antinuclear protest. In the words of protestor John Lindsay-Poland, they
sought to make visible that "every contract this lab gets has blood on it,"
whether due to military assault or because dollars spent on defense could
have been spent on AIDS research or care.[1] The protesters were members
of Enola Gay, a group of radical white gay men active in the antinuclear
and Central American solidarity movements and whose name reappro-
priated the moniker of the plane that dropped the atomic bomb on
Hiroshima, Japan. Their action was the first recorded instance of civil
disobedience to confront AIDS.[2]

In June 1985 a person with AIDS named John Lorenzini chained
himself to the doors of the San Francisco office of the US Department of
Health and Human Services to protest federal inaction on the epidemic.
Lorenzini was inexperienced in activism but had sought advice and
mentoring from Bill Blackburn, an HIV-negative gay man who had frequently served as a police liaison at antinuclear and Central American
solidarity protests.[3] Blackburn met with Lorenzini several times to help
him plan his protest, and on the day of the action he chained Lorenzini
to the doors of the federal building, holding a banner reading "People

with A.I.D.S. Chained to a Sick Society," while Lorenzini wore a T-shirt that proclaimed "I am a person with AIDS." Lorenzini won a conversation with the acting director of the office before police briefly detained him. This was the second recorded instance of civil disobedience to confront AIDS.

The actions by Enola Gay and John Lorenzini foreshadowed a much larger current to come: the AIDS direct action movement, which sprang up around the United States throughout 1986 and 1987. The birth of direct action against AIDS is usually attributed solely to AIDS Coalition to Unleash Power, or ACT UP, founded in March 1987 in New York City. However, echoing this book's challenges to Stonewall exceptionalism, this chapter intervenes against narratives that imagine ACT UP as formed spontaneously and as the only group to lead street protests against the crisis of AIDS. The most simplistic origin stories of ACT UP locate its catalyst in Larry Kramer's March 1987 speech at New York's Lesbian and Gay Community Services Center. While Kramer's speech was an important event and did help to spark ACT UP's founding, two other AIDS groups that had formed several months earlier in New York laid groundwork for ACT UP. One was the Silence = Death Project, a collective of artists that later formed into the group Gran Fury. As commemorated by participant Avram Finkelstein, the collective sought to create a simple, graphically compelling poster that would "advertise" the scale of the AIDS crisis and the need for action. Its members initiated the project in summer 1986 and worked on it for six months, debating iconography and fonts and "stud[ying] the work of other [artist] collectives, like the Guerrilla Girls," before coming up with the design of a black background and pink triangle—an inverted version of the symbol the Nazis used to identify homosexuals—above the words "SILENCE = DEATH." The bottom of the poster read in smaller font: "Why is Reagan silent about AIDS? What is really going on at the Center for Disease Control, the Food and Drug Administration, and the Vatican? Gays and lesbians are not expendable . . . Use your power . . . Vote . . . Boycott . . . Defend yourselves . . . Turn anger, fear, grief into action." The collective wheatpasted the poster around Manhattan in February 1987, and when ACT UP formed the next month, it "surrendered its use to the group" by providing posters and paying for the first run of buttons.[4] Deborah Gould has traced the other effort that seeded ACT UP: a direct action group called the Lavender Hill Mob that also formed in New York City in summer 1986. The members of this group "disrupted a CDC [Centers for Disease Control] conference on mandatory testing" in February 1987 and attended Kramer's March speech "as much to see who the other angry ones were as to hear Larry speak."[5] Thus, the power of Kramer's speech lay not only in his words and charisma but also in the existing political analyses, networks, and skills that his audience members brought.

AIDS direct action found multiple and overlapping sources around the United States. In the Bay Area, it was initiated and mentored by gay and lesbian radicals whose histories ranged from gay liberation through Central American solidarity. As early as 1983, the Lesbian and Gay Task Force of the campaign for Proposition N, an initiative that declared San Francisco's opposition to US intervention in El Salvador, adopted the slogan "Money for AIDS, Not War." Similar connections structured Enola Gay's action at Livermore Labs in 1984 and John Lorenzini's civil disobedience in 1985. By summer 1986, while New Yorkers formed the Silence = Death Project and the Lavender Hill Mob, San Francisco activists created Citizens for Medical Justice (CMJ)—and these radicals took action first, before their peers in New York.

CMJ cited the Central American solidarity organization Pledge of Resistance as an inspiration and worked closely with two existing lesbian and gay left groups, Lesbians and Gays Against Intervention (LAGAI) and Stand Together, to confront state and federal AIDS policy. When these activists joined civil disobedience at Concord Naval Weapons Station to block the shipments of weapons to El Salvador, they highlighted the links between the US inaction speeding deaths from AIDS and the US actions fueling war in Central America. By summer 1987, San Francisco activists from CMJ and other groups formed the AIDS Action Pledge, which they modeled explicitly on the Pledge of Resistance. Calls for "Money for AIDS, not war," "Fight AIDS, not Nicaragua," and "Condoms, not contras" circulated nationally, including at the first AIDS protest in front of the White House.[6] The politics linking anti-militarism to AIDS direct action reached a powerful scale in fall 1987 through the March on Washington for Lesbian and Gay Rights and through civil disobedience at the Supreme Court Building. San Francisco's AIDS Action Pledge and New York's ACT UP collaborated to create the AIDS Coalition to Network, Organize, and Win (ACT NOW), a national group that adopted the language of the AIDS Action Pledge as a statement of principles.[7] Back in San Francisco, the call for "Money for AIDS, Not War" filled city streets when lesbian, gay, and AIDS activists led thousands to protest the US invasion of Honduras in March 1988.

This chapter analyzes the formation of AIDS direct action in the Bay Area, concentrating primarily on Citizens for Medical Justice and the

AIDS Action Pledge and secondarily on the formation of ACT UP San Francisco and Stop AIDS Now Or Else. Direct action against AIDS culminated two decades of work by the gay and lesbian left even as it marked the start of a new queer politics. Through it, lesbian and gay leftists adapted their long-standing political commitments in order to meet a new crisis. And while early AIDS activists acknowledged their radical past, such recognition faded as divisions emerged between single-issue and multi-issue AIDS politics and as more and more activists died, leaving their histories behind them. By the late 1980s and early 1990s, these deaths left newcomers to AIDS and queer activism unaware of radical memories gone missing.

. . .

The first reports of what would become known as AIDS appeared from the US Centers for Disease Control, and then the *New York Times,* in July 1981.[8] The San Francisco Department of Public Health would later contend that the first local cases appeared in May 1981 and that 127 cases were present in San Francisco by the end of that year.[9] Nationally, by the end of 1986—the year the first sustained AIDS direct action groups were founded—the US epidemic had reached 28,712 cumulative diagnoses and 24,559 cumulative known deaths.[10] The first markedly effective drug, AZT, was not available until early 1987, and even though it marked an important advance, AZT made some people with AIDS worse and not better. Until the introduction of effective anti-retroviral drug therapy in 1996, death from AIDS appeared certain, many people were diagnosed fairly late in their illness, and most died very quickly.

As initial discussions of AIDS bounced from dismissal to suspicion to fear, gay men influenced by the feminist health care movement formed the first community-based responses. In 1983, a group of gay men with AIDS attended the Second National AIDS Forum and wrote a document known as the Denver Principles. They created the term "people with AIDS" (PWAs) to replace "AIDS patient" or "AIDS victim" and insisted on the rights of PWAs to respect, quality medical care, and active involvement in their own care.[11] People with AIDS Coalitions formed around the country, and two coauthors of the Denver Principles, Michael Callen and Richard Berkowitz, wrote the influential booklet *How to Have Sex in an Epidemic,* formulating the first safer-sex guidelines (1983). Activists did all this before the HIV virus had been identified, before transmission factors were precisely known, and before any form of testing other than diagnosis of illness was available.

Across the early and mid-1980s AIDS activism centered almost exclusively on prevention efforts and AIDS service organizations (or ASOs, which worked to provide everything from practical support such as meals to assistance in navigating medical paperwork and job discrimination). In 1983 the University of California, San Francisco, and the San Francisco Department of Public Health established the first dedicated AIDS clinic in the United States at San Francisco General Hospital. This epitomized the "San Francisco model" in HIV/AIDS care, which brought health and social services to one location and fostered collaborations between city agencies and ASOs. But, as Jennifer Brier has shown, a problem emerged as early prevention activism effectively "marketed" gay sexuality and safer sex as white.[12] Black, Latino, and other activists of color began to craft independent outreach efforts and, by the latter 1980s, had developed significant work in AIDS prevention and care. Key early efforts in this regard in the Bay Area included the Third World AIDS Advisory Task Force (founded in 1985) and the Latino AIDS Project (created in 1987 by the Instituto Familiar de la Raza, a Mission District community health organization; see chapter 5).

As AIDS direct action developed, it too was largely white; this was true of Enola Gay, of John Lorenzini and Bill Blackburn, and of most members of Citizens for Medical Justice, the AIDS Action Pledge, and ACT UP groups. Race also operated through an ideological divide between "treatment" and "social action" agendas, also termed single- versus multi-issue politics. Tensions between these agendas became heightened by 1988 and led multiple ACT UP groups, including the one in San Francisco, to split apart between 1990 and 1992. The treatment agenda, often characterized as a call for "drugs into bodies," centered on expanding and speeding up the research and availability of AIDS drugs and drug regimens. The social action agenda looked to the conditions in which people with HIV and AIDS lived and became sick; it sought to put "bodies into health care" and to consider how problems of housing discrimination, incarceration, immigration, sex work, and racism, sexism, and poverty affected both the spread of the virus and access to and efficacy of medical care. Treatment and social action agendas could certainly converge; for example, demands for drug trials sought to ensure greater inclusion of people of color and women in research, and work to lower drug costs challenged drug companies' profit margins. But the divide between treatment and social action was significant and overlapped with demographics. Those emphasizing treatment tended to be well-educated white men, often relatively new to activism, while those invested in a social action agenda included more women, people of color, and working-class people, as well as more long-time leftists.[13]

Anti-militarist responses to AIDS not only fueled a multi-issue politics but also built on cultural comparisons between the epidemic and war. Rhetoric about "AIDS casualties" or referring to AIDS as "living in wartime" became common by the mid-1980s as activists strove to communicate the depth of the crisis. Vito Russo declared in a 1988 speech at an ACT UP demonstration in Albany, New York: "Living with AIDS is like living through a war which is happening only for those people who happen to be in the trenches. Every time a shell explodes, you look around and you discover that you've lost more of your friends, but nobody else notices."[14] Activists drew parallels to the Holocaust and other genocides, as in the pink triangle and "Silence = Death." As Marita Sturken has observed, they also posed comparisons to US deaths in the Vietnam War, drawing power from public memories of the Vietnam conflict that fused stigma with grief.[15] These parallels imagined people with AIDS as soldiers or veterans rather than as civilian targets, reinforcing a dynamic in which both the Vietnam War and AIDS were viewed principally through the deaths of young white men. The NAMES Project AIDS Memorial Quilt echoed the then-controversial Vietnam Veterans Memorial by reconfiguring a wall of names and memorabilia as hand-sewn fabric panels on the ground. And when participants at ACT UP's Ashes Action in October 1992 scattered their loved ones' human remains over the White House fence, their actions harkened back to the April 1971 protest by Vietnam Veterans Against the War, in which several hundred veterans threw their medals onto the steps of the US Capitol.[16]

Activists compared AIDS and the Vietnam War as catalysts for radical organizing. A participant in a 1987 ACT UP New York demonstration described protesters as expressing "the kind of anger not seen on white American faces since Vietnam"—a framing whose racialization captured the sense of betrayal of privilege present in each movement.[17] A 1988 newsletter by the AIDS Action Pledge used similar comparisons to call for multi-issue and multiracial coalition. It introduced Martin Hiraga, a member of ACT UP in Rochester, New York, first arrested at age twelve "for throwing blood on missiles at an anti–[Vietnam] war demonstration." Noting that he was Japanese American, it quoted him as saying, "It is easy to throw away people who society does not think are important."[18] Mark Kostopoulos, a member of ACT UP Los Angeles, reminded AIDS activists that the anti–Vietnam War movement had been split between a "single-issue" focus and "link[ing] up with people fighting racism," and he argued that only radical coalitions could end the AIDS crisis.[19]

While some connections between AIDS and anti-militarism were symbolic, others were very concrete. The Central American solidarity movement offered immediate resources and lessons, particularly through the use of civil disobedience. Bay Area AIDS activists drew particular inspiration from the Pledge of Resistance, an organization that had formed in late 1983 in response to the US invasion of Grenada and by fall 1984 had established a national network against US intervention. Those who joined the Pledge of Resistance signed a statement that read:

> If the United States invades, bombs, sends combat troops, or otherwise significantly escalates its intervention in Central America, I pledge to join with others to engage in acts of nonviolent civil disobedience as conscience leads me at U.S. federal facilities, including U.S. federal buildings, military installations, Congressional offices, offices of the Central Intelligence Agency, the State Department, and other appropriate places. I pledge to engage in nonviolent civil disobedience in order to prevent or halt the death and destruction which such U.S. military action causes the people of Central America.[20]

More than forty thousand people signed within four months of the Pledge's creation, with the first mass signing taking place on October 9, 1984, in downtown San Francisco. Active through 1993, the Pledge of Resistance summoned tens of thousands of people to protests around the country and proved central in building sustained, effective opposition to US intervention in Central America. The Bay Area proved to be a hub for this anti-intervention organizing, and the Pledge of Resistance maintained a national office in San Francisco. The Pledge especially fueled AIDS direct action through its reliance on affinity groups—small networks, generally no more than a dozen people, who coordinated acts of civil disobedience and organized through shared identities and interests.[21] Such networks, which had also been central to the antinuclear movement, proved significant for lesbian, gay, and AIDS activists because they allowed political and social autonomy and because they could function as a kind of connective tissue across movements, helping activists adapt tactics and analyze political links.

It is important to note that the practices of Central American solidarity marked by the Pledge of Resistance and other anti-intervention groups differed from those analyzed in previous chapters. In chapters 4 and 5, solidarity operated through direct exchange between US and Central American people and explicit support for—even at times involvement in—the Sandinista Revolution. These dimensions of solidarity were highly transnational and relatively multiracial, linking US citizens and expatriates with Nicaraguans and with Central American migrants and refugees. Through brigades and other forms of direct exchange, lesbian, gay, and AIDS activists engaged in transnational political dialogue about sexuality and feminism and organized grassroots AIDS prevention across borders. By contrast, the Pledge of Resistance centered on using street protests and civil disobedience inside the United States. Although guided by leaders in the Central American diaspora, anti-intervention protests principally mobilized people in the United States and explicitly targeted US policy. This made anti-intervention an invaluable model for AIDS activists seeking to challenge the US federal government, but it also meant that the activists who adapted anti-militarist civil disobedience to confront AIDS engaged Central American solidarity in less transnational, less multiracial, and more domestic ways. These differences helped to explain why, as AIDS activism grew, many newcomers came to view anti-militarism as tangential to fighting the epidemic and changing the politics of sexuality.

. . .

In June 1986 lesbian and gay activists were hit with three frightening political threats. The first was a new Justice Department policy that allowed federal contractors to fire employees with HIV/AIDS if they feared casual transmission.[22] Second came the placement of an AIDS quarantine measure on California's November 1986 ballot, backed by extremist demagogue Lyndon LaRouche.[23] Finally, on June 30, the US Supreme Court upheld Georgia's sodomy law in the *Bowers v. Hardwick* case.[24] In a 5–4 ruling, the Court excluded sodomy from the domain of sexual privacy and compared consensual homosexual intimacy, especially anal sex, to rape. Writers in gay and lesbian newspapers argued that *Hardwick* denied them even the safety of the closet and that the ruling defined homosexuals as socially worthless—"better off dead."[25] Coupled with the LaRouche initiative and Justice Department ruling, *Hardwick* seemed to cement into US law a rejection of the physically and socially "diseased." A growing number of gay, lesbian, and bisexual people argued that federal and state responses to AIDS held their sexual and social freedom at stake.

Citizens for Medical Justice (CMJ) in San Francisco and the Lavender Hill Mob in New York City formed in direct response to these events. Both were founded in summer 1986, after the *Hardwick* ruling, but

CMJ holds the distinction of carrying out civil disobedience first. Keith Griffith, one of CMJ's key founders, publicized the group in a July 1986 letter to the *San Francisco Sentinel* that called for activism against both the Court's ruling and AIDS. Over the summer, CMJ organized itself as an affinity group, later noting in publicity that though such groups were "new to the AIDS struggle . . . for the last several years [they] have been the backbone of every major nonviolent peace or anti-nuclear direct action in this country."[26] Other gay and lesbian affinity groups in the Bay Area at this time included Enola Gay, the Revolting Lesbians, and FORMICA FAG (Fags Organizing to Resist Militarism in Central America–Fight AIDS Group; as member Henry (Camo) Bortman laughingly recalled, they chose their acronym because Formica was the "countertop material of the gay nation").[27] CMJ shared a structure and politics with these groups but differed in centering on the express goal of demanding AIDS funding and challenging AIDS discrimination.

CMJ carried out its first action on September 24, 1986, at California's state capitol. The group traveled to Sacramento and demanded a meeting with Governor George Deukmejian, who had said he would not sign a bill banning discrimination against people with AIDS. When Deukmejian refused to meet with them, CMJ sat down and blocked his office entrance. Eight members of the group were arrested. In a brochure created after the action, they described civil disobedience as a means of using "our very bodies as a means of laying our case before the conscience of the local and national community."[28] Although CMJ was a small group, its action won it acclaim from the broader gay and lesbian community. The *San Francisco Sentinel* named CMJ founder Keith Griffith its 1986 "Man of the Year" for his role in organizing the Sacramento action "despite the absence of support from the state's so-called gay leadership."[29]

While CMJ was forming, other activists in the Bay Area were organizing to confront an "AIDS quarantine" measure, Proposition 64, backed by Lyndon LaRouche. A statewide campaign backed by national donors led the mobilization against LaRouche. However, a more radical coalition called Stand Together challenged both Proposition 64 and Proposition 63, which sought to declare English the official language of California.[30] The difference between the "No on 64" campaign and Stand Together echoed divides that had appeared in 1978, when only a few groups—principally Lesbian Schoolworkers and the Third World Gay Caucus—challenged both the antigay Proposition 6 and the death penalty measure Proposition 7. Similar to the earlier radical groups, Stand

Together brought together members of LAGAI, the affinity group Revolting Lesbians, and Out of Control, a network supporting lesbian political prisoners. It also produced multilingual materials and conducted grassroots voter outreach in Bay Area communities of color.[31] Stand Together drafted a "pledge of non-cooperation" with AIDS quarantine should the LaRouche measure pass, and it described "English-only" as an attack on immigrants and refugees driven north by US-sponsored wars. Voters ultimately rejected the LaRouche initiative by a 3-to-1 margin but approved "English-only" at the same overwhelming rate.

After the November 1986 election, the members of Stand Together continued to link AIDS to Central American solidarity by joining civil disobedience at the Concord Naval Weapons Station, which was located some thirty miles east of San Francisco and served as a hub for arms shipments, including the white phosphorus sent to the right-wing government of El Salvador. Activists had staged antinuclear and solidarity protests at Concord since the early 1980s, often placing their bodies on the station's railroad tracks. On September 1, 1987, Vietnam veteran Brian Wilson lost both his legs and suffered a skull fracture when he lay down on the tracks and was hit by a train whose crew had been ordered not to stop.[32] Nearly three months before the attack on Wilson, on June 13, 1987, members of LAGAI and CMJ joined a thousand others at Concord in an action summoned by the Pledge of Resistance. They highlighted their presence by wearing medical isolation suits labeled "Quarantine the War Machine," stretching quarantine tape across the gate where railroad cars loaded with weapons were set to leave, and carrying two black coffins through the crowd—one labeled "Killed By Contra Terror" and the other "Killed by AIDS."[33] Displaying and chanting the slogans "Fund condoms, not contras" and "Money for AIDS, not war," they won front-page coverage in the *San Francisco Sentinel,* at the time one of the Bay Area's largest gay and lesbian newspapers. Months later, LAGAI drew contrasts between war-making and the needs of people with AIDS by staging an action at a military recruiting center; participants threw condoms full of red paint, spray-painted pink triangles, and criticized the military as exploiting working-class people, including gay men and lesbians who signed up to escape hostile families.[34]

During this same time, activists from CMJ, Stand Together, and LAGAI joined forces to organize a larger and more sustained effort: the AIDS Action Pledge. An important step in the development of this group came when CMJ leader Keith Griffith approached Eileen Hansen, a longtime radical but a newcomer to San Francisco. Hansen's activist history stretched from the anti–Vietnam War movement and War on Poverty organizing to lesbian feminism, Central American solidarity, and anti-apartheid work. She had moved to San Francisco from Boston in late 1985 with the express goal of fighting AIDS and been surprised to find, in her words, no "street activism" against the epidemic.[35] Following the Enola Gay action and John Lorenzini's protest, another effort at civil disobedience—the AIDS/ARC Vigil, begun at San Francisco's Civic Center on October 27, 1985—had stumbled because of its lack of ties to broader radicalism, and soon became more an encampment than a targeted protest.[36] Aware of both the vigil's frustrations and Hansen's expertise, Griffith approached Hansen for advice about "moving forward CMJ." She pointed to how the Pledge of Resistance had "asked people to commit to being in the struggle till we won, basically—it may sound lofty . . . but the fact that individuals committed to that has its own form of power."[37] Across the first half of 1987, Hansen, Griffith, LAGAI leader Kate Raphael, and others met to discuss goals and structure for what would become the AIDS Action Pledge (AAP). One newcomer to activism in the planning group, Michelle Roland, worked as Griffith's boyfriend's Shanti volunteer (Shanti provided practical and emotional support for people with AIDS).[38]

The AIDS Action Pledge held its first public meeting in San Francisco on August 27, 1987. Directly echoing the Pledge of Resistance, it asked signers to commit not only to legal protest against AIDS but also to "to engage, as conscience leads me," in "nonviolent direct action, including civil disobedience," or to demonstrate in support of those who did.[39] The group drew approximately one hundred initial signers and thirty-five core participants and welcomed activists to join while maintaining autonomous affinity groups.[40] Its first action, held in early September 1987, protested President Reagan's recently formed AIDS Commission, which was visiting San Francisco and had received widespread criticism for appointing several antigay conservatives but no AIDS activists or people with AIDS.[41] José Fernandez, head of the AAP's Public Education and Media committee, introduced the AAP as a new organization centered on civil disobedience and described protesters as performing "guerrilla theater to expose the farce of Reagan's AIDS Commission."[42] Protesters chanted the by now familiar slogans "Condoms, not contras!" and "Money for AIDS, not for war—U.S. out of El Salvador."[43]

As the AAP finalized its agenda in fall 1987, it sharpened its concern over the divide between military and social spending into an analysis of the disproportionately racialized, classed, and global effects of the AIDS epidemic. This shift expanded the simple call for "Money for AIDS, not for war" into a more detailed and sophisticated analysis of how such money should be spent. The AAP solidified six core demands:

1. Massive funding to end the AIDS epidemic, made available from local, state and federal governments for research, care, education, anonymous testing programs and any and all treatments.

2. A federally funded education program which is comprehensive and sex positive, and which promotes safer sex, addiction recovery and IV hygiene.

3. Centrally coordinated research for AIDS treatments, cures and vaccines.

4. A free, nationalized health care system guaranteeing equal access, regardless of ability to pay.

5. Public accountability, especially to affected communities, regarding any AIDS-related research, funding and programs, to be controlled by the communities affected by AIDS.

6. A worldwide, culturally-sensitive funding program focused on ending the AIDS epidemic. The program would be initiated and financed by the United States, in cooperation with international health organizations. The U.S. would encourage the financial participation of other developed nations, with implementation controlled by the recipient nations.[44]

The last of these demands showed that AAP members understood the limits of a one-size-fits-all model of prevention and care that had been initiated to respond to white, largely middle-class gay men in the United States, who faced serious personal, social, and economic losses from AIDS but who were nonetheless more privileged than many in the expanding epidemic. Calls for "culturally-sensitive" programs pointed to activists' awareness of new efforts both locally and internationally, including the Latino AIDS Project and the Nicaragua AIDS Education Project (chapter 5). The AAP's demand for U.S. funding of a global AIDS program "controlled by the recipient nations," as well as its demand that AIDS funding "be taken primarily from the military budget," translated values from Central American solidarity and showed the group's roots in the gay and lesbian left.

Like ACT UP, the AAP declined to define itself as an exclusively lesbian and gay group, seeking instead to recognize the impact of the epidemic across sexual identities. And although the AAP did not become the vehicle for queer sexual politics that ACT UP did, it paid significant attention to prostitutes' rights thanks to the leadership of sex work organizer and AAP member Carol Leigh.[45] The group also opposed quarantining, mandatory testing, discrimination against prisoners and undocumented immigrants with HIV/AIDS, and "inflammatory, isolating language" such as "AIDS blood" or "AIDS victim."

The timing of the AAP's formation connected it tightly to the October 1987 March on Washington for Lesbian and Gay Rights. Many Bay Area activists planned to travel to Washington, DC, especially to participate in a national gathering on AIDS direct action and a day of civil disobedience at the Supreme Court. Early AAP meetings revolved around planning for the Court action, with training led by "preparers," people experienced in civil disobedience. Some of these sessions were held at the San Francisco Women's Building, reinforcing connections to networks of Central American solidarity as well as to antinuclear activism.[46] Kate Raphael led one such training with John Ashby, an HIV-positive member of the anti-militarist affinity group Enola Gay.[47] Penn Garvin was another "preparer" who brought experience in the Pledge of Resistance and became a leader in the AAP. As she noted in an AAP newsletter, nonviolence workshops taught both practical skills and movement history, helping AIDS activists see themselves as tied to past and ongoing efforts, especially "civil rights, anti-war, and women's movements."[48]

Although the AAP offered people ways to participate with less risk of arrest (for example, by monitoring police or speaking with media), it encouraged more people to consider arrest by helping them practice what might occur and by discussing whether individual health or legal needs might be turned into points of collective struggle at an action. Clearly, arrest and jail were risky: people of color, women, and queer people were routinely beaten and mistreated, people with AIDS were denied access to medicine, and noncitizens could be deported. Bail and fines entailed costs, especially for those with prior records, and although the AAP and other groups sought to maintain a bail fund, it could not always be guaranteed. Acknowledging these issues opened the door to making actions more inclusive and, as Eileen Hansen put it, prompted a "larger conversation . . . about how can you do more? How can we radicalize people and get them to take stronger positions, and learn on a personal level what they're capable of?"[49] Hansen acted as the AAP's media representative and played a key role in its connections to the March on Washington, devoting most of her time in 1987 to helping organize the action at the Supreme Court and serving as the central point of contact for Bay Area participants. She acted as the West Coast representative in the committee that wrote the Supreme Court action's handbook, *Out and Outraged*.[50] The day before the Court's action, AIDS activists convened a meeting that founded the national AIDS direct action movement; the AAP proved central here as well.

The impact of *Bowers* and AIDS, combined with the influences of the Central American solidarity, antinuclear, and anti-apartheid movements, pushed the 1987 March on Washington for Lesbian and Gay Rights toward a more left agenda than that seen at similar national marches in 1979 and 1993.[51] Activists set the 1987 march's agenda at meetings in June and November 1986 in New York. At the second of these, following a proposal from the Lesbian and Gay Network of the antinuclear Mobilization for Survival, organizers adopted "Money for AIDS, not war" as a "galvanizing slogan."[52] Significantly, an anti-apartheid demand and a call to "end U.S. intervention in the Third World" prompted more "rancorous debate," as some contended they would distract attention from more narrowly defined lesbian, gay, and AIDS issues.[53] But proponents of multi-issue sexual politics succeeded in adding reproductive freedom and "an end to racism in the U.S. and to apartheid in South Africa" to the demands, along with legal protections for lesbian and gay people and people with AIDS. The final lineup at the March on Washington highlighted coalition as four straight-identified speakers proclaimed their support: UFW leader Cesar Chavez, National Organization for Women president Eleanor Smeal, comedian Whoopi Goldberg, and the Reverend Jesse Jackson, whose appearance at the march was his first speech after declaring his candidacy for president.[54]

Held on October 11, 1987, the March on Washington drew an estimated 650,000 people to the Capitol, and it stood as only one in six days of events held from October 8 through 13. Activists unveiled the AIDS Memorial Quilt for the first time, displaying an initial 1,920 handmade panels—each the size of a grave—on the National Mall. The week also included gatherings of the National Coalition of Black Lesbians and Gays, the Latina/o coalition LLEGÓ, the bisexual organization BiNet, and a "Liberation Contingent" of gay and lesbian leftists. Reflecting more liberal politics, two thousand couples celebrated a symbolic wedding in front of the IRS building, while advocates of military inclusion held a ceremony at the Tomb of the Unknown Soldier honoring gay veteran Sergeant Leonard Matlovich—the man whose campaign had prompted Bay Area Gay Liberation to split into leftist and liberal factions in 1976.[55] AIDS activists held their national meeting October 12, while the Supreme Court action occupied October 13. Rebecca Hensler, then a nineteen-year-old student at Brown University, was inspired to join the Court action after taking part in the march and being shocked by the "media blackout" that followed. Her day at the Court marked her very first arrest. The action and the civil disobedience training "made me want to be an activist" and by the next summer launched her into ACT UP San Francisco.[56]

An estimated 840 people were arrested at the Supreme Court Building while 4,000 to 5,000 supporters rallied.[57] Compared to other acts of civil disobedience in the nation's capital, the arrests ran second only to an April 1971 demonstration against the Vietnam War. The day's civil disobedience was simple: protesters sought to demonstrate on the steps of the Supreme Court, an act that was illegal because federal law prohibits pickets, marches, or other political speech in the 252-foot zone between the public sidewalk and the Court's front doors.[58] Thus, people took direct action simply by walking onto the Court plaza and sitting down.[59] As they made clear throughout the day, they did this to protest *Bowers v. Hardwick* and the weak federal response to AIDS. The action occupied a full day and shut down the entrance to the Supreme Court for the first time in its history. Protesters crossed barricades in thematic waves that included sodomy laws, AIDS funding, and lesbians, each composed of multiple affinity groups—many assembled that weekend. They used campy and creative tactics to face off with violent police, who included DC cops in blue, court officers in gray, and the Capitol Hill riot squad in badgeless black, whom activists called the Darth Vaders. Women from the Seneca Peace Encampment created a spider's web of yarn to make it difficult for police to isolate people for arrest, and a group of Radical Faeries threw pink confetti while seated in passive resistance on the ground. Both these acts reflected the histories of activism that brought participants to the day.[60] Police carried out rough assaults and expressed disgust for people with AIDS by wearing bright-yellow rubber gloves; activists mocked officers' misunderstanding and fear with a chant that soon became beloved: "Your gloves don't match your shoes; you'll see it on the news!"[61]

The handbook for the Supreme Court action, *Out and Outraged*, stands as a rich archive of the left histories that informed and were cited that day. An opening statement declared:

> We act together so we cannot be defeated one by one. We act in the tradition of the labor movement, the suffragist movement, the civil rights movement, the women's movement, the anti-war movement, and in solidarity with Central Americans and Black South Africans fighting for self-determination.

Through these movements we have learned that substantial gains come through prolonged and persistent direct action.[62]

This theme was repeated and expanded throughout the handbook in a series of essays that explained tactics of civil disobedience, narrated the growth of direct action against AIDS, analyzed anti-racism in the lesbian and gay movement, and recounted lesbian and gay involvement in Central American solidarity. Some portions of the guide, particularly those on the practical details of civil disobedience, were reprinted from antinuclear manuals or lesbian and gay publications. The handbook also included a brief essay by San Francisco activist John Lorenzini describing his June 1985 civil disobedience at the Department of Health and Human Services and highlighting his mentorship by Central American solidarity activist Bill Blackburn.[63]

By focusing on civil disobedience, *Out and Outraged* defined lesbian and gay liberation through resistance to state authority rather than through legal inclusion. In her essay "C.D. in D.C.," activist Jessica Shubow defined civil disobedience as an assertive subversion of both individual and state violence and a way to forge radical purpose: "When we commit civil disobedience, we act with unity and discipline on a time-table dictated by our own desire for self-determination. . . . Civil disobedience is but a heightened replay of our daily lives. We politicize our resistance through our unity."[64] Several other essays elaborated on these themes by linking sexual freedom to military noncompliance. In "Coming Out as Non-Violent Direct Action," Sean McShee echoed rhetoric from the gay liberation era by stating that "we must not look to our militaristic society for images or courage," but rather draw inspiration from cultures of leather and drag.[65] San Francisco activist Jim Denison—a leader in the AAP—offered the essay "Gay People and Central America," which cited the Pledge of Resistance, LAGAI, and the Victoria Mercado Brigade.[66] Elva Perez-Treviño, a member of the march's People of Color Task Force, noted that the conjoined domestic and foreign agendas of the right had "impelled the Lesbian and Gay community to address racism at home and has enabled the community to take up . . . the oppressiveness of U.S. foreign policy."[67]

Preparation for civil disobedience also informed the national AIDS activist gathering organized by the AAP and New York's ACT UP. This meeting initiated a national grouping called AIDS Action Now, soon renamed the AIDS Coalition to Network, Organize, and Win (ACT NOW). ACT NOW linked the AIDS Action Pledge, ACT UP New York, and AIDS direct action groups around the country.[68] It adopted the AIDS Action Pledge as "points of unity" and, as a first major project, called for a week of nationwide AIDS protests to be held from April 29 to May 7, 1988.[69] In January 1988 it pooled funds to hire as full-time coordinator San Francisco activist Terry Beswick, who held the position for six months before turning it over to Scott Sanders in Washington, DC.[70] This leadership continued to rotate over the next few years, with ACT UP San Francisco member Arawn Eibhlyn serving as coordinator in 1990.[71] Meanwhile, New York's influence was felt as the growing number of AIDS direct action groups around the country adopted ACT UP's name, visual materials, and rhetoric.

After October 1987's powerful events, activists around the country returned home and threw themselves into organizing. In the Bay Area, AAP members turned their attention to their first major local action: a march and civil disobedience at the West Coast distribution center of Burroughs-Wellcome, the pharmaceutical company that manufactured the AIDS drug AZT.[72] To prepare, the AAP organized such forums as "The Economics of AIDS," noting that while Burroughs-Wellcome had responded to ACT UP demands by cutting the cost of AZT by 20 percent, even its lowered price—$8,000 a year—was out of reach for most people in the United States and virtually all of those in poorer countries.[73] In addition, many people with AIDS experienced AZT as highly toxic and became even sicker on the drug. The AAP demanded public investigation into AZT's effectiveness, Burroughs-Wellcome's costs and profits, and the company's so-called "payment" of $55,000 to the National Institutes of Health on the day it was granted sole rights to AZT's distribution.[74] The organization also hoped but was unable to initiate a boycott of Burroughs-Wellcome's over-the-counter medicines Actifed, Sudafed, and Neosporin.[75]

The AAP offered people a range of ways to participate in targeting Burroughs-Wellcome. Supporters could attend a kick-off rally in the Castro or donate to the fundraising effort, which raised $2,500 for AAP and local AIDS service organizations including the Asian AIDS Project, Black Coalition on AIDS, Indian AIDS Project, and Latino AIDS Project.[76] Those unable to march could ride in a "comfort van and medi-support," join in a carpool, or take light rail. A number of local groups endorsed or participated, including LAGAI, the queer-inclusive radical groups Women Against Imperialism and the Prairie Fire Organizing Committee, the Central American solidarity groups CISPES and the Pledge of Resistance, fellow AIDS groups Mobilization Against

AIDS and ACT UP Los Angeles, and both of San Francisco's gay Democratic clubs.[77]

The West Coast office of Burroughs-Welcome was located in Burlingame, fifteen miles south of San Francisco. On January 24, 1988, the AAP drew three hundred people to a kick-off rally in San Francisco, while eighty-five people began the march south. They covered twelve miles the first day, spending the night in a friendly Catholic church. AAP member Michelle Roland recalls that the march passed through neighborhoods with "a lot of working-class and elderly people" and that the stay at the church evoked activists' previous links to the farmworkers' movement and Central American solidarity.[78] On the morning of January 25, marchers completed the remaining three miles to the Burroughs-Wellcome office, and a total of two hundred people assembled for the action.[79]

Once at Burroughs-Wellcome, activists scaled ladders to the company's roof and hung banners declaring "Burroughs UnWellcome" and "End AIDS Profiteering" (figure 16). Nineteen people took position on the roof in three affinity groups—the first made up of gay men with AIDS—and all were arrested for trespassing.[80] Michelle Roland was one of three women detained, and two people with AIDS, Terry Sutton and Branch Hastings, were denied access to their AZT while held by police.[81] Other protesters chanted "Health care—not Contra aid!" and demanded that the drug be provided to people with AIDS on the African continent. They carried giant lavender hearts labeled with the names of people who had died of AIDS, displayed a fifteen-foot-tall puppet of a "Burroughs-Wellcome Vice President" with its pockets stuffed with money, and held placards decrying AZT's high price.[82]

The AAP's action at Burroughs-Wellcome drew the attention of local TV news stations and the lesbian and gay press and solidified the group's reputation in the growing AIDS movement. It also highlighted the presence of longtime gay and lesbian leftists in AIDS direct action. One of the first people to be arrested was Hank Wilson, a central leader of Bay Area Gay Liberation (BAGL) in the mid-1970s. Another, Henry (Camo) Bortman, was a member of Enola Gay and the Prairie Fire Organizing Committee who had been active in both BAGL and the radical gay men's group the June 28 Union. The histories that these and other activists brought to the AAP shaped its rhetoric. As protester Larry Glover told *Coming Up!*, "The connection between capitalism and the profiteering on this epidemic is so blatant that I feel that if people simply know the price of the drug, it's gonna make them do an analysis of the political and economic system."[83] In an AAP newsletter soon after the action,

FIGURE 16. Civil disobedience by the AIDS Action Pledge at the
Burroughs-Wellcome office in Burlingame, California, January 25,
1988. Photograph by Rick Gerharter. Courtesy Rick Gerharter.

Eileen Hansen argued that though the demand of free AZT was unlikely
to be won, it highlighted the larger goal of free and nationalized health
care and the AAP's desire to "push activists to new levels. . . . We invite
participation from all who have a radical vision."[84]

The histories that fueled the AAP sent it to the streets when the Reagan administration escalated the threat of war in Central America. As
highlighted in the first pages of this book, in March 1988 President

Reagan—falsely claiming that the forces of Nicaragua's Sandinista government had crossed into Honduras—sent 3,200 US soldiers to the region to prepare for a full-scale military assault. His action was turned back in the face of protests in 150 US cities and objections from Congress. San Francisco activists organized ten days of demonstrations lasting from March 17 through 26, including marches that brought downtown traffic to a standstill and produced more than five hundred arrests.[85] A "Gay and Lesbian Task Force"—a temporary coalition led by the AIDS Action Pledge and including LAGAI and many affinity groups—served as one of four groups leading the protests, joined by the Pledge of Resistance, CISPES, and the Nicaragua Information Center.[86] Catherine Cusic, recently active in AIDS brigades that collaborated with activists and Sandinista officials in Nicaragua, gave a speech at the Federal Building on the first night of the actions, and LAGAI and AAP members Kate Raphael and Terry Sutton spoke at the closing rally.

In addition to being prominent in protests throughout the week, the AAP and lesbian and gay groups organized their own, specifically queer protests on Friday March 18 and Tuesday March 22. The first of these, somewhat hastily assembled, numbered 2,000 to 3,000 people and marched from the Castro to the Federal Building, with protesters pausing to throw (fake-)bloodstained money at the US Mint. The second march was more planned and drew more than 4,000 people. Protestors carried a forty-foot-wide banner that read "Gays, Lesbians Say No War" and chanted "Quarantine the war machine, not people with AIDS," "Money for AIDS, not war," and "We're dykes and faggots and we're here to say, down with the army and the CIA" (figure 17).[87] Rally speakers reflected the strong networks built in lesbian and gay solidarity and lesbian and gay of color organizing, as they included Gloria Canas of the Salvadoran refugee group CRECE; Fernando Arenas, who was a Colombian immigrant active in Amaranto, a group of gay and lesbian Latin American immigrants; the Latino AIDS educator Guillermo Gonzales; Rebecca Gordon, author of *Letters from Nicaragua*; and Pat Norman, a black lesbian who coordinated the San Francisco Department of Public Health's community response to AIDS.[88]

The March 1988 anti-intervention protests were significant to both the larger history of the gay and lesbian left and to the course of AIDS direct action, and they mattered for several reasons. For one, they asserted a prominent queer presence in actions whose most immediate targets lay outside sexual politics. Although this was no surprise for any-

FIGURE 17. The AIDS Action Pledge and others march against U.S. intervention in Central America, San Francisco, March 18, 1988. Photograph by Rick Gerharter. Courtesy Rick Gerharter.

one familiar with past gay and lesbian radicalism, it prompted reconsiderations from others, queer or straight, who might not have been paying attention. Coverage of the protests in both mainstream and gay and lesbian newspapers around the Bay Area made it evident that straight people found the scale of the queer presence in the protests surprising, even though gay and lesbian activists had played prominent roles in solidarity work for years. Perhaps AIDS made the ties between sexuality and other politics more visible, whereas claims of gay and lesbian freedom through socialist alliance with Nicaragua had been easier to ignore. Tying AIDS to Central America also helped to remake the meaning of the epidemic, shifting it from a problem of pathology or deviance to one of the "human needs" that might be met by cutting the military budget.

In addition, the March 1988 protests drew in a number of gay and lesbian people who had previously embraced a more liberal or left-liberal politics. Two leaders of the march on Friday March 18 were Cleve Jones, then best known as the founder of the AIDS Memorial Quilt, and Gilbert Baker, the creator of the rainbow "pride" flag. Neither had been significantly involved in Central American solidarity before, but Baker told gay radical Tede Matthews that lesbian activist Catherine Cusic's speech on March 17 "ignited me to do something," while Jones said, "I fear any move towards militarism and not only because of diversion of funds from AIDS. Gay people always suffer in the social climate generated by an increase in militaristic rhetoric."[89] Jones's statement showed how the anti-militarism of the lesbian and gay left helped to drive the radicalizing impact of AIDS.

For all their significance, the March 1988 anti-intervention protests might have produced greater political power if straight activists had responded with greater support for AIDS and queer organizing. As the AIDS crisis expanded, the contrast grew sharper between, on the one hand, a lesbian, gay, and AIDS movement that showed up to protest US intervention in Central America and, on the other hand, a Central American solidarity movement that said little about queer lives or AIDS. By 1990 LAGAI concluded: "It has been a constant struggle for us, in a city with over 150,000 gay people, to keep the CASM [Central American Solidarity Movement] from scheduling major mobilizations that conflict with Lesbian/Gay Freedom Day. . . . They want us to organize for mobilizations at the Concord Naval Weapons Station, yet are not there when we organize demonstrations against the Concord Traditional Values Coalition."[90] While LAGAI kept the faith with Central American solidarity, its critique evidenced frustration.

Despite these conflicts, the AAP continued to encourage AIDS activists around the country to join actions against US intervention in Central America and to build alliances with solidarity groups. It sent clippings about the March 1988 protests to member groups of ACT NOW, wrote about these issues in its newsletter, and took part in solidarity protests around the Bay Area. During ACT NOW's week of actions in late April and May 1988, the AAP's events included contingents at a solidarity march, a May Day protest, and the Concord Naval Weapons Station.[91] This did not mean that the AAP defined AIDS only through Central American solidarity; it also held a forum on women and AIDS, a march on the Social Security office to demand disability payments to people with AIDS, a protest at the Immigration and Naturalization Service cosponsored with the Latino Coalition on AIDS, and an "AIDS Treatment Tour" with actions at the California Department of Health, the Food and Drug Administration, and the National Institutes of Health.[92] Still, the AAP stood out in emphasizing anti-militarism as entwined with demands for HIV/AIDS treatment, care, and funding.

In July 1988 the AIDS Action Pledge changed its name to ACT UP San Francisco, a decision that aligned with national trends and made its work more recognizable.[93] Along with ACT UP New York and ACT NOW, ACT UP San Francisco continued to embrace the text of the AIDS

Action Pledge as a broad statement of politics.[94] Increasingly, however, anti-militarism became relegated to the background, and conflicts sharpened between treatment and social action agendas. People of color in ACT UP San Francisco formed the Bayard Rustin Coalition to address both the racialized impact of HIV/AIDS and "racial insensitivity" in the group itself. This small group claimed "roots . . . in the alliances of diverse groups—White, Black, Latino, Asian, Lesbian and Gay—who fight against unjust wars, and strive for equal rights for all people," and held that "what is especially of concern about ACT-UP/SF is that ACT-UP/SF militantly denies its own racism."[95] Debates between treatment and social action agendas also fell out as differences between West Coast and East Coast groups, especially leading up to a national ACT UP action in October 1988. While New Yorkers wanted to concentrate demands on drug approval by the Food and Drug Administration (FDA), San Francisco activists also sought to address health care access at the National Institutes of Health and to more explicitly raise issues of race and gender in the epidemic. After what ACT UP San Francisco recorded as "intense fights over the phone," the narrower focus on the FDA won out, and the ACT NOW conference before the action was "tense."[96]

The FDA action was certainly powerful and militant: driven by the rising urgency of the epidemic, it was ACT UP's largest protest yet. Called "Shut Down the FDA," it drew 1,500 people and extensive media coverage and won a shorter timeline for drug testing as well as a pathway to "parallel trials" (these allowed more people access to testing new drugs even if they were too sick or otherwise ineligible for traditional clinical research).[97] The action's success drew more and more newcomers into ACT UP San Francisco, though these new activists joined just as an accelerating number of more experienced activists were dying.[98] Meanwhile, the civil disobedience handbook for "Shut Down the FDA" focused entirely on the FDA's structure and on policy regarding AIDS drugs and treatment, offering none of the anti-militarist context for direct action that the *Out and Outraged* handbook for the Supreme Court action had done. This had the effect of limiting new activists' knowledge of the genealogies behind the AIDS movement.

Amidst this shift, a group of AIDS activists in San Francisco formed Stop AIDS Now Or Else (SANOE). The members of SANOE—including Kate Raphael, Henry (Camo) Bortman, Terry Sutton, Arawn Eibhlyn, David Stern, Stephen Fish, and many others—were primarily white radicals with experience in ACT UP San Francisco, the AAP, LAGAI, and other efforts. SANOE was larger than an affinity group but worked separately

FIGURE 18. Stop AIDS Now Or Else (SANOE) blocks the Golden Gate Bridge, January 31, 1989. Photograph by Rick Gerharter. Courtesy Rick Gerharter.

from ACT UP, in part to set its own agenda and in part to protect ACT UP from legal charges. Calling themselves a "non-violent direct action network with the purpose of actively resisting AIDS genocide," SANOE carried out dramatic, high-visibility protests, often including civil disobedience, that called public attention to AIDS as a life-or-death crisis.[99] The group's first action began at 7:27 A.M. on January 31, 1989, when eighty activists stopped traffic on the Golden Gate Bridge. Some sat down across the lanes while others unfurled banners reading "AIDS = Genocide," "Silence = Death," and "Fight Back," creating a massive traffic jam (figure 18). Others distributed fliers to drivers asking, "Are you sick and tired of being stuck on this bridge?" and comparing commuters' sense of frustration to the situation of people with AIDS who were desperate for care, research, and funding.[100] They asked drivers to demand anti–AIDS discrimination policies at their jobs and to join in pressuring government officials for change. The action won extensive press coverage, though also many angry public responses.[101]

SANOE took action at a time of rising fury and grief, emotions that were heightened when Terry Sutton—one of the key organizers of the AAP, of ACT UP San Francisco, and of the Golden Gate Bridge action—died of AIDS on April 11, 1989. Though by no means the only activist lost, Sutton's death left a large emotional as well as political hole. Rebecca Hensler, by then also a member of ACT UP San Francisco, counted Sutton as one of her most important political mentors and recalls that he routinely "put himself at risk for others," for example, refusing to be released early when arrested at the FDA.[102] Within two weeks of Sutton's passing, his friends and comrades honored him with a memorial march, and they held the FDA and the drug company Astra responsible for his death by denying him access to the drug foscarnet.[103] Sutton's leadership was exemplary, yet his death was cruelly ordinary, preceded and followed by the losses of other AAP, LAGAI, and SANOE activists. Indeed, by the time of SANOE's second action, two other men who had taken part in the bridge action—Don Wright and Jim Allen— had also died, and others would die soon.[104] Kate Raphael observed that "media commentators are saying that the AIDS crisis has peaked, that AIDS is last year's disaster," even while deaths rolled on and the rates of people of color with HIV/AIDS rose.[105] In the words of ACT UP New York member Douglas Crimp, "Frustration, anger, rage, and outrage, anxiety, fear, and terror, shame and guilt, sadness and despair—it is not surprising that we feel these things; what is surprising is that we often don't," but are left with "only a deadening numbness or constant depression."[106] Crimp called on AIDS activists to not deny any of their responses to the epidemic, but rather to fuse "mourning *and* militancy" so as to remain psychically whole.[107] But as his words made clear, emotional well-being was hard to find amidst so much death.

SANOE kept moving. On September 8, 1989, fifty-four activists bought standing-room-only tickets to the opening night of the San Francisco Opera. Entering the hall in evening wear, they interrupted the performance just as the lights went down and the orchestra began to play, moving into the aisles, unfolding banners, and distributing a flier made to look like an alternate opera program. They blew whistles, chanted, raised banners, and above the din of audience reaction, read a statement:

> We see resources being spent on Opera openings and missiles and bombers but NOT to save lives. . . . We're here because we're under attack by AIDS and violence and bigotry that has increased with the AIDS epidemic. We're lesbians, gay men, and friends. Together we are fighting back. We demand a change in Government priorities NOW. This is a state of emergency. We are living in wartime.[108]

SANOE called on operagoers to use their wealth and political connections to speak up and create change that could make AIDS "more of a chronic manageable disease and less of a death sentence," especially given recent cuts to California's AIDS budget, President George H. W. Bush's declaration that federal funds would be spent only on research and prevention rather than patient care or treatment, and the exceedingly short life expectancy of Latino residents of San Francisco diagnosed with AIDS (just sixty days, because lack of health care delayed diagnosis and accelerated the course of illness).[109] Apart from a few scattered "bravos," SANOE received a very hostile reaction from opera patrons. When the orchestra began playing the "Star Spangled Banner" to interrupt the protest, the crowd sang along, and as SANOE left the hall, audience members grabbed at activists' whistles, threw punches, and yelled threatening antigay language. One woman ran into the lobby to spray the departing activists with mace.[110] In initial press coverage, the *San Francisco Chronicle* incorrectly stated that SANOE members had committed violence and had to be forced out of the hall by police; under pressure the newspaper issued a correction that acknowledged that protesters had left on their own and that audience members were the evening's only physical aggressors.[111]

A month after the opera house action, on October 6, 1989, ACT UP San Francisco participated in a national day of action coordinated through ACT NOW.[112] It marched from downtown to the Castro, covering thirty blocks and stopping at the by now familiar sites of the San Francisco Federal Building and US Mint. The action sought "to focus attention on the neglect of people with AIDS by the Bush administration, governmental spending on military as opposed to health, . . . and [inadequate resources for] the San Francisco health care model."[113] Once in the Castro, demonstrators spray-painted body outlines on the asphalt to create a "Permanent Quilt"—what Kate Raphael terms "a subtle dig at the Names Project [AIDS Memorial Quilt] which many of us felt had gone from a powerful protest to a kind of a feel-good way of beautifying the epidemic."[114] (Friends had also made a AIDS Memorial Quilt panel for Terry Sutton that read: "Terry Sutton hated this quilt and so do we!") Police carried out an unusual level of harassment along the march route and arrested ACT UP's police liaison very early on—a tactic that weakened marchers' ability to communicate with one another and to respond to officers' presence. As the march concluded in the Castro, protesters were met by a phalanx of officers in riot gear who closed the street and sidewalks, declared martial law in the neighborhood, and ordered the crowd to leave. Officers began to use motorcycles to scatter the crowd, and when people began a sit-in to protest these tactics, the police carried out a brutal dispersal, charging people with nightsticks and arresting participants—indeed, charging people using nonviolent resistance with assault.[115] Protesters chanted the helmet number of an officer who had left a nineteen-year-old attending his first ACT UP demonstration unconscious and requiring several stitches. Police declared the entire Castro an "illegal assembly" and occupied the neighborhood until 10:00 P.M.; the night became known as the Castro sweep.[116]

Five days after the Castro sweep, ACT UP San Francisco and ACT NOW demanded the resignation of SFPD chief Frank Jordan, disciplinary actions against officers, and a public accountability plan. Activists speculated that the SFPD may have carried out the attack in retaliation for SANOE's opera action or to punish ACT UP for its opposition to Mayor Art Agnos's baseball stadium plan.[117] Some of the injured eventually won a lawsuit against the city, though LAGAI and other groups raised the concern that the official complaint process and investigation would produce increased surveillance of activists, as had happened during a grand jury investigation of the SFPD's recent beating of UFW leader Dolores Huerta.[118] Gay journalist Tim Kingston situated the sweep in broader histories of SFPD repression centered on Latino and African American neighborhoods and on leftists. He cited repeated SFPD harassment of Central American solidarity activists, including Salvadoran refugees, and noted a State Department memo to the SFPD urging surveillance of Central American groups. "Seasoned observers of the SFPD," he concluded, "say ACT UP is just the latest target."[119]

ACT UP San Francisco might have been able to respond more forcefully to the Castro sweep by building alliances against police harassment and surveillance had the Bay Area not been hit by the Loma Prieta earthquake on October 17, 1989. The quake measured a magnitude of 6.9 and hit at 5:04 P.M.—at the start of rush hour and just minutes before the start of Game 3 of the World Series between the Oakland Athletics and San Francisco Giants in Candlestick Park. It devastated the Nimitz Freeway in West Oakland (forty-two people died there, of a total of sixty-three earthquake-related deaths), caused a collapse on the two-decker Bay Bridge, and produced significant building damage and structure fires in San Francisco's Marina District. Massive damage to infrastructure affected millions of people, and the disaster's economic and social effects derailed activism for weeks and even months. Many people who had previously given to AIDS service organizations redirected their contributions to earthquake relief, and some stopped donating time or money at all because of the effects of the quake on their lives.

While activists continued to organize after Loma Prieta, their work slowed for a time, and SANOE wisely shifted its next action to Southern California. On New Year's Day, 1990, fourteen activists (backed by a "support team" of more than thirty) halted the nationally televised Rose Parade by walking in front of a float called "First Symbols of Freedom" and unfurling banners reading "Emergency, Stop the Parade, 70,000 Dead of AIDS." Many were arrested, and SANOE held fundraisers in Los Angeles and Laguna Beach (then a liberal and gay enclave in conservative Orange County) to cover their court costs.[120] At the end of January, the group held a "commemorative walk" across the Golden Gate Bridge, but cognizant of the trauma of the Bay Bridge destruction, participants walked legally along the viewing platform and did not block traffic. Their commemoration highlighted the rising incidence of HIV and AIDS among black women and drew endorsement from many AIDS organizations, including several working in Bay Area communities of color. SANOE held its last action on May Day, 1990, when it occupied the offices of the Immigration and Naturalization Service in Los Angeles and San Francisco. A total of sixty people participated, with twenty-four arrested in the north and thirteen in the south. The group's bilingual press release noted that they occupied the office at closing time so as not to interfere with immigrants seeking to meet with officials or complete paperwork. Their key demands included an end to immigration laws that barred HIV-positive and gay and lesbian immigrants, as well as sanctuary for refugees from Guatemala, El Salvador, and other governments responsible for political repression and torture.[121]

Meanwhile, ACT UP was turning its focus to planning for protests at the 6th International AIDS Conference, to be held in San Francisco in late June 1990. The week of actions is commemorated today as a mark of ACT UP's mobilizing power and as an instance when the AIDS movement recaptured national attention. The HIV "travel ban"—one of the policies SANOE had protested—meant that international activists with HIV were barred from the conference as well as from US medical care. In part because of this policy, ACT UP San Francisco, ACT NOW, and other ACT UP groups decided to shut down the city with protests in the streets rather than entering conference halls. They made one exception for an action to interrupt a speech by Louis Sullivan, the secretary of health and human services.[122]

In addition to daily street protests, ACT UP held a forum analyzing the broad context of HIV/AIDS, with speakers addressing the immigration ban, HIV/AIDS in prison, policies toward sex workers and IV drug

FIGURE 19. Women's March outside the International
AIDS Conference, San Francisco, June 22, 1990.
Photograph by Rick Gerharter. Courtesy Rick Gerharter.

users, and the intersections of homophobia and racism in both the
domestic and international pandemic.[123] A Women's March highlighted
the epidemic's links to incarceration, the regulation of sex work, and
racist and sexist systems of health care (figure 19). Conference protests
indicated a clear investment in a multi-issue politics and showed how
proponents of a social action response to AIDS were turning ever greater
attention to criminalization and poverty. Indeed, organizing to confront
HIV/AIDS in prisons would grow through the early 1990s and inform
the prison abolition movement.

Yet the June 1990 protests also propelled conflicts that led to ACT UP San Francisco splitting into two groups and losing energy. The immediate catalyst of this split was a debate, begun soon after the International AIDS Conference, over whether ACT UP San Francisco should lease an office space. Combined with growing expenditures on publicity and media, this office was estimated to have required an annual budget of around $100,000, a significant jump for the group. (Although ACT UP New York operated on a larger budget thanks to East Coast donors, ACT UP San Francisco had not reached anywhere near this financial scale.)[124] Many activists noted that the office space was inaccessible to wheelchairs, which meant some people with AIDS would not be able to enter.[125] As debate over the plan grew heated, consensus became impossible. By the end of summer 1990, a significant contingent of longtime activists left ACT UP entirely, while others split into two factions, one that retained the name ACT UP San Francisco and another that called itself ACT UP Golden Gate. ACT UP San Francisco embraced a social action agenda (committees included Universal Health Care, Prison Issues, and Needle Exchange) but soon became a much smaller and weaker group, while ACT UP Golden Gate pursued a treatment agenda and remained somewhat larger, though it too faded.[126] In 1994 ACT UP San Francisco suffered an even deeper wound when a small group of newcomers to the city took over the organization and redirected its efforts toward HIV denialism, or the belief that HIV does not cause AIDS. The 1994 takeover has often been misrepresented as the cause of the San Francisco–Golden Gate split, a narrative that contributes to the erasure of radical political histories. But, reinforcing the earlier timeline and debate, ACT UP New York also experienced a definitive split between treatment and social action in early 1992 and began to fade thereafter.[127]

For many of those who left ACT UP in San Francisco after summer 1990, the debate over office space was never the central concern. Instead, departing activists expressed frustration with patterns of red-baiting, misogyny, white and middle-class privilege, and "business activism" that they had seen in the group and that they felt had worsened as ACT UP expanded. Two lesbian leftists central to LAGAI and SANOE, Kate Raphael and Deeg Gold, wrote a statement that termed the office debate a red herring, since ultimately neither ACT UP San Francisco nor ACT UP Golden Gate rented the space at all. They lambasted ACT UP both in San Francisco and in New York for becoming a "product to be packaged and sold," composed of "young, hip, mostly white, attractive" people who "weren't those old-style radicals . . . [and] would condense our politics into twenty seconds for the news." They argued that though the phrase "We're dying" had been frequently used to shut down efforts to discuss sexism or leftist coalition, people with AIDS "were generally disempowered" through a lack of attention to accessibility at protests and control of decision making by HIV-negative gay men.[128]

Fellow SANOE and ACT UP San Francisco member Arawn Eibhlyn concurred with Raphael and Gold in observations about People with Immune System Disorders (PISD), a caucus of ACT UP members who had AIDS, were HIV-positive, or had other (non-HIV-related) immune illness. The members of PISD included people of various genders and sexualities, but all sought to address the social and economic consequences of chronic and fatal illness in a society without a real safety net.[129] The fact that the group existed at all hinted at the ways both HIV-positive people and the social action agenda could sometimes feel pushed to the margins of ACT UP. Related to this development, Raphael and Gold lamented how anti-war organizing, abortion rights, and homelessness had come to be seen as "distractions" from AIDS, arguing, "The attempt is to take AIDS out of the social context that most PWA's experience, and to look at it as just a medical issue for people who have the necessities of life, and access to health care." They described this view as a betrayal of the roots of the AIDS direct action movement.[130]

The fractures within ACT UP had begun amidst earlier losses of movement history, and in their immediate aftermath—even as queer radicalism continued—a much more liberal agenda for LGBT politics gained power. Queer activists protested the first Gulf War in early 1991, but their actions along with the military conflict were short-lived. Instead, the decline of multi-issue politics in the AIDS direct action movement enabled something quite different: new mobilizing for gay and lesbian inclusion in the US military. As radicals protested this goal, they mourned their diminished political power along with their dead and dying friends.

Epilogue

In 1991, Henry (Camo) Bortman posed for a poster declaring "Not *Every* Boy Wants to Be a Soldier" (figure 20). Dressed in a long pink gown that set off his wavy brown hair and graying beard, Bortman gazed at the blossoms of a cherry tree and rested a protest sign on the ground, apparently pausing for reflection at the end of a march. A subtle manicure matched his gown, while a hint of chest hair drew the eye to his décolletage. Bortman was by this time a longtime radical who had been part of gay and AIDS groups including Bay Area Gay Liberation, the June 28 Union, the affinity group FORMICA FAG, the AIDS Action Pledge, and Stop AIDS Now Or Else. He was also a part of the Prairie Fire Organizing Committee, an anti-racist white organization that had evolved out of the Weather Underground; this was the group that produced "Not *Every* Boy Wants to Be a Soldier," printing the image in its magazine *Breakthrough* and distributing it as a poster at the 1993 March on Washington for Gay, Lesbian, and Bi Equal Rights and Liberation. "Not *Every* Boy" challenged a central agenda item of that march: gay, lesbian, and bisexual inclusion in the US military.

The politics of military inclusion proved ascendant as the Cold War ended and a neoliberal order gained sway. Over the early 1990s, gay and lesbian liberals drew new energy to military inclusion through the cases of Sergeants Leonard Matlovich, Miriam Ben-Shalom, and Perry Watkins and through challenges to discrimination in college ROTC programs.[1] In 1992 presidential candidate Bill Clinton sought support

FIGURE 20. "Not *Every* Boy Wants to Be a Soldier," 1991.
Fireworks, John Brown Education Fund, Queer Caucus of PFOC,
Breakthrough Magazine. Courtesy Lincoln Cushing/Docs Populi.

from prominent gay donors and promised to end the ban on gay men
and lesbians in the military if elected. Three months after Clinton's
inauguration, the March on Washington for Gay, Lesbian, and Bi Equal
Rights and Liberation put forward a call to "Lift the Ban," but by summer 1993, President Clinton agreed to the compromise known as
"Don't Ask, Don't Tell," which advocates for inclusion viewed as a
betrayal. That policy resulted in a net increase in the expulsion of gay,
lesbian, and bisexual people from the military and was also observed to
fuel sexual harassment and rape—since assailants used lesbian-baiting
to coerce women into sex, and gay-baiting to ensure that men who were
assaulted kept quiet.[2] A combination of legislation, court order, and
certification by top military leaders brought an end to the ban in 2011.
The Department of Defense is now implementing transgender inclusion,

though many trans activists have rejected this goal based on their broader opposition to US militarism.[3]

Queer opposition to military inclusion in the 1990s held direct legacies from the gay and lesbian left. In the Bay Area, many who had participated in ACT UP, SANOE, LAGAI, and related groups protested both the First Gulf War and military inclusion. Their efforts began on the heels of ACT UP San Francisco's single-issue versus multi-issue split. LAGAI members debated military inclusion on national television in an episode of the NBC talk show hosted by Sally Jesse Raphael, and by June 1992 they began a counterrecruitment project, "We Like Our Queers Out of Uniform." Their materials for this project included accounts of draft resistance and military discrimination, as well as practical advice for resisting military enrollment or leaving once enrolled. LAGAI further highlighted the military prosecution of Gulf War conscientious objectors and included the account of a black lesbian who had been the target of an antigay witch hunt in the navy.[4]

While LAGAI decried discrimination within military branches, it more forcefully opposed inclusion because it held that "the military isn't a job program for young people. It's the muscle behind u.s. imperialism"—a tool used both outside and inside the United States to counter grassroots resistance.[5] As evidence of the continuities between foreign and domestic repression, the group pointed to the deployment of the army and marines in the 1992 Los Angeles uprising that followed the Rodney King police brutality verdict. LAGAI also criticized the growth of gay and lesbian alliances with police, holding that it was "bizarre" and "insulting" to bring police into annual pride celebrations since "Stonewall was a riot against police violence."[6] Moreover, the group asserted that the San Francisco Police Department used gay and lesbian officers to undermine queer activism, pointing to two lesbian SFPD officers who had allegedly infiltrated the radical group Queer Nation and used their observations to prosecute participants of the AB 101 Veto Riots. (These occurred in San Francisco in September 1991 when Governor Pete Wilson vetoed a state bill that would have banned job discrimination on the basis of sexual orientation.)[7]

While still significant, anti-militarist and anti-imperialist politics were increasingly shunted to the margins of gay, lesbian, and queer activism in the early 1990s. LAGAI member Tede Matthews marked this change in a 1992 essay in which he described having evaded the Vietnam War draft and concluded by wistfully stating, "Although I feel in my heart that being gay was linked with my refusal to be a murderer in a racist war, that obviously is not true for all lesbians and gay men."[8] For Matthews, anti-war commitment had been such a central tenet of gay liberation that it defined how he understood his gayness itself. But he was compelled to recognize that this was only one conception of sexual identity.

The displacement of anti-militarism and anti-imperialism in gay, lesbian, and queer politics was driven both by the losses wrought by AIDS—Matthews died in July 1993—and by the supposed defeat of socialism at the end of the Cold War.[9] With the left as a whole in upheaval, the United States's already minimal commitments to social welfare—though under attack since the 1970s—became further decimated by neoliberal policies built on privatization, "personal responsibility," and "law and order."[10] A wave of prison construction and lengthened prison sentences, begun in the 1980s, accelerated in the 1990s alongside attacks on immigrants and on social benefits. In 1994, California voters approved "three strikes" sentencing that imposed automatic life sentences for all third felonies (Proposition 184) and barred undocumented immigrants from accessing public services (Proposition 187). The same year, President Bill Clinton signed the Violent Crime Control and Law Enforcement Act, which dramatically increased budgets for policing and prisons, created sixty new federal death penalty offenses, and eliminated funding that would allow prisoners to get a college education.[11] In 1996 Clinton signed the Personal Responsibility and Work Opportunity Reconciliation Act, characterized as "welfare reform," which cut aid and increased poverty rates by imposing time limits, requiring stricter enforcement of child support (including making failure to pay a crime), eliminating support for unmarried parents under age eighteen and for undocumented immigrants, and allowing states to tie anti-poverty benefits to heterosexual marriage promotion.[12] California voters meanwhile overturned affirmative action (Proposition 209, in 1996), sent youth to adult prisons, and banned same-sex marriage (Propositions 21 and 22 in the year 2000).[13] Each of these losses placed radicals, progressives, and liberals on the defensive, consuming energy and triggering heightened needs for services that government agencies could not or would not offer any longer. Meanwhile, in cities around the country but especially in the Bay Area, rising housing costs and gentrification made it increasingly difficult to build and live in radical countercultures.

The changes of the 1990s and 2000s divided a good deal of gay and lesbian rights work from agendas of economic, racial, and reproductive justice. National gay and lesbian organizations (gradually, though unevenly, including bisexual and transgender people and issues) gained influence while prioritizing military inclusion and marriage equality, goals that many radicals criticized as homonormative.[14] Advocates increasingly won recognition by defining gay and lesbian identities as merely personal differences rather than as means to challenge privatization or state violence. Some policies claimed as victories against harm, including hate crime laws and "quality of life" policing, aligned with trends toward longer prison sentencing, the containment of public sexuality, and harsher regulation of queer and trans people of color.[15] As Lisa Duggan argues, against earlier frameworks of liberation, gay and lesbian "rights" have increasingly been incorporated into a "superficial 'multiculturalism'" that reifies gay and lesbian people as white and affluent and redirects attention from redistributive goals.[16] Proponents of the rights agenda came to present it as the ultimate horizon of freedom, seeming to leave no other possibilities for change. Such rhetoric accelerated after September 11, 2001, when calls for gay and lesbian military inclusion were reshaped into a "homonationalism" that aligns US gay and lesbian freedom with the "Global War on Terror."[17]

And yet, through the 1990s and since, radicals also built a new sexual politics, one labeled queer. By opposing assimilation, queer politics draws attention to the constructed violence of heteronormativity and undermines views of sexual identity as fixed, natural, or inherent. Activists and scholars have used such mutability to embed queerness in broader radical challenges to social and economic norms, thereby posing a direct contrast to neoliberals' reliance on the argument that homosexual, bisexual, and transgender identities are involuntary or inborn.

Writing in 1992, Douglas Crimp argued that queer politics' power lay in its construction of "identity" itself as relational. A cultural critic and a member of ACT UP New York, Crimp called on his fellow activists and theorists to "rethink identity politics" as not predicated on essential characteristics, but rather as a way of expressing "relational . . . political identifications that constantly remake" their meaning. Crimp illustrated this point through ACT UP New York's needle exchange campaign, which he argued expanded the meaning of "queer" to refer to more than sexuality alone: "It's not that 'queer' doesn't any longer encompass [activists'] sexual practices; it does, but it also entails a *relation* between those practices and other circumstances that make very different people vulnerable both to HIV infection and to the stigma, discrimination, and neglect that have characterized the societal and governmental response to the constituencies most affected by the AIDS epidemic."[18]

Crimp's argument stood in tense relationship with the history of the gay and lesbian left. On the one hand, his call for a "relational" view of identity resonated strongly with two decades of activism that had continually redefined sexual freedoms through opposition to US imperialism and war. Implicitly, Crimp echoed the claim that Tede Matthews had embraced from the early 1970s forward. But Crimp did not acknowledge the gay and lesbian left as part of the background of queer critique; in fact, the perceived absence of the gay and lesbian left was key to his argument. Crimp narrated a capsule history of gay and lesbian politics in three stages: first, gay liberation was sparked through "identification with other political movements," principally Black Power and feminism; second, gay liberation split apart as it failed to sustain radical alliances, reducing it to two narrower modes of either "essentialist separatism" or a "liberal politics of minority rights"; third, "the AIDS crisis brought us face to face with the consequences of both our separatism and our liberalism," triggering queer activists to remake the original affiliations seen in gay liberation.[19] Crimp's account relied on exceptionalist views of both Stonewall and ACT UP as isolated, spontaneous vehicles of change.

Certainly, both separatism and liberal rights have been long-standing strands of gay and lesbian politics, and both gained strength between Stonewall and ACT UP. But Crimp was incorrect to present them as the only modes of politics developed in the 1970s or 1980s. Throughout those decades, gay and lesbian leftists challenged both separatism and liberalism, crafting a broader, more complex, and more sustained array of politics than Crimp understood. The gay and lesbian left continued the "identification with other political movements" that Crimp believed was practiced only at the outset of gay liberation. It had been "rethinking identity politics" for decades by defining sexual liberation through radical solidarity. It offered queer politics a genealogy, even if that was a genealogy Crimp did not know.

This is not to say that the gay and lesbian left was simply queer politics by another name, or vice versa. By and large, gay and lesbian leftists only sometimes embraced destabilized views of gender and sexuality. They generally failed to incorporate, and in some cases expressed criticism of, bisexual and transgender identities, butch-femme expression, and BDSM. Likewise, queer activists of the 1990s did not always pursue multi-issue radicalism. A single-issue view of sexual politics especially appeared in Queer Nation, which emerged out of ACT UP New York in 1990 and then mushroomed to other cities. San Francisco's Queer Nation was active from June 1990 through 1991 and produced an offshoot, the San

Francisco Street Patrol, that lasted through 1992. Queer Nation's street theater, marked by "mall invasions" and kiss-ins, powerfully claimed public space and challenged the everyday nature of heterosexual privilege and hostility. Yet, as Cathy Cohen argues, the group relied on "simple dichotomies between the heterosexual and everything 'queer'" that failed to distinguish heterosexuality from heteronormativity or to consider how all sexualities are stratified by and intersected through race, class, and gender.[20] Christina Hanhardt adds that the San Francisco Street Patrol supported "draconian policing" and relied on racialized, classed constructions of crime to "bash back" against harassment and violence.[21] Invested in public expressions of sexuality and mobilizing through militant anger, Queer Nation differed sharply from both the "gay nationalism" of 1970s Alpine County and the "homonationalism" of the post-9/11 era. But it relied on white and middle-class definitions of both "straight" and "queer," and aspects of its work defined sexual freedom and safety in alliance with US state violence.

Building on her critique of Queer Nation, Cathy Cohen calls for a different kind of queer politics, one "inclusive of all those who stand on the outside of the dominant constructed norm of state-sanctioned white middle- and upper-class heterosexuality."[22] Her "outside" includes not only all those who identify as other than heterosexual, but also those whose heterosexuality is racialized and classed as pathological or unworthy of respect. Cohen specifically brings mothers on welfare, people in jails and prisons, and the so-called "underclass" into queer politics. Recognizing this expansive potential of "queer" challenges the shape-shifting discourses of perversity, criminality, and dependence. While Cohen ties herself explicitly to left critique, she does not simply resuscitate a gay and lesbian left vision; rather, she names a power in queer radicalism that remained obscured in activism relying on more stable conceptions of "gay" and "lesbian" as well as "black" or "Central American." Expanding on Douglas Crimp's analysis, Cohen suggests that radical change becomes most powerful when it remakes not simply the content but the structure of belonging: "The multiplicity and interconnectedness of our identities . . . provide the most promising avenue for the *destabilization and radical politicization* of these same categories."[23] By focusing on such multiplicity and interconnectedness, we can approach our identities as not fixed but "strategically oriented," defined from a "shared marginal relationship to dominant power that normalizes, legitimizes, and privileges."[24] Roderick Ferguson's queer of color critique offers another way to name this sexual politics.[25]

Over the past several years many queer and trans radicals, especially queer and trans people of color, have answered calls like Cohen's by voicing ever stronger and clearer refusals of intertwined sexual, racial, gender, and class norms. They have built a radical queer politics that works against gentrification and privatization and for economic justice, immigrant rights, prison abolition, and Palestinian solidarity. Like the gay and lesbian left, recent queer radicalism stands as both a product of and a challenge to its broader context. The gay and lesbian left grew out of the Cold War and drew on socialist feminism and Third World internationalism. Contemporary queer radicalism emerges against a neoliberalism that would swallow it whole, and it gains power from what Chris Dixon observes as the convergence of "anti-racist feminism, prison abolitionism, and anarchism" in radical activism writ large.[26] That convergence can be seen through markers both inside and outside the United States, including the Zapatista uprising in Chiapas, Mexico, in 1994 and the anti-globalization protests at the World Trade Organization in Seattle in 1999; the 1998 Critical Resistance conference, which fostered a dramatic growth in anti-prison organizing; the 2000 gathering Color of Violence, which produced the radical women of color network INCITE!; and post-9/11 organizing against war, Islamophobia, and xenophobia.[27] More recently, the transformations of 2011—Arab Spring, the Occupy movement, and multiple global protests against austerity—have pulled a new generation toward anti-capitalist critique and exposed many to decentralized models of organizing.

Certainly, while queer people have been a strong presence across many recent movements, there remains a difference between queer participation in radicalism generally and the creation of a new queer radicalism itself—even one that uses the expansive definition of "queer" that Cathy Cohen identifies. But this is indeed what stands out as emerging in the past several years: activists have increasingly crafted a queer politics that is unmistakably queer-identified, that is a site of community built through sexuality and gender, and that is woven tightly into a broader radical grid. Multiple markers speak to this shift.

One important turning point came in 2008, when the simultaneous election of President Barack Obama and voter approval of California's anti–gay marriage Proposition 8 prompted some observers to declare that "gay is the new black."[28] Compelled to counter such specious comparisons between race and sexuality, a broad range of queer activists sharpened their challenges to single-issue LGBT politics. Their responses ran alongside and intersected with transnational queer critiques organized through Palestinian solidarity, which gained strength through the first decade of the twenty-first century and especially following the 2008–9 Gaza War. Much as the Central American solidarity movement fueled gay and lesbian radicalism in the 1980s, queer radicalism today has been profoundly affected by Palestinian solidarity, especially the Boycott, Divestment, and Sanctions (BDS) movement, which calls for Israel to comply with international law by ending its occupation of the West Bank and Gaza Strip and respecting the rights of Palestinian residents and refugees. Queer activists have especially challenged "pinkwashing," a term used to name the Israeli government's effort to minimize criticism by emphasizing its limited tolerance for Israelis who are gay or lesbian. Critiques of pinkwashing have grown in response to the Israeli government's marketing campaign "Brand Israel," which promotes the country as welcoming to US, European, and Canadian gay tourists. Queers Undermining Israeli Terrorism (QUIT), created in 2000 as an outgrowth of San Francisco's LAGAI, began in 2007 to pressure the Frameline LGBT Film Festival to refuse sponsorship from the Israeli consulate, and won temporary success in 2008 and 2009. A similar network, Queers Against Israeli Apartheid, is active in Seattle, Toronto, New York, Chicago, Auckland, and other cities; the Seattle chapter of Jewish Voices for Peace is predominately queer; and in Palestinian society queer radicals organize through al-Qaws, Aswat, and Palestinian Queers for BDS.[29]

Another turning point for queer radicalism, particularly in the United States, could be seen in 2012 and 2013 with the rise of "undocuqueer" activism, the campaign to free Chelsea Manning, and the growth of Black Lives Matter. Undocuqueer activism describes immigrant organizers, principally youth and young adults, who claim identities as both queer and undocumented. These leaders have adapted queer strategies of coming out to challenge the stigma attached to undocumented immigration status, and they have demanded an end to the legal, economic, and social consequences of being undocumented as well as of violating norms of sexuality and gender. They have also pushed larger immigrant rights groups to be more attentive to queer politics, winning a significant collaboration between the Not1More campaign against immigrant deportation and the smaller group Familia: TransQueer Liberation Movement. Responding to widespread gender and sexual violence in detention centers and transgender immigrants' calls for asylum, Not1More has demanded the release of transgender and many other detainees and highlighted transgender and queer immigrants' vulnerabilities amidst deportation.[30] In spring 2015 the campaign played an important role in winning freedom for Guatemalan immigrant Nicoll Hernandez-Polanco, a transgender woman who had been subjected to repeated rape and harassment from both guards and other immigrants while she was held in a detention facility in Arizona, and it backed activist Jennicet Gutierrez when she challenged President Obama regarding queer immigrants' detention.[31]

In summer 2013 US Army intelligence specialist Chelsea Manning was convicted under the Espionage Act for revealing the extent of US-sponsored torture, contractor abuse, and civilian deaths in Afghanistan and Iraq. Manning had identified publicly as gay for a number of years, and she came out as transgender the day after she was sentenced in August 2013; her support campaign incorporated queer and trans recognition both before and after her gender announcement. In April 2013 Manning was selected as grand marshal of the San Francisco Pride parade, then saw this honor immediately revoked when the president of the Pride organization's board declared the nomination should "never have been allowed to happen."[32] Activists organized a support contingent anyway and selected Daniel Ellsberg—the former military analyst who released the Pentagon Papers in 1971, and who is straight—to accept the honor on Manning's behalf.[33] In the end, Manning's supporters formed the single-largest contingent in the parade, with some two thousand people marching behind a banner that read "Pride in Our Whistleblower." The eighty-two-year-old Ellsberg rode in a float, waving at the crowds and wearing a hot-pink feather boa.

At this writing, the most powerful recent expression of a new queer politics has come through Black Lives Matter. The co-creators of the hashtag #BlackLivesMatter—Alicia Garza, Patrisse Cullors, and Opal Tometi—have emphasized not only that Garza and Cullors identify as queer but also that gender and sexual regulation are central to how the "normality defined by White supremacy" devalues black lives.[34] In her "Herstory of #BlackLivesMatter," Garza writes that "Black Lives Matter affirms the lives of Black queer and trans folks, disabled folks, Black undocumented folks, folks with records, women and all Black lives along the gender spectrum. It centers those that have been marginalized within Black liberation movements. It is a tactic to (re)build the Black liberation movement." In her claiming of "herstory," Garza insists on the authorship and leadership of black queer women and pushes back against the gendered, sexualized, classed, and racialized politics of black respectability. As she notes, she, Cullors, and Tometi created the hashtag #BlackLivesMatter after "17-year-old Trayvon Martin was posthumously placed on trial for his own murder and the killer, George Zimmerman, was not held accountable for the crime." Martin's "posthumous trial" attacked him for such offenses as wearing a hoodie sweatshirt and using marijuana, and while Martin was himself heterosexual and cis-gender, Black Lives Matter has shown that attacks on his character were inextricable from larger and racialized panics about sexual and gender norms. It has exposed links between hysteria over sagging pants, attempts to justify police murders, and laws against what activist Monica Jones and others term "walking while trans."[35] Through Garza, Cullors, and Tometi; through the strongly queer Black Youth Project (BYP) 100; and through many other dimensions of its decentralized work, the Black Lives Matter movement answers Cohen's call to bring the so-called "underclass" into queer politics. It bridges queer critique with many earlier dimensions of black liberation, including Ella Baker's insistence that civil rights activists must "reach out to the town drunk" and the Black Panther Party's goal of organizing the "brothers on the block."[36]

Black Lives Matter, bolstered by related efforts such as #SayHerName and #SayTheirNames, reminds us that both Lamia Beard, a transgender black woman in Norfolk, and Tanisha Anderson, a cisgender black woman in Cleveland, have been among those killed by vigilantes and police. It clarifies that discourses of thugs and riots are also discourses about parenting, family, and sexuality and that the criminalization of child support was one of the many reasons North Charleston resident Walter Scott had cause to run from police.[37] Alicia Garza accentuates this point when she frames anti-black racism as the hinge in a broader system. Indeed, speaking to nonblack people in much the same terms Cathy Cohen speaks to those who are straight, she affirms that "#Black-LivesMatter doesn't mean your life isn't important—it means that Black lives, which are seen as without value within White supremacy, are important to your liberation. . . . When Black people get free, everybody gets free." Reflecting the importance that Black Lives Matter holds to a wide range of queer activists, San Francisco Pride selected Alicia Garza as community grand marshal in 2015 and Black Lives Matter as organizational grand marshal in 2016, and it designated its 2016 theme as "For Racial and Economic Justice." Significantly, the SFPD implemented an unprecedented level of policing at 2016 Pride, which occurred two weeks after the gun massacre at Pulse nightclub in Orlando. In response, Black Lives Matter-Bay Area and two of the year's other grand marshals, trans and prison activist Janetta Johnson and the sex worker organization St. James Infirmary, withdrew from Pride events, citing concern over the harm police might bring to their members and other people of color. The Pride board expressed support for their decision, stating, "Increasing police presence in our community is not the solution."[38]

The historical gay and lesbian left differs in significant ways from the queer activism of the present. Although the earlier movement was committed to demonstrations of anti-imperialism and anti-militarism, it proved inconsistent in its analysis of racism and its membership remained largely white. By contrast, a commitment to people of color leadership and an understanding of racism in and as state violence have become central to contemporary queer radical critique. Such differences between past and present should not be overlooked; rather, we should seek to understand them in greater depth by pursuing more histories of radical activism.

In both its successes and its missteps, the history of the gay and lesbian left offers us a host of lessons today. One of these rests in the movement's commitment to imagine a world beyond the present—to imagine something else. Fighting back against attack—saying "no" to what we do not want—is absolutely necessary but can never be enough. The gay and lesbian left not only challenged repression but imagined and pursued the future, as through its efforts toward socialist feminism, its backing of a revolutionary underground, and its work in solidarity with Nicaragua. Aspirations for a new world sustained its work for change.

Second, internationalism and transnationalism were central to the gay and lesbian left's aspirational power. Gay and lesbian leftists understood that sexual regulation was imbricated with racism, imperialism, and war, and this understanding advanced their work toward radical sexual politics. Contemporary queer organizing can be strengthened by laying claim to this vision.

The history of the gay and lesbian left also cautions us to consider the gaps that appear as certain locations of struggle begin to appear less relevant or assaults seem to fade. It is striking that US lesbian, gay, bisexual, transgender, and queer radicals' awareness of Central American politics virtually evaporated after the late 1980s, leaving few sustained connections. Nicaragua's current, and now neoliberal, Sandinista government is isolating feminist activists and pursuing a massively privatized interocean canal, yet transnational queer links with Nicaragua seem nowhere to be found today. Likewise, in 2009, responses were scarce when the US-backed coup in Honduras led to harsh persecution of LGBT people there. We must question what makes some sites of solidarity attractive while others are left ignored, and continually assess our practices of solidarity lest they become inattentive or narcissistic.

Ultimately, the history of the gay and lesbian left underscores the transformative potential of sexual politics and of the rethinking of identity writ large. Identity can summon powerful affiliations with others precisely because it can be continually remade. This malleability is both an opportunity and a challenge; now as in the past, queer people who are privileged by race, nation, or class may not see themselves as "getting free" with others who do not look like them, live like them, or experience police stops or border checkpoints as they do. As privileges expand for some, previous radical affiliations will surely change. Yet we can seize new affiliations, and make new futures, by understanding and critically using our queer pasts.

Notes

1. Reagan's action occurred on the same day Oliver North and other defendants were indicted on Iran-Contra charges. In the ensuing two weeks activists staged more than two hundred protests in 150 US cities. Christian Smith, *Resisting Reagan: the U.S. Central America Peace Movement* (Chicago: University of Chicago Press, 1996), 85; and Doyle McManus and David Lauter, "Statements on Honduras Stir Skepticism in Congress," *Los Angeles Times*, March 19, 1988. On Bay Area gay and lesbian participation, see Tede Matthews, "Coming Out for Peace: Lesbians and Gays Play Major Role in Protests," *San Francisco Sentinel* (April 8, 1988), 8; and "Gays, Lesbians Spearhead Peace Demos," *San Francisco Sentinel* (March 25, 1988), 3.

2. Raphael, Gonzalez, and Matthews, quoted in Matthews, "Coming Out for Peace," 14.

3. On the concept of scales, see Neil Smith, "Contours of a Spatialized Politics," *Social Text* 33 (1992): 55–81.

4. In Britain, the gay left found particularly important expression in the latter 1970s through the publication *Gay Left,* the best-known member of whose staff was Jeffrey Weeks. During the UK miners' strike of the mid-1980s, lesbian and gay leftists organized Lesbians and Gays Support the Miners (LGSM), recently celebrated in the film *Pride* (2014) and resuscitated since 2015 as Lesbians and Gays Support the Migrants. See Emily K. Hobson, "Pits and Perverts: A Review of *Pride,*" Outhistory blog, November 13, 2014; Diarmaid Kelliher, "Solidarity and Sexuality: Lesbians and Gays Support the Miners 1984–5," *History Workshop Journal* 77 (spring 2014): 240–62.

5. Roger Harkenrider, quoted in *Word Is Out: Stories of Some of Our Lives,* dir. Mariposa Film Group (New Yorker Films, 1977).

6. On the Gay Liberation Theater, see chapter 1; on Stonewall and the Gay Liberation Front, see, especially, Martin Duberman, *Stonewall* (New York: Penguin, 1993); Terrence Kissack, "Freaking Fag Revolutionaries: New York's Gay Liberation Front, 1969–1971," *Radical History Review* 62 (1995): 104–34; KC Diwas, "Of Consciousness and Criticism: Identity in the Intersections of the Gay Liberation Front and the Young Lords Party" (MA thesis, Department of Women's History, Sarah Lawrence College, 2005); and David Carter, *Stonewall: The Revolution That Sparked the Gay Revolution* (New York: St. Martin's Griffin, 2010).

7. Konstantin Berlandt, "Konstantin Berlandt in FANTASYLAND," *Gay Sunshine* 7 (June–July 1971), 14.

8. Multiple organizations—for example, the Lavender & Red Union, the Lavender Left, and the Workers World Party—used or use the metaphor "lavender and red." However, no one group or ideological formation can claim the phrase as its own.

9. Roderick Ferguson, *Aberrations in Black: Toward a Queer of Color Critique* (Minneapolis: University of Minnesota Press, 2004), 126–27.

10. The term "intersectionality" was coined by Kimberlé Crenshaw, in "Demarginalizing the Intersection of Race and Sex: A Black Feminist Critique of Antidiscrimination Doctrine, Feminist Theory, and Antiracist Politics," *University of Chicago Legal Forum* 1989:1 (1989): 139–67; and "Mapping the Margins: Intersectionality, Identity Politics, and Violence against Women of Color," *Stanford Law Review* 43: 6 (1991): 1241–99. It is important to note here that Ferguson does not simply continue women of color feminism. Rather, he cites it as central to his concept of "queer of color critique" and thereby expands the breadth of intersectional analysis. Queer of color critique draws on Marxist analysis and sociology but rejects those traditions' tendencies to view queer black subjects as "deviant" or "pathological." Here Ferguson draws extensively on José Esteban Muñoz's concept of "disidentification"; see, for example, Ferguson, *Aberrations in Black*, 4, 8, 11.

11. Gloria Anzaldúa and Cherríe Moraga, eds., *This Bridge Called My Back: Writings by Radical Women of Color*, 2nd ed. (San Francisco: Kitchen Table Press, 1983; 1st ed., Watertown, MA: Persephone Press, 1981).

12. See, for example, David Deitcher, ed., *The Question of Equality: Lesbian and Gay Politics in America since Stonewall* (New York: Scribner, 1995); Elizabeth Armstrong, *Forging Gay Identities: Organizing Sexuality in San Francisco, 1950–1994* (Chicago: University of Chicago, 2002).

13. My thanks to one of my anonymous manuscript readers, who used the term "Stonewall exceptionalism" to describe my draft of this argument.

14. Paul Buhle coined the term "good sixties/bad sixties" to summarize Todd Gitlin's argument in Gitlin's *Years of Protest, Days of Rage* (New York: Bantam, 1993); Paul Buhle, "Madison Revisited," *Radical History Review* 57 (1993): 248. A declension narrative is apparent in popular memory and in much other scholarship on the period, including James Miller, *Democracy Is in the Streets: From Port Huron to the Siege of Chicago* (Cambridge, MA: Harvard University Press, 1987); David Farber, *The Age of Great Dreams: America in the 1960s* (New York: Hill and Wang, 1994). See also Andrew Hunt, "'When

Did the Sixties Happen?': Searching for New Directions," *Journal of Social History* 33: 1 (1999): 147–61.

15. See, especially, Nikhil Pal Singh, *Black Is a Country: Race and the Unfinished Struggle for Democracy* (Cambridge, MA: Harvard University Press, 2004); Cynthia Young, *Soul Power: Culture, Radicalism, and the Making of a U.S. Third World Left* (Durham, NC: Duke University Press, 2006); Vijay Prashad, *The Darker Nations: A People's History of the Third World* (New York: The New Press, 2007); Dan Berger, *Captive Nation: Black Prison Organizing in the Civil Rights Era* (Chapel Hill: University of North Carolina Press, 2014); Laura Pulido, *Black, Brown, Yellow, and Left: Radical Activism in Los Angeles* (Berkeley: University of California Press, 2005); Benita Roth, *Separate Roads to Feminism: Black, Chicana, and White Feminist Movements in America's Second Wave* (Cambridge: Cambridge University Press, 2004); Kimberly Springer, *Living for the Revolution: Black Feminist Organizations, 1968–1990* (Durham, NC: Duke University Press, 2005); Maylei Blackwell, *¡Chicana Power! Contested Histories of Feminism in the Chicana Movement* (Austin: University of Texas Press, 2011). Two other important works relevant to the Bay Area are Daryl J. Maeda, *Chains of Babylon: The Rise of Asian America* (Minneapolis: University of Minnesota Press, 2009); and Jason Ferreira, "'With the Soul of a Human Rainbow': Los Siete, Black Panthers, and Third Worldism in San Francisco," in *Ten Years That Shook the City: San Francisco, 1968– 1978*, ed. Chris Carlsson (San Francisco: City Lights Books, 2011): 30–47.

16. Three examples are Tede Matthews and Simeon White, both discussed in this book, and Tommi Avicolli Mecca, who lived in Philadelphia during the period this book addresses but later moved to San Francisco. Mecca is now an important housing and anti-gentrification activist.

17. Aaron Lecklider, "Coming to Terms: Homosexuality and the Left in American Culture," *GLQ: A Journal of Lesbian and Gay Studies* 18: 1 (2012): 179–95; other especially useful work includes Daniel Hurewitz, *Bohemian Los Angeles and the Making of Modern Politics* (Berkeley: University of California Press, 2007); Gary Holcomb, *Claude McKay, Code Name Sasha: Queer Black Marxism and the Harlem Renaissance* (Gainesville: University Press of Florida, 2009); Dayo Gore, "Making Space for Pauli Murray: Transformations in Queer Politics and a Queer Life," paper presented at the annual meeting of the American Historical Association, January 2, 2015 (New York, New York).

18. Peter Drucker, "Introduction: Remapping Sexualities," in *Different Rainbows*, ed. Drucker (London: Gay Men's Press, 2000), 34.

19. M. Jacqui Alexander, "Not Just (Any) Body Can Be a Citizen: The Politics of Law, Sexuality and Postcoloniality in Trinidad and Tobago and the Bahamas," *Feminist Review* 48 (fall 1994): 5–23.

20. Lillian Guerra, "Gender Policing, Homosexuality, and the New Patriarchy of the Cuban Revolution, 1965–70," *Social History* 35: 3 (August 2010): 268–89; Julio Capó Jr., "Queering Mariel: Mediating Cold War Foreign Policy and U.S. Citizenship among Cuba's Homosexual Exile Community, 1978– 1994," *Journal of American Ethnic History* 29: 4 (summer 2010), 78–106; Ian K. Lekus, "Queer Harvests: Homosexuality, the U.S. New Left, and the Venceremos Brigades to Cuba," *Radical History Review* 89 (spring 2004): 57–91.

21. Lekus, "Queer Harvests," 61.

22. On the remaking of sex, see Patrick Moore, *Beyond Shame: Reclaiming the Abandoned History of Radical Gay Sexuality* (Boston: Beacon Press, 2004).

23. The original phrasing was apparently "feminism is a theory, lesbianism is a practice"; see Nancy Chater and Lilith Finkler, "'Traversing Wide Territories': A Journey from Lesbianism to Bisexuality," in *Plural Desires: Writing Bisexual Realities,* ed. Bisexual Anthology Collective (Toronto: Sister Vision Press, 1995), 36. I use the formulation with "the" because it became better known and therefore carried greater influence. While Ti-Grace Atkinson is not central to this book, her mentorship within black feminism, traced in Sherie Randolph's biography of Flo Kennedy, reflected dynamics similar to those that structured the gay and lesbian left. Sherie M. Randolph, *Florynce "Flo" Kennedy: The Life of a Black Feminist Radical* (Chapel Hill: University of North Carolina Press, 2015).

24. Raymond Williams, *Keywords: A Vocabulary of Culture and Society* (New York: Oxford University Press, 1976); Bruce Burgett and Glenn Hendler, eds., *Keywords for American Cultural Studies* (New York University Press, 2007).

25. In addition to the citations above, see Becky Thompson, "Multiracial Feminism: Recasting the Chronology of Second Wave Feminism," *Feminist Studies* 28:2 (2002), especially 338–341; Jennifer Nelson, *Women of Color and the Reproductive Rights Movement* (New York: New York University Press, 2003); Anne M. Valk, *Radical Sisters: Second-Wave Feminism and Black Liberation in Washington, D.C.* (Urbana: University of Illinois Press, 2008).

26. Cary Cordova, "The Mission in Nicaragua: San Francisco Poets Go to War," in *Beyond el Barrio: Everyday Life in Latina/o America,* ed. Gina M. Pérez, Frank Guridy, and Adrian Burgos (New York: New York University Press, 2010), 211–32.

27. Most of those with whom I spoke who described themselves as bisexual were women, but a few were men. The total number of those describing themselves in this way was just a handful. Whenever someone mentioned a bisexual identity or sexual practice, I asked if they wanted me to note this in the book; none asked me to do so. (In addition, all interviewees quoted were provided excerpts of the manuscript citing them in order to obtain corrections of fact.) My questions about how to name sexual identity consistently produced interesting discussions about sexual labels and fluidity. Some of my interviewees suggested that the labels "lesbian" and "gay" could function much like "queer" to name a range of sexual practices, including bisexuality, along with a generally radical sexual politics. Most drew distinctions between political affiliations and sexual behavior and felt that participants in "lesbian," "gay," and "queer" activism might be presumed to have a range of sexual practices. In general, although my interviewees struck me as fairly unconcerned about whether readers might presume anything specific about their sex lives, most suggested that the boundaries between lesbian, gay, and bisexual identities were more fraught in the 1970s, 1980s, and 1990s than now.

28. According to the census, the populations of San Francisco, Oakland, and Berkeley were fairly flat from 1970 to 1990—San Francisco roughly 715,000,

Oakland 350,000, and Berkeley 100,000. For detailed census figures, see the Bay Area Census compiled by the Metropolitan Transportation Commission and Association of Bay Area Governments (www.bayareacensus.ca.gov). In general, census numbers should be treated carefully as they offer only limited insight into dynamics of outmigration, undocumented immigration, homelessness, and imprisonment.

29. This is to say that noting the presence or absence of queer people of color is not the same as analyzing the distinctive goals or logics of queer of color activism. See Kevin J. Mumford, *Not Straight, Not White: Black Gay Men from the March on Washington to the AIDS Crisis* (Chapel Hill: University of North Carolina Press, 2016).

CHAPTER 1. BEYOND THE GAY GHETTO

1. "Brothers Slain," *Berkeley Tribe* (August 28–September 4, 1970), 3.

2. Stevens, *San Francisco Free Press* 1:4 (November 1–14, 1969); "No Vietnamese Ever Called Me a Queer!" flier, Thorpe File, San Francisco History Center, San Francisco Public Library (hereafter cited as Thorpe File, SFPL).

3. Hay resigned his membership in the CPUSA shortly before founding Mattachine in response to the Communist Party's ban on homosexual members. However, he remained in contact with many in the Los Angeles left, including the Civil Rights Congress. Emily K. Hobson, "Policing Gay LA: Mapping Racial Divides in the Homophile Era, 1950–1967," in *The Rising Tide of Color: Race, State Violence, and Radical Movements across the Pacific*, ed. Moon-Ho Jung (Seattle: University of Washington Press, 2014), 189–212.

4. Marc Stein, "Canonizing Homophile Sexual Respectability: Archives, History, and Memory," *Radical History Review* 120 (fall 2014): 53–73.

5. Nan Alamilla Boyd, *Wide Open Town: A History of Queer San Francisco to 1965* (Berkeley: University of California Press, 2005); for another example, see Hobson, "Policing Gay LA."

6. Timothy Stewart-Winter argues that division between homophile organizing and queer street life was less present in Chicago, in part because of the severity of police abuse; relatedly, he finds that homophile and gay liberation groups maintained common ground across the 1960s and 1970s by challenging the police. See Timothy Stewart-Winter, *Queer Clout: Chicago and the Rise of Gay Politics* (Philadelphia: University of Pennsylvania Press, 2016). Another way to analyze homophile and gay liberationist divides is to track individual activists' stories. Some homophile activists who were more radical, particularly on issues of militarism and race, moved into gay liberation groups, making homophile groups more conservative through their departure.

7. These practices have been widely discussed; see especially Jeffrey Escoffier, "The Political Economy of the Closet," in *Homo Economics: Capitalism, Community, and Gay and Lesbian Life*, ed. Amy Gluckman and Betsy Reed (New York: Routledge, 1997), 128.

8. Bob Damron quoted in ibid.

9. Susan Stryker, *Transgender History* (Berkeley, CA: Seal Press, 2008), 67–69.

10. Christina B. Hanhardt, *Safe Space: Gay Neighborhood History and the Politics of Violence* (Durham, NC: Duke University Press, 2013); for further context, see Christopher Lowen Agee, *The Streets of San Francisco: Policing and the Creation of a Cosmopolitan Liberal Politics, 1950–1972* (Chicago: University of Chicago Press, 2014). Stewart-Winter finds that the black press in Chicago sympathetically discussed police exploitation of queer life, and he argues that the black press may have posed analogies between race and sexuality before homophile activists did; Stewart-Winter, *Queer Clout*, 65.

11. *Screaming Queens: The Riot at Compton's Cafeteria*, dir. Victor Silverman and Susan Stryker (San Francisco: Independent Television Service [ITVS], 2005); Stryker, *Transgender History*, 64–65.

12. Stryker, *Transgender History*, 75–76.

13. On boundary marking around transgender identities, see David Valentine, *Imagining Transgender: An Ethnography of a Category* (Durham, NC: Duke University Press, 2007); and Susan Stryker, "(De)Subjugated Knowledges: An Introduction to Transgender Studies," in *The Transgender Studies Reader* [I], ed. Susan Stryker and Stephen Whittle (New York: Routledge, 2006): 1–17.

14. Boyd, *Wide Open Town*; Josh Sides, *Erotic City: Sexual Revolutions and the Making of Modern San Francisco* (New York: Oxford University Press, 2010). By the late 1970s the neighboring Mission District would follow the Castro as a heavily lesbian area in which lesbian community became a vector for debates over gentrification; see Hanhardt, *Safe Space*.

15. Hanhardt, *Safe Space*, 81.

16. Donna Jean Murch, *Living for the City: Migration, Education, and the Rise of the Black Panther Party in Oakland, California* (Chapel Hill: University of North Carolina Press, 2010), 8, 141.

17. Ibid., 6. Robyn Spencer notes that the rhetoric of self-defense spoke in particular ways to Panther women; see, especially, Robyn C. Spencer, "Engendering the Black Freedom Struggle: Revolutionary Black Womanhood and the Black Panther Party in the Bay Area, California," *Journal of Women's History* 20:1 (spring 2008): 90–113, as well as her forthcoming work *The Revolution Has Come: Black Power, Gender, and the Black Panther Party in Oakland* (Durham, NC: Duke University Press, 2016).

18. Murch, *Living for the City*, 133.

19. Ibid., 148.

20. Ibid., 153.

21. Joshua Bloom and Waldo E. Martin Jr., *Black against Empire: The History and Politics of the Black Panther Party* (Berkeley: University of California Press, 2013), 272–83; Daryl Maeda, *Chains of Babylon: The Rise of Asian America* (Minneapolis: University of Minnesota, 2009).

22. Maeda, *Chains of Babylon*, 81.

23. "Homo Revolt: 'Don't Hide It,'" *Berkeley Barb* (March 28-April 3, 1969), 5; Hanhardt, *Safe Space*, 85.

24. Quoted in Betty Luther Hillman, "'The Most Profoundly Revolutionary Act a Homosexual Can Engage In': Drag and the Politics of Gender Presentation in the San Francisco Gay Liberation Movement, 1964–1972," *Journal of the History of Sexuality* 20:1 (January 2011): 178.

25. Susan Stryker and Jim Van Buskirk, *Gay by the Bay: A History of Queer Culture in the San Francisco Bay Area* (San Francisco: Chronicle Books, 1996), 53. See also Sides, *Erotic City*, 92–95.

26. CHF newsletters, one dated April 29, 1969, another undated, in Thorpe File, SFPL (capitalization in the original).

27. "Homo Revolt: 'Don't Hide It.'" See also Morgan Pinney, "Gay Liberation: a movement without a model," undated manuscript (c. 1971), Berlandt File, San Francisco History Center, SFPL, 3.

28. Wittman's biography is discussed in Ian K. Lekus, "Queer and Present Dangers: Homosexuality and American Anti-war Activism during the Vietnam Era," PhD dissertation, Duke University (2003); and in Mab Segrest, *Memoir of a Race Traitor* (Boston: South End Press, 1994). See also Wittman, "Us and the New Left," *Fag Rag*, 23–24 (fall 1978), 22–23. In 1974, Wittman founded a gay commune in Oregon; he also later published *RFD*, a magazine on rural gay life. He died in 1986 of complications from AIDS.

29. Carl Wittman, "A Gay Manifesto," in *Out of the Closets: Voices of Gay Liberation,* ed. Karla Jay and Allen Young (New York: Douglas, 1972), 330–42.

30. Ibid.

31. Varda Ono [One], "Come Together Right Now Over Us: Women's Liberation and Gay Liberation; An Alliance for the Seventies," *Gay Sunshine* 1:4 (December 1970): 3 (incorrect capitalization in the original). For a related critique, see Allan Bérubé, "How Gay Stays White and What Kind of White It Stays," in *My Desire for History: Essays in Gay, Community, and Labor History,* ed. John D'Emilio and Estelle B. Freedman (Chapel Hill: University of North Carolina Press, 2011): 202–30.

32. Mattachine convened two follow-up meetings on July 9 and 16; a non-Mattachine group first met on July 24 and adopted the name Gay Liberation Front at a meeting on July 31. The first GLF meetings were held at the Alternate U, used for multiple radical convenings at this time. Carter, *Stonewall*, 210–19.

33. Benjamin Shepherd, "Play as World-Making: From the Cockettes to the Germs, Gay Liberation to DIY Community Building," in *The Hidden 1970s: Histories of Radicalism,* ed. Dan Berger (New Brunswick, NJ: Rutgers University Press, 2010): 177–94.

34. Stryker and Van Buskirk, *Gay by the Bay,* 53; Sides, *Erotic City*, 96.

35. Committee for Homosexual Freedom/Gay Liberation Front flier, October 1969, Charles Thorpe Papers, 1987-02, GLBT Historical Society, San Francisco (hereafter Thorpe File, GLBTHS); also found in Ephemera–LGBT Groups, GLBTHS. The protest promoted in this flier became known as the "Friday of the Purple Hand" because *Examiner* staff threw purple printer's ink on gay activists, who then marked the *Examiner* building with purple handprints and were assaulted by police.

36. On the CHF's and Leo Laurence's use of masculinist rhetoric, see Betty Luther Hillman, *Dressing for the Culture Wars: Style and the Politics of Self-Presentation in the 1960s and 1970s* (Lincoln: University of Nebraska Press, 2015), 103, 111.

37. An early critique of the homophile movement as a "ghetto" appeared in Leo Ebreo, "A Homosexual Ghetto?" *The Ladder* (1965), reprinted in *We Are Everywhere: A Historical Sourcebook of Gay and Lesbian Politics,* ed. Mark Blasius and Shane Phelan (New York: Routledge, 1997), 340–43.

38. Quoted in Hillman, *Dressing for the Culture Wars,* 97.

39. "Gay . . . Gay?" flier, undated [late 1969], Thorpe File, SFPL (emphasis in original).

40. Chapter 6 of Jennifer Le Zotte, *From Goodwill to Grunge: Secondhand Economies and Styles* (Chapel Hill: University of North Carolina Press, forthcoming).

41. "Fuck the 'Human Rights Commission'!" (flier calling for GLF meeting on March 12 [1970]),Thorpe File, SFPL. As the citation of the Tenderloin suggested, these views of the gay ghetto also understood sex work as exploitation; Pinney, "Gay Liberation: a movement without a model," 17. For another use of "ghetto" to describe a gay neighborhood, see Stewart-Winter, *Queer Clout,* 103.

42. On minoritarian versus universalist conceptions of gayness, see Eve Sedgwick, *Epistemology of the Closet* (Berkeley: University of California Press, 1990); and Marc Stein, *City of Sisterly and Brotherly Loves: Lesbian and Gay Philadelphia, 1945–1972* (Philadelphia: Temple University Press, 2004).

43. Bérubé, "How Gay Stays White."

44. Justin David Suran, "Coming Out Against the War: Antimilitarism and the Politicization of Homosexuality in the Era of Vietnam," *American Quarterly* 53:3 (2001): 460.

45. Los Angeles GLF, "Revolutionary Homosexual Draft Resistance," n.d. 1970, Thorpe File, GLBTHS.

46. Robert O. Self, *All in the Family: The Realignment of American Democracy since the 1960s* (New York: Hill and Wang, 2013), 84–85, 96–97.

47. Suran, "Coming Out Against the War," 463.

48. Lekus, "Queer and Present Dangers," 5, 30. See also Gael Graham, "Flaunting the Freak Flag: *Karr v. Schmidt* and the Great Hair Debate in American High Schools, 1965–1975," *Journal of American History* 91:2 (September 2004): 522–43; and Ian K. Lekus, *Queer and Present Dangers: Masculinity, Sexuality, and the Sixties* (Chapel Hill: University of North Carolina Press, forthcoming).

49. Lekus, "Queer and Present Dangers," 38, 252.

50. "Bring the Beautiful Boys Home Now!" Vietnam Moratorium flier, n.d. [October 1969], Thorpe File, SFPL.

51. Gary Alinder, interview by Reid Condit, December 6, 1996, Voices of the Oral History Project of the GLBTHS, San Francisco (GLBTHS), 22. By late 1971 a smaller and less collectively run group, headed by Winston Leyland, seized control and continued to publish *Gay Sunshine* through 1982.

52. Benton also founded a short-lived gay liberation group called the Effeminists, which, among other proposals, held that antigay discrimination operated as a form of imperialism and that gay men ought to reject penetration of all kinds as anti-egalitarian. *The Effeminist,* no. 2 (c. 1969–1970), 1; Benton, "Sex-

ism, Racism, . . ." 4, and Benton, "gay is the most," *Gay Sunshine*, no. 2 (October 1970). Other dimensions of effeminism, less centered on Benton, revolved around childrearing and gay fatherhood; Daniel Winunwe Rivers, *Radical Relations: Lesbian Mothers, Gay Fathers, and Their Children in the United States since World War II* (Chapel Hill: University of North Carolina Press, 2013), 114–21.

53. "Boycott," *Berkeley Tribe* (September 18–25, 1970), 4. In October 1970, Benton became the first gay liberationist speaker at a major antiwar demonstration; Suran, "Coming Out Against the War," 453, 466, 473.

54. Hal Tarr, "A Consciousness Raised," in *Smash the Church, Smash the State! The Early Years of Gay Liberation,* ed. Tommi Avicolli Mecca (San Francisco: City Lights Books, 2009), 22. See also Stephen Vider, "'The Ultimate Extension of Gay Community': Communal Living and Gay Liberation in the 1970s," *Gender & History* 27:3 (November 2015): 865–81.

55. Tarr, "A Consciousness Raised," 29.

56. See Murch, *Living for the City,* 144; *Berger, Captive Nation;* Tracye Matthews, "'No One Ever Asks What a Man's Role in the Revolution Is': Gender Politics and Leadership in the Black Panther Party, 1966–1971," in *Sisters in the Struggle: African American Women in the Civil Rights-Black Power Movement,* ed. Bettye Collier and V. P. Franklin (New York: New York University, 2001), 230–55.

57. See, especially, Spencer, "Engendering the Black Freedom Struggle"; Murch, *Living for the City,* 169; and Bloom and Martin, *Black against Empire,* 302–3.

58. Ian K. Lekus, "Losing Our Kids: Queer Perspectives on the Chicago Seven Trial," in *The New Left Revisited,* ed. John McMillian and Paul Buhle (Philadelphia: Temple University Press, 2003): 199–213; Kissack, "Freaking Fag Revolutionaries"; John Knoebel, interview by Christopher de la Torre, "40 Years after Stonewall" series, July 2, 2009, https://christopherdelatorre.com.

59. Third World Gay Revolution, "What We Want, What We Believe," in *Out of the Closets,* 365–66; Red Butterfly, "Gay Liberation" (1970), Anson Reinhart Papers, GLBT Historical Society (GLBTHS), San Francisco (hereafter Reinhart Papers, GLBTHS); Pinney, "Gay Liberation: a movement without a model," 26. On the formation of Third World Gay Revolution in Chicago, see Stewart-Winter, *Queer Clout,* 91.

60. Members of the GLF and Radicalesbians at Antioch College in Yellow Springs, Ohio, issued a strong denunciation of the Brigades policy, arguing that most gay and lesbian people were working class but that economic privilege made it easier to come out (quoted in Lekus, "Queer and Present Dangers," 415). See also "Venceremos," *Gay Sunshine*, no. 1 (August 1970). Throughout 1971 and 1972 *Gay Sunshine* remained an important venue for discussions of gay socialism, of antigay exclusions in Cuba, and of Latin American sexual politics more generally; see Gay Committee of Returned Brigadistas, "North American Gays Protest," *Gay Sunshine*, no. 9 (October–November 1971), 2; "Letter from Cuba," *Gay Sunshine*, no. 15 (October–November 1972), 13; "Mexico G.L.F.," *Gay Sunshine*, no. 11 (February–March 1972), 2; "Argentina: GAY MANIFESTO," translated by Allen Young, *Gay Sunshine*,

no. 15 (October–November 1972), 7; Allen Young, "Gays in Brazil: 24/'Veado,'" *Gay Sunshine,* no. 13 (June 1972), 4; Allen Young, "¿Cuba Si?" *Gay Sunshine,* no. 13 (June 1972), 13; Zack Mansfield, "The Gay Soul of Socialism," *Gay Sunshine,* no. 15 (October–November 1972), 4.

61. Brigada Venceremos Policy on Gay Recruitment, 1972, Race-Class Articles folder, Sally Gearhart Papers, GLBT Historical Society (GLBTHS), San Francisco (hereafter Gearhart Papers, GLBTHS); Lekus, "Queer Harvests," 78; Lekus, "Queer and Present Dangers," 419–20. See also Guerra, "Gender Policing"; B. Ruby Rich and Lourdes Arguelles, "Homosexuality, Homophobia, and Revolution: Notes toward an Understanding of the Cuban Lesbian and Gay Male Experience, Part I," *Signs* 9:4 (1984): 683–99, and "Homosexuality, Homophobia, and Revolution: Notes toward an Understanding of the Cuban Lesbian and Gay Male Experience, Part II," *Signs* 11:1 (1985): 120–36; Roger Lancaster, *Life Is Hard: Machismo, Danger, and the Intimacy of Power in Nicaragua* (Berkeley: University of California Press, 1992), 253; and Ileana Rodriguez, *Women, Guerrillas, and Love: Understanding War in Central America* (Minneapolis: University of Minnesota Press, 1996).

62. Elsa Knight Tompson, interview with Huey Newton, KPFA, August 11, 1970, KP 020, Freedom Archives, San Francisco.

63. I follow the pagination of the reprint of "A Letter from Huey" in Len Richmond and Gary Noguera, eds., *The Gay Liberation Book: Writings and Photographs on Gay (Men's) Liberation* (San Francisco: Ramparts Press, 1973), 142–45.

64. Ibid., 143.

65. Bloom and Martin, *Black against Empire,* 306. See also Amy Abugo Ongiri, "Prisoner of Love: Affiliation, Sexuality, and the Black Panther Party," *Journal of African American History* 94:1 (winter 2009): 69–86.

66. GLF Los Angeles Press Release (Don Kilhefner and Tony de Rosa), October 6, 1970, Thorpe File, GLBTHS.

67. Knoebel, interview by de la Torre.

68. Stein, *City of Sisterly and Brotherly Loves,* 333; see also Marc Stein, "'Birthplace of the Nation': Imagining Lesbian and Gay Communities in Philadelphia, 1969–70," in *Creating a Place for Ourselves,* ed. Brett [Genny] Beemyn (New York: Routledge, 1997), 253–88; and George Katsiaficas, "Organization and Movement: The Case of the Black Panther Party and the Revolutionary People's Constitutional Convention of 1970," in *Liberation, Imagination, and the Black Panther Party: A New Look at the Panthers and Their Legacy,* ed. Kathleen Cleaver and George Katsiaficas (New York: Routledge, 2001), 145.

69. Registration Form (Revolutionary People's Plenary Session), Revolutionary Peoples Constitutional Convention, Berkeley Free Church Collection (GTU 89-5-016), Graduate Theological Union Archives, Berkeley, CA.

70. Katsiaficas, "Organization and Movement," 142, 146.

71. Stein, "'Birthplace of the Nation,'" 268; Knoebel, interview by de la Torre.

72. Katsiaficas, "Organization and Movement," 147.

73. Ibid., 149; Revolutionary Peoples Constitutional Convention materials, Berkeley Free Church Collection (GTU 89-5-016).

74. Martha Shelley, "Subversion in the Women's Movement: What is To Be Done?" n.d. [c. 1970], Indo-Chinese Women's Conference Folder 3, Anne Roberts Women's Movement Collection Fund, Simon Fraser University (courtesy Judy Tzu-Chun Wu).

75. "Gay Sisters Speak," *Berkeley Tribe* (October 30–November 6, 1970), 8–9; Stein, *City of Sisterly and Brotherly Loves,* 336; "Gay Sisters Speak." See also "Woman-Identified Women" [report on RPCC], Indo-Chinese Women's Conference Folder 3, Anne Roberts Women's Movement Collection Fund, an account of the lesbian workshop at the Panthers' RPCC that was signed by New York Radicalesbians Marlene Elkin, Donna Gottschald, Lois Hart, Brenda Howard, Arlene Kisner, Debbie Muldovan, and "Shoshana" (a pseudonym likely used to honor Patricia Swinton, a white radical implicated in a series of political bombings in 1969 and who by 1970 lived underground under that alias).

76. See, for example, "Gay Workshop," *Berkeley Tribe* (November 13–20, 1970), 11.

77. "Let Freedom Ring," *Berkeley Tribe* (November 13–20, 1970), 4; "Regional Conference" [report], *Berkeley Tribe* (November 20–27, 1970), 13; Barbara, Karen & Sally, "Washington: Two Views," *Berkeley Tribe* (December 12–19, 1970), 8. A group of predominately white women, many of them lesbian, had also held their own meeting at Glide Memorial Church a few weeks before the Regional Conference; see "women-identified-women," *Berkeley Tribe* (November 6–13, 1970), 5.

78. Stein, *City of Sisterly and Brotherly Loves,* 339.

79. Barbara, Karen & Sally, "Washington: Two Views." These activists also conducted a protest at a local bar where a man wearing lipstick had been refused service. At the bar, employees and patrons attacked two black gay men and a Puerto Rican gay man; a fight ensued and police arrested a group that became termed the "DC 12." Local GLFers continued to protest these arrests until the DC 12 were released a month later; see Hal Tarr, "A Consciousness Raised," in *Smash the Church, Smash the State!* 25.

80. Barbara, Karen & Sally, "Washington: Two Views"; "Conceiving a New Nation," *Berkeley Tribe* (December 12–19, 1970), 10.

81. "Brother Don Has a Dream," undated flier (clipping from *Los Angeles Free Press,* June 1970), Thorpe File, GLBTHS. See also Paul Eberle, "Gays plan to liberate a county," *Los Angeles Free Press,* October 25, 1970 (n.p.).

82. "Brother Don Has a Dream" and "Help Build the Stonewall Nation," Thorpe File, GLBTHS. "Help Build the Stonewall Nation" calls for September 20, 1970, meeting in Los Angeles.

83. This population and geography information is reported in the Alpine Liberation Front information packet, Thorpe File, GLBTHS. This packet also states that the county's total population included 298 Washoe Indian people. The California census for 1970 is recorded as counting 484 total residents, 367 of whom were white, 97 Native American, 19 Filipina/o (mostly men), and 1 African American (a man). While it is certainly possible that Washoe people were undercounted in the census, it remains unclear where ALF activists found the figure of 298 Washoe residents.

84. "The Great Gay Conspiracy," *San Francisco Examiner,* October 18, 1970; "Brother Don Has a Dream," and "Alpine Liberation" flier, Thorpe File, GLBTHS.

85. "Brother Don Has a Dream."

86. "Homosexuals Weigh Move to Alpine County," *Los Angeles Times* (October 19, 1970), 3.

87. Alpine County Project, file II (of two files), Subject Files Collection, ONE National Gay and Lesbian Archives, Los Angeles (hereafter ACP [file no.], ONE); Charles Foley, "The Gay Front plans a takeover," *London Observer* November 29, 1970, ACP file I, ONE.

88. Lee Dye, "Claim 479 to Move In: Homosexuals Describe Plan to Take Over Alpine County," *Los Angeles Times* October 21, 1970, ACP file I, ONE; "gaycity," *Berkeley Tribe,* October 30, 1970, copied in Alpine Liberation Front (ALF) packet published as a fundraising tool (most likely January 1971), Thorpe File, GLBTHS; investments as reported by the Alpine Message Center, cited in "AlpLib for Washos Too," *Berkeley Barb* (December 11–17, 1970), 4, Thorpe File, GLBTHS; proposals from Economics Research Associates and Ladd & Kelsey, Architects, in ACP file II, ONE.

89. "GAY vs GOSPEL," *San Francisco Good Times,* October 30, 1970, reprinted in ALF Packet, Thorpe File, GLBTHS.

90. "Gay Mecca No. 1," *Time,* November 2, 1970 (n.p), ACP file I, ONE.

91. "Brother Don Has a Dream"; see also Don Jackson, "Help Build the Stonewall Nation," which calls for a September 20, 1970, meeting, Thorpe File, GLBTHS; and "Planning the City of Gay," *Spokane Natural,* September 18–October 2, 1970, Don Jackson file, ONE National Gay and Lesbian Archives, Los Angeles (hereafter ONE).

92. Publicity photo, c. 1970, ACP file I, ONE.

93. Don Jackson, "We Are All Fugitives," *Gay Sunshine,* no. 14 (August 1972), 4. On this and other gay liberationist prison activism, see Regina Kunzel, *Criminal Intimacy: Prison and the Uneven History of Modern American Sexuality* (Chicago: University of Chicago Press, 2008).

94. "Gay Lib in Alpine County," *Daily Californian* (UC Berkeley), October 22, 1970, clipping in Thorpe File, GLBTHS. See also "BAG-FUN," *Berkeley Tribe* (October 16–23, 1970), 20.

95. Robert Allen Warrior and Paul Chaat Smith, *Like a Hurricane: The American Indian Movement from Alcatraz to Wounded Knee* (New York: New Press, 1996); *Alcatraz Is Not an Island,* directed by James M. Fortier (Pacifica, CA: Diamond Island Productions, 2001).

96. Don Jackson, "Gay Say They Ain't Guil-Tay!" *Berkeley Barb,* October 23, 1970, Don Jackson file, ONE. See also Paul Eberle, "Gays plan to liberate a county," *LA Free Press,* October 25, 1970, ACP file I, ONE; Don Jackson, "Pro Alpine," *Berkeley Tribe,* November 6, 1970, ibid.

97. Don Jackson to Stan Williams and Gay Nationalists, report on BAGFUN (Bay Area Gays for Unification and Nationalism) proposal, ACP file II, ONE.

98. Kilhefner quoted in "Alpine County Hopes for Snow," *San Francisco Chronicle,* October 22, 1970, clipping in Thorpe File, GLBTHS.

99. Untitled clipping from *Daily Californian*, October 21, 1970, Thorpe File, GLBTHS.

100. "gaycity," *Berkeley Tribe* (October 30–November 6, 1970), 20. Jackson added, "For those who are not hardy enough to endure the hardships of the pioneer life, Gay Nationalists are planning the take over of a city within 15 miles of San Francisco." The "gaycity" article was distributed in the Alpine Liberation Front Packet (Thorpe File, GLBTHS).

101. Kilhefner quoted in "Alpine County Hopes for Snow." See also letter from San Francisco men Tom, Doug, and Mel in ACP file II, ONE; and Don Jackson, "Mountain Women," *Berkeley Barb*, ACP file II, ONE.

102. "Gay Radical Says Alpine Indian Turf," *Berkeley Barb*, n.d., Alpine Liberation Front Packet, Thorpe File, GLBTHS. My critiques are informed by Scott Lauria Morgensen, *Spaces Between Us: Queer Settler Colonialism and Indigenous Decolonization* (Minneapolis: University of Minnesota Press, 2011); Philip J. Deloria, *Playing Indian* (New Haven: Yale University Press, 1998); and Shari M. Huhndorf, *Going Native: Indians in the American Cultural Imagination* (Ithaca, NY: Cornell University Press, 2001).

103. "No One to Listen: Gays' Outline for Invasion," *San Francisco Examiner*, November 27, 1970, clipping in Thorpe File, GLBTHS.

104. Don Jackson to Stan Williams and Gay Nationalists, ACP File II, ONE.

105. Alpine Liberation Front Packet, Thorpe File, GLBTHS. Materials on Washoe people were collected by Jefferson Fuck Poland, leader of San Francisco's Sexual Liberation League and Psychedelic Venus Church.

106. "Berkeley GLF opts out," *The Advocate* (November 25–December 8, 1970), 9; see also Nick Benton, "Alpine Put Down," *Berkeley Tribe* (October 30–November 6, 1970), 9; "Gay Unit Rejects Alpine Takeover," *Los Angeles Times*, n.d., ACP File I, ONE.

107. "Berkeley GLF opts out."

108. Benton, "Alpine Put Down." The clipping of this article notes this editorial was also printed in the *San Francisco Chronicle*.

109. "From Gay Flames," *Gay Sunshine*, no. 3 (1970) n.p., clipping in Thorpe File, GLBTHS.

110. "off the snow pigs," *Gay Sunshine*, n.d., 4, clipping in Thorpe File, GLBTHS.

111. *Front Lines* (LA GLF newsletter), Alpine Liberation Front Packet, Thorpe File, GLBTHS.

112. Alpine Liberation Front Packet, Thorpe File, GLBTHS.

113. Don Jackson to Stan Williams and the Gay Nationalists, GLF of Los Angeles (n.d.), ACP File II, ONE. See also Leo Laurence, "A Gay County?" *Berkeley Barb*, October 16, 1970, ACP File I, ONE.

114. Voter registration and absentee voting swelled in the 1972 election, suggesting that vacation home owners may have registered to vote in Alpine to stop the gay colony; "Alpine taking no chances?" *The Advocate*, December 6, 1972, ACP File I, ONE. In June 1971, Robert Humphries, Mike Haggerty, and Donald Dill were found "not guilty of misdemeanor fraud charges resulting from street solicitation of funds last fall for the Alpine County gay colonization

project"; "L.A. judge finds Alpine fund raiser innocent," *The Advocate,* June 23, 1971, ACP File II, ONE.

115. *Gay Sunshine,* no. 5 (January 1971), 2; "Third World People Unite!," *Gay Sunshine,* no. 5 (January 1971), 2.

116. "Pigs Shoot Gay Brother," *Berkeley Tribe* (December 18–25, 1970), 7.

117. Robinson, "The Stud Shooting: From a Black Viewpoint," *Gay Sunshine,* no. 5 (January 1971), 2; "Showdown," *Gay Sunshine,* no. 5 (January 1971), 1–2.

118. See also Gary Alinder, "Where are the Gay Black Panthers?" *Gay Sunshine,* no. 5 (January 1971), 15; Pinney, "Gay Liberation: a movement without a model," 8.

119. Richard R. Moser, *The New Winter Soldiers: GI and Veteran Dissent during the Vietnam Era* (New Brunswick, NJ: Rutgers University Press, 1996), 92, 100, 150; Ian K. Lekus, "Interview with Amber Hollibaugh," *Peace & Change* 29:2 (April 2004): 266–321; "Where We're At," *All Hands Abandon Ship* (June 1970), 2; "Letter from a Navy Wife," *All Hands Abandon Ship* (August 1970), 5.

120. "Come Out!" *All Hands Abandon Ship* 5 (March 1971): 3; "G.I.G.L.," *All Hands Abandon Ship* 5 (March 1971): 9. GIGL produced *GIGLE,* or *GI Gay Liberation Experience.* See also Moser, *New Winter Soldiers,* 93–95; *Shakedown* 2:2 (April 24, 1970); *GI News and Discussion Bulletin,* no. 4 (April 1971), 96; "Your Uncle Sam is a Male Chauvinist Pig: Prostitution," *All Hands Abandon Ship* 3:4 (September 1972), 7A; "Forward Macho," *Hansen Free Press* 2:1 (March 15, 1973).

121. Andrew Hunt, *The Turning: A History of Vietnam Veterans against the War* (New York: New York University Press, 1999), 136–37; Vince Muscari, "Gay Brigade," *Gay Sunshine,* no. 11 (February–March 1972), 10.

122. "Gay Peace Treaty Preamble," Gay May Day Tribe, n.d. [1971], Thorpe File, SFPL; Gay May Day Tribe, "America: We Won't Let You Murder Anymore!" n.d. [1971], Thorpe File, SFPL. Sexism and the War," n.d. [1970?], Thorpe File, SFPL.

123. Mark Turner and Al Crofts (Roger Casement Collective, Oakland), "Gays Against War: April 24 San Francisco," *Gay Sunshine,* no. 7 (June–July 1971), 5.

124. On this campaign, see Murch, *Living for the City.* The campaign reflected splits within the Panthers, with some seeing it as slick or sold out.

125. Ibid., 200–201; see also Self, *American Babylon.*

126. This alliance building included both the commitments highlighted by the Gay Men's Political Action Group and the Alice B. Toklas Democratic Club, as well as bilingual ballots. Cesar Chávez and many longtime black civil rights and left-liberal leaders endorsed the Seale and Brown campaigns; Murch, *Living for the City,* 211, 272.

127. "People's Campaign Supports Gay Rights," *Black Panther* 9:22 (March 17, 1973), 6, 13. To a degree, the Gay Men's Political Action Group's alliance with the Oakland Black Panther Party foreshadowed gay-black electoral coalitions that developed in Chicago and other cities during the 1970s and 1980s and that are discussed in Stewart-Winter, *Queer Clout.* However, both the Polit-

ical Action Group and the Black Panther Party approached race and sexuality in more radical terms than the minoritarian interest-group framing that came to dominate liberal gay involvement in electoral politics.

128. "Ericka Huggins at Gay Meeting for Bobby and Elaine," *Black Panther,* 9:26 (1973): 7. The *Panther* noted that another of the group's activities would be a screening of Jean Genet's film *Un Chant d'Amour* (Song of Love), on gay men in prison.

129. These ties included a forum, "Gay Men at Work," in October 1973 and participation in the boycott of Coors beer, which activists targeted for several years because of its anti-union policies, racism, and funding of right-wing groups (see chapter 3). Michael Novick, "East of the Bay: Gay Men at Work," *Vector* (November 1974), 13; Novick, "East of the Bay: Coors Beer Boycott," *Vector* (January 1975), 13.

CHAPTER 2. A MORE POWERFUL WEAPON

1. Saxe first stated these words at her arrest and expanded on them at a plea deal in June. "Statement of Susan Saxe," June 9, 1975, Susan Saxe Subject File, Lesbian Herstory Archives, Brooklyn, NY (hereafter LHA).

2. Joan Nestle, "A Fem's Feminist History," in *The Feminist Memoir Project: Voices from Women's Liberation,* ed. Rachel Blau DuPlessis and Ann Snitow (New Brunswick, NJ: Rutgers University Press, 2007), 339.

3. Berger, *Captive Nation,* 68; Emily Thuma, "'Not a Wedge, But a Bridge,': Prisons, Feminist Activism, and the Politics of Gendered Violence, 1968–1987," PhD dissertation, New York University (2010).

4. See, especially, Ferguson, *Aberrations in Black*; Hanhardt, *Safe Space*; Springer, *Living for the Revolution*; Emily Thuma, "Against the 'Prison/Psychiatric State': Anti-Violence Feminisms and the Politics of Confinement in the 1970s," *Feminist Formations* 26:2 (summer 2014): 26–51; Emily Thuma, "Lessons in Self-Defense: Gender Violence, Racial Criminalization, and Anti-carceral Feminism," *WSQ: Women's Studies Quarterly* 43:3–4 (fall–winter 2015), 52–71; Tamara Lee Spira, "Intimate Internationalisms: 1970s 'Third World' Queer Feminist Solidarity with Chile," *Feminist Theory* 15:2 (summer 2014): 119-140; Paola Bacchetta, "Dyketactics! Notes Towards an Un-silencing," in Mecca, *Smash the Church, Smash the State,* 218–31; José Esteban Muñoz, *Disidentifications: Queers of Color and the Performance of Politics* (Minneapolis: University of Minnesota Press, 1999); Cathy Cohen, "Punks, Bulldaggers, and Welfare Queens: The Radical Potential of Queer Politics?" in *Black Queer Studies: A Critical Anthology,* eds. E. Patrick Johnson and Mae J. Henderson (Durham, NC: Duke University Press, 2005), 21–51; Linda Garber, *Identity Poetics: Race, Class, and the Lesbian-Feminist Roots of Queer Theory* (New York: Columbia University Press, 2001).

5. On Daughters of Bilitis and the transition to lesbian feminism, see Marcia M. Gallo, *Different Daughters: A History of Daughters of Bilitis and the Rise of the Lesbian Rights Movement* (New York: Seal Press, 2006).

6. Timothy B. Tyson, *Radio Free Dixie: Robert F. Williams and the Roots of Black Power* (Chapel Hill: University of North Carolina Press, 1999); Charles

E. Cobb, *This Nonviolent Stuff'll Get You Killed* (New York: Basic Books, 2014); Akinyele Omowale Umoja, *We Will Shoot Back: Armed Resistance in the Mississippi Freedom Movement* (New York: New York University Press, 2014); Bloom and Martin Jr., *Black against Empire*.

7. Judy Tzu-Chun Wu, *Radicals on the Road: Internationalism, Orientalism, and Feminism during the Vietnam War Era* (Ithaca, NY: Cornell University Press, 2013), 159. See also Agatha Beins, "Radical Others: Women of Color and Revolutionary Feminism," *Feminist Studies* 41:1 (2015): 150–83.

8. Shelley, "Subversion in the Women's Movement." A rhetoric of retributive violence against men was also circulated by Valerie Solanas's *SCUM Manifesto* and by the radical feminist group Cell 16; on Cell 16 see Roxanne Dunbar-Ortiz, *Outlaw Woman: A Memoir of the War Years, 1960–1975,* rev. ed. (Norman: University of Oklahoma Press, 2014; original ed., 2001), and Randolph, *Florynce "Flo" Kennedy,* 148.

9. Dan Berger, *Outlaws of America: the Weather Underground and the Politics of Solidarity* (Oakland, CA: AK Press, 2005).

10. For more on the underground and draft resistance, see Matt Meyer and Paul Magno, "Hard to Find: Building for Nonviolent Revolution and the Pacifist Underground," in *The Hidden 1970s: Histories of Radicalism,* ed. Dan Berger (New Brunswick, NJ: Rutgers University Press, 2010), 250–266.

11. See discussion by Bettina Aptheker in *Free Angela Davis and All Political Prisoners,* directed by Shola Lynch (Santa Monica, CA: Lions Gate, 2012).

12. Thuma, "Lessons in Self-Defense," 62.

13. Kunzel, *Criminal Intimacy,* 11–12. See also *Gay Sunshine,* no. 14 (1972), and Regina Kunzel, "Lessons in Being Gay: Queer Encounters in Gay and Lesbian Prison Activism," *Radical History Review,* no. 100 (winter 2008): 11–36.

14. Regina Kunzel briefly discusses these efforts in *Criminal Intimacy,* chapter 6. My thanks also to Laura Briggs, who observes that approximately "10% of all issues of GCN [*Gay Community News*] went to prisons (which was not a small commitment, given the high cost of mailing)" and that members of the newspaper's collective survived on "poverty wages"; Laura Briggs, comments to author, July 29, 2015.

15. See note 21 in the introduction.

16. Sidney Abbott and Barbara Love, *Sappho Is a Right-On Woman* (New York: Stein and Day, 1972). See also Gill Valentine, "Making Space: Lesbian Separatist Communities in the United States," in *Contested Countryside Cultures: Otherness, Marginalization, and Rurality,* ed. Paul Cloke and Jo Little (New York: Routledge: 1997), 109–22; Anne Valk, "Living a Feminist Lifestyle: The Intersection of Theory and Action in a Lesbian Feminist Collective," *Feminist Studies* 28:2 (summer 2002): 303–32; Anne Enke, "Smuggling Sex through the Gates: Race, Sexuality, and the Politics of Space in Second Wave Feminism," *American Quarterly* 55:4 (2003): 635–67 and Anne Enke, *Finding the Movement: Sexuality, Contested Space, and Feminist Activism* (Durham, NC: Duke University Press, 2007); Valk, *Radical Sisters*; Wu, *Radicals on the Road*; Roth, *Separate Roads to Feminism*; Alice Echols, *Daring to Be Bad: Radical Feminism in America, 1967–1975* (Minneapolis: University of Minnesota Press, 1989).

17. Laura Browder, *Her Best Shot: Women and Guns in America* (Chapel Hill: University of North Carolina Press, 2008), 137. See also Mary F. Beal, *Safe House: A Casebook Study of Revolutionary Feminism in the 1970s* (Eugene, OR: Northwest Matrix, 1976), 5; and Mary F. Beal, *Amazon One* (Little, Brown & Co., 1975), the latter a novel fictionalizing the gender and sexual politics of the Weather Underground.

18. Davis discusses this characterization in *Free Angela Davis and All Political Prisoners*; see also Berger, *Captive Nation*.

19. On black lesbians as criminal, see, for example, Cookie Woolner, "'Women Slain in Queer Love Brawl': African American Women, Same-Sex Desire, and Violence in the Urban North, 1920–1929," *Journal of African American History* 100:3 (summer 2015): 406–27.

20. Judy Grahn, *A Simple Revolution: The Making of an Activist Poet* (San Francisco: Aunt Lute Books, 2012), 77 (hereafter cited as Grahn, *ASR*). Grahn attended Howard from June 1964 through December 1965 after completing junior college. On the influence of Grahn's poetry in lesbian feminism, see Chelsea del Rio, "Voicing Gay Women's Liberation: Judy Grahn and the Shaping of Lesbian Feminism," *Journal of Lesbian Studies* 19 (2015): 357–66, and Kristen Hogan, *The Feminist Bookstore Movement: Lesbian Antiracism and Feminist Accountability* (Durham, NC: Duke University Press, 2016).

21. Grahn, *ASR*, 115, 203. The straight women's group included Beth Oglesby, then the wife of Carl Oglesby, a leader in SDS. Peter Adair, a friend of Wendy Cadden's from Antioch, filmed the events at People's Park and later filmed the free concert at Altamont. He would go on to form the Mariposa Film Group, which in the late 1970s made the gay and lesbian documentary *Word Is Out*. Robert Duncan never attended the gay men's poetry group, but it later organized Man Root Press.

22. Randolph, *Florynce "Flo" Kennedy*, 112.

23. Judy Grahn, "On the Development of a Purple Fist" (speech given at NACHO), November 1969, Berkeley, CA), D.E. Bertelson Papers, GLBTHS. This essay was later published in the *San Francisco Free Press* and in other venues.

24. Grahn, *ASR*, 119. See also Gay Women 1970–[197]1, Gay Movement 1965–1982 (Carton 8, Folder 20), Social Protest Collection, Bancroft Library, University of California, Berkeley.

25. Grahn, *ASR*, 129.

26. Vider, "'The Ultimate Extension of Gay Community,'" 866.

27. Pat Parker, 1975 pre-interview for *Word Is Out*, Peter Adair Papers, 1973–1986 (Folder 56), GLC 70, San Francisco History Center, SFPL. See also *Last Call at Maud's*, directed by Paris Poirier (San Francisco: Frameline, 1993).

28. See, for example, Leslie Cagan, "Something New Emerges: The Growth of a Socialist Feminist," in *They Should Have Served That Cup of Coffee*, ed. Dick Cluster (Boston: South End Press, 1979), 243. Cagan defines her decision to live collectively as inspired by her experience living in Cuba. See also Enke, *Finding the Movement*; Valk, *Radical Sisters*; Valentine, "Making Space"; Judy Grahn, "Ground Zero: The Rise of Lesbian Feminism," in *The Judy Grahn Reader* (San Francisco: Aunt Lute Books, 2009), 314.

29. On the racial and gender politics of toplessness, see Enke, *Finding the Movement*.

30. Grahn, *ASR*, 153. Alice Molloy's former lover Natalie Lando had put down the money for the house and lived nearby; Molloy was the home's central anchor. Grahn and Cadden lived there from 1971 through 1976; previously they had anchored the San Francisco apartment and Carol Wilson the Benvenue Street house. The Lesbian Mothers' Union was led by Pat Norman and Daughters of Bilitis founders Phyllis Lyon and Del Martin. On ICI: A Woman's Place and its relationship to A Woman's Press and to GWL, see Hogan, *The Feminist Bookstore Movement*, especially 98–101. Hogan notes that ICI: A Woman's Place developed multiracial leadership by 1974 but split apart over issues of race in the early 1980s, with former GWL members Alice Molloy, Carol Wilson, and Natalie Lando locking out two women of color and two white women who were pushing an anti-racist agenda.

31. For analysis of these dynamics, see Hanhardt, *Safe Space*.

32. Grahn, *ASR*, 154–155, 159; Grahn, "Ground Zero," 314; Adrienne Skye Roberts, "We thought the world we built would be forever: An interview with Lenn Keller," *Open Space: Art, Culture, Bay Area* (June 16, 2012), http://openspace.sfmoma.org/2012/06/we-thought-the-world-we-built-would-be-forever-an-interview-with-lenn-keller/ (accessed May 19, 2016).

33. Grahn, "Ground Zero," 312; Grahn, *ASR*, 122.

34. "Women Unite! Rapists Assailed," *Berkeley Tribe* (November 6–13, 1970), 12–13.

35. Grahn, *ASR*, 139.

36. On SFWAR see Grahn, *ASR*, 147; Maria Bevacqua, "Reconsidering Violence against Women: Coalition Politics in the Antirape Movement," ed. *Feminist Coalitions: Historical Perspectives on Second-Wave Feminism in the United States*, ed. Stephanie Gilmore (Urbana: University of Illinois Press, 2008), 163–77; Catherine O. Jacquet, "Responding to Rape: Contesting the Meaning of Sexual Violence in the United States, 1950–1980" (PhD dissertation, University of Illinois, Chicago, 2012). On gender in the Oakland Black Panther Party, see Spencer, "Engendering the Black Freedom Struggle," and Spencer, *The Revolution Has Come*.

37. Grahn, "Ground Zero," 316.

38. On radical and feminist styles see Randolph, *Florynce "Flo" Kennedy*, 154; Hillman, *Dressing for the Culture Wars*; Tanisha C. Ford, *Liberated Threads: Black Women, Style, and the Global Politics of Soul* (Chapel Hill: University of North Carolina Press, 2015).

39. Hart quoted in Stein, "'Birthplace of the Nation,'" 270. See also Stein, *City of Sisterly and Brotherly Loves*, 335; and Diana Block, *Arm the Spirit: A Woman's Journey Underground and Back* (Oakland, CA: AK Press, 2009), 42.

40. "We Have to Be Our Own Spark: An Interview with 'Gente' Third-World Lesbian Softball Team," *The Lesbian Tide* (July 1974), 6–7, 25–28 (quote on 25). Gente's members included Sandi Ajida (a musician), Dodici Azpadu (a novelist and professor), Judith Casselberry (a musician and later a professor of Africana studies), Matu Feliciano (a musician), Joanne Garrett, Barbara "B.G." Glass, Pat Norman, Anita Oñang, Linda Tillery (a musician

who had grown up in the Fillmore, performed with Janis Joplin and Cream, and in 1978 recorded a solo album with Olivia Records), and Linda Wilson (earlier a member of GWL) and. Pat Parker's poem "gente" reflected on the group; see Pat Parker, *Movement in Black: The Collected Poetry of Pat Parker, 1961–1978* (Ithaca, NY: Firebrand Books, 1990).

41. Wu, *Radicals on the Road*, 9.

42. Key examples in the United States included the Black Liberation Army, New World Liberation Front, FALN, and George Jackson Brigade; see, especially, Daniel Burton-Rose, *Guerrilla USA: The George Jackson Brigade and the Anticapitalist Underground of the 1970s* (Berkeley: University of California Press, 2010). On women's radical violence in Germany, see Patricia Melzer, *Death in the Shape of a Young Girl: Women's Political Violence in the Red Army Faction* (New York: New York University Press, 2015).

43. Burton-Rose, *Guerrilla USA*, 33, 36–37; Bay Area Research Collective (BARC), "The Trial of Little and Remiro," *Dragon* 2 (September 1975), 5. Bay Area Research Collective, Carton 2, Folder 2, Louise Merrill Papers, GLBTHS. Through its publication *Dragon,* the Bay Area Research Collective reported on and expressed support for the SLA, the New World Liberation Front, the Red Guerrilla Family, the Black Liberation Army, the George Jackson Brigade, and other formations; it also covered state attacks at Pine Ridge and elsewhere.

44. Comedian Richard Pryor used this narrative for humor about racial and sexual taboos; Richard Pryor, *Richard Pryor Meets Richard & Willie and the SLA,* Laff Records A188, LP, 1976.

45. Bay Area Research Collective, "Symbionese Liberation Army: support/criticize/love them," n.d., Bay Area Research Collective, Carton 2, Folder 2, Louise Merrill Papers, GLBTHS. On broader discourses of homosexual criminality, see Joey L. Mogul, Andrea J. Ritchie, and Kay Whitlock, *Queer (In) Justice: The Criminalization of LGBT People in the United States* (Boston: Beacon Press, 2012).

46. Ruth Mahaney, interview by author, June 27, 2013, San Francisco.

47. Lucinda Franks, "Annals of Crime: Return of the Fugitive," *New Yorker* (June 13, 1994), 54; on mainstream media sensationalism regarding Saxe's sexuality, see Anne McSweeney, "'Hijacking the Movement': The Saxe-Alpert Controversy, Media Politics, and the Making of Radical Feminism in the U.S., 1974–1976" (B.A. thesis, Wesleyan University, 2008), 51.

48. Bay Area Research Collective, Folder 2, Carton 2, Louise Merrill Papers, GLBTHS.

49. *The Women's Gun Pamphlet: A Primer on Handguns* (Oakland, CA: Women's Press Collective, 1975), 38. See also Grahn, *ASR,* 202, 215.

50. "Who Are the Dangerous People?" *The Lesbian Tide* (July 1974), 12. This same article noted that an unnamed women's press printed some of Hall's poetry to Mizmoon after the LAPD firebombing. See also Julie Lee (New Jersey D.O.B.), Letters to the Collective, *The Lesbian Tide* (July 1974), 19.

51. Randolph, *Florynce "Flo" Kennedy,* 197.

52. Alpert was incorrect in her number; the total number of deaths at Attica was forty-three. Emily Thuma notes that Naomi Jaffe left women's liberation for the WUO because some feminists saw those who died at Attica as "chauvinists";

Thuma, "'Not a Wedge, but a Bridge,'" 55. On debates about Alpert, see also Becky Thompson, *A Promise and a Way of Life: White Antiracist Activism* (Minneapolis: University of Minnesota Press, 2001).

53. Randolph details Kennedy mentoring Atkinson especially; Randolph, *Florynce "Flo" Kennedy*, 124–25.

54. Burton-Rose, *Guerrilla USA*, 35.

55. Valeri turned state's evidence and was quickly released; Bond died in prison, allegedly while attempting to escape; and Gilday died in prison in 2011. On Gilday, see David Abel, "Apologetic in the End, William Gilday Dies," *Boston Globe*, September 16, 2011. On the cases in general and especially on Power, see Franks, "Annals of Crime."

56. See, for example, "FBI Countered: The Grand Jury Project," *on our way: Cambridge Women's Center Newsletter* (June 1975), 1, 3; Burton-Rose, *Guerrilla USA*, 184–85, 302.

57. Three of the Lexington 6 served sentences; Franks, "Annals of Crime," 54.

58. Lezzie Fair [pseud.], "Sisters! Read This Carefully—The Hassle You Save May Be Your Own!" [n.d.; c. April 1975], Susan Saxe Subject File, LHA.

59. Jeanne Cordova and Ann Dozci, "Power or Paralysis," *The Lesbian Tide* (May–June 1975), 4, 7, Susan Saxe Subject File, LHA.

60. "Susan Saxe Statement June 9, 1975," *on our way: Cambridge Women's Center Newsletter* (June 1975), 5–7.

61. Barbara Deming, *Remembering Who We Are*, 2nd ed. (St. Augustine, FL: Pagoda, 1981), 159.

62. Susan Saxe Defense Fund (Philadelphia, care of Lawyers Guild), "To All Our Sisters and Concerned Brothers," June 11, 1975, Susan Saxe Subject File, LHA. See also Cagan, "Something New Emerges," 255.

63. Cagan, "Something New Emerges," 255.

64. Susan Saxe Defense Fund, "Support Susan Saxe" brochure [c. 1975], Susan Saxe Subject File, LHA.

65. Susan Saxe Defense Fund (Philadelphia, care of Lawyers Guild), "To All Our Sisters and Concerned Brothers." As examples of critiques of Saxe, see unattributed flier critiquing Saxe and Power (Susan Saxe Subject File, LHA); Jill Johnston, "The Myth of Bonnies without Clydes: Lesbian Feminism and the Male Left," *Village Voice* (April 28, 1975), 14; and Barbara Deming, "Seeing Us As We Are Not" [1979 pamphlet, War Resisters League], in *Remembering Who We Are*, 124–34.

66. Susan Saxe Defense Committee Newsletter, No. 1, Susan Saxe Defense Committee folder (Carton 2, Folder 24), Louise Merrill Papers, GLBTHS.

67. As examples, see "Editorial," *off our backs*, March 31, 1975; Eugene Women's Union, "Who Is Susan Saxe?" brochure [c. mid-1975–1976], and flier for New York City poetry benefit held February 7, 1976 (both in Susan Saxe Subject File, LHA). Gay leftist men were largely absent from support of Saxe; for a gay leftist's critique of this absence, see Tom Kennedy, "Susan Saxe: Prisoner of War," *Magnus: a socialist journal of gay liberation*, No. 2 (summer 1977): 31–34.

68. Nancy Wechsler, "Susan Saxe Pleads Guilty to Lesser Charges," *Gay Community News,* January 29, 1977; Susan Saxe, "Why I Bargained for a Reduced Sentence," *Majority Report* (February 19–March 4, 1977), 11.

69. The Cambridge Women's Center's list of defense funds in June 1975 was representative, including Garcia, Little, the Lexington 6, "Shoshana" (Pat Swinton), Kenneth Edelin (the gynecologist in an abortion case), and Ella Ellison (a black woman charged with murder of a police officer because of the flimsy accusation of other suspects).

70. One parallel that activists did not discuss, presumably because it was too volatile, was the case of Valerie Solanas. The founder of the Society for Cutting Up Men (SCUM) and author of the *SCUM Manifesto,* Solanas had attempted to murder Andy Warhol in 1968. Flo Kennedy initially defended Solanas and sought to build a case that defined her actions as political tactics to gain feminism a legal and media voice; at the same time, Kennedy rejected Solanas's separatism, and she withdrew her support after Solanas insulted her. Randolph, Florynce "Flo" Kennedy, 145–50.

71. Victoria Law, "Sick of the Abuse: Feminist Responses to Sexual Assault, Battering, and Self-Defense," in *The Hidden 1970s: Histories of Radicalism,* ed. Dan Berger (New Brunswick, NJ: Rutgers University Press, 2010), 39–56; Bevacqua, "Reconsidering Violence against Women"; Thuma, "'Not a Wedge, but a Bridge.'"

72. Merrill had recently been central to the Bay Area Women's Affirmative Action Union, which organized around fair hiring of women at local libraries and highlighted the cases of both black and white women. For an overview of the defense committee's fundraising and other work, see Louise Merrill for Inez Garcia Defense Committee, "Dear Friend," December 27, 1976, Carton 2, Folder 13, Inez Garcia Defense Committee, Louise Merrill Papers, GLBTHS.

73. Law, "Sick of the Abuse"; Berger, *Captive Nation,* 212; Danielle McGuire, *At the Dark End of the Street: Black Women, Rape, and Resistance; A New History of the Civil Rights Movement from Rosa Parks to Black Power* (New York: Vintage Books, 2011).

74. Activists frequently cited this reaction as evidence of the negative power of the criminal legal system; see, for example, *The Feminist* 1: 2 (February 1975): 1; *The Feminist* 1:3 (April 1975): 1.

75. Law, "Sick of the Abuse," 41.

76. Planning for the February 1975 protest was highlighted in *The Feminist* 1:2 (February 1975): 1; and further reported in *The Feminist* 1;3 (April 1975): 1. See also Block, *Arm the Spirit.*

77. Thuma, "Lessons in Self-Defense," 61; Block, *Arm the Spirit,* 53, 55–57; Bevacqua, "Reconsidering Violence against Women." Berger also places some blame on men leading prison activism for failing to collaborate with feminists; *Captive Nation,* 173.

78. "We need the power to defend ourselves! They offer us more of the protection racket!" *The Feminist* 1:3 (April 1975): 2.

79. Parker, 1975 pre-interview for *Word Is Out.*

80. Law, "Sick of the Abuse," 43; see also Thuma, "'Not a Wedge, but a Bridge,'"; Grahn, *ASR*, 219.

81. In addition, media attention in 1976 included a play and a TV movie, *The People vs. Inez Garcia.*

82. In November 1976 Garcia joined a rally celebrating the acquittal of three members of the San Quentin 6, prison radicals who had been accused of an escape attempt during which guards murdered George Jackson. This strengthened the framing of Garcia as a political prisoner; Berger, *Captive Nation*, 228.

83. By the latter part of the 1970s, the impact of collective defense could be seen in the George Jackson Brigade, a multiracial armed group in the Pacific Northwest half of whose members identified as gay, bisexual, or lesbian; Lesbians Against Police Violence, formed in San Francisco; and the Boston-based Combahee River Collective. In 1973 two of the lesbians in the George Jackson Brigade formed a group to support lesbian and other women prisoners; in 1975 they traveled the country meeting with prison activists and attended the trials of Assata Shakur and Pat Swinton, the latter of whose supporters were divided into pro- and anti-Alpert camps. On the George Jackson Brigade, see Burton-Rose, *Guerrilla USA*. On Lesbians Against Police Violence, see Hanhardt, *Safe Space*. On the Combahee River Collective, see Springer, *Living for the Revolution*, and Thuma, "Against the 'Prison/Psychiatric State.'"

CHAPTER 3. LIMP WRISTS AND CLENCHED FISTS

1. Michael Olden, "I am Faggot," *Gay Sparks* (San Francisco) 1:1 (January–February 1975), Gay Sparks/Dish Rag Folder, Tede Matthews Archive, San Francisco (hereafter cited as Matthews Papers).

2. Guerra, "Gender Policing"; Rich and Arguelles, "Homosexuality, Homophobia, and Revolution, Part I," and "Homosexuality, Homophobia, and Revolution, Part II."

3. Brigada Venceremos Policy on Gay Recruitment, 1972, Race-Class Articles folder, Gearhart Papers, GLBTHS; Lekus, "Queer Harvests," 78; Lekus, "Queer and Present Dangers," 419–20.

4. The Berkeley-based *Gay Sunshine* was a key venue for discussion of Cuba. See "Venceremos," *Gay Sunshine*, no. 1 (August, 1970); Gay Committee of Returned Brigadistas, "North American Gays Protest," *Gay Sunshine*, no. 9 (October–November 1971), 2; "Letter from Cuba," *Gay Sunshine*, no. 15 (October–November 1972), 13; Allen Young, "¿Cuba Si?" *Gay Sunshine*, no. 13 (June 1972), 13; Zack Mansfield, "The Gay Soul of Socialism," *Gay Sunshine*, no. 15 (October–November 1972), 4. Coverage of gay life elsewhere in Latin America typically drew comparisons to Cuba; see "Mexico G.L.F.," *Gay Sunshine*, no. 11 (February–March 1972), 2; "Argentina: GAY MANIFESTO," *Gay Sunshine*, no. 15 (October–November 1972), 7; Allen Young, "Gays in Brazil," *Gay Sunshine*, no. 13 (June 1972), 4.

5. Max Elbaum, *Revolution in the Air: Sixties Radicals Turn to Lenin, Mao, and Che* (New York: Verso Books, 2002), 5, 136, 154. The New Communist Movement (NCM) reached its height between 1972 and 1974 but disintegrated by the end of the 1970s; as it receded, some participants formed the Line of

March, which later informed the Alliance against Women's Oppression (see chapter 5). On the Third World Left, see Pulido, *Black, Brown, Yellow, and Left*; Young, *Soul Power*; and Singh, *Black Is a Country*.

6. "New Mvt. Strategy," *Gay Sunshine*, no. 14 (August 1972), 4.

7. Elbaum, *Revolution in the Air*, 133.

8. "Position Paper of the Revolutionary Union on Homosexuality and Gay Liberation," attached to Los Angeles Research Group statement (1975), Anson Reinhart Papers, GLBTHS. A useful analysis of the circulation of similar rhetoric in the Latin American left can be found in James N. Green and Florence Babb, "Introduction," *Latin American Perspectives* 29:2 (March 2002): 3–23.

9. Steve Hamilton, "On the History of the Revolutionary Union (Part II)," *Theoretical Review* 14 (January–February 1980): 8; Elbaum, *Revolution in the Air*, 139. On Hamilton's political history, see Lekus, "Queer and Present Dangers."

10. Reflecting its ties to the NCM, the group described its orientation as a "*pre*-pre-party formation"; Lavender & Red Union (LRU), *The Lavender & Red Book: A Gay Liberation/Socialist Anthology* (Los Angeles: Lavender & Red Union/Peace Press, 1976), 52, 55. On opposition to antigay policies, see, especially, "Is Genocide . . ." (July 1974), reprinted both in *Lavender & Red Book*, 27, and *Come Out Fighting* No. 12–13 (March–April 1976); and LRU, "PRSC Exclusion" (October 1974), reprinted in *Lavender & Red Book*, 28. On critiques of gay and lesbian radicals who did not foreground class, see LRU, "The GCSC Strike," in *Lavender & Red Book*, 21–22. LRU also collaborated with a semisecret network of lesbian communists called the Los Angeles Research Group; Los Angeles Research Group, "Toward a Scientific Analysis of the Gay Question," Cudahy, California, 1975, Anson Reinhart Papers, GLBTHS (also held in Mike Conan Collection, Southern California Library for Social Studies and Research, donated by Max Elbaum). By 1977, LRU split into two smaller factions, one of which joined the antigay Spartacist League. Revolutionary Faction, Lavender & Red Union/Red Flag Union, "Documents of Struggle: Gay Liberation Through Socialist Revolution," 1978, Ephemera— Subjects (Socialism), GLBTHS.

11. Barbara Epstein, "Ambivalence about Feminism," in DuPlessis and Snitow, *The Feminist Memoir Project*, 124–48; Amy Kesselman, with Heather Booth, Vivian Rothstein, and Naomi Weisstein, "Our Gang of Four: Friendship and Women's Liberation," in DuPlessis and Snitow, *The Feminist Memoir Project*, 25–53. On socialist-feminism more broadly, see Mary Ann Clawson, "Looking for Feminism: Racial Dynamics and Generational Investments in the Second Wave," *Feminist Studies* 34:3 (fall 2008): 526–55; Elizabeth Lapovsky Kennedy, "Socialist Feminism: What Difference Did It Make to the History of Women's Studies?" *Feminist Studies* 34:3 (fall 2008): 497–525; Judith Kegan Gardiner, "What Happened to Socialist Feminist Women's Studies Programs? A Case Study and Some Speculations," *Feminist Studies* 34:3 (fall 2008): 558–84; and Nancy Holstrom, "Introduction," in Holstrom, ed., *The Socialist Feminist Project: A Contemporary Reader in Theory and Politics* (New York: Monthly Review Press, 2002), 1–12; Valk, *Radical Sisters*; Enke, *Finding the Movement*; and Echols, *Daring to Be Bad*.

12. See, especially, "Berkeley-Oakland Women's Union Principles of Unity" (1973), Berkeley-Oakland Women's Union, 1975, Berkeley-Oakland Women's Union file, GLBTHS; "Presentation to Vietnam-US Women's Conference, February 25, 1975," Berkeley-Oakland Women's Union file, GLBTHS.

13. For overviews, see Tom Kennedy, "A Closer Look at Socialist Feminism," *Magnus*, no. 1 (summer 1976), 27; John D'Emilio, "By Way of Introduction: Notes from One Gay Life," in *Making Trouble: Essays on Gay History, Politics, and the University* (New York: Routledge, 1992), xiii–xliv. On the influence of socialist feminism in the later 1970s Lavender Left and New American Movement, see Kennedy, "Socialist Feminism"; Judy MacLean, "Lesbians and the Left," in Gay and Lesbian Task Force of the New American Movement (Socialist Feminist Commission), *Working Papers on Gay/Lesbian Liberation and Socialism* (Blazing Star, Chicago: New American Movement, 1979), 3–6, Ephemera—Organizations (N-Miscellaneous), GLBTHS; Peter Drucker, "The Lavender Left: An Evaluation," in "Spring 1981 Discussion Bulletin on Socialist-Feminism" (Solidarity), "Socialism" folder (Box S2), Lesbian Legacy Collection (hereafter LLC), ONE; Lavender Left Subject File, ONE; and Bay Area Socialist School folder, Ephemera—Organizations, GLBTHS. My analysis stands in contrast to that of Jim Downs, who leaves the feminist dimensions of the 1970s gay left unexplored; Downs, *Stand By Me: The Forgotten History of Gay Liberation* (New York: Basic Books, 2016).

14. "Bases of Unity of the Revolutionary Gay Men's Union," n.d., Miscellaneous Folder, Matthews Papers. See also "Revolutionary Gay Men's Union Principles of Unity," n.d., Miscellaneous Folder, Matthews Papers.

15. Tim Corbett and rama [Charlie Hinton] (authors hereafter cited as Corbett and Hinton), "Practice Makes Powerful: Can Gays Get It Together in San Francisco? A Political Analysis of Bay Area Gay Liberation," *Magnus*, no. 2 (summer 1977), 37–47.

16. "Faggots, Sissies, Queens" (flier, c. early 1974), Designed Folder, Matthews Papers.

17. Tede Matthews, undated autobiographical notes, Bay Area Gay Liberation (BAGL) Folder, Matthews Papers; Matthews, "I was a teenage draft dodger," *We Like Our Queers Out of Uniform* (San Francisco: Lesbians and Gays Against Intervention, 1991).

18. The term "genderfuck" began to see wide circulation in 1972, when it appeared in a *Rolling Stone* article about glam rock; see Le Zotte, *From Goodwill to Grunge*.

19. Matthews' gender expression shifted further over time, by the 1980s becoming more butch, but he did not disavow his earlier feminine presentation.

20. Tede Matthews interview, 1977 (final interview for *Word Is Out*), Box 43, Folder 155F, Peter Adair Papers (GLC 70), James C. Hormel Gay and Lesbian Center, San Francisco Public Library (hereafter Hormel Center, SFPL). See also Matthews in *Word Is Out* (1977), and in Nancy Adair and Casey Adair, *Word Is Out: Stories of Some Of Our Lives* (San Francisco: New Glide, 1978). Although this explanation of drag has often been attributed to RuPaul, it is likely that RuPaul either adapted it from Matthews or that it had multiple sources in queer culture.

21. Modern Times's role as a community center and activist hub echoed patterns being established among women's bookstores in the Bay Area and beyond; see Hogan, *The Feminist Bookstore Movement.*

22. On Matthews's experiences, see Tede Matthews interview, September 26, 1975 (preliminary interview for *Word Is Out*), Box 43, Folder 155F, Peter Adair Papers (GLC 70), Hormel Center, SFPL; on the self-defense classes and Mahaney's and others' views, see Mahaney, interview by author, and Ruth Mahaney, email correspondence with author, February 16, 2016.

23. "Combating Sexism: a study group for pro-feminist gay males," (flier, c. fall 1974), Favorite Leaflets Folder, Matthews Papers. The study group was held at 37 Sanchez, the address of the *Gay Sparks* collective.

24. "Faggots Against Rape" (flier, c. October 1974), Sex Roles—Sissies Folder, Matthews Papers.

25. Matthews autobiographical notes, Matthews Papers.

26. Matthews interview, 1977; Greg Youmans, *Word Is Out: A Queer Film Classic* (Vancouver: Arsenal Pulp Press, 2011).

27. Larry Mitchell and Ned Asta, *The Faggots and Their Friends between Revolutions* (San Francisco: Calamus Books, 1977).

28. Scott Herring, "Out of the Closets, into the Woods: *RFD,* Country Women, and the Post-Stonewall Emergence of Queer Anti-Urbanism," *American Quarterly* 59 (2007): 341–72.

29. Dennis Altman, "What Changed in the Seventies?" in *Homosexuality: Power and Politics,* ed. Gay Left Collective (London: Allison & Busby, 1980), 52. See also Rivers, *Radical Relations,* 114–21. The photograph discussed here is held in the Marie Ueda Photographs Collection, GLBTHS.

30. Matthews interview, 1975.

31. Andrew Holleran, "The Petrification of Clonestyle," *Christopher Street* 69 (1982): 14–18.

32. Greg Grandin, *Empire's Workshop: Latin America, the United States, and the Rise of the New Imperialism* (New York: Holt Paperbacks, 2007); Peter Winn, "The Furies of the Andes: Violence and Terror in the Chilean Revolution and Counterrevolution," in *A Century of Revolution: Insurgent and Counter-insurgent Violence during Latin America's Long Cold War,* ed. Greg Grandin and Gilbert M. Joseph (Durham, NC: Duke University Press, 2010); Macarena Goméz-Barris, *Where Memory Dwells: Culture and State Violence in Chile* (Berkeley: University of California Press, 2008); "Pinochet's regime official victims' list increased by 9.800 to 40.018," *Merco Press,* August 19, 2011.

33. For a detailed account of this report, see LeRoy Ashby and Rod Gramer, *Fighting the Odds: The Life of Senator Frank Church* (Pullman: Washington State University Press, 1994), especially 411–50.

34. Mark Feldstein, "The Last Muckraker," *Washington Post* (July 28, 2004), A19.

35. Ashby and Gramer, *Fighting the Odds,* 468. Idaho Senator Frank Church chaired both these investigations. COINTELPRO had first been exposed in 1971 through a break-in committed by activists.

36. Charlie Hinton, interview by author, July 29, 2011, by telephone.

37. Margaret Power, "The U.S. Movement in Solidarity with Chile in the 1970s," *Latin American Perspectives* 36:6 (November 2009): 46–66. On Chilean solidarity more broadly, see Van Gosse, "Unpacking the Vietnam Syndrome: The Coup in Chile and the Rise of Popular Anti-interventionism," in *The World the Sixties Made: Politics and Culture in Recent America*, ed. Van Gosse and Richard Moser (Philadelphia: Temple University Press, 2003), 100–113.

38. "Chilean Fascists Terrorize Gays," *Body Politic* 14 (July–August 1974): 7; Carlos Manuel, "Junta Coup Comes Down Hard on Chilean Gays," *Vector* (June 1974), 16–17, 35, clipping in Latina/o Lesbian Gay Folder, Matthews Papers.

39. Gays in Solidarity with the Chilean Resistance, "Solidarity With Chilean Gays" (flier, c. September 1974), Designed Folder, Matthews Papers.

40. Stuart may also have been active in the Gay Men's Political Action Group of Oakland.

41. Gays in Solidarity with the Chilean Resistance, "Solidarity With Chilean Gays"; Matthews interview, 1975.

42. Tede Matthews, "Poem for Pop-Eye," read at Gays in Solidarity with the Chilean Resistance event, September 1975; audio recording held by James Green and in the files of Tamara Lea Spira, transcription provided courtesy Tamara Lea Spira. Wilbert "Popeye" Jackson had been a leader of the United Prisoners Union, which assisted in organizing the Symbionese Liberation Army's food giveaway. In December 1974, when gay and prison activists in San Francisco organized the "Stonewalls Prison Conference," speakers included Jackson along with Morris Kight of Los Angeles's Gay Community Service Center (see Stonewalls Prison Conference flier, Ephemera—Subjects (Protests), GLBTHS). Jackson was assassinated in early June 1975 while sitting in a parked car at 2 A.M. with his girlfriend and fellow activist Sally Voye. A communiqué attributed to the New World Liberation Front claimed responsibility for the murder, but the SLA's front group the Bay Area Research Collective held that this communiqué came from government sources; see Orphans of Amerika/Bay Area Research Collective, "Fight the Set-Up," June 11, 1975, Symbionese Liberation Army Collection, Freedom Archives. Ultimately, a member of a group known as Tribal Thumb was convicted for Jackson and Voye's murder; Berger, *Captive Nation*, 258.

43. "Fruits of the Chilean Junta: Rape, Torture, Death—and Resistance," *off our backs* 5:10 (December 1975): 4; "Chile," *Come Out Fighting*, November 1975 (back cover); Matthews, "Coming Out for Peace," 8.

44. "Chile," *Gay Sparks* 1:1 (January–February 1975): 11–12; see also "Imperialism" in same issue, 9–10, 12. Tede Matthews was part of the editorial collective of *Gay Sparks* and active in both RGMU and GSCR.

45. "Imperialism," *Gay Sparks*. *Gay Sparks*'s analysis is backed by that of Robert O. Self, *American Babylon: Race and the Struggle for Postwar Oakland* (Princeton: Princeton University Press, 2005). The magazine, whose slogan was "Limp Wrists, Clenched Fists," was produced at the same house and by some of the same activists as the "Combating Sexism" study group, which also supported Inez Garcia. On the Garcia case and gay men as subjects of

rape, see "The Politics of Sexual Terrorism," *Gay Sparks* 1 (January–February 1975).

46. Randy Shilts, *The Mayor of Castro Street: The Life and Times of Harvey Milk* (New York: St. Martin's, 1982; reprint, New York: St. Martin's Griffin, 2008), 92–93.

47. Corbett and Hinton, "Practice Makes Powerful," 38; Hal Offen, "Gay liberation growing with BAGL," *The Voice of the Gay Students Coalition* (San Francisco), no. 3 (April 18, 1975), reprinted as flier, Ephemera—Organizations (BAGL), GLBTHS.

48. "Can Gay People Get It Together in San Francisco?" John Kyper Papers, GLBTHS.

49. Tom Ammiano, "My Adventures as a Gay Teacher," in Mecca, *Smash the Church, Smash the State*, 40–42.

50. Corbett and Hinton, "Practice Makes Powerful."

51. Miriam Frank, *Out in the Union: A Labor History of Queer America* (Philadelphia: Temple University Press, 2014), 78 and 90.

52. Ammiano, "My Adventures as a Gay Teacher"; Sara R. Smith, "Organizing for Social Justice: Rank-and-File Teachers' Activism and Social Unionism in California, 1948–1978" (Ph.D. dissertation, University of California, Santa Cruz, 2014), 419.

53. "A Call For Labor Leadership and Action on Human Rights," Labor Committee of Bay Area Gay Liberation to Delegates at the Eleventh Constitutional Convention of the AFL-CIO, San Francisco, October 2, 1975, Ephemera—Organizations (BAGL), GLBTHS.

54. "Labor Supports *Our* Rights—Do We Support *Labor's?*" flier, October 1976, Ephemera—Organizations (BAGL), GLBTHS.

55. "Boycott the Mindshaft [*sic*]" (flier c. September 1975) and "Joint Statement by the Management of the Mindshaft [*sic*] and the Negotiations Committee of BAGL," September 24, 1975, Ephemera—Organizations (BAGL), GLBTHS. Also see "Bill of Rights for Patrons and Employees of Gay Establishments," flier, San Francisco Gay Liberation, n.d., John Kyper Papers, GLBTHS.

56. Hinton, interview by author.

57. See, for example, "Lesbian Mother Witch Hunt" (flier, c. April 1976), BAGL Folder, Matthews Papers. On gay and lesbian custody activism in general, see Rivers, *Radical Relations*.

58. John D'Emilio, interview by author, June 28, 2011, by telephone.

59. Corbett and Hinton, "Practice Makes Powerful," 38.

60. "Gay Freedom Day Sunday June 29, 1975: March for Gay Rights, Join the Stonewall Gay Liberation Contingent," Gay Day folder, Stonewall Contingent, Matthews Papers.

61. On solidarity work generally, see Offen, "Gay liberation growing with BAGL," and Corbett and Hinton, "Practice Makes Powerful"; on the May Day exclusion, see ibid., 39. The May Day event was held on May 4, 1975, in Oakland's San Antonio Park and was organized principally by CASA (El Centro de Acción Social y Autónomo). BAGL had been promised a booth before the event but was not allowed to set it up, ostensibly because it had not prepared the booth in time for pre-approval, but more clearly because of straight activists' discomfort.

62. Estella Habal, *San Francisco's International Hotel: Mobilizing the Filipino American Community in the Anti-eviction Movement* (Philadelphia: Temple University Press, 2007), 3, 111–12; Trinity Ordona, "Coming Out Together: An Ethnohistory of the Asian and Pacific Islander Queer Women's and Transgendered People's Movement of San Francisco" (PhD dissertation, University of California, Santa Cruz, 2000), 94; Elbaum, *Revolution in the Air,* 139. Opponents of BAGL's presence included the Chinese American group Wei Min She and the Revolutionary Communist Party, or RCP (a descendant of RU). As Ordona notes, the gay and lesbian members in KDP were Melinda Parras, Trinity Ordona, and Syl Savellano ("Coming Out Together").

63. "3rd World Gay Caucus," flier, November 1975, Ephemera—Organizations (BAGL), GLBTHS; see also "Gays Speak Out Against Racism," Third World Committee of Bay Area Gay Liberation, n.d.; and "BAGL Bulletin," 1:7 (November 1975), both in Ephemera—Organizations (BAGL), GLBTHS.

64. Horacio N. Roque Ramírez, "'That's My Place!': Negotiating Racial, Sexual, and Gender Politics in San Francisco's Gay Latino Alliance, 1975–1983," *Journal of the History of Sexuality* 12:2 (April 2003): 225, 228. GALA operated out of offices in the League of United Latin American Citizens (LULAC) building in the Mission District, as well as the Gay Community Center in the Castro; Carmen Vázquez, interviewed by Kelly Anderson, 2005, Voices of Feminism Oral History Project, Sophia Smith Collection, Smith College, 31–32.

65. Brian Freeman, interview by author, June 24, 2013, San Francisco. Freeman grew up in Boston, attended the University of Pennsylvania, and participated in gay activism in Philadelphia before moving to San Francisco in 1977.

66. Corbett and Hinton, "Practice Makes Powerful," 39–40.

67. Ibid.; Offen, "Gay liberation growing with BAGL."

68. Elbaum, *Revolution in the Air,* 51–52; Van Gosse, *Where the Boys Are: Cuba, the Cold War, and the Making of a New Left* (New York: Verso Press, 1993), 145–47. This critique circulated in the gay press in 1970–71 when the SWP and its affiliate organization the Young Socialist Alliance overturned their bans on gay and lesbian members; see Philip Derbyshire, "Sects and Sexuality: Trotskyism and the Politics of Homosexuality," in Gay Left Collective, *Homosexuality,* 104–15; "SWP Infiltration," *Lesbian Organizer* (August 1971), 2; John Kyper, "Coming Out and into the GLF: Banned No More in Boston," in Mecca, *Smash the Church, Smash the State,* 37; "SF News," *Gay Sunshine,* no. 12 (April 1972), 2; Karen Bancroft, "On Gay Liberation," *Young Socialist Discussion Bulletin,* 15:7 (1971), Reinhart Papers, GLBTHS; Laura Miller, "Gay Liberation Task Force," *Young Socialist Organizer,* April 1971, Reinhart Papers, GLBTHS; and Socialist Workers Party Discussion Bulletins, Reinhart Papers, GLBTHS. Notably, the Young Socialist Alliance and Socialist Workers Party were entirely separate from the Young People's Socialist League (YPSL) and Socialist Party of America/USA. Openings for gay and lesbian recognition developed in the YPSL as early as 1952, but the group was effectively disbanded by the mid-1960s; see Chris Phelps, "A Neglected Document on Socialism and Sex," *Journal of the History of Sexuality* 16:1 (January 2007): 1–13. In 1980, David McReynolds became the first openly gay man to run for president on the Socialist Party USA ticket, but he earned minimal gay and lesbian support;

see Martin Duberman, *A Saving Remnant: The Radical Lives of Barbara Deming and David McReynolds* (New York: The New Press, 2011); Gert Hekma, Harry Oosterhuis, and James Steakley, eds., "Leftist Sexual Politics and Homosexuality: A Historical Overview," *Journal of Homosexuality* 29:2–3 and 4 (1995): 1–40.

69. Corbett and Hinton, "Practice Makes Powerful"; "The Little Red Camp Songbook," June 28 Union, Ephemera—Organizations, GLBTHS.

70. One member, Michael Bumblebee, was an active supporter of the American Indian Movement; Philip Maldari worked with the radio station KPFA, through, for example, the gay show *Fruit Punch*; and Henry (Camo) Bortman had attended the Black Panthers' Revolutionary People's Constitutional Convention in 1970, had been a member of the Lost Kidz Tribe (which traveled the country in a school bus named General Harriet, for Harriet Tubman), and once baled hay in drag; as Bortman recalls with amusement, "it was a very fluid time" (Henry (Camo) Bortman, interview by author, May 31, 2011, San Francisco).

71. Hinton, interview by author; see also Corbett and Hinton, "Practice Makes Powerful," and Green, "Feathers and Fists: Socialists and the Brazilian Gay Liberation Movement in the 1970s," self-interview, 15 (in possession of the author, courtesy of James Green).

72. Bortman and Novick were accepted into the Prairie Fire Organizing Committee. The PFOC developed after the Weather Underground Organization released its book *Prairie Fire: The Politics of Revolutionary Anti-Imperialism* in 1974. Many radicals, including socialist feminists, gay men, and lesbians, cited *Prairie Fire*'s discussion of cultural imperialism as useful to gay liberation, but were also critical of PFOC's resistance to autonomous gay and feminist organizing. See June 28 Union, "Criticism of the June 28 Union" (c. 1976–1977), 12, Ephemera—Organizations, GLBTHS.

73. On the official bicentennial, see Natasha Zaretsky, *No Direction Home: The American Family and the Fear of National Decline, 1968–1980* (Chapel Hill: University of North Carolina Press, 2007).

74. KDP, the Puerto Rican Socialist Party, the American Indian Movement, the Republic of New Afrika, the Philadelphia Workers' Organizing Committee, socialist-feminist women's unions, June 28 Union, and other groups attended Hard Times and became active in the Counter-Bicentennial. The Weather Underground Organization folded soon after, and Prairie Fire split into a Bay Area group that retained the name PFOC and a New York group called the May 19 Communist Organization. Berger, *Outlaws of America*, 225–28.

75. Corbett and Hinton, "Practice Makes Powerful," 43; Kennedy, "A Closer Look at Socialist Feminism"; Amber Hollibaugh, "Right to Rebel," in Gay Left Collective, *Homosexuality*, 212. Hollibaugh's essay has been reprinted in her essay collection, *My Dangerous Desires: A Queer Girl Dreaming Her Way Home* (Durham, NC: Duke University Press, 2000). Kennedy notes that he became an activist in the anti-war movement and first had contact with socialist feminism in the summer of 1975 through the New American Movement, or NAM, which grew as the NCM faded.

76. Sam Blazer, Charles Hinton, Tom Kennedy, Michael (Miguel) Rosner, Denny Smith, and Richard Wilson, *Magnus: a journal of collective faggotry*,

no. 1 (summer 1976), and no. 2 (summer 1977). The issue was dedicated to Michael Krauss, a member of Magnus, RGMU, Gays in Solidarity with the Chilean Resistance, the June 28 Union, the Counter-Bicentennial, and other efforts, who had recently been killed in a bicycle accident.

77. "THREE July Programs," flier, July 1976, Ephemera—Organizations (BAGL), GLBTHS; "Gays and Classism: Workshops . . . Skit!" (flier, c. March 1976), Designed Folder, Matthews Papers. A comment posted by Michael Ogelsby on Tede Matthews's obituary on the GLBTHS and *Bay Area Reporter* obituary database (obit.glbthistory.org) offers insight into the last of these events.

78. "Join the Stonewall Contingent," 1976 (c. June), Ephemera—Organizations (S-Miscellaneous), GLBTHS; "Second Annual BAGL Birthday Party," flier, January 1977, Ephemera—Organizations (BAGL), GLBTHS.

79. Stonewall Contingent, "Stonewall Gay Funnies," 1976, Ephemera—Organizations, GLBTHS.

80. Corbett and Hinton, "Practice Makes Powerful," 44; the vote was also reported as 69–17. The anti-imperialist agenda retained the "mass action" structure first linked to the "rights" approach. See also "What does the future hold for BAGL? BAGL Evaluation Workshop," October 1976; "Progressive Gay Caucus [of BAGL]—Principles of Unity," n.d. (fall 1976); and "Second Annual BAGL Birthday Party," flier, January 1977, all in Ephemera—Organizations (BAGL), GLBTHS.

81. Hanhardt, *Safe Space.*

82. In a related development, the radical gay magazine *Magnus* held that gay oppression began through religious persecution of witches and pagans in early modern Europe and was globalized through European colonialism. In 1979 the Bay Area Socialist School hosted a seminar, "Politics and Gay History," led by members of the new San Francisco Gay History Project, cofounded by Jeffrey Escoffier, a member of the New American Movement and later a well-known scholar. Bay Area Socialist School class calendar, Spring 1979, Ephemera—Organizations, GLBTHS.

83. "Progressive Gay Caucus [of BAGL]—Principles of Unity"; "International Workers' Day/Vietnamese Liberation Celebration," flier, April 1977; and "Independence & Self Determination for Puerto Rico!" (flier c. 1977), all in Ephemera—Organizations (BAGL), GLBTHS.

84. Program & Structure Proposal—Rough Draft, spring 1977, and "Bay Area Gay Liberation June Newsletter," 1978, both in Ephemera—Organizations (BAGL), GLBTHS.

85. Frank, *Out in the Union,* 90; Miriam Frank, "Organized Labor, Gay Liberation, and the Battle against the Religious Right, 1977–1994," *Notches: (re)marks on the history of sexuality,* March 17, 2015.

86. Milk stood to the left of the Society for Individual Rights (SIR) and San Francisco's Alice B. Toklas Democratic Club, and he helped to form a more progressive gay and lesbian Democratic Club that now bears his name.

87. Hinton, interview by author.

88. March Fong Eu (California secretary of state), California Voters Pamphlet, General Election, November 7, 1978.

89. Fred Fejes, *Gay Rights and Moral Panic: The Origins of America's Debate on Homosexuality* (London: Palgrave Macmillan, 2008), 181–82.

90. Smith, "Organizing for Social Justice," 391.

91. Fejes, *Gay Rights and Moral Panic*, 182–86.

92. Michael Ward and Mark Freeman, "Defending Gay Rights: The Campaign against the Briggs Initiative in California," *Radical America* 13:4 (July–August 1979): 22. By December 1977, activists founded the Coalition against the Briggs Initiative (CABI), which dissolved in March 1978 but produced two major offshoots, the Bay Area Coalition against the Briggs Initiative (BACABI) and the Coalition against the Briggs Initiative–Los Angeles (CABILA). These two groups coordinated voter outreach and grassroots organizing undertaken by smaller, local groups across Northern and Southern California. Goodstein's Concerned Voters of California (CVC) and an allied group, Southern California Women for Understanding, raised money from wealthy donors and funded the campaign's few, very muted TV and radio advertisements. Yolanda Retter, "Lesbian Activism in Los Angeles, 1970–79," in *Queer Frontiers: Millennial Geographies, Genders, and Generations*, ed. Joseph A. Boone et al. (Madison: University of Wisconsin Press, 2000): 196–221; Lillian Faderman and Stuart Timmons, *Gay L.A.: A History of Sexual Outlaws, Power Politics, and Lipstick Lesbians* (Berkeley: University of California Press, 2009); Shilts, *Mayor of Castro Street*.

93. Diane Ehrensaft and Ruth Milkman, interview with Amber Hollibaugh, "Sexuality and the State: the Defeat of the Briggs Initiative and Beyond," *Socialist Review* 9:3 (May–June 1979): 1–11.

94. Ward and Freeman, "Defending Gay Rights," 24.

95. Craig and Mahaney in "Milk Skimmed," panel at GLBT Historical Society, San Francisco, February 19, 2009 (notes in author's possession).

96. Hollibaugh, in Ehrensaft and Milkman, "Sexuality and the State." See also Amber Hollibaugh and Cherríe Moraga, "What We're Rollin Around in Bed With: Sexual Silences in Feminism—A Conversation toward Ending Them" (1981), in *My Dangerous Desires*, 62–84.

97. Smith, "Organizing for Social Justice"; Frank, *Out in the Union*, 90–92.

98. Hollibaugh, in Ehrensaft and Milkman, "Sexuality and the State," 7; Ward and Freeman, "Defending Gay Rights." See also "Who Is the Real Threat to Children?" flier, 1977, Ephemera—Organizations (BAGL), GLBTHS.

99. The conference also highlighted the death penalty measure Proposition 7, the property tax cap Proposition 13, and the Supreme Court's anti–affirmative action ruling in *Bakke*. Conference sponsors included the East Bay chapter of the mainline anti-Briggs coalition (EBACABI), the socialist-feminist group Radical Women, BAGL and its Progressive Caucus, the Gay Caucus of HERE Local 2, Union Women's Alliance to Gain Equality (Union WAGE), Lesbian Schoolworkers, Gay Teachers and School Workers, Lesbians and Gay Men (Los Angeles), Gay Teachers (Los Angeles), Nontraditional Employment for Women, and Join Hands (a support group for gay prisoners). Endorsing organizations included Straights for Gay Rights; the Mi Casa, Su Casa Coalition (affiliated with the Puerto Rican Women's Organization); Asian Feminist Group; Black Teachers

Caucus of San Francisco; Gay Asian Support Group; Committee to Defend Reproductive Rights; Sonoma County Residents Against Prop 6 (SCRAP 6); Jews Against Briggs (Los Angeles); President Samille Gooden of AFSCME Local 1695; Coalition of Black Trade Unionists of Northern California; Gay American Indians; and chair Larry Gurley of the National Black Caucus of the American Federation of Teachers. "Statewide Workers Conference Against Briggs/Prop 6, for straight, gay, organized and unorganized workers," September 9–10, 1978, Stonewall Organization Papers, GLBTHS. See also Smith, "Organizing for Social Justice," 403.

100. *Radical America* 13:4 (July–August 1979).

101. Berger, *Outlaws of America,* 234–36. Berger notes that the scheme to bomb Briggs's office was encouraged by undercover FBI provocateurs. See also Bob Lederer, "Three Decades of Queer Solidarity and Radical Struggle: A Rich History," in *Let Freedom Ring: A Collection of Documents from the Movement to Free U.S. Political Prisoners,* ed. Adolfo Perez Esquivel (Montreal: Kersplebedeb, 2008), 395–400; and Judith Bissell [Siff] and Leslie Mullin, "Free the L.A. 5!" *Breakthrough: Political Journal of the Prairie Fire Committee* 2:1 (spring 1978): 54–63.

102. In addition, after the election the Third World Fund, a group based at Glide Church and separate from the Third World Gay Caucus, criticized white gay groups for not opposing Proposition 7; Smith, "Organizing for Social Justice," 428.

103. This poster was designed by Rodrigo Reyes and its photo was taken by Efren Ramírez; both of these men were active in GALA, as well as the Third World Gay Caucus. Individuals in the photo included Blackberri and Brian Freeman, among others.

104. Freeman, interview by author.

105. According to member Lois Helmbold, Lesbian Schoolworkers' spin-off from Gay Teachers and School Workers was an "organic" development rather than a "split" (Hanhardt, *Safe Space,* 119). Gay Teachers and School Workers was led by Tom Ammiano and Hank Wilson (Smith, "Organizing for Social Justice," 421–22, 426).

106. "Don't Let it Happen Here" slideshow, Lesbian Schoolworkers slideshow, GLBTHS. See also "Dear Legislator" form letter, 1978, Wages Due Lesbians file, LLC, ONE; Lesbian Schoolworkers, "Vote No on 6 & 7" flier, Paula Lichtenberg Papers, Box 1, Lesbian Schoolworkers file, GLBTHS.

107. Lesbian Schoolworkers, "THE BRIGGS' INITIATIVE—NOT A SINGLE ISSUE" flier, Ephemera—Subjects (Briggs), GLBTHS.

108. Hanhardt, *Safe Space,* 117.

109. Ibid., 117, 135.

110. LAPV, "Principles of Unity," History and Structure of LAPV (folder), Meg Barnett Papers (1989-05), GLBTHS. See also "Open Letter to Mayor Feinstein," flier, February 15, 1979, Ephemera—Subjects (Wages Due Lesbians), GLBTHS.

111. LAPV Press Release, April 23, 1979, Ephemera—Subjects (Police Relations, 1970s), GLBTHS.

112. Hanhardt, *Safe Space*, 133. See also "Count the Contradictions," Lesbians Against Police Violence (folder), Meg Barnett Papers, GLBTHS; GALA, "Gays vs. *La Raza?*" (letter to the editor), *Plexus* 4:9 (January 1977): 3; Monica Lozano, "Mission Solidarity" (letter to the editor), *Plexus* (July 1979), 2; Jan Adams, "Lozano Taken To Heart" (letter to the editor), *Plexus* (August 1979), 3; "Gay Oppression: A Socialist Perspective," *Turnover: Magazine of Politics & Food*, no. 26 (August–September 1978).

113. Peter Plate, interviewed in "Writing the Left Coast: Peter Plate, in Conversation with Christian Parenti," *Brooklyn Rail*, January 1, 2002, http://brooklynrail.org/2002/01/books/writing-the-left-coast-peter-plate-in-conversation-with-christian-parenti (accessed May 2, 2016).

114. Mahaney, interview by author.

115. Pam David and Lois Helmbold, for Lesbians Against Police Violence, "San Francisco: Courts and Cops vs. Gays," *Radical America* 13:4 (July–August 1979): 27–32.

116. Today, a different bar at the former location of the Elephant Walk bears the commemorative name Harvey's. This is at the intersection of 18th and Castro.

117. Plate, interview by Parenti, "Writing the Left Coast." See also "White Night" flier (n.d., c. October 1981), May 21st folder, Matthews Papers.

118. "America the Beautiful???" flier, 1979, Ephemera—Subjects (White Night Riots), GLBTHS.

119. "Happy Birthday," flier (n.d., c. May 22, 1979), May 21st folder, Matthews Papers.

120. "We Got Cooled Out Tuesday, But We Rioted Monday," May 1979, Stonewall File (Stonewall organization), GLBTHS. Activists also created campy pseudonyms, including Bardykes United Against Police Repression, Politically Correct Lesbians, Daly City Committee for the Elimination of the Ruling Class, and People for a Police-Free Future.

121. LAPV, "Were you at the riot Monday night? Don't talk to the cops," n.d. (1979), Ephemera—Subjects (Protests), GLBTHS.

122. Others arrested accepted plea bargains; Billy Budd (his real name) allegedly committed suicide in jail.

123. Plate, interview by Parenti, "Writing the Left Coast." On the memory of May 21, see David Lamble, "A Night of Fury Remembered: The Voices of May 21st," *Coming Up!* (May 1982), 1–2.

CHAPTER 4. 24TH AND MISSION

1. See figure 9, chapter 3.

2. Cordova, "The Mission in Nicaragua," 213.

3. Carol Seajay, who had worked at the North Oakland bookstore ICI: A Woman's Place (originally affiliated with Gay Women's Liberation), cofounded the bookstore Old Wives' Tales on Valencia Street in 1976; the bookstore was collectively run and sought to respond to its Mission District location by building a section of bilingual books. Hogan, *The Feminist Bookstore Movement*, 31, 40. Modern Times was also located in the neighborhood.

4. Lisa McGirr, *Suburban Warriors: The Origins of the New American Right* (Princeton: Princeton University Press, 2002), 15.

5. Walter LaFeber, *Inevitable Revolutions: The United States in Latin America*, 2nd ed. (New York: W. W. Norton, 1993), 29, 30–31; Michel Gobat, *Confronting the American Dream: Nicaragua under U.S. Imperial Rule* (Durham, NC: Duke University Press, 2005); Thomas D. Schoonover, *The United States in Central America, 1860–1911: Episodes of Social Imperialism and Imperial Rivalry in the World System* (Durham, NC: Duke University Press, 1991). A succession of US policies enabled control: the Monroe Doctrine, the Roosevelt Corollary, the Tobar Doctrine (1922), the Clark Memorandum (1928), FDR's "Good Neighbor" policy, the Rio Pact (1948), the Miller Doctrine (1950), and the Nixon Doctrine (1969).

6. For a summary of the Somoza regime, see Maria Cristina García, *Seeking Refuge: Central American Migration to Mexico, the United States, and Canada* (Berkeley: University of California Press, 2006).

7. LaFeber, *Inevitable Revolutions*, 83–84, 96–97, 111; William Blum, *Killing Hope: U.S. Military and CIA Interventions since World War II* (Monroe, ME: Common Courage Press, 1995).

8. LaFeber, *Inevitable Revolutions*, 11; see also ibid., 163; García, *Seeking Refuge*, 14.

9. María Josefina Saldaña-Portillo, in *The Revolutionary Imagination in the Americas and the Age of Development* (Durham, NC: Duke University Press, 2003), analyzes Sandinista policy in relation to race, ethnicity, and land ownership. Leftist scholarship in English by and about the Sandinistas during the 1980s includes Dennis Gilbert, *Sandinistas: The Party and the Revolution* (New York: Blackwell, 1988); Salvador Cayetano Carpio, *Listen, Compañero: Conversations with Central American Leaders, El Salvador, Guatemala, Nicaragua* (San Francisco: Solidarity, 1983); idem, *Sandinistas Speak—Tomas Borgé et al.* (New York: Pathfinder Press, 1982); and Marlene Dixon and Susanne Jonas, eds., *Revolution and Intervention in Central America* (San Francisco: Synthesis, 1983).

10. For a discussion of the earthquake and the expropriation of aid, see, especially, Omar Cabezas, *Fire from the Mountain: The Making of a Sandinista* (New York: Crown, 1985), 21–23; see also LaFeber, *Inevitable Revolutions*, 165, 226; Saldaña-Portillo, *Revolutionary Imagination*, 111, 117; and García, *Seeking Refuge*, 15.

11. Lancaster, *Life Is Hard*, 4.

12. Elbaum, *Revolution in the Air*, 270.

13. Cordova, "The Mission in Nicaragua," 213.

14. LaFeber, *Inevitable Revolutions*, 233–34; Mauricio Solaún, *U.S. Intervention and Regime Change in Nicaragua* (Lincoln: University of Nebraska Press, 2005); Morris H. Morley, *Washington, Somoza, and the Sandinistas: State and Regime in U.S. Policy toward Nicaragua, 1969–1981* (Cambridge: Cambridge University Press, 1994).

15. Somoza was assassinated in Paraguay in 1980. LaFeber, *Inevitable Revolutions*, 234. On Tellez, see, especially, Margaret Randall, "To Change Our Own Reality and the World: A Conversation with Lesbians in Nicaragua," *Signs: Journal of Women in Culture and Society* 18:4 (1993): 908.

16. Thomas W. Walker, *Reagan versus the Sandinistas: The Undeclared War on Nicaragua* (Boulder, CO: Westview Press, 1987); Peter Kornbluh, *Nicaragua: The Price of Intervention; Reagan's War Against the Sandinistas* (Washington, DC: Institute for Policy Studies, 1987). The International Court of Justice ruled in *The Republic of Nicaragua v. United States of America* (1986) that the United States had violated international law by mining the harbors and funding the Contras, and the court awarded reparations to Nicaragua. On polls, see LaFeber, *Inevitable Revolutions*, 279 (for 1981 poll), 292 (1983 poll), 304 (from January 1984 to late 1986, support was never higher than 35%).

17. The US Senate confirmed the cocaine trafficking through the Kerry Committee Report, formally known as the "Senate Subcommittee Report on Drugs, Law Enforcement, and Foreign Policy: A Report Prepared by the Subcommittee on Terrorism, Narcotics, and International Relations of the Committee on Foreign Relations, U.S. Senate," December 1988 (Washington, DC: U.S. Government Printing Office, 1989). See also Robert Parry, "How John Kerry Exposed the Contra-Cocaine Scandal," *Salon*, October 25, 2004.

18. LaFeber, *Inevitable Revolutions*, 352.

19. Key sources on the solidarity movement at large include Héctor Perla Jr., "Si Nicaragua Venció, El Salvador Vencerá: Central American Agency in the Creation of the U.S.-Central American Peace and Solidarity Movement," *Latin American Research Review* 43:2 (2008): 136–58; idem, "Heirs of Sandino: the Nicaraguan Revolution and the US-Nicaragua Solidarity Movement," *Latin American Perspectives* 36:6 (November 2009): 80–100; Norma Stoltz Chinchilla, Nora Hamilton, and James Loucky, "The Sanctuary Movement and Central American Activism in Los Angeles," *Latin American Perspectives* 36:6 (November 2006): 101–26; Van Gosse, "'The North American Front': Central American Solidarity in the Reagan Era," in *Reshaping the U.S. Left,* ed. Mike Davis and Michael Sprinkler (New York: Verso Press, 1988); idem, "El Salvador Is Spanish for Vietnam," in *The Immigrant Left in the United States,* ed. Paul Buhle and Dan Georgakas (Albany: State University of New York Press, 1996); Sharon Erickson-Nepstad, "Creating Transnational Solidarity: The Use of Narrative in the U.S.-Central America Peace Movement," *Mobilization* 6:1 (2001): 21–36; Ana Patricia Rodriguez, *Dividing the Isthmus: Central American Transnational Histories, Literatures, and Cultures* (Austin: University of Texas Press, 2009); Margaret Keck and Kathryn Sikkink, *Activist beyond Borders* (Ithaca, NY: Cornell University Press, 1998); Smith, *Resisting Reagan*; and Clare Weber, *Visions of Solidarity: U.S. Peace Activists in Nicaragua from War to Women's Activism and Globalization* (Boston: Lexington Books, 2006).

20. LaFeber, *Inevitable Revolutions*, 295; see also García, *Seeking Refuge*; Smith, *Resisting Reagan*; and Ross Gelbspan, *Break-Ins, Death Threats, and the FBI: The Covert War against the Central America Movement* (Boston: South End Press, 1991).

21. Tim Kingston, "Break-In at the Women's Building," *Coming Up!* (April 1987), 10.

22. See, especially, Roxanne Dunbar-Ortiz, *Blood on the Border: A Memoir of the Contra War* (Boston: South End Press, 2005; paperback ed., with new afterword by the author, Norman: University of Oklahoma Press, 2016).

23. Cordova, "The Mission in Nicaragua," 214–15.

24. The figure of 50,000 Nicaraguans is from Alejandro Murguía, "Poetry and Solidarity in the Mission District," in *Ten Years That Shook the City: San Francisco 1968–1978,* ed. Chris Carlsson with Lisa Ruth Elliott (San Francisco: City Lights Books, 2011), 61–70.

25. "Reflecciones de la Raza," radio broadcast, December 30, 1972, KPFA/Pacifica Radio, RP 052, Freedom Archives, San Francisco. Anti-Somoza sentiment also grew within the United States after priests testified before Congress in 1975 and 1976 about atrocities committed by the National Guard, including rape, electric shocks, and other torture (as discussed by both Perla, "Si Nicaragua Venció, El Salvador Vencerá," and LaFeber, *Inevitable Revolutions*).

26. Cordova, "The Mission in Nicaragua," 217; Perla, "Si Nicaragua Venció, El Salvador Vencerá," 144; Murguía, "Poetry and Solidarity"; J.J. Barrow, "When the Mission Ran with the Rebels," *MissionLocal,* February 23, 2011, http://missionlocal.org/2011/02/when-the-mission-ran-with-rebels/ (accessed May 3, 2016). Other organizations that Perla names as active beginning in the late 1970s in both San Francisco and Washington, DC, and that were catalyzed by Central American activists include Casa Nicaragua, the Committee in Solidarity with the People of Nicaragua, NICA, the Nicaragua Taskforce, Los Muchachos de DC, and the Washington Area Nicaragua Solidarity Organization.

27. Cordova, "The Mission in Nicaragua," 221–22; Juan Felipe Herrera, "Riffs on Mission District *Raza* Writers," in *Reclaiming San Francisco: History, Politics, Culture,* ed. James Brook, Chris Carlsson, and Nancy J. Peters (San Francisco: City Lights Books, 1998), 226.

28. Herrera, "Riffs on Mission District *Raza* Writers," 225.

29. Cordova, "The Mission in Nicaragua," 222–23, 226; Herrera, "Riffs on Mission District *Raza* Writers," 226.

30. Sushawn Robb, *Mothering the Movement: The Story of the San Francisco Women's Building* (Denver: Outskirts Press, 2012), 5.

31. Ibid., 143–44; Vázquez, interviewed by Anderson, 2005, 47–48. Diane Jones also echoed these points; Diane Jones, interview by author, June 3, 2011, San Francisco, and email correspondence to author, February 2, 2016. Robb attributes the idea of the merger to Vázquez.

32. On both AAWO and ties to solidarity, see Robb, *Mothering the Movement*; Elbaum, *Revolution in the Air*; and Vázquez, interview by Anderson, 2005. Vázquez notes that, following SFPD brutality toward activists who protested a visit by Salvadoran president Duarte, building staff refused to rent meeting space to an organization of women police.

33. Cordova, "The Mission in Nicaragua," 226 (Alicia and Bergman's travel to Nicaragua); "MaestraPeace Mural," The Women's Building, womensbuilding.org/the-mural (accessed May 3, 2016).

34. Maylei Blackwell, "Translenguas: Mapping the Possibilities and Challenges of Transnational Women's Organizing across Geographies of Difference," in *Translocalities/Translocalidades: Feminist Politics of Translation in the Latin/a Americas,* ed. Sonia E. Alvarez et al. (Durham, NC: Duke University Press, 2014), 302; see also Araceli Esparza, "Cherríe Moraga's Changing Con-

sciousness of Solidarity," in *The Un/Making of Latina/o Citizenship: Culture, Politics, and Aesthetics,* ed. Ellie D. Hernández and Eliza Rodriguez y Gibson (New York: Palgrave Macmillan, 2014), 145–66.

35. Cordova, "The Mission in Nicaragua," 211, 220.

36. Roberto Vargas, "My World Incomplete/To Complete My World," in Carlsson, with Elliot, *Ten Years That Shook the City,* 92–94.

37. Paul Albert, interviewed by Michael Hoffman, June 3, 2012, courtesy of Michael Hoffman. Hoffman is producing a documentary film, *Abrazos de San Pancho,* on the Nicaraguan solidarity movement in San Francisco.

38. Roberto Gurdián, interview by author, July 21, 2012, Los Angeles.

39. Margaret Randall, interview with Rita Arauz, in *Sandino's Daughters Revisited: Feminism in Nicaragua* (New Brunswick, NJ: Rutgers University Press, 1994), 267. Ruth Mahaney recalls two other Nicaraguans—sisters, both of whom were lesbian—who brought discussions of Nicaraguan solidarity to college classes Mahaney taught; Mahaney, interview by author.

40. Siobhan Somerville, "Sexual Aliens and the Racialized State: A Queer Reading of the 1952 U.S. Immigration and Nationality Act," in *Queer Migrations: Sexuality, U.S. Citizenship, and Border Crossings,* ed. Eithne Luibhéid and Lionel Cantú Jr. (Minneapolis: University of Minnesota Press, 2005), 75–91; Marc Stein, "All the Immigrants Are Straight, All the Homosexuals Are Citizens, but Some of Us Are Queer Aliens: Genealogies of Legal Strategy in *Boutilier v. INS,*" *Journal of American Ethnic History* 29:4 (summer 2010): 45–77; Margot Canaday, *The Straight State: Sexuality and Citizenship in Twentieth-Century America* (Princeton, NJ: Princeton University Press, 2011).

41. BAGL Newsletter, June 1978, Ephemera—Organizations (BAGL), GLBTHS; Aurora Levins Morales, "Gays in Nicaragua: An Interview with Roberto Gurdián," *Coming Up* (July 1983), 1.

42. Gurdián quoted in Levins Morales, "Gays in Nicaragua."

43. Albert, interview by Hoffman; see also photo by Emmanuelle Gomez in Gay People for the Nicaraguan Revolution (GPNR) brochure, c. 1979, Vertical Files: United States organizations and individuals (Gay People for the Nicaraguan Revolution), Canadian Lesbian and Gay Archives.

44. Farthing was raised in Montreal and moved to Boston in the early 1970s after deciding that, as a Canadian of English descent, she was unable to commit to assimilating herself fully into Quebecois society as she believed English-speaking people ought to do. She was active in Gay McGill, Gay Montreal, and the Montreal Women's Center. In Boston she worked as the news editor for *Gay Community News* and at Project Lambda, the first organization in the United States to provide services to gay teenagers. She moved to San Francisco in the mid-1970s, taking a job with the city mental health department on a project addressing lesbian drug users and, prior to her trip to Cuba, had become involved in activist efforts including a Haight-Fillmore gay-straight coalition against housing speculation and a group of radical lesbian and gay mental health workers called the DAFODIL Alliance (Dykes and Faggots Organized to Defeat Institutionalized Liberalism). Linda Farthing, interview by author, February 5, 2016, via Skype.

45. Farthing, interview by author; Linda Farthing, email correspondence to author, January 31, 2016.

46. Capó, "Queering Mariel"; Susana Peña, *¡Oye Loca! From the Mariel Boatlift to Gay Cuban Miami* (Minneapolis University of Minnesota Press, 2013).

47. Albert, interview by Hoffman.

48. Farthing, interview by author.

49. Farthing, interview by author. Farthing adds that this session was modeled on similar ones she had carried out in Massachusetts among social workers, court staff, and others who interacted with gay and lesbian youth.

50. Albert, interview by Hoffman.

51. Farthing states that GPNR raised most of its funds from garage sales: "We were garage sale queens" (Farthing, interview by author).

52. "GPNR: Nicaragua," *Plexus* 8:2 (April 1981): 7; Gay People for the Nicaraguan Revolution, "Lesbian Attends International Solidarity Convention," press release, March 5, 1981, Vertical Files: United States organizations and individuals: Gay People for the Nicaraguan Revolution, Canadian Lesbian and Gay Archives.

53. All quotes in this paragraph come from GPNR brochure, c. 1979.

54. Farthing, interview by author.

55. Ibid.

56. GPNR brochure.

57. See also Emily K. Hobson, "'Si Nicaragua Venció': Lesbian and Gay Solidarity with the Revolution," *Journal of Transnational American Studies* 4:2 (fall 2012): 1–26.

58. 1981 Lesbian/Gay Freedom Day Guide, Carton 8, Folder 19, Social Protest Collection, Bancroft Library, University of California, Berkeley. See also undated Casa Nicaragua flier, Ephemera—Organizations (Casa Nicaragua), GLBTHS.

59. Audre Lorde, "When Will the Ignorance End? Keynote Speech at the National Third World Lesbian and Gay Conference, Washington, DC, October 13, 1979," *off our backs* 9:10 (November 1979).

60. Daniel Tsang, "Third World Lesbians and Gays Meet," *Gay Insurgent* 6 (Summer 1980): 11.

61. Rodrigo Reyes, "Latino Gays: Coming Out and Coming Home," *Coming Up!* (December 1981), 3. The Mexican conference was hosted by Mexico's Frente Homosexual de Acción Revolucionaria, or Revolutionary Homosexual Action Front. In 1983, a group of five women from the San Francisco Women's Building traveled to Peru to attend the second Latin American and Caribbean feminist conference; the women stayed at the home of Lucrecia Bermudez, a Peruvian lesbian and Women's Building staff member whose family lived in Lima (Lucrecia Bermudez, interview by author, December 7, 2010 , San Francisco). GPNR member Linda Farthing participated in the trip (Farthing, interview by author).

62. Roque Ramírez, "'That's My Place!'"; and Horacio N. Roque Ramírez, "Claiming Queer Cultural Citizenship: Gay Latino (Im)Migrant Acts in San Francisco," in *Queer Migrations: Sexuality, U.S. Citizenship, and Border Crossings,* ed. Eithne Luibhéid and Lionel Cantú Jr. (Minneapolis: University of Minnesota Press, 2005), 161–88.

63. Ana Patricia Rodriguez, "Refugees of the South: Central Americans in the U.S. Latino Imaginary," *American Literature* 73:2 (June 2001): 389.

64. In *Coming Up!*, see John Kyper, "Mexico: A Movement Under the Gun" (July 1981), 2; Monica Lozano, "Gay Latino/Latina Alliance" (September 1981), 2; Cris, "International Feminism: Lesbian and Gay in Argentina" (March 1982), 1, 5; Aurora Levins Morales, "Breaking the Silence: Gays and the Cuban Revolution" (June 1982), 15; Rodrigo Reyes, "On the Fourth of July: 'What America Means to Me'" (July 1982), 1, 2; John Kyper, "Lesbian/Gay Activists Organize Movement in Mexico" (September 1982), 1–2; and John Kyper, "Gay in Cuba" (August 1983), 1, 15.

65. Reyes, "On the Fourth of July."

66. John Kyper, "New Year's in the New Nicaragua," *Coming Up!* (July 1982), 1, 2.

67. A previous group, the UC Nuclear Weapons Conversion Project, had targeted Livermore through legal advocacy and fueled activists' shift to the labs in 1981. Livermore Action Group, "Livermore Weapons Lab Blockade/Demonstration Handbook, June 21, 1982" (Berkeley, CA: Livermore Action Group, 1982) (hereafter LAG Handbook), 6–10. On the antinuclear movement in general, see, especially, Barbara Epstein, *Political Protest and Cultural Revolution: Nonviolent Direct Action in the 1970s and 1980s* (Berkeley: University of California Press, 1993); Noel Sturgeon, *Ecofeminist Natures: Race, Gender, Feminist Theory, and Political Action* (New York: Routledge, 1997); Sasha Roseneil, *Common Women, Uncommon Practices: The Queer Feminisms of Greenham* (London: Cassell, 2000); Lawrence S. Wittner, *Toward Nuclear Abolition: A History of the World Nuclear Disarmament Movement, 1971 to the Present* (Palo Alto, CA: Stanford University Press, 2003).

68. Wallace Turner, "170 Arrested as Nuclear Protestors Seek to Block Laboratory on Coast," *New York Times*, February 2, 1982, A12; Jill Clark, "Lesbians, Gays Busted at Anti-nuke Blockade," *Gay Community News* 9:50 (July 10, 1982). LAG's 1982 and 1983 blockade coincided with global actions; the 1982 march in New York City drew a million people, and the 1983 "International Day of Nuclear Disarmament" saw protests around the world. Of all these, LAG's blockade produced the greatest number of arrests, with at least 832 reported. David L. Langford, "At Least 1,200 Protestors Arrested in 'Day of Nuclear Disarmament,'" *Philadelphia Inquirer*, June 21, 1983, A4.

69. Sue Zemel, "Nuclear Freeze: Time Is Running Out," *Coming Up!* (December 1981), 3, 8.

70. Many gay men in the antinuclear movement were also active in the Radical Faeries, whose views of the pagan European past and Native North America echoed the settler colonialism that threaded through antinuclear work as a whole; see Scott Morgensen, *Spaces Between Us*. On materialist and anti-essentialist feminism in the antinuclear movement, see, especially, Sturgeon, *Ecofeminist Natures*, 73, 113; Women's Pentagon Action, "Unity Statement" (1980), *Social Justice* 27:24 (82; winter 2000): 160–63; Pam McAllister, ed., *Reweaving the Web of Life: Feminism and Nonviolence* (Vancouver: New Society Publishers, 1982); and Catriona Mortimer-Sandilands and Bruce Erickson,

Queer Ecologies: Sex, Nature, Politics, Desire (Bloomington: Indiana University Press, 2010).

71. "Nonviolence Process: Guidelines for Nonviolence," in LAG Handbook, 32; see also Barbara Epstein, "The Culture of Direct Action: Livermore Action Group and the Peace Movement," *Socialist Review* 15:4–5 (July 1985): 33.

72. "Nonviolence Process: Guidelines for Nonviolence," 32.

73. On the consensus process and "blocking," see LAG Handbook, 42.

74. Ibid., 35, 48.

75. Kate Raphael, email communication to author, February 6, 2016. On the numbers of lesbians among women arrested in the 1982 blockade, see Epstein, "The Culture of Direct Action," 12, 126, 131; and Clark, "Lesbians, Gays Busted at Anti-nuke Blockade." See also Clark, "Anti-Nuke Tactics Confound Livermore Jailers," and Tede Matthews, "Peter Adair: A Change of Heart," *Coming Up!* (January 1983), 3, 5.

76. Clark, "Anti-Nuke Tactics Confound Livermore Jailers"; "News Notes," *Gay Community News* 9:45 (June 5, 1982).

77. Clark, "Lesbians, Gays Busted at Anti-nuke Blockade." On LAG's views of sexual desire more broadly, see "Overcoming Masculine Oppression," LAG Handbook, 40 (originally written by Bill Moyers through his work with Movement for a New Society). Epstein offers a different take by noting that pagans in LAG played "truth or dare" within one another in jail; Epstein, "The Culture of Direct Action," 41.

78. Kate Raphael, interview by author, June 2, 2011, San Francisco (hereafter Raphael, interview by author, 2011). On similar scheduling conflicts in Central American solidarity activism, see the conclusion of chapter 6. Raphael adds that in 1983, the length of the stay in jail caused people to miss the lesbian and gay march, and so they held "pride" celebrations in jail, "which elicited some homophobia from straight activists as well as the guards" (Raphael, email to author, 2016).

79. Tim Wolfred of Gays Against Nuclear Power, quoted in Zemel, "Nuclear Freeze"; Randy Alfred's *The Gay Life* (radio program), May 8, 1979. Abalone's blockades began to expand in the wake of the Three Mile Island nuclear accident in 1979, and in September 1981 Abalone held a major blockade that lasted over two weeks and sent nineteen hundred people to jail, the largest single group of arrests in the history of the antinuclear movement; Epstein, "The Culture of Direct Action," 11.

80. Raphael, interview by author, 2011. On Pledge of Resistance and Witness for Peace, see, especially, Smith, *Resisting Reagan*. Evidence of how these shifts were tracked in the Bay Area gay and lesbian press may be found in Marjory Nelson, "World March for Disarmament," *Coming Up!* (June 1982), 1, 15; Barbara Ustanko, "A Guide for Peace Activists," *Coming Up!* (September 1984), 27; Ustanko, "A Resource Guide for Central American Solidarity Activists," *Coming Up!* (October 1984), 26–27.

81. Ruth Grabowski, interview by author, June 19, 2014, San Francisco.

82. Ruth Grabowski, Kim Marshall, and Kathy Phillips, "The Lesbian & Gay Task Force of the El Salvador Initiative Campaign," *Coming Up!* (October

1983), 2–3; Lesbians and Gays Against Intervention, "Principles of Unity," n.d. (c. 1984), LAGAI folder, Box 2, Marcy Rein Collection, GLBTHS.

83. Grabowski, Marshall, and Phillips, "Lesbian & Gay Task Force."

84. Lesbians and Gays Against Intervention, "Principles of Unity."

85. Raphael, interview by author, 2011. LAGAI also had conflicts with others in the solidarity movement about whether to hold events in Catholic churches, in one instance because of the Church's refusal to allow Dignity, the organization of gay and lesbian Catholics, to hold mass at St. Mary's Cathedral, but more broadly because of concerns about the "the Church's role in enforcing misogyny and homophobia throughout the culture" (Raphael, email to author, 2016).

86. "Alliances: Lesbians and Gay Men in Solidarity," was held on February 11, 1984, and included music, a "Gay Guerrillas" performance, and six speakers: Lucrecia Bermudez on lesbians and gays in Peru; Bill Kraus, "assistant to Rep. Sala Burton, recently returned from El Salvador"; Colombian gay activist Guillermo Ballesteros; Tita Caldwell of the Women's Committee on Central America and Guatemala News and Information Bureau; Merri Besden on Grenada; and Federico Jimenez of the National Committee to Free Puerto Rican Prisoners of War. Alliances flier and 1984 organizational description, LAGAI folder, Box 2, Marcy Rein Collection, GLBTHS.

87. Grabowski, Marshall, and Phillips, "Lesbian & Gay Task Force"; see also John Kyper, "Nicaragua under Attack," *Coming Up!* (April 1983), 2.

88. Mahaney, interview by author.

89. San Francisco Women's Centers/Women's Building Newsletter, June 1984, Newsletters, San Francisco Women's Centers/Women's Building (hereafter SFWC/WB), GLBTHS; Mel Gussow, "Theater: 'Last Tango' from San Francisco," *New York Times,* November 27, 1982; *Crossing Borders* program, San Francisco Mime Troupe file, Hank Tavera Collection (41/28), Ethnic Studies Library, University of California, Berkeley; "Friends of the San Francisco Mime Troupe . . . Help Send the Troupe to Nicaragua," flier (c. 1986), San Francisco Mime Troupe file, Hank Tavera Collection (41/28), Ethnic Studies Library, UC Berkeley.

CHAPTER 5. TALK ABOUT LOVING IN THE WAR YEARS

Portions of this chapter were previously published as "'Si Nicaragua Venció': Lesbian and Gay Solidarity with the Revolution," *Journal of Transnational American Studies* 4:2 (fall 2012): 1–26.

1. Delegates' affiliations included the International Council of African Women, Women for Women in Lebanon, the ACLU, KPFA radio, the gay and lesbian caucus of the Boston Rainbow Coalition, the San Francisco Women's Building, and the Alliance Against Women's Oppression. Alliance Against Women's Oppression/Somos Hermanas newsletter, fall 1984, Somos Hermanas (35/1); Somos Hermanas (50/6), both in SFWC/WB, GLBTHS.

2. Vázquez, interview by Anderson, 50.

3. Ibid., 51.

4. Cherríe Moraga, *Loving in the War Years: Lo que nunca pasó por sus labios,* 2nd ed. (Boston: South End Press, 2000; 1st ed., 1983); and Anzaldúa

and Moraga, eds., *This Bridge Called My Back,* first published in 1981 and 1983, with successive editions in 1988 [Spanish], 2002, and 2015).

5. Esparza, "Cherríe Moraga's Changing Consciousness of Solidarity." See also Sandy Soto, "Where in the Transnational World Are Women of Color?" in *Women's Studies for the Future: Foundations, Interrogations, Politics,* ed. Elizabeth Lapovsky Kennedy and Agatha Beins (New Brunswick, NJ: Rutgers University Press, 2005), 111–24.

6. Moraga, *Loving in the War Years,* 23–24.

7. Vázquez, interview by Anderson, 50.

8. Moraga, *Loving in the War Years,* 23–24.

9. Ibid., 44 (emphasis in original).

10. Sara Ahmed, *The Cultural Politics of Emotion* (London: Routledge, 2004), 189 (spelling in the original).

11. Blackwell, "Translenguas," 317. Similarly, M. Jacqui Alexander and Chandra Talpade Mohanty remind us to continually test out our commitments through networks of "responsibility, accountability, engagement"; Alexander and Mohanty, "Introduction: Genealogies, Legacies, Movements," in *Feminist Genealogies, Colonial Legacies, Democratic Futures,* ed. Alexander and Mohanty (New York: Routledge, 1997), xix.

12. Esparza, "Cherríe Moraga's Changing Consciousness of Solidarity," 164.

13. Other accounts of Nicaraguan gay and lesbian organizing and CEP-SIDA include Karen Kampwirth, "Organizing the *Hombre Nuevo Gay:* LGBT Politics and the Second Sandinista Revolution," *Bulletin of Latin American Research* 33:3 (2014): 319–33; Cymene Howe, *Intimate Activism: The Struggle for Sexual Rights in Postrevolutionary Nicaragua* (Durham, NC: Duke University Press, 2013); Randall, "To Change Our Own Reality and the World"; Margaret Randall, "Coming Out as a Lesbian Is What Brought Me to Social Consciousness: Rita Arauz," in *Sandino's Daughters Revisited,* 265–85; Florence E. Babb, "Out in Nicaragua: Local and Transnational Desires after the Revolution," *Cultural Anthropology* 18:3 (2003): 308; and *Sex and the Sandinistas,* directed by Linda Broadbent (Women Make Movies, 1991).

14. Blackwell, "Translenguas," 299–300.

15. Ibid., 305. As another example, Blackwell notes that in Britain the term "black" includes Caribbean and South Asian people, whereas in the United States it refers only to people of African descent.

16. In the Americas, these debates were often articulated through critiques of Cuba and Cuban solidarity; see, in particular, Guerra, "Gender Policing"'; Lekus, "Queer Harvests"'; Rich and Arguelles, "Homosexuality, Homophobia, and Revolution, Part I"; Capó, "Queering Mariel"; Susana Peña, *¡Oye Loca!*

17. Jones, interview by author.

18. For one account of these brigades, see Janice Irvine, "'Gay Man in a Dyke Squad': *Brigadistas* Inspired by Nicaraguans," *Gay Community News* (March 17, 1984), 3.

19. Rebecca Gordon, *Letters from Nicaragua* (San Francisco: Spinsters/Aunt Lute Press, 1986); Raphael, interview by author, 2011.

20. Important sources on feminism and sexuality in the Sandinista Revolution include Cymene Howe, "Gender, Sexuality, and Revolution: Making Histories and Cultural Politics in Nicaragua 1979–2001," in *Gender, Sexuality, and Power in Latin America since Independence*, ed. William E. French and Katherine Elaine Bliss (Lanham, MD: Rowman & Littlefield, 2007), 230–60; Karen Kampwirth and Victoria Gonzáles-Rivera, *Radical Women in Latin America: Left and Right* (University Park: Penn State University Press, 2001); Norma Stoltz Chinchilla, "Revolutionary Popular Feminism in Nicaragua: Articulating Class, Gender, and National Sovereignty," *Gender and Society* 4:3 (1990): 370–97; idem, "Revolutionary Popular Feminism in Transition in Nicaragua: 1979–1994," in *Women in the Latin American Development Process*, ed. Chris Bose and Edna Acosta-Belen (Philadelphia: Temple University Press, 1995), 242–71; Maxine Molyneux, "Mobilization without Emancipation? Women's Interest, State, and Revolution in Nicaragua," *Feminist Studies* 11:2 (1985): 227–54; and Lancaster, *Life Is Hard*. On women's and feminist mobilization before the revolution, see Victoria Gonzáles-Rivera, *Before the Revolution: Women's Rights and Right-Wing Politics in Nicaragua, 1821–1979* (University Park: Penn State University Press, 2012).

21. See, especially, Lorraine Bayard de Volo, *Mothers of Heroes and Martyrs: Gender Identity Politics in Nicaragua, 1979–1999* (Baltimore: Johns Hopkins University Press, 2001).

22. Ernesto (Che) Guevara, "Socialism and Man in Cuba" (1965), in *Che Guevara Reader: Writings on Guerrilla Strategy, Politics and Revolution*, 2nd ed., ed. David Deutschmann (Melbourne, Australia: Ocean Press, 2003), 212–30. For critiques, see especially Guerra, "Gender Policing"; Rich and Arguelles, "Homosexuality, Homophobia, and Revolution"; Lekus, "Queer Harvests"; and Rodriguez, *Women, Guerrillas, and Love*.

23. Victoria Gonzáles-Rivera and Karen Kampwirth are developing a history of LGBT Nicaragua both before and since 1979. See Victoria González-Rivera, "The Alligator Woman's Tale: Remembering Nicaragua's 'First Self-Declared Lesbian,'" *Journal of Lesbian Studies* 18:1 (2014): 75–87.

24. Millie Thayer, "Identity, Revolution, and Democracy: Lesbian Movements in Central America," *Social Problems* 44:3 (1997): 386–407.

25. Lancaster, *Life Is Hard*, 254, 237–45.

26. Randall, "To Change Our Own Reality and the World," 916; see also Howe, "Gender, Sexuality, and Revolution," and the film *Sex and the Sandinistas*.

27. Cymene Howe, "Undressing the Universal Queer Subject: Nicaraguan activism and transnational identity," *City & Society* 14:2 (2002): 254.

28. Ibid., 241–43.

29. "Celebrate—Demonstrate—March," July 19, 1981, John Kyper Papers, GLBTHS.

30. Margaret Randall, *Sandino's Daughters: Testimonies of Nicaraguan Women in Struggle*, rev. ed. (New Brunswick, NJ: Rutgers University Press, 1995; original edition, London: Zed Books, 1981). The book was also published in Spanish in 1981 and 1983, Portuguese in 1983, and Turkish in 1985.

31. Vázquez, interview by Anderson, 49.

32. Pam David, interview by author, August 13, 2010, San Francisco.

33. Marcia M. Gallo, interview by author, August 16, 2010, Berkeley.

34. John Kyper, "New Year's in the New Nicaragua," *Coming Up!* (July 1982), 1. Similarly, in 1986 the Boston gay organization United Fruit created the parodic calendar "Hunks of Nicaragua.".

35. An example of heterosexual desire within Nicaraguan solidarity can be seen in the publication and reception of Gioconda Belli's memoir *The Country Under My Skin* (New York: Anchor, 2002).

36. Hiram Pérez, *A Taste for Brown Bodies: Gay Modernity and Cosmopolitan Desire* (New York: New York University Press, 2015). See also Emily K. Hobson, "'Si Nicaragua Venció.'"

37. Gurdián, quoted in Levins Morales, "Gays in Nicaragua," 1 (emphasis in original).

38. Gordon, *Letters from Nicaragua*.

39. Ibid., 42–43. See also Jan Adams's statements in ibid., 26–27.

40. For her later self-critique, see Rebecca Gordon, "The Price of Visibility: Book Review of *Queers in Space: Communities, Public Places, Sites of Resistance*" (by Gordon Brent Ingram, Anne-Marie Bouthillete, and Yolanda Retter), *Women's Review of Books* 15:6 (1998): 7–8.

41. Gordon, *Letters from Nicaragua*, 43.

42. Smith quoted in ibid., 16.

43. Bermudez, interview by author.

44. See also Lucrecia Bermudez, "Me siento marginada," in *Compañeras: Latina Lesbians*, ed. Juanita Ramos (New York: Routledge, 1994), 227–31. Bermudez settled in San Francisco in 1980 and became active in Gay People for Nicaragua, the San Francisco Women's Building, La Conexion Latina (a group of Latina lesbians), Amaranto (gay and lesbian Latin American immigrants), and other groups.

45. Vázquez, interview by Anderson, 49.

46. Ibid., 62; Bermudez, interview by author.

47. Vázquez, interview by Anderson, 49. Vázquez had worked in the Puerto Rican Socialist Party in New York and the League of United Latin American Citizens in San Francisco, and from 1980 to 1984 she served in the central leadership of the San Francisco Women's Building.

48. On the Third World Women's Alliance and AAWO, see Springer, *Living for the Revolution*; and Elbaum, *Revolution in the Air*. On the Women's Building, see Robb, *Mothering the Movement*.

49. The first public report of the trip was AAWO, "Somos Hermanas (We Are Sisters) Women's Tour to Nicaragua," *Coming Up!* (September 1984), 9.

50. Rose Appleman, "First West Coast Conference on Women in Central America, Somos Hermanas: Embracing Our Sisters in Solidarity," *Coming Up!* (April 1985), 9–10. The March conference received support from MADRE, Friends of Nicaraguan Culture, CHRICA, the Victoria Mercado Brigade, and the Women's Building. On Nairobi, see Carmen Vázquez, "6,000 Women at African Conference Conclude U.N. Decade of the Women, Strategize for the Future," *Coming Up!* (August 1985), 12–13.

51. Elsa Granados, "Haciendo conexiones," in *Esta puente, mi espalda: Voces de mujeres tercermundistas en los Estados Unidos,* ed. Cherríe Moraga and Ana Castillo (San Francisco: Ism Press, 1988), 201–3; discussed in Esparza, "Cherríe Moraga's Changing Consciousness of Solidarity," 158–159.

52. Somos Hermanas brochure, c. 1986 (50/6), SFWC/WB, GLBTHS.

53. Somos Hermanas mailing, 1989 (50/11), SFWC/WB, GLBTHS.

54. Vázquez, interview by Anderson; Jones, interview by author. Vázquez and Jones represented Somos Hermanas on the 1987 visit.

55. On Fuentes's history, see Cary Cordova, "The Heart of the Mission: Latino Art and Identity in San Francisco" (PhD dissertation, American Studies, University of Texas, Austin, 2005).

56. Marcia Gallo states that she has taken the poster everywhere she has lived or worked since 1985. Gallo, personal email correspondence with author, July 6, 2010.

57. For a critique of universalism in women of color and transnational feminism during this time, see Chandra Mohanty, "Under Western Eyes: Feminist Scholarship and Colonial Discourses," *boundary* 2 (1984): 333–58. For a more recent analysis, see Soto, "Where in the Transnational World Are Women of Color?"

58. Grabowski, interview by author.

59. Quotes from Ruth Grabowski, "Int'l Lesbian/Gay Brigade to Nicaragua," *Coming Up!* (September 1984), 9.

60. "Lesbian/Gay Work Brigade Readies for Nicaragua Trip; Plans Benefit," *Coming Up!* (December 1984), 8.

61. On the collective at Old Wives' Tales, see Carol Fields, interview by author, June 20, 2014, Oakland; and Hogan, *The Feminist Bookstore Movement.* On Victoria Mercado, see Canyon Sam, "For Victoria," *Coming Up!* (July 1982), 2; and Bettina Aptheker, "Mercado, Victoria 'Vicky' (1951–1982)," in *Latinas in the United States: A Historical Encyclopedia,* Vol. 2, ed. Vicki L. Ruiz and Virginia Sánchez (Bloomington: Indiana University Press, 2006), 451–52. Mercado had been involved in the campaign to defend Angela Davis and was an activist in the ILWU (International Longshore and Warehouse Union). She and a friend were killed when they went to meet a man who had agreed to buy Mercado's used car.

62. Among the participants were Carol Fields, Regina Gabrielle, Margaret Benson Thompson, Ellen Gavin, Ruth Grabowski, and Phil Tingley (Kiowa). Those who helped organize the brigade but did not go included Marisa Monasterio, a close friend of Victoria Mercado's; Maria Cora, who had participated in the Somos Hermanas delegation the previous year; Puerto Rican lesbian Margarita Benitez; longtime gay leftist and social butterfly Tede Matthews; and David Stern, who would soon become a central leader in San Francisco's ACT UP. On Cora's role in Somos Hermanas, see "Somos Hermanas (We Are Sisters) Women's Tour to Nicaragua," 9. Six of those tied to the project—Benitez and all the men—later died of AIDS-related causes; for Benitez's experience, see Margarita Benitez, "Learning to Live with AIDS," *Sinister Wisdom* 47 (summer–fall 1992), 25–27.

63. Hogan, *The Feminist Bookstore Movement,* 40, 45, and 79. Hogan draws a contrast between Old Wives' Tales and ICI: A Woman's Place, which

split during the early 1980s over questions of antiracism. A Woman's Place had been founded in 1970 as an outgrowth of Gay Women's Liberation (GWL, discussed in chapter 2). In 1982 three of its original collective members and former GWL members—Alice Molloy, Carol Wilson, and Natalie Lando—locked out four others who had been advocating antiracism—two women of color and two white women. This conflict was widely reported in the feminist press, and while the "Locked Out Four" regained control of A Woman's Place, the bookstore closed in 1985. The original GWL women went on to form Mama Bears bookstore in North Oakland, while one of those locked out joined Old Wives' Tales. On these events, see Hogan, *The Feminist Bookstore Movement*, 98–101.

64. Ellen Gavin, interview by author, December 15, 2010, Los Angeles.

65. Grabowski, interview by author.

66. Ibid.

67. Ellen Gavin, "Nicaragua: Front Line Report," *San Francisco Sentinel,* July 18, 1985.

68. Fields, interview by author; Alliance Against Women's Oppression/ Somos Hermanas newsletter, fall 1984 (35/1), SFWC/WB, GLBTHS. Somos Hermanas noted that it countered this response by explaining that the members all traveled from the United States but "represented those sectors of women most oppressed by racism, sexism, and Reagan's budget cuts and war policies." For a related example of views of women of color abroad, see Audre Lorde's description of her time in Mexico in *Zami: A New Spelling of My Name* (Trumansburg, NY: Crossing Press, 1982).

69. Fields, interview by author. Solidarity activists often kept quiet about Sandinista policies toward indigenous and black Nicaraguans, press censorship, and election delays, and these silences reflected both their desire to follow the Sandinista leadership and their often limited framework for analyzing racism and sovereignty. In response to Sandinista policy, Miskitu people split into pro- and anti-Sandinista groups (the latter were recruited into the contras). The FSLN then split the Zelaya region into two zones, creating black and indigenous self-rule in the revolution. For a leftist account of Sandinista indigenous policy and the transnational effort to reshape it, see Dunbar-Ortiz, *Blood on the Border*. For a critical analysis of Sandinista land policy more broadly, see Saldaña-Portillo, *Revolutionary Imagination*.

70. Fields, interview by author. Fields grew up in Ohio and had moved to the Bay Area at age twenty, in August 1978, drawn especially by its black political cultural and arts scene. Upon her arrival she joined the women's rugby team and, through that affiliation, lesbian activism; she also completed degrees at San Francisco State University, where she took courses from Angela Davis and bell hooks, among others. After the Victoria Mercado Brigade she also became active in Nia, a black lesbians' group.

71. Gavin, "Nicaragua: Front Line Report," 12–13; see also Ellen Gavin, email correspondence to author, February 1, 2016.

72. Victoria Mercado Brigade event program, Folder 20, Women Against Imperialism (hereafter WAI) Collection, Freedom Archives. Event sponsors and advertisers named in the program included LAGAI, Somos Hermanas (espe-

cially Carmen Vázquez and Lucrecia Bermudez); the Human Rights and Justice Program of the American Friends Services Committee; CISPES; CHRICA; the Nicaragua Network; the Vanguard and Capp Street Foundations; Woman's Press; Swingshift; the Nicaragua Information Center; Prairie Fire Organizing Committee; Women Against Imperialism; Jewish Women for a Secular Middle East; the Woman to Woman Campaign to Support the Women's Associations of Nicaragua and El Salvador; the bookstores Old Wives' Tales, Modern Times, and A Woman's Place; the Enola Gay affinity group; and several law offices and individuals associated with organizations.

73. The Philadelphia Lesbian and Gay Work Brigade was sponsored by the Philadelphia American Friends Service Committee and financially supported by two local gay men. My thanks to Bob Siedle-Khan for informing me of this project. In addition, a largely lesbian construction project established in Nicaragua, the Mujeres Constructoras in Condega, was assisted by a brigade of lesbian activists from Boston in the late 1980s; Lucy Grinnell, email correspondence with author, January 11, 2011.

74. Martha Sacasa, interview by author, January 8, 2014, Managua, Nicaragua; Joel Zúñiga Traña, interview by author, January 10, 2014, Managua, Nicaragua (hereafter Zúñiga); Lupita Sequeira, interview by author, January 11, 2014, Matagalpa, Nicaragua. These interviews were conducted in Spanish and translations are my own.

75. Gurdián, interview by author.

76. Zúñiga, interview by author; Julie Light, interview by author, June 26, 2013, Oakland.

77. Zúñiga, interview by author.

78. Sacasa and Sequeira, interviews by author; Brenda Flores (pseudonym of Lupita Sequeira), quoted in Kim Irving, "Lesbian Sandinista Speaks Out," *Rites* 3:9 (March 1987): 13.

79. List of activists and friends included in Amy Bank to Amanda Newstetter, July 1, 1990, Amanda Newstetter Archive, San Francisco. My thanks to Amy Bank and Amanda Newstetter for providing access to these materials.

80. Julieta Martínez, email correspondence with author, February 16, 2016.

81. Sequeira, interview by author.

82. Amy Bank, interview by author, June 25, 2013, via Skype (hereafter Bank interview 1 or Bank (1)); Amy Bank, interview by author, January 18, 2014, Managua, Nicaragua (hereafter Bank interview 2).

83. Light, interview by author.

84. Bank interviews 1 and 2; Light, interview by author. One of the other buyers was María Josefina (Josie) Saldaña-Portillo, a researcher, writer, and activist then living in Nicaragua and working for the periodical *Envío*, published by the Instituto Histórico Centroamericano. Saldaña-Portillo later went on to graduate school and became a scholar of race, globalization, and Latina/o cultural studies. Josefina Saldaña-Portillo, email communication to author, April 24, 2014, and February 16, 2016.

85. Amy Bank, group letter, October 13 1986, Newstetter Archive.

86. Light, interview by author.

87. Light, interview by author. Ellen Gavin, Catherine Cusic, and Leonel Argüello have also recalled attending parties at the house; Gavin, interview by author; Catherine Cusic, interview by author, June 24, 2013, San Francisco; Leonel Argüello, interview by author, January 17, 2014, Managua, Nicaragua.

88. Arauz in Randall, "Coming Out as a Lesbian"; Zúñiga, interview by author; Bank interview 1.

89. Light, interview by author; Bank interview 1.

90. Sequeira, quoted in Irving, "Lesbian Sandinista Speaks Out."

91. Bank interviews 1 and 2; Sequeira and Zúñiga, interviews by author.

92. Sequeira, interview by author.

93. Bank interview 1; on Arauz, see Amy Bank to Amanda Newstetter, February 27, 1987, Newstetter Archives. In this letter, Bank asked Newstetter to keep this information confidential.

94. Zúñiga and Bank (1), interviews by author.

95. Zúñiga and Bank (1), interviews by author. The quiebre is also noted by Arauz, in Randall, "Coming Out as a Lesbian." Commemorations of the quiebre are issued primarily by the LGBTI activist network associated with the MRS, or Movimiento Renovador Sandinista (Sandinista Renovation Movement), which was founded through a break from the FSLN. Zúñiga is associated with the MRS and is an activist in its LGBTI working group, the Red Nacional de la Diversidad Sexual Renovadora.

96. Bank (1) and Light, interviews by author; on the pressure on Light to inform on the press corps, see Julie Light, email communication to author, March 22, 2016.

97. Zúñiga, interview by author.

98. Arauz, in Randall, "Coming Out as a Lesbian"; see also Bank, in Randall, "To Change Our Own Reality and the World."

99. Light, interview by author. See also Randall, Sandino's Daughters Revisited.

100. Amy Bank, group letter, February 11, 1987, Newstetter Papers.

101. Amy Bank, group letter, May 10, 1987, Newstetter Papers.

102. Melissa Smith and Robert Drickey, "Education for Primary Health Care: A Report on the U.S.-Nicaragua Colloquia on Health," Mobius 5:3 (July 1985): 136. Sandinista policy followed guidelines set out by the WHO- and UNICEF-sponsored International Conference on Primary Health Care held in September 1978 in Alma-Ata, USSR (now Almaty, Kazakhstan).

103. Argüello, interview by author; Ana Quirós, interview by author, January 10, 2014, Managua, Nicaragua. Quirós, also a cofounder of CISAS, held the codirectorship with Maria Hamlin Zuniga (no relation to Joel Zúñiga); at this writing Quirós is director of CISAS.

104. Argüello is Nicaraguan, and Quirós was born in Mexico to Costa Rican parents and raised in Costa Rica and the United States.

105. Alexis X. Jetter, "Trailing the Cops and the Demonstrators," Coming Up! (September 1984), 12, 54.

106. Naomi Schapiro, "AIDS Brigade: Organizing Prevention," in AIDS: The Women, ed. Ines Rieder and Patricia Ruppelt (San Francisco: Cleis Press, 1988), 211.

107. The group changed its name after learning that *crica* is a Puerto Rican vulgarity equivalent to "cunt"; the fact that members had not known of this connotation earlier reflected their Central American, Mexican, and Chicana/o knowledge of Spanish. My thanks to Estelle Schneider for alerting me to the context of this name change.

108. Smith and Drickey, "Education for Primary Health Care."

109. Cusic and Quirós, interviews by author; Sue Zemel, "Visiting the New Nicaragua," *Coming Up!* (March 1984), 9, 21. Zemel's article, based on an interview with Cusic, noted that Cusic spoke about lesbian and gay support for Central American solidarity during her visit to the colloquium, emphasizing both the Proposition N campaign and the role of "gay Latins" in solidarity work.

110. Argüello, interview by author. Given these conditions, Nicaragua could easily have developed an extremely high rate of HIV/AIDS; Argüello credits the low rate to the Sandinistas' ban on the commercialization of blood products, which had been instituted to end a Somoza-era blood bank that exploited people in deep poverty.

111. "Health: Taking AIDS Seriously," *Envío*, no. 92 (March 1989).

112. Argüello, interview by author.

113. Dan Belmm, "AIDS Education Nicaragua Style," *Coming Up!* (May 1988), 14–15.

114. Derek Coursen, "AIDS Education in Nicaragua," *Nicaragua through Our Eyes: The Bulletin of Committee of US Citizens Living in Nicaragua (CUS-CLIN)* 3:6 (1987): 8. On the recognition of Kraus, see Cusic, interview by author.

115. Cusic, interview by author.

116. Cathy Cockrell, "Nicaragua Faces AIDS: San Francisco Activists Advise the Sandinistas," *San Francisco Sentinel* (February 5, 1988), 12; Schapiro, "AIDS Brigade," 212; Coursen, "AIDS Education in Nicaragua," 5. On the general response to the AIDS brigade, see Amy Bank to Amanda Newstetter, December 3, 1986, Newstetter Archive.

117. Schapiro, "AIDS Brigade," 213.

118. Dora María Tellez, interview by author, January 15, 2014, Managua, Nicaragua (this interview was conducted in Spanish and the translation is my own); Argüello, interview by author.

119. Dan Wohlfeiler, "NICA-AIDS" report (January 5, 1988), 1, courtesy Dan Wohlfeiler. Wohlfeiler also carried toilet paper, gefilte fish, and motorcycle parts—the first a scarce commodity thanks to the U.S.-backed economic blockade, the second to mark the upcoming Passover with Amy Bank and others, and the third to ensure Wohlfeiler and Cusic's transportation in Managua, as Cusic had obtained an old bike that needed repair (Dan Wohlfeiler, interview by author, March 7, 2014, Berkeley; Dan Wohlfeiler, email communication to author, March 24, 2016).

120. Cusic and Wohlfeiler, interviews by author. In addition, Nicaraguan activists did not know that Leonel Argüello and Dora María Tellez had not been told of the *quiebre*.

121. Cusic, interview by author; Cusic, email communication to author, July 10, 2013; Quirós, interview by author. The head of the Human Rights Commission was Vilma Nuñez de Escorcia.

122. Wohlfeiler, interview by author.

123. Wohlfeiler, "NICA-AIDS" report, 11.

124. Ibid., 19. Wohlfeiler also noted that both the gay men in the workshop and the women epidemiologists from MINSA "seemed more than willing to talk openly and crack jokes" about sex (ibid., 17).

125. Argüello, interview by author. MINSA had separately received ELISA test kits from supporters in Europe, but could not use them without reagents.

126. In 1990 Perpich was the named plaintiff in a federal suit (*Perpich v. Department of Defense*) seeking to allow governors to prevent state National Guard units from being deployed internationally. He lost.

127. Leonel Argüello, public interview in San Francisco, July 1987, courtesy Ellen Gavin. See also Argüello, interview by author.

128. Bank, quoted in Coursen, "AIDS Education in Nicaragua," 8.

129. Tellez and Zúñiga, interviews by author.

130. Zúñiga, interview by author.

131. Tellez, interview by author.

132. Tellez said that the lack of any official FSLN policy on homosexuality at that time—whether for or against—meant that she and Argüello did not need to seek party approval to support CEP-SIDA or to support gay and lesbian leadership within it. No date was recorded for the Tellez meeting, but a report published in 1988 by an Irish solidarity group states that the gay and lesbian group received MINSA training by October. Kieran Rose, "Lesbians and Gay Men," in *Nicaragua: An Unfinished Canvas*, ed. Nicaraguan Book Collective (Dublin: Nicaraguan Book Collective, 1988): 84. Rose was a union and gay activist who took part in the "First Irish Coffee Brigade" to Nicaragua in 1988 and, while there, met the lesbian and gay group. Like US activists, he contrasted Nicaraguan AIDS policy to his own country's criminalization of homosexuality.

133. Schapiro, "AIDS Brigade," 212.

134. On the number of outreach workers, see Howe, *Intimate Activism*, 44; on condoms, see Light, interview by author.

135. Bank interview 1. The film was *Ojos que no ven*, directed by Jose Gutierrez-Gomez (Instituto Familiar de la Raza and Latino AIDS Project, 1987). See also Bank, quoted in Coursen, "AIDS Education in Nicaragua," 9.

136. For background on these efforts, see Jennifer Brier, *Infectious Ideas: U.S. Political Responses to the AIDS Crisis* (Chapel Hill: University of North Carolina Press, 2009); and Horacio N. Roque Ramírez, "Gay Latino Histories/ Dying to Be Remembered: AIDS Obituaries, Public Memory, and the Queer Latino Archive," in *Beyond El Barrio: Everyday Life in Latina/o America*, ed. Adrian Burgos, Frank Andre Guridy, and Gina M. Perez (New York: New York University Press, 2010), 103–28.

137. Tim Kingston, "The First Six Months: Latino AIDS Project Grapples with the Epidemic," *Coming Up!* (September 1987), 5, 7–8.

138. Schapiro, "AIDS Brigade," 211.

139. In the revolution's wake, several NGOs emerged that addressed HIV/ AIDS, lesbian and gay concerns, and women's rights; three key organizations were Fundación Nimehuatzin and Fundación Xochiquetzal, both of which addressed HIV/AIDS, and Puntos de Encuentro, a feminist organization working for women's rights. See especially Howe, *Intimate Activism*, 46, and the Puntos de Encuentro website, puntosdeencuentro.org.

140. Cockrell, "Nicaragua Faces AIDS," 1, 12. Nicaraguan activists also recall ACT UP New York member Jeff Gates working to organize support for CEP-SIDA.

141. A painter, Aguilar presented his work in an exhibit at Modern Times Bookstore from July 6 through August 31, 1988; called "Flores en el crater/ Flowers in the crater," the exhibit was organized through the collaboration of Tede Matthews and several other solidarity activists. Aguilar lives in the Bay Area today.

142. "AIDS Education Nicaragua Style," reception invitation, c. 1988, Instituto Familiar de la Raza, Ephemera Collection—Organizations, GLBTHS; see also Skye Morrison, "Amaranto: Latin Lesbians and Gays Organize," *Coming Up!* (October 1988), 8–9; and Amy Bank, group letter, December 5, 1988, Newstetter Archive.

143. Dan Belmm, "AIDS Education Nicaragua Style," *Coming Up!* (May 1988), 14–15. On the surgeon general mailing and federal responses to AIDS, see Brier, *Infectious Ideas*, and Jennifer Brier, "The Immigrant Infection: Images of Race, Nation, and Contagion in the Public Debates on AIDS and Immigration," in *Modern American Queer History*, ed. Allida Black (Philadelphia: Temple University Press, 2001), 253–70.

144. Schapiro, "AIDS Brigade," 214; on earlier cases of Nicaraguans living outside the country, see Wohlfeiler, "NICA-AIDS" report, 5. According to Argüello, eighteen of the foreigners with HIV/AIDS were Spaniards and straight IV drug users visiting on a drug rehabilitation brigade sponsored by Tomás Borge and known as "el Patriarca"; they were expelled from the country after refusing to adhere to safer-sex guidelines (Argüello, interview by author).

145. Wohlfeiler, interview by author; Bank, in Coursen, "AIDS Education in Nicaragua," 8–9.

146. Tede Matthews to Amy Bank, October 10, 1988, Amy Bank Archive, Berkeley, CA. On mourning in the Mission as related to both AIDS and Central America, see Horacio N. Roque Ramírez, "My Community, My History, My Practice," *Oral History Review* 29:2 (summer–autumn 2002): 87–91; Roque Ramírez, "Gay Latino Histories/Dying to Be Remembered"; Cordova, "The Heart of the Mission."

147. Zúñiga, interview by author.

148. Amy Bank, letter to Amanda Newstetter (January 24, 1989), 2, Newstetter Archive; Zúñiga, interview by author.

149. Jeffrey Gates, CEP-SIDA flier, c. 1989–1990, Organizational Files: CEP-SIDA, LHA; *Sex and the Sandinistas*.

150. Arauz, in Randall, *Sandino's Daughters Revisited*, 275. See also Randall, "To Change Our Own Reality and the World"; and Howe, "Undressing the Universal Queer Subject."

151. Lupita Sequeira, in *Sex and the Sandinistas*. For a brief discussion of the mural that Sequeira notes, see Barbara Lowe et al., *Human Rights for All? Global View of Lesbian and Gay Oppression and Liberation* (London: Reading International Support Center, 1992).

152. Zúñiga, interview by author.

CHAPTER 6. MONEY FOR AIDS, NOT WAR

1. John Lindsay-Poland, quoted in Scott Brookie, "Blood and Money: Gay Men Protest Military Spending," *Gay Community News* 12:14 (October 20, 1984): 3.

2. The first civil disobedience in New York City took place in November 1985 and was less informed by anti-militarism. David Summers, the board chair of New York's PWA Coalition, was arrested when he attempted to enter a New York City Council hearing where he was scheduled to address a resolution on closing bathhouses. Sean Strub, *Body Counts: A Memoir of Politics, Sex, AIDS, and Survival* (New York: Scribner, 2014), 186; Jane Rosett, "The Buddy Line," *Poz*, March 1997.

3. John Lorenzini, "AIDS and Civil Disobedience," in *Out and Outraged: Non-Violent Civil Disobedience at the U.S. Supreme Court—For Love, Life & Liberation, October 13, 1987: C.D. Handbook,* 23–24 (Carton 1, Folder 33: March on Washington, Arawn Eibhlyn Papers, GLBTHS); Bill Blackburn, interview by author, July 2, 2014, by telephone. Just a few weeks before Lorenzini's action, Blackburn had taken part in the Men's Peace Encampment, in which seventy-five gay and straight men marched to the Concord Naval Weapons Station and performed a "keening," or ritual act of crying, at the gate; this action was modeled on, and employed to honor, tactics used by many women in the antinuclear movement. On the Men's Peace Encampment, see John Lindsay-Poland, "Men's Peace Camp," *Collective Networker Newsletter,* no. 83 (April 1985), 2; "Men's Action" flier, June 12, 1985 (courtesy John Lindsay-Poland); and Blackburn, interview by author.

4. This account draws principally on Avram Finkelstein, "The Silence = Death Poster," LGBT@NYPL (New York Public Library blog), November 22, 2013, http://www.nypl.org/blog/2013/11/22/silence-equals-death-poster (accessed May 26, 2016); see also Avram Finkelstein, "AIDS 2.0," *Poz* (January 10, 2013); Avram Finkelstein, interviewed by Sarah Schulman, January 23, 2010, ACT UP Oral History Project (actuporalhistory.org).

5. Deborah B. Gould, *Moving Politics: Emotion and ACT UP's Fight Against AIDS* (Chicago: University of Chicago Press, 2009), 130–31.

6. Tim Kingston, "Gay Leaders Hit the Streets," *Coming Up!* (July 1987), 6–7, 35. On the D.C. protest, see Strub, *Body Counts*; Gould, *Moving Politics*; and Marc Stein, *Rethinking the Gay and Lesbian Movement* (New York: Routledge, 2012).

7. At least two members of ACT UP New York, Jim Eigo and Jeff Gates, also had histories in Central American solidarity, but they were relatively unique in New York as compared to the Bay Area.

8. Lawrence K. Altman, "Rare Cancer Seen in 41 Homosexuals," *New York Times*, July 3, 1981.

9. Willi McFarland, ed., *Atlas of HIV/AIDS in San Francisco 1981–2000* (San Francisco: San Francisco Department of Public Health AIDS Office, 2002), 44.

10. "Thirty Years of HIV/AIDS: Snapshots of an Epidemic," amfAR, Foundation for AIDS Research, http://www.amfar.org/thirty-years-of-hiv/aids-snapshots-of-an-epidemic/ (accessed May 8, 2016).

11. See, especially, Strub, *Body Counts*; and Martin Duberman, *Hold Tight Gently: Michael Callen, Essex Hemphill, and the Battlefield of AIDS* (New York: The New Press, 2014).

12. Brier, *Infectious Ideas*, 54; see also 69, 171.

13. In addition, backers of a social action agenda were at times mistakenly characterized as HIV-negative because they prioritized identities as people of color or some other group. Gould, *Moving Politics*, 369–72; Brier, *Infectious Ideas*; and discussions in *United in Anger: A History of ACT UP*, directed by Jim Hubbard (2012).

14. Vito Russo, "Why We Fight," speech at ACT UP demonstration in Albany, New York, May 9, 1988, reprinted in full in Jeffrey Schwartz, "Vito Russo's 'Why We Fight': Revisiting the Explosive 1988 AIDS Speech," *Huffington Post*, July 11, 2012.

15. Marita Sturken, *Tangled Memories: The Vietnam War, the AIDS Epidemic, and the Politics of Remembering* (Berkeley: University of California Press, 1997), 195; see also *Maya Lin: A Strong Clear Vision*, directed by Freida Lee Mock, 1994.

16. Indeed, GIs and veterans had led some of the most spectacular protests against the Vietnam War, and the challenges their organizing posed to traditional masculinity and citizenship—including through ties to gay liberation—lay at the heart of the conflict's troubled public memory. Hunt, *The Turning*; Simeon Man, "Radicalizing Currents: The GI Movement in the Third World," in *The Rising Tide of Color: Race, State Violence, and Radical Movements across the Pacific*, ed. Moon-Ho Jung (Seattle: University of Washington Press, 2014), 266–97; Zaretsky, *No Direction Home*; *Sir! No Sir!* directed by David Zeiger (Docurama, 2005).

17. Gould, *Moving Politics*, 243.

18. Keith Griffith, "Activists Mobilize for Spring AIDS Actions," *AIDS Action Call: The Newsletter of the AIDS Action Pledge* (April 1988), 1, 14–15.

19. Ibid., 15.

20. Emergency Response Network, *¡Basta! No Mandate for War: A Pledge of Resistance Handbook*, ed. Ken Butigan, Terry Messman-Rucker, and Marie Pastrick (Philadelphia: New Society, 1986). Records of the national Pledge of Resistance and of the Bay Area Pledge of Resistance/Emergency Response Network are held at the Graduate Theological Union Archives, Graduate Theological Union, Berkeley.

21. Important sources on affinity groups and direct action in the antinuclear, anti-apartheid, and Central American solidarity movements include Epstein,

Political Protest and Cultural Revolution; Smith, *Resisting Reagan*; Bradford Martin, *The Other Eighties: A Secret History of America in the Age of Reagan* (New York: Hill & Wang, 2012); Michael Stewart Foley, *Front Porch Politics: The Forgotten Heyday of American Activism in the 1970s and 1980s* (New York: Hill & Wang, 2013). Anti-apartheid activism at UC Berkeley reached its height in April 1986 through the divestment movement, and street protest in the Central American solidarity movement accelerated during 1986 and 1987 as a result of the Iran-Contra scandal and Sanctuary trials (which targeted priests and others who provided safe haven to Central American refugees in the United States).

22. Gould, *Moving Politics*, 138.

23. Kevin Roderick, "LaRouche Backers Qualify AIDS Measure for Fall Vote," *Los Angeles Times*, June 25, 1986.

24. On *Hardwick*, see George Chauncey, "What Gay Studies Taught the Court: The Historians' Amicus' Brief in *Lawrence v. Texas*," *GLQ* 10:3 (2004): 509–38.

25. Stein, *Rethinking the Gay and Lesbian Movement*, 157–58. See also Gould, *Moving Politics*, 138, 141; Strub, *Body Counts*, 188.

26. Citizens for Medical Justice brochure, c. late 1987, Carton 2, Citizens for Medical Justice folder, Eibhlyn Papers, GLBTHS. See also Citizens for Medical Justice, "CMJ Information and History," n.d., Carton 2, ibid.

27. Bortman, interview by author. In fall 1984 Enola Gay also staged a mock "invasion" of Angel Island, located in the San Francisco Bay, to protest the US invasion of the island of Grenada in the prior year; see Brookie, "Blood and Money."

28. Citizens for Medical Justice brochure, c. late 1987. As shown in the Deukmejian action, not all of CMJ's work tied AIDS to Central America; for example, in 1987 CMJ also held an action at the San Francisco Federal Building to protest a US Department of Labor rule that required HIV tests for applicants to the Job Corps youth program. Charles Linebarger, "AIDS Dominates 1987 Politics, Social Life," *San Francisco Sentinel* (January 1, 1988), 7.

29. "Man and Woman of the Year '86," *San Francisco Sentinel* (December 26, 1986), 1–6; also noted in Gould, *Moving Politics*, 150. The *Sentinel's* "Woman of the Year" for 1986 was Pat Norman, a black lesbian and psychologist who coordinated the San Francisco Department of Public Health's response to AIDS.

30. On Proposition 63 and the politics of English-only, see Daniel Martinez HoSang, *Racial Propositions: Ballot Initiatives and the Making of Postwar California* (Berkeley: University of California Press, 2010).

31. Alex MacDonald, "64: The Last 35 Days," *Coming Up!* (October 1986), 1, 4–5. On fundraising for "No on 64," see Strub, *Body Counts*, 188–90. Strub helped raise $50,000 for the campaign through a direct mail appeal signed by the heads of the NGLTF, HRCF, Lambda, and other national lesbian and gay organizations.

32. Wilson, a cofounder of Veterans for Peace, had been deemed a "domestic terrorist" by the Reagan administration. Fifty thousand protestors converged on Concord to protest the attack, and activists maintained a twenty-four-hour vigil at the station for years to follow. S. Brian Wilson, *Blood on the Tracks: The Life and Times of S. Brian Wilson* (Oakland, CA: PM Press, 2011).

33. Corinne Lightweaver, "Arms Protest: Alice Walker Arrested at Weapons Station," *San Francisco Sentinel* (June 19, 1987), 1, 11.

34. Caden Gray, "Forty March on Recruiting Center," *San Francisco Sentinel* (January 15, 1988), 3. This article reported on the follow-up action on behalf of those arrested at the initial protest in September 1987; one of those arrested was Kate Raphael.

35. Eileen Hansen, interview by author, June 18, 2014, San Francisco.

36. On October 27, 1985, two men with AIDS, Steve Russell and Frank Bert, decided to chain themselves to the Health and Human Services Building at the end of a legally permitted rally by the legislative group Mobilization for AIDS. This was the same site John Lorenzini had targeted. Russell and Bert demanded FDA authorization of drugs available outside the United States, funding for a cure, and disability benefits for people diagnosed with ARC ("AIDS related complex," a diagnosis considered less severe than AIDS that predated widespread testing for HIV). Faced with no immediate government reaction, they established an encampment that by the end of 1985 included more than one hundred participants. The San Francisco Board of Supervisors passed a resolution to grant ARC the same medical priority as AIDS and to address AIDS discrimination, and in November two thousand people joined the vigil after a march commemorating Harvey Milk and George Moscone; many posted placards memorializing friends who had died. Activist Cleve Jones, who sought to defuse anger that night and inhibited sharper protest, later held that the placards placed at the vigil inspired the AIDS Memorial Quilt (Gould, *Moving Politics*, 107–8). The AIDS/ARC Vigil soon became primarily a support site for homeless people both with and without AIDS. It received ongoing coverage by journalist Alex McDonald in *Coming Up!* In addition, the AIDS Action Pledge extended support to the vigil during a period of arrests; Jean-Jacques Zenger, "Pledge Joins Vigil Protest," *AIDS Action Call: The Newsletter of the AIDS Action Pledge* (January 1988), 10, Box 120, AIDS History Project Records, ONE; "A People of Color Day for Protest and Civil Disobedience!" flier, AIDS Action Pledge Folder, Ephemera Collection, GLBTHS.

37. Hansen, interview by author.

38. Michelle Roland, interview by author, June 16, 2014, by telephone; Hansen, interview by author.

39. Eileen Hansen, "Pledge for Our Lives," *AIDS Action Call: The Newsletter of the AIDS Action Pledge* (autumn–winter 1987), 1–2. See also Eileen Hansen, "Long Live Activism" (letter to the editor), *Bay Area Reporter,* April 24, 2012; and Carol Leigh in "Not Over: The Legacy of ACT UP," *KPFA Women's Magazine,* March 24, 2012, archived at kpfawomensmagazine.blogspot.com, March 30, 2012.

40. "AIDS Action Pledge Proposal," n.d., AIDS Action Pledge Folder, Ephemera Collection, GLBTHS. A January 14, 1988, document lists the coordinating committee as Jim Denison, Michael Ryan, Arawn Eibhlyn, Terry Beswick, and Keith Griffith. AAP newsletters named Keith Griffith and Jean-Jacques Zenger as editors and cited a range of committees and contact people, including Action and Resistance (Daniel Parker, later replaced by Jim Denison); Public Education and Media (José Fernandez, later replaced by Terry Sutton);

Fundraising (Terry Beswick, later replaced by William Gersten); Newsletter (Keith Griffith); Think Tank (Penn Garvin). By 1988, additional committees were Outreach (Arawn Eibhlyn) and Zaps (Terry Sutton).

41. "AIDS Action Pledge 1988," video, Reel 549, Charles Cyberski Videos, GLBTHS. This fourteen-minute video centered on the September 1987 AIDS Commission protest, but combined it with clips from the March on Washington and the unveiling of the AIDS Memorial Quilt. See also "ACT UP History," n.d., Carton 1, Folder 6: ACT UP History, Eibhlyn Papers, GLBTHS. On the AIDS Commission more generally, see Stein, *Rethinking the Gay and Lesbian Movement,* 157–58.

42. "AIDS Action Pledge 1988" video.

43. "ACT UP History."

44. "AIDS Action Pledge: of protest and support, for love and life," undated fliers, Box 8, Folder 3, ACT UP/LA Collection, ONE.

45. Leigh, "Not Over"; Carol Leigh, "In Search of Scapegoats: Mandatory AIDS Testing Law Alert," *AIDS Action Call: The Newsletter of the AIDS Action Pledge* (January 1988), 5; Jim Dickey, "AIDS Prison: Separate and Unequal," *AIDS Action Call: The Newsletter of the AIDS Action Pledge* (April 1988), 6–7, 10, 14 (a reprint of an article originally published in February 1988 in the *San Jose Mercury News*); Keith Griffith, "Urgent: California Legislators May Cripple AIDS Policies," *AIDS Action Call: The Newsletter of the AIDS Action Pledge* (April 1988), 11–13.

46. "AIDS Action Pledge . . . The AAP needs YOU!!!" flier, n.d. (c. September 1987), AIDS Action Pledge Folder, Ephemera Collection, GLBTHS.

47. Kate Raphael, interview by author, June 17, 2014, San Francisco.

48. Penn Garvin, "Do I Have to Take an 8-Hour Training Just to Get Arrested?" *AIDS Action Call: The Newsletter of the AIDS Action Pledge* (April 1988), 5–6.

49. Hansen, interview by author.

50. Ibid.

51. Stein, *Rethinking the Gay and Lesbian Movement,* 146–47. See also Epstein, *Political Protest and Cultural Revolution,* 166.

52. Amin Ghaziani, *The Dividends of Dissent: How Conflict and Culture Work in Lesbian and Gay Marches on Washington* (Chicago: University of Chicago Press, 2008), 102–3.

53. Ibid., 104–5.

54. Tim Kingston, "Painting the Town Pink," *Coming Up!* (November 1987), 6–10, 13.

55. Matlovich had been diagnosed with AIDS in 1986 and died in June 1988. For summaries of groups, see Ghaziani, *Dividends of Dissent,* 122; and Tim Kingston, "March on Washington," *Coming Up!* (October 1987), 6–7, 47. In "Painting the Town Pink," Kingston noted that the California contingent in the march was estimated at anywhere from 10,000 to 50,000 people. LAGAI coordinated the Liberation Contingent with the Lavender Left from Los Angeles and the Gay and Lesbian Liberation and Solidarity Committee (formerly known as DAFFODIL) from New York; activists from Boston, Chicago, Seattle, Los Angeles, New York, and the Bay Area attended. On the Liberation Contin-

gent, see "Gay Liberation, Not Just Gay Rights!" 1987; and LAGAI Update, November 6, 1987, both in LAGAI folder, Box 2, Marcy Rein Collection, GLBTHS.

56. Rebecca Hensler, interview by author, July 7, 2014, via Skype.

57. Kingston, "Painting the Town Pink"; "C.D. Training Offered," *AIDS Action Call: The Newsletter of the AIDS Action Pledge* (autumn–winter 1987), 2. Official arrest figures were not released; Kingston estimated 840 arrests based on lawyers' accounts, and the AAP newsletter stated "nearly 840." Gould, citing the *Advocate*, states over 800 (*Moving Politics*, 132), Ghaziani estimates 650 to 850 (*Dividends of Dissent*, 123), and Stein puts the number at 600 (*Rethinking the Gay and Lesbian Movement*, 165). The majority of those arrested pled guilty or paid fees, but nine—including San Francisco activist Terry Blankenship—pled not guilty as a further act of noncooperation and returned to DC for trial; see "The Supreme Court Protest Goes On!" *AIDS Action Call: The Newsletter of the AIDS Action Pledge* (autumn–winter 1987), 6.

58. This restriction was referenced in the CD handbook. The law was recently criticized following *McCullen v. Coakley* (2014), in which the Court struck down a Massachusetts law providing a similar "buffer zone" in front of clinics that provide abortion services.

59. *Out and Outraged*, 2.

60. Kingston, "Painting the Town Pink."

61. Ibid. See also "For Love, Life and Liberation: First Person Accounts of the Lesbian and Gay Nonviolent Civil Disobedience at the U.S. Supreme Court, October 13, 1987," collected at supremecourtcd.org. Most material on this site was originally collected by Terry Sutton, with more recent work by Markley Morris and Eileen Hansen.

62. *Out and Outraged*, 2.

63. Lorenzini, "AIDS & Civil Disobedience," 23–24. Deborah Gould, noting that the Chicago gay paper the *Windy City Times* published a feature article on John Lorenzini in September 1986, interprets this to mean that his story was brought out again when useful because of possibilities for mobilizing in the aftermath of *Hardwick* (Gould, *Moving Politics*, 149).

64. Jessica Shubow, "C.D. in D.C . . . Civil Disobedience and the Lesbian/Gay Community," in *Out and Outraged*, 5–6.

65. Sean McShee, "Coming Out as Non-violent Direct Action," in *Out and Outraged*, 7. See also Flowing Margaret Johnson, "Direct Action and Lesbian/Gay Rights," in ibid., 44; and "Nonviolent Civil Disobedience" in ibid., 49–50.

66. Jim Denison, "Gay People and Central America," in *Out and Outraged*, 48.

67. Elva Peréz-Treviño, "Joining Racism and Homophobia," in *Out and Outraged*, 49. Keith Griffith's contribution to the handbook highlighted lesbian feminist health care activism as a model for AIDS activism; Griffith, "Quality Healthcare Is a Civil Right," in ibid., 21.

68. Organizational chart, Folder 27: ACT UP, Stephen Fish Papers, GLBTHS.

69. "Agitate, Educate, Organize!" agenda, October 12, 1987, AIDS Action Pledge Folder, Ephemera Collection, GLBTHS; "ACT UP History." On the week of actions, see Frank Richter, "AIDS Protest Week Planned," *AIDS Action*

Call: The Newsletter of the AIDS Action Pledge (autumn–winter 1987), 3; Jean-Jacques Zenger, "Major Progress in National Organizing," *AIDS Action Call: The Newsletter of the AIDS Action Pledge* (January 1988), 11; Keith Griffith, "Activists Mobilize for Spring AIDS Actions," *AIDS Action Call: The Newsletter of the AIDS Action Pledge* (April 1988), 15.

70. Scott Sanders, "Dear Friends" (ACT NOW Steering Committee meeting notes), July 8, 1988, courtesy Eileen Hansen.

71. Arawn Eibhlyn, "Fighting AIDS Is More Than a Fashion Statement," *Breakthrough: Political Journal of Prairie Fire Organizing Committee* (winter 1990), 10–17.

72. Tim Kingston, "Activists Hit the Roof: Burlingame Cops Hit the Ceiling, Arrest 19," *Coming Up!* (February 1988), 5; "Burroughs-Wellcome: Crimes against People," *San Francisco Sentinel* (January 29, 1988), 1, 6–7, 15; Gould, *Moving Politics,* 400.

73. The dollar's value roughly doubled from 1988 to 2016, meaning that at the time of this book's publication, AZT's lowered price of $8,000 would be equivalent to just over $16,000.

74. "How Much Will They Charge for the Cure?" flier, January 1988, AIDS Action Pledge Folder, Ephemera Collection, GLBTHS; "AIDS Profiteering: A Bitter Pill to Swallow, March on Burroughs-Wellcome," flier (January 1988), AIDS Action Pledge Folder, Ephemera Collection, GLBTHS.

75. "Proposed opinion piece for publicizing the B-W boycott," n.d. (c. March 1988); Memo from AIDS Action Pledge to ACT NOW Member Organizations, March 31, 1988, both in AIDS Action Pledge Folder, Ephemera Collection, GLBTHS. The boycott idea was inspired by the 1970s boycott of Nestlé for its global promotion of infant formula rather than breast milk.

76. AAP Coordinating Committee, "Dear Friend," January 14, 1988, AIDS Action Pledge Folder, Ephemera Collection, GLBTHS; "AIDS Profiteering"; "March Raises $2,500 for Pledge," *AIDS Action Call: The Newsletter of the AIDS Action Pledge* (February–March 1988), 11, Hank Tavera Collection (35/24), Ethnic Studies Library, UC Berkeley.

77. "Thank You!" *AIDS Action Call: The Newsletter of the AIDS Action Pledge* (January 1988), 8.

78. Roland, interview by author.

79. "March Raises $2,500 for Pledge"; "ACT UP History."

80. Jean-Jacques Zenger, "Pledge to Do Protest March—Burroughs-Wellcome Is the Target," *AIDS Action Call: The Newsletter of the AIDS Action Pledge* (January 1988), 1–2; Keith Griffith, "19 Face Arraignment for B-W Action," *AIDS Action Call: The Newsletter of the AIDS Action Pledge* (January 1988), 3–4. In addition to marching and joining the civil disobedience, supporters could pledge funds for each mile activists walked. See also Gould, *Moving Politics,* 400.

81. Those arrested included Terry Beswick, Henry (Camo) Bortman, Dan Carmell, Arthur Evans, Ray Fidler, William Gersten, Keith Griffith, Don Harris, Branch Hastings, Michael Kensinger, Deborah Lafferty, Rohn Maggio, Phillip Morgan, Michelle Roland, Eric Slade, Terry Sutton, Lynn Taylor, Hank Wilson, and Jean-Jacques Zenger. Griffith, "19 Face Arraignment," 9.

82. George Mendenhall, "Wildness Awakens Burlingame: 19 Arrests at AZT Firm," *San Francisco Sentinel* (January 29, 1988), 7.

83. Kingston, "Activists Hit the Roof."

84. Eileen Hansen, "Unreasonable Demands or Unreasonable System?" *AIDS Action Call: The Newsletter of the AIDS Action Pledge* (February–March 1988), 11, Hank Tavera Collection (35/24), Ethnic Studies Library, UC Berkeley.

85. Reagan's action occurred on the same day Oliver North and other defendants were indicted on Iran-Contra charges. In the ensuing two weeks activists staged more than two hundred protests in 150 US cities. Smith, *Resisting Reagan,* 85; Doyle McManus and David Lauter, "Statements on Honduras Stir Skepticism in Congress," *Los Angeles Times,* March 19, 1988. On Bay Area gay and lesbian participation, see Matthews, "Coming Out for Peace"; and "Gays, Lesbians Spearhead Peace Demos."

86. Lance Williams and Norman Melnick, "Who Leads Honduras Protests: 4 Groups Cooperating in S.F. Demonstrations," *San Francisco Examiner,* March 22, 1988, A-6. The spokesperson for the task force was Arawn Eibhlyn, a member of Prairie Fire and later a leader in ACT UP San Francisco.

87. *AIDS Action Call: The Newsletter of the AIDS Action Pledge* (April 1988), 11; "Homosexuals Lead 2,000 in S.F. Protest," *San Jose Mercury News* (March 23, 1988), 14A; Torri Minton, "A Long, Peaceful S.F. March on War," *San Francisco Chronicle,* March 23, 1988; Norman Melnick, "Fund AIDS Research, Not War, Gays Demand during S.F. Trek," *San Francisco Examiner,* March 23, 1988, A13; Matthews, "Coming Out for Peace"; "Gays, Lesbians Spearhead Peace Demos."

88. Matthews, "Coming Out for Peace."

89. Baker and Jones, quoted in ibid.

90. Lesbians and Gays Against Intervention, cited in "Central America Symposium: Where Do We Go from Here?" *Breakthrough: Political Journal of Prairie Fire Organizing Committee* (fall 1990): 24. See also Women Against Imperialism, cited in the same symposium.

91. Joanie Marquardt for AIDS Action Pledge, "Dear Friends," May 12, 1988, AIDS Action Pledge Folder, Ephemera Collection, GLBTHS.

92. Other events during the week included a grieving ceremony and a statewide march and CD in Sacramento. AIDS Action Pledge Folder, Ephemera Collection, GLBTHS; "Spring AIDS Actions '88," *AIDS Action Call: The Newsletter of the AIDS Action Pledge* (April 1988), 8–9. The "Stop Social Insecurity" protest can be observed in AIDS Action Pledge, "Stop Social Insecurity," April 29, 1988 (video), Reel 320, Charles Cyberski Collection, GLBTHS.

93. Gould, *Moving Politics,* 220; Mike Hippler, "Pissed Off and Inspired: ACT UP Encourages Defiance," *Bay Area Reporter* (November 17, 1988), 11. In one of its last protests prior to this shift, the AAP cosponsored a protest targeting the FDA on June 27, 1988 ("AIDS: A National Emergency," flier [June 1988], and "News Advisory: Protestors Call for Emergency Meeting with FDA, Demand Access to Promising Treatments," both in AIDS Action Pledge Folder, Ephemera Collection, GLBTHS).

94. For example, its March 1989 calendar of events listed a protest for peace in El Salvador, a march for reproductive rights, and an anti-nuclear action at the Nevada Test Site. ACT UP San Francisco newsletter, 1:2 (March 1989), Hank Tavera Collection (35:25), Ethnic Studies Library, UC Berkeley.

95. Bayard Rustin Coalition, "Racism within ACT-UP/SF," n.d., Hank Tavera Collection (35: 25), Ethnic Studies Library, UC Berkeley.

96. On fights over the phone, see "ACT UP History"; on tension at the ACT NOW conference, see Hensler, interview by author.

97. Gould, *Moving Politics,* 401. On the 1992 implementation, see United States Food and Drug Administration, "First AIDS Drug Tested under Parallel Track Policy; Other d4T Related Press Releases," October 5, 1992 (archived at AIDSinfo.nih.gov).

98. Eileen Hansen recalls meetings at this point averaging four hundred people; Hansen, "Long Live Activism."

99. SANOE press release, May 1, 1990, Folder 26: SANOE, Stephen Fish Papers, GLBTHS.

100. These fliers demanded greater government accountability, affordable health care for all, no mandatory testing or quarantine (for prostitutes, prisoners, immigrants, or others), and an end to anti–gay and lesbian violence. Stop AIDS Now or Else (SANOE), "Are you sick and tired of being stuck on this bridge?" flier, January 31, 1989, Carton 1, Folder 5: Golden Gate Bridge AIDS Protest, Eibhlyn Papers, GLBTHS.

101. Arl Nadel, "The Golden Gate Bridge Blockade" (compilation of news footage), Youtube.com, April 4, 2011 (accessed May 9, 2016); Ted Kerr, "AIDS Activism and Beyond: Radical Queer Politics of the '80s and '90s," *Visual AIDS,* April 11, 2013, https://www.visualaids.org/events/detail/aids-activism-and-beyond (accessed May 9, 2016).

102. Hensler, interview by author. Hensler cited Joanie Marquardt, a member of ACT UP San Francisco's PISD (People with Immune System Disorders) Caucus, as another important mentor.

103. Sutton had developed the disease CMV, a common AIDS complication that causes blindness. He initially sought to treat the CMV with ganciclovir (DHPG), but that drug was toxic in combination with AZT. He then sought access to foscarnet to replace the AZT, but was denied inclusion in the drug's research trials because he had previously taken ganciclovir and lacked the funds to pay for his own hospitalization in Houston—the only place he could sidestep the trials' protocol. "Who Killed Terry Sutton?" memorial and march flier, April 24, 1989; Michelle Roland, Speech at Memorial Rally and March for Terry Sutton, April 24, 1989, both in Carton 1, Folder 14: Memorial for Terry Sutton, Eibhlyn Papers, GLBTHS; Dennis McMillan, "Activist Terry Sutton Dies of AIDS," *Bay Area Reporter,* April 20, 1989.

104. SANOE, "Stop AIDS Now or Else Stops the Opera!!!" flyer and press release, September 8, 1989, Folder 26: SANOE, Stephen Fish Papers, GLBTHS.

105. Raphael quoted in SANOE Press Release, January 23, 1990, Folder 26: SANOE, Stephen Fish Papers, GLBTHS.

106. Douglas Crimp, "Mourning and Militancy," *October* 51 (winter 1989), 16.

107. Ibid., 18 (emphasis in original).

108. SANOE, "Stop AIDS Now or Else Stops the Opera!!!"

109. SANOE (Opera House Chapter), "AIDS—the Epidemic: a dramatic evening in three Acts," action flyer September 8, 1989, Folder 26: SANOE, Stephen Fish Papers, GLBTHS.

110. Stephen Fish, open letter, September 12, 1989, Folder 26: SANOE, Stephen Fish Papers, GLBTHS.

111. SANOE, "San Francisco Chronic Liar," parody flier, October 7, 1989, *San Francisco Chronicle* clippings, Folder 26: SANOE, Stephen Fish Papers, GLBTHS; Stephen Fish, May 4, 1948–February 8, 1991 (obituary), *Bay Area Reporter*, February 21, 1991 (archived at obit.glbthistory.org). See also "San Francisco Opera Debut Is Disrupted by AIDS Group," *New York Times*, September 10, 1989.

112. "Living with AIDS and Fighting Back: Friday, October 6, 1989," Folder 27: ACT UP, Stephen Fish Papers, GLBTHS.

113. "ACT UP Condensed History," n.d., Carton 1, Folder 6, Eibhlyn Papers, GLBTHS.

114. Kate Raphael, "This Day in History: Martial Law in the Castro," *Democracy Sometimes* blog, October 6, 2011, http://democracy-sometime .blogspot.com/2011/10/this-day-in-history-martial-law-in.html (accessed May 26, 2016).

115. ACT UP [San Francisco]/ACT NOW press statement, October 11, 1989, Carton 2: October 6, 1989, Eibhlyn Papers, GLBTHS; Raphael, "This Day in History."

116. Gerard Koskovich, "San Francisco Journal: Stonewall for a New Generation," *Outweek* (November 5, 1989), 32–33, 65; Gerard Koskovich, "Remembering a Police Riot: The Castro Sweep of October 6, 1989," in *Out in the Castro: Desire, Promise, Activism,* ed. Winston Leyland (San Francisco: Leyland, 2002); Gerard Koskovich, "Castro Sweep Police Riot: 1989 Outweek Article," public Facebook post, October 5, 2009; Matthew S. Bojko, "20 years ago, Police Shut Down the Castro," *Bay Area Reporter,* October 1, 2009; Waiyde Palmer, "Today is the 23rd Anniversary of the Castro Sweep: Looking Back on that Historic and Infamous Night," *Hoodline,* October 6, 2012.

117. Agnos had aggressively courted gay voters for this measure, in part because they were expected to turn out in large numbers to prevent the repeal of a new city law that had established domestic partner benefits. In November, voters, influenced by the recent Loma Prieta earthquake, rejected the stadium proposal. They also repealed the domestic partner law but passed a modified domestic partner initiative in 1990. In 1996 voters approved a different ballpark measure in the same location as Agnos's proposed site, but with a different design and no direct public funding (though significant infrastructure improvements and abatements).

118. ACT UP/S.F./ACT NOW, "What happened the night of Oct. 6th?" flier; LAGAI, "If you are thinking of filing an OCC complaint please read this first!" n.d. (October 1989), both in Carton 2, October 6, 1989 Folder, Eibhlyn Papers, GLBTHS; ACT UP/ACT NOW, "What we experienced as ACT UP and as the Lesbian/Gay Community, . . ." undated flier (c. late 1989), Folder 27: ACT UP, Stephen Fish Papers, GLBTHS.

119. Tim Kingston, "Nightstick Justice," *San Francisco Bay Times* (formerly *Coming Up!*) (December 1989), 4–7.

120. SANOE (Rose Parade Chapter), "Protest by AIDS Activists Halts Procession," flyer for fundraiser held February 4, 1990, in Laguna Beach, Folder 26: SANOE, Stephen Fish Papers, GLBTHS. See also "We Reigned in Their Parade!" flyer for fundraiser held January 21, 1990, in Los Angeles, ibid.

121. SANOE, "Open the Borders! Stop AIDS Now!" INS action flier, May 1, 1990, Folder 26: SANOE, Stephen Fish Papers, GLBTHS; "37 AIDS Activists Arrested at 2 Protests," *Los Angeles Times,* May 2, 1990.

122. "ACT UP Condensed History," n.d., Carton 1, Folder 6, Eibhlyn Papers, GLBTHS; Jon Van, "AIDS Activists Disrupt Speech by Sullivan," *Chicago Tribune,* June 25, 1990.

123. ACT UP/S.F. and ACT NOW, "Speaking Across Borders," n.d. (June 1990), Carton 2: 6th International Conference Folder, Eibhlyn Papers, GLBTHS.

124. On New York's budget, see Strub, *Body Counts*; on the budget required for the proposed San Francisco office space, see "The ACT-UP Split," *OUT!* (newsletter of Lesbians and Gays Against Intervention), 2:2 (December 1990): 5–6 (courtesy Eileen Hansen).

125. Hensler, interview by author.

126. ACT UP San Francisco and ACT UP Golden Gate double-sided flier, n.d., Carton 1, Folder 6, Eibhlyn Papers, GLBTHS. See also Gould, *Moving Politics,* 347.

127. Brier, *Infectious Ideas,* 179–83; Gould, *Moving Politics,* 338, 391. Within ACT UP New York, the Treatment and Data Committee split off in 1991 to become a separate organization, the Treatment Action Group. See Maxine Wolfe, "AIDS and Politics: Transformations of Our Movement" (speech given at the National Gay and Lesbian Task Force Town Meeting for the Gay Community, 1989), in Blasius and Phelan, *We Are Everywhere,* 638–41.

128. In addition, a document criticizing the office plan, written by Raphael, Gold, and two other activists, was defaced with slogans such as "100,000 dead from AIDS, where were you?" "The ACT-UP Split."

129. "ACT UP PISD Caucus," n.d. (c. March 1989), Folder 27: ACT UP, Stephen Fish Papers, GLBTHS; Eibhlyn, "Fighting AIDS Is More Than a Fashion Statement."

130. "The ACT-UP Split." A note in the newsletter states that this article was written by "Deeg [Gold], with some help from Kate [Raphael]." Courtesy Eileen Hansen.

EPILOGUE

1. Vicki Eaklor, *Queer America: A People's GLBT History of the United States* (New York: The New Press, 2008), 198, 200–201. See also Tim McFeeley, "Getting It Straight: A Review of the 'Gays in the Military' Debate," in *Creating Change: Sexuality, Public Policy, and Civil Rights,* ed. John D'Emilio, William B. Turner, and Urvashi Vaid (New York: St. Martin's Press, 2000), 236–50; Allan Bérubé, "How Gay Becomes White and What Kind of White It Stays," *My Desire for History: Essays in Gay, Community, and Labor History,* ed. John D'Emilio

and Estelle B. Freedman (Chapel Hill: University of North Carolina Press, 2011), 202–30; Aaron Belkin, *Bring Me Men: Military Masculinity and the Benign Façade of American Empire, 1892–2001* (New York: Oxford University Press, 2012).

2. See, for example, Doug Ireland, "Gay-Baiting under Don't Ask, Don't Tell," *The Nation*, July 3, 2000.

3. Matthew Rosenberg, "Pentagon Moves to Allow Transgender People to Serve Openly in the Military," *New York Times*, July 13, 2015; Sunnivie Brydum, "U.S. Transgender Military Ban Could End in May," *The Advocate*, August 26, 2015; Chris Geidner, "Meet the Trans Scholar Fighting against the Campaign for Out Trans Military Service," *Buzzfeed*, September 9, 2013.

4. LAGAI, "We Like Our Queers out of Uniform: A Counter-Recruitment and Anti-Draft Outreach Packet for Lesbians and Gay Men" (San Francisco, June 1992), archived at Against Equality under Themes: Military, http://faggotz.org/againstequality/We_Like_Our_Queers_Out_Of_Uniform.pdf (accessed May 15, 2016). The navy witch hunt is detailed in Janine Abernathy, "It Was a Big Mistake," in ibid.

5. LAGAI, "Who What Why When, . . ." in ibid. (lowercase "u.s." in original).

6. LAGAI, "Queer Cops? No Thanks!" in ibid.

7. Scott Harris and George Ramos, "Gay Activists Vent Rage over Wilson's Veto," *Los Angeles Times*, October 1, 1991; "All the Rage: Stories from the AB 101 Veto Riot of 1991," panel at the GLBT History Museum, September 29, 2011; "20 Years Ago Today in Gay History: The AB 101 Veto Riot Would've Blown Your Mind," *Autostraddle*, September 30, 2011; Faderman and Timmons, *Gay L.A.*, 325. The two officers accused of infiltrating Queer Nation were Lea Militello and Sally DeHaven; both remained on the force, with Militello retiring in 2011.

8. Tede Matthews, "I Was a Teenage Draft Dodger," in LAGAI, "We Like Our Queers Out of Uniform."

9. Further telling evidence can be seen in a panel held in June 1991 at the San Francisco Women's Building, "Queer Relations: The Lesbian/Gay Movement and the U.S. Left." The event's speakers described themselves as far more welcomed by straight radicals at that time than they had been in the past, but deeply uncertain about the directions of the left as a whole. Sponsors of the event included LAGAI, Modern Times Bookstore, and the recently founded International Lesbian and Gay Human Rights Commission. Speakers were Harry Hay, Pat Norman, Carmen Vázquez, Tede Matthews, Angie Fa, José Medina, and Arawn Eibhlyn. Event flier, Lesbians & Gays Against Intervention (LAGAI) folder, Ephemera—Organizations, GLBTHS; "Queer Relations," *Crossroads* 15 (November 1991).

10. Lisa Duggan, *The Twilight of Equality? Neoliberalism, Cultural Politics, and the Attack on Democracy* (Boston: Beacon Press, 2003); Self, *All in the Family*.

11. See, especially, Ruth Wilson Gilmore, *Golden Gulag: Prisons, Surplus, Crisis, and Opposition in Globalizing California* (Berkeley: University of California Press, 2007); Beth E. Richie, *Arrested Justice: Black Women, Violence,*

and America's Prison Nation (New York: New York University Press, 2012); Heather Ann Thompson, "Why Mass Incarceration Matters: Rethinking Crisis, Decline, and Transformation in Postwar American History," *Journal of American History* 97:3 (December 2010): 703–34.

12. On the rhetoric, implementation, and consequences of the 1996 law, see Sharon Hays, *Flat Broke with Children: Women in the Age of Welfare Reform* (New York: Oxford University Press, 2004); Alejandra Marchevsky and Jeanne Theoharis, *Not Working: Latina Immigrants, Low-Wage Jobs, and the Failure of Welfare Reform* (New York: New York University Press, 2006); Laura Briggs, *Somebody's Children: The Politics of Transracial and Transnational Adoption* (Durham, NC: Duke University Press, 2012).

13. On Proposition 209 and its predecessors, see HoSang, *Racial Propositions*.

14. While the activists whose lives and work I analyze in this book maintain a sharp critique of military inclusion, they are more divided in their views of marriage equality. Most agree that marriage is a privatizing institution, and some are highly critical of it. However, many see marriage equality as important both pragmatically and culturally. Some are married themselves, though they hold varying interpretations of marriage in their own lives (e.g., in the choice to hold a wedding or not, terms for referring to partners or spouses, the wearing of rings, practices of monogamy or open relationships, and so on).

15. See, especially, Dean Spade, *Normal Life: Administrative Violence, Critical Trans Politics, and the Limits of the Law* (Boston: South End Press, 2011); Hanhardt, *Safe Space*; and the work of Against Equality (www.againstequality .org).

16. Duggan, *The Twilight of Equality?* 44, 46; see also Urvashi Vaid, *Virtual Equality: The Mainstreaming of Gay and Lesbian Liberation* (New York: Anchor Books, 1996).

17. Jasbir Puar, *Terrorist Assemblages: Homonationalism in Queer Times* (Durham, NC: Duke University Press, 2007); Anna M. Aganthangelou, Daniel Bassichis, and Tamara L. Spira, "Intimate Investments: Homonormativity, Global Lockdown, and Seductions of Empire," *Radical History Review* 100 (winter 2008): 120–43.

18. Douglas Crimp, "Right On, Girlfriend!" *Social Text* 33 (1992): 12, 16.

19. Ibid., 13–14.

20. Cohen, "Punks, Bulldaggers, and Welfare Queens," 22. For another and earlier, though less extended, leftist critique of Queer Nation and "queer nationalism," see Mab Segrest, "A Bridge, Not a Wedge" (1993 speech to Creating Change), in *Memoir of a Race Traitor*, 229–46.

21. Hanhardt, *Safe Space*, 177–82.

22. Cohen, "Punks, Bulldaggers, and Welfare Queens," 25–26.

23. Ibid., 45 (emphasis in original).

24. Ibid., 43.

25. Ferguson, *Aberrations in Black*.

26. Chris Dixon, *Another Politics: Talking across Today's Transformative Movements* (Berkeley: University of California Press, 2014), 5.

27. Texts relevant to these shifts include INCITE! Women of Color against Violence, ed., *Color of Violence: the INCITE! Anthology* (Boston: South End

Press, 2006); idem, *The Revolution Will Not Be Funded: Beyond the Non-profit Industrial Complex* (Boston: South End Press, 2009); "Igniting the Kindred: Visions of Queer Radicalism," *Left Turn*, April–May 2009; Eric Stanley and Nat Smith, eds., *Captive Genders: Trans Embodiment and the Prison Industrial Complex* (Oakland, CA: AK Press, 2011); Mogul, Ritchie, and Whitlock, *Queer (In)Justice*; Ryan Conrad, ed., *Against Equality: Queer Revolution Not Mere Inclusion* (Oakland, CA: AK Press, 2014).

28. This claim was broadcast especially through a cover article in *The Advocate*: Michael Joseph Gross, "Gay Is the New Black?" November 16, 2008. Similar questions are explored in a more sophisticated way in *The New Black*, directed by Yoruba Richen (Promised Land Film, 2013).

29. For one introduction to this work, see Sarah Schulman, *Israel/Palestine and the Queer International* (Durham, NC: Duke University Press, 2012).

30. For background, see Alisa Solomon, "Trans/Migrant: Christina Madrazo's All-American Story," in *Queer Migrations: Sexuality, U.S. Citizenship, and Border Crossings,* ed. Eithne Luibhéid and Lionel Cantú (Minneapolis: University of Minnesota Press, 2005), 3–29; Karma R. Chávez, *Queer Migration Politics: Activist Rhetoric and Coalitional Possibilities* (Urbana: University of Illinois Press, 2013).

31. See, for example, Prerna Lai, "How Queer Undocumented Youth Built the Immigrant Rights Movement," *HuffPost Queer Voices*, March 28, 2013; "ICE Ignores Requests to Release Transgender Woman from Detention #FreeNicoll," #Not1More http://www.notonemoredeportation.com/portfolio/freenicoll/ (accessed May 15, 2016); "End the Deportation and Detention of the LGBTQ Migrant Community," Familia: Trans Queer Liberation Movement, April 23, 2015, http://familiatqlm.org/not1more/end-the-detention-and-deportation-of-the-lgbtq-migrant-community/ (accessed May 15, 2016); "Transgender Asylum Seeker Faces Abuse in Immigration Detention," Transgender Law Center, n.d., http://transgenderlawcenter.org/archives/11347 (accessed May 15, 2016); Mitch Kellaway, "Immigration Advocates Demand Release of Abused Trans Asylum Seeker," *The Advocate*, January 24, 2015. The LGBTQ organization GetEqual—originally founded during the push to end Don't Ask Don't Tell—began a decisive shift toward a more radical queer politics in 2013 and 2014, in large part because of the influence of undocuqueer organizing as well as the growth of Black Lives Matter.

32. Caitlin Carmody, "San Francisco Pride, Chelsea Manning, and Queer Assimilation," *FoundSF*, n.d., http://foundsf.org/index.php?title=San_Francisco_Pride,_Chelsea_Manning,_and_Queer_Assimilation (accessed May 15, 2016).

33. "Bradley Manning San Francisco Pride Supporters Come Out in the Thousands," *Huffington Post*, July 2, 2013. After the year's parade, the San Francisco Pride board retroactively declared Manning an "Honorary Grand Marshal"; Lucas Grindley, "San Francisco Pride Apologizes, Honors Chelsea Manning," *The Advocate*, April 13, 2014.

34. Alicia Garza, "A Herstory of #BlackLivesMatter," *Feminist Wire*, October 7, 2014.

35. Mitch Kelloway, "Phoenix Drops 'Walking While Trans' Charges against Monica Jones," *The Advocate*, February 27, 2015.

36. Jelani Cobb references historian Barbara Ransby as highlighting Baker's call to "reach out to the town drunk" in his essay on Black Lives Matter, "The Matter of Black Lives," *The New Yorker,* March 14, 2016. See also Barbara Ransby, *Ella Baker and the Black Freedom Movement* (Chapel Hill: University of North Carolina Press, 2003), and Keeanga-Yamahtta Taylor, *From #BlackLivesMatter to Black Liberation* (Chicago: Haymarket Books, 2016).

37. Christopher Mathias, "One-Eighth of South Carolina Inmates Were Jailed over Child Support Payments; Walter Scott Was One of Them," *Huffington Post,* April 10, 2015.

38. Coverage of the grand marshal selections includes Joe Fitzgerald, "Meet Alicia Garza, Pride's Community Grand Marshal Who Helped Coin 'Black Lives Matter,'" *San Francisco Examiner,* June 24, 2015; "Black Lives Matter to Help Lead San Francisco Pride Parade," *The Grio,* March 16, 2016; Daniel Reynolds, "San Francisco Pride Names Black Lives Matter as Grand Marshal," *The Advocate,* March 17, 2016. On the withdrawal from 2016 Pride, see, for example, Julia Carrie Wong, "Black Lives Matter pulls out of San Francisco gay pride over policing," *The Guardian,* June 24, 2016; and Victoria M. Massie, "Why Black Lives Matter just pulled out of San Francisco Pride," *Vox,* June 25, 2016.

Bibliography

INTERVIEWS BY AUTHOR

Leonel Argüello. January 17, 2014, Managua, Nicaragua.
Amy Bank. June 15, 2013, via Skype. January 18, 2014, Managua, Nicaragua.
Lucrecia Bermudez. December 7, 2010, San Francisco.
Bill Blackburn. July 2, 2014, by telephone.
Henry (Camo) Bortman. May 31, 2011, San Francisco.
Catherine Cusic. June 24, 2013, San Francisco.
John D'Emilio. June 28, 2011, by telephone.
Pam David. August 13, 2010, San Francisco.
Linda Farthing. February 5, 2016, via Skype.
Carol Fields. June 20, 2014, Oakland.
Brian Freeman. June 6, 2013, San Francisco.
Marcia M. Gallo. August 16, 2010, Berkeley.
Ellen Gavin. December 15, 2010, Los Angeles.
Ruth Grabowski. June 19, 2014, San Francisco.
Roberto Gurdián. July 21, 2012, Los Angeles.
Eileen Hansen. June 18, 2014, San Francisco.
Rebecca Hensler. July 7, 2014, via Skype.
Charlie Hinton. July 29, 2011, by telephone.
Diane Jones. June 3, 2011, San Francisco.
Julie Light. June 26, 2013, Oakland.
Ruth Mahaney. June 27, 2013, San Francisco.
Ana Quirós. January 10, 2014, Managua, Nicaragua.
Kate Raphael. June 2, 2011, and June 17, 2014, San Francisco.
Michelle Roland. June 16, 2014, by telephone.
Martha Sacasa. January 8, 2014, Managua, Nicaragua.
Lupita Sequeira. January 11, 2014, Matagalpa, Nicaragua.

Dora María Tellez. January 15, 2014, Managua, Nicaragua.
Dan Wohlfeiler, March 7, 2014, Berkeley.
Joel Zúñiga Traña. January 10, 2014, Managua, Nicaragua.

ARCHIVAL SOURCES

Bancroft Library, University of California, Berkeley
    Social Protest Collection
Canadian Gay and Lesbian Archives
Ethnic Studies Library, University of California, Berkeley
    Hank Tavera Collection
Freedom Archives, San Francisco
    Women Against Imperialism (WAI) Collection
GLBT Historical Society (GLBTHS), San Francisco
    Meg Barnett Papers, 1989-05
    Berkeley-Oakland Women's Union, 2005-25
    Konstantin Berlandt Papers, 1995-03
    D. E. Bertelson Papers, 2000-01
    Charles Cyberski Videos, 1994-03
    Arawn Eibhlyn Papers, 1973–1995
    Ephemera—Individuals, Organizations, and Subjects
    Stephen Fish Papers, 1991-19
    Sally Gearhart Papers, 1993-27
    John Kyper Papers, 2005-19
    Lesbian Schoolworkers, 2003-26
    Stephen Lowell Papers, 1996-5
    Louise Merrill Papers, 2003-40
    Oral Histories
    Marcy Rein, 1998-14
    Anson Reinhart Papers, 1994-25
    San Francisco Women's Centers/Women's Building, 1996-15
    Stonewall (Organization) Papers, 1989-9
    Charles Thorpe Papers, 1987-02
Graduate Theological Union, Berkeley
    Berkeley Free Church, GTU 89-5-016
International Gay Information Center, New York Public Library
    Ephemera Collection—Organizations and Subjects
Lesbian Herstory Archives, Brooklyn (LHA)
    Geographic Files—San Francisco, Nicaragua
    Organization Files
    Subject Files
    Susan Saxe Collection
    Third World Conference
ONE National Gay and Lesbian Archives, Los Angeles
    1979 March on Washington Collection
    ACT UP/LA Collection
    AIDS History Project Records

Lesbian Legacy Collection
ONE Subject Files Collection
Anne Roberts Women's Movement Collection Fund, Simon Fraser University, Vancouver, British Columbia
San Francisco History Center, San Francisco Public Library
Peter Adair Papers, GLC 70
Charles Thorpe Papers
Southern California Library for Social Studies and Research
Gay Left Periodicals and Files
Liberty Hill Foundation Records
Voices of Feminism Oral History Project, Sophia Smith Collection, Smith College

PRIVATE COLLECTIONS

Amy Bank Archive, Berkeley
Bill Blackburn, Napa, California
Ellen Gavin, Los Angeles
Eileen Hansen, San Francisco
Michael Hoffman, San Diego
Robert Levering, San Francisco
John Lindsay-Poland, Oakland
Tede Matthews Archive, San Francisco
Amanda Newstetter Archive, San Francisco
Dan Wohlfeiler, Berkeley

SELECTED NEWSPAPERS AND MAGAZINES

The Advocate
The AIDS Action Call: The Newsletter of the AIDS Action Pledge
All Hands Abandon Ship
Bay Area Reporter
Berkeley Barb
Berkeley Tribe
Coming Up!/San Francisco Bay Times
The Feminist
Gay Community News
Gay Sparks
Gay Sunshine
GIGLE (G.I. Gay Liberation Experience)
Hansen Free Press
The Lesbian Tide
Los Angeles Free Press
Magnus
off our backs
Plexus
San Francisco Sentinel

Shakedown

MOVING IMAGE SOURCES

Alcatraz Is Not an Island. Directed by James M. Fortier. Diamond Island Productions, 2001.

Free Angela Davis and All Political Prisoners. Directed by Shola Lynch. Lions Gate, 2012.

Last Call at Maud's. Directed by Paris Poirier. Frameline, 1993.

The New Black. Directed by Yoruba Richen. Promised Land Film, 2013.

Ojos que no ven. Directed by Jose Gutierrez-Gomez. Instituto Familiar de la Raza and Latino AIDS Project, 1987.

Screaming Queens: the Riot at Compton's Cafeteria. Directed by Victor Silverman and Susan Stryker. Independent Television Service (ITVS), 2005.

Sex and the Sandinistas. Directed by Linda Broadbent. Women Make Movies, 1991.

Sir! No Sir! Directed by David Zeiger. Docurama, 2005.

United in Anger: A History of ACT UP. Directed by Jim Hubbard. Jim Hubbard and Sarah Schulman, 2012.

Word Is Out: Stories of Some of Our Lives. Directed by Mariposa Film Group. New Yorker Films, 1977.

SELECTED PUBLISHED PRIMARY SOURCES AND MEMOIRS

Abbott, Sidney, and Barbara Love. *Sappho Is a Right-On Woman: A Liberated View of Lesbianism.* New York: Stein and Day, 1972.

Adair, Nancy, and Casey Adair. *Word Is Out: Stories of Some Of Our Lives.* San Francisco: New Glide, 1978.

Anzaldúa, Gloria, and Cherríe Moraga, eds. *This Bridge Called My Back: Writings by Radical Women of Color.* 2nd ed. San Francisco: Kitchen Table Press, 1983. 1st ed., Watertown, MA: Persephone Press, 1981.

Bermudez, Lucrecia. "Me siento marginada." In *Compañeras: Latina Lesbians,* 227–31. Edited by Juanita Ramos. New York: Routledge, 1994.

Blasius, Mark, and Shane Phelan, eds. *We Are Everywhere: A Historical Sourcebook of Gay and Lesbian Politics.* New York: Routledge, 1997.

Block, Diana. *Arm the Spirit: A Woman's Journey Underground and Back.* Oakland, CA: AK Press, 2009.

Cabezas, Omar. *Fire from the Mountain: The Making of a Sandinista.* New York: Crown, 1985.

Cagan, Leslie. "Something New Emerges: The Growth of a Socialist Feminist." In *They Should Have Served That Cup of Coffee,* 225–58. Edited by Dick Cluster. Boston: South End Press, 1979.

Deming, Barbara. *Remembering Who We Are.* 2nd ed. St. Augustine, FL: Pagoda, 1981.

Dunbar-Ortiz, Roxanne. *Blood on the Border: A Memoir of the Contra War.* Boston: South End Press, 2005; Norman: University of Oklahoma Press, 2016.

———. *Outlaw Woman: A Memoir of the War Years, 1960–1975*. Revised edition. Norman: University of Oklahoma Press, 2014; original edition, 2001.

DuPlessis, Rachel Blau, and Ann Snitow, eds. *The Feminist Memoir Project: Voices from Women's Liberation*. New Brunswick, NJ: Rutgers University Press, 2007.

Emergency Response Network. *¡Basta! No Mandate for War: A Pledge of Resistance Handbook*. Edited by Ken Butigan, Terry Messman-Rucker, and Marie Pastrick. Philadelphia: New Society, 1986.

Garza, Alicia. "A Herstory of #BlackLivesMatter." *Feminist Wire*, October 7, 2014.

Gay Left Collective, ed. *Homosexuality: Power and Politics*. London: Allison & Busby, 1980.

Gordon, Rebecca. *Letters from Nicaragua*. San Francisco: Spinsters/Aunt Lute Press, 1986.

Grahn, Judy. "Ground Zero: The Rise of Lesbian Feminism." In *The Judy Grahn Reader*, 312–17. San Francisco: Aunt Lute Books, 2009.

———. *A Simple Revolution: The Making of an Activist Poet*. San Francisco: Aunt Lute Books, 2012.

Granados, Elsa. "Haciendo conexiones." In *Esta puente, mi espalda: Voces de mujeres tercermundistas en los Estados Unidos*, 201–3. Edited by Cherríe Moraga and Ana Castillo. San Francisco: Ism Press, 1988.

Guevara, Ernesto (Che). "Socialism and Man in Cuba" (1965). In *Che Guevara Reader: Writings on Guerrilla Strategy, Politics and Revolution*, 2nd ed., 212–30. Edited by David Deutschmann. Melbourne, Australia: Ocean Press, 2003.

Jay, Karla, and Allen Young, eds. *Out of the Closets: Voices of Gay Liberation*. New York: Douglas, 1972.

Lavender & Red Union, ed. *The Lavender & Red Book: A Gay Liberation/ Socialist Anthology*. Los Angeles: Lavender & Red Union/Peace Press, 1976.

McAllister, Pam, ed. *Reweaving the Web of Life: Feminism and Nonviolence*. Vancouver: New Society, 1982.

Mecca, Tommi Avicolli, ed. *Smash the Church, Smash the State! The Early Years of Gay Liberation*. San Francisco: City Lights Books, 2009.

Mitchell, Larry, and Ned Asta. *The Faggots and Their Friends Between Revolutions*. San Francisco: Calamus Books, 1977.

Moraga, Cherríe. *Loving in the War Years: Lo que nunca pasó por sus labios*. 2nd ed. Boston: South End Press, 2000. 1st ed., 1983.

Out and Outraged: Non-Violent Civil Disobedience at the U.S. Supreme Court—For Love, Life & Liberation, October 13, 1987: C.D. Handbook.

Richmond, Len, and Gary Noguera, eds. *The Gay Liberation Book: Writings and Photographs on Gay (Men's) Liberation*. San Francisco: Ramparts Press, 1973.

Rose, Kieran. "Lesbians and Gay Men." In *Nicaragua: An Unfinished Canvas*, 83–85. Edited by Nicaraguan Book Collective. Dublin: Nicaraguan Book Collective, 1988.

Schapiro, Naomi. "AIDS Brigade: Organizing Prevention." In *AIDS: The Women*, 211–16. Edited by Ines Rieder and Patricia Ruppelt. San Francisco: Cleis Press, 1988.

The Women's Gun Pamphlet: A Primer on Handguns. Oakland, CA: Women's Press Collective, 1975.

SECONDARY SOURCES

Aganthangelou, Anna M., Daniel Bassichis, and Tamara L. Spira. "Intimate Investments: Homonormativity, Global Lockdown, and Seductions of Empire." *Radical History Review* 100 (winter 2008): 120–43.

Agee, Christopher Lowen. *The Streets of San Francisco: Policing and the Creation of a Cosmopolitan Liberal Politics, 1950–1972.* Chicago: University of Chicago Press, 2014.

Ahmed, Sara. *The Cultural Politics of Emotion.* London: Routledge, 2004.

Alexander, M. Jacqui. "Not Just (Any) Body Can Be a Citizen: The Politics of Law, Sexuality and Postcoloniality in Trinidad and Tobago and the Bahamas." *Feminist Review* 48 (fall 1994): 5–23.

Alexander, M. Jacqui, and Chandra Talpade Mohanty, eds. *Feminist Genealogies, Colonial Legacies, Democratic Futures.* New York: Routledge, 1997.

Aptheker, Bettina. "Mercado, Victoria 'Vicky' (1951–1982)." In *Latinas in the United States: A Historical Encyclopedia,* Vol. 2, pp. 451–52. Edited by Vicki L. Ruiz and Virginia Sánchez. Bloomington: Indiana University Press, 2006.

Armstrong, Elizabeth. *Forging Gay Identities: Organizing Sexuality in San Francisco, 1950–1994.* Chicago: University of Chicago, 2002.

Ashby, LeRoy, and Rod Gramer. *Fighting the Odds: The Life of Senator Frank Church.* Pullman: Washington State University Press, 1994.

Babb, Florence E. "Out in Nicaragua: Local and Transnational Desires after the Revolution." *Cultural Anthropology* 18:3 (2003): 304–28.

Bayard de Volo, Lorraine. *Mothers of Heroes and Martyrs: Gender Identity Politics in Nicaragua, 1979–1999.* Baltimore: Johns Hopkins University Press, 2001.

Beal, Mary F. *Safe House: A Casebook Study of Revolutionary Feminism in the 1970s.* Eugene, OR: Northwest Matrix, 1976.

Beins, Agatha. "Radical Others: Women of Color and Revolutionary Feminism." *Feminist Studies* 41:1 (2015): 150–83.

Belkin, Aaron. *Bring Me Men: Military Masculinity and the Benign Façade of American Empire, 1892–2001.* New York: Oxford University Press, 2012.

Berger, Dan. *Captive Nation: Black Prison Organizing in the Civil Rights Era.* Chapel Hill: University of North Carolina Press, 2014.

———. *Outlaws of America: The Weather Underground and the Politics of Solidarity.* Oakland, CA: AK Press, 2005.

Bérubé, Allan. "How Gay Becomes White and What Kind of White it Stays." In *My Desire for History: Essays in Gay, Community, and Labor History,* 202–30. Edited by John D'Emilio and Estelle B. Freedman. Chapel Hill: University of North Carolina Press, 2011.

Bevacqua, Maria. "Reconsidering Violence against Women: Coalition Politics in the Antirape Movement." In *Feminist Coalitions: Historical Perspectives on Second-Wave Feminism in the United States,* 163–77. Edited by Stephanie Gilmore. Urbana: University of Illinois Press, 2008.

Blackwell, Maylei. ¡Chicana Power! Contested Histories of Feminism in the Chicano Movement. Austin: University of Texas Press, 2011.

———. "Translenguas: Mapping the Possibilities and Challenges of Transnational Women's Organizing Across Geographies of Difference." In Translocalities/Translocalidades: Feminist Politics of Translation in the Latin/a Americas, 299–320. Edited by Sonia E. Alvarez et al. Durham, NC: Duke University Press, 2014.

Bloom, Joshua, and Waldo E. Martin Jr. Black against Empire: The History and Politics of the Black Panther Party. Berkeley: University of California Press, 2013.

Blum, William. Killing Hope: U.S. Military and CIA Interventions since World War II. Monroe, ME: Common Courage Press, 1995.

Boyd, Nan Alamilla. Wide Open Town: A History of Queer San Francisco to 1965. Berkeley: University of California Press, 2005.

Brier, Jennifer. "The Immigrant Infection: Images of Race, Nation, and Contagion in the Public Debates on AIDS and Immigration." In Modern American Queer History, 253–70. Edited by Allida Black. Philadelphia: Temple University Press, 2001.

———. Infectious Ideas: U.S. Political Responses to the AIDS Crisis. Chapel Hill: University of North Carolina Press, 2009.

Briggs, Laura. Somebody's Children: The Politics of Transracial and Transnational Adoption. Durham, NC: Duke University Press, 2012.

Browder, Laura. Her Best Shot: Women and Guns in America. Chapel Hill: University of North Carolina Press, 2008.

Buhle, Paul. "Madison Revisited." Radical History Review 57 (1993): 242–49.

Burgett, Bruce, and Glenn Hendler, eds. Keywords for American Cultural Studies. New York: New York University Press, 2007.

Burton-Rose, Daniel. Guerrilla USA: The George Jackson Brigade and the Anticapitalist Underground of the 1970s. Berkeley: University of California Press, 2010.

Canaday, Margot. The Straight State: Sexuality and Citizenship in Twentieth-Century America. Princeton, NJ: Princeton University Press, 2011.

Capó, Julio, Jr. "Queering Mariel: Mediating Cold War Foreign Policy and U.S. Citizenship among Cuba's Homosexual Exile Community, 1978–1994." Journal of American Ethnic History 29: 4 (summer 2010): 78–106.

Carter, David. Stonewall: The Riots That Sparked the Gay Revolution. New York: St. Martin's Griffin, 2010.

Chater, Nancy, and Lilith Finkler. "'Traversing Wide Territories': A Journey from Lesbianism to Bisexuality." In Plural Desires: Writing Bisexual Realities, 14–36. Edited by the Bisexual Anthology Collective. Toronto: Sister Vision Press, 1995.

Chávez, Karma R. Queer Migration Politics: Activist Rhetoric and Coalitional Possibilities. Urbana: University of Illinois Press, 2013.

Clawson, Mary Ann. "Looking for Feminism: Racial Dynamics and Generational Investments in the Second Wave." Feminist Studies 34:3 (fall 2008): 526–55.

Cobb, Charles E. This Nonviolent Stuff'll Get You Killed. New York: Basic Books, 2014.

Cobb, Jelani. "The Matter of Black Lives." *The New Yorker,* March 14, 2016.

Cohen, Cathy J. "Punks, Bulldaggers, and Welfare Queens: The Radical Potential of Queer Politics." In *Black Queer Studies: A Critical Anthology,* 21–51. Edited by E. Patrick Johnson and Mae J. Henderson. Durham, NC: Duke University Press, 2005.

Conrad, Ryan, ed. *Against Equality: Queer Revolution, Not Mere Inclusion.* Oakland, CA: AK Press, 2014.

Cordova, Cary. "The Heart of the Mission: Latino Art and Identity in San Francisco." PhD dissertation, American Studies, University of Texas at Austin, 2005.

———. "The Mission in Nicaragua: San Francisco Poets Go to War." In *Beyond el Barrio: Everyday Life in Latina/o America,* 211–32. Edited by Gina M. Pérez, Frank Guridy, and Adrian Burgos. New York: New York University Press, 2010.

Crenshaw, Kimberlé. "Demarginalizing the Intersection of Race and Sex: A Black Feminist Critique of Antidiscrimination Doctrine, Feminist Theory, and Antiracist Politics." *University of Chicago Legal Forum* 1989:1 (1989): 139–67.

———. "Mapping the Margins: Intersectionality, Identity Politics, and Violence Against Women of Color." *Stanford Law Review* 43: 6 (1991): 1241–99.

Crimp, Douglas. "Mourning and Militancy." *October* 51 (winter 1989): 3–18.

———. "Right On, Girlfriend!" *Social Text* 33 (1992): 2–18.

D'Emilio, John. "By Way of Introduction: Notes from One Gay Life." In *Making Trouble: Essays on Gay History, Politics, and the University,* xiii–xliv. New York: Routledge, 1992.

Deitcher, David, ed. *The Question of Equality: Lesbian and Gay Politics in America since Stonewall.* New York: Scribner, 1995.

Del Rio, Chelsea. "Voicing Gay Women's Liberation: Judy Grahn and the Shaping of Lesbian Feminism." *Journal of Lesbian Studies* 19 (2015): 357–66.

Deloria, Philip J. *Playing Indian.* New Haven: Yale University Press, 1998.

Diwas, KC. "Of Consciousness and Criticism: Identity in the Intersections of the Gay Liberation Front and the Young Lords Party." MA thesis, Department of Women's History, Sarah Lawrence College, 2005.

Dixon, Chris. *Another Politics: Talking across Today's Transformative Movements.* Berkeley: University of California Press, 2014.

Downs, Jim. *Stand By Me: The Forgotten History of Gay Liberation.* New York: Basic Books, 2016.

Drucker, Peter, ed. *Different Rainbows.* London: Gay Men's Press, 2000.

Duberman, Martin. *Hold Tight Gently: Michael Callen, Essex Hemphill, and the Battlefield of AIDS.* New York: The New Press, 2014.

———. *A Saving Remnant: The Radical Lives of Barbara Deming and David McReynolds.* New York: The New Press, 2011.

———. *Stonewall.* New York: Penguin, 1993.

Duggan, Lisa. *The Twilight of Equality? Neoliberalism, Cultural Politics, and the Attack on Democracy.* Boston: Beacon Press, 2003.

Eaklor, Vicki. *Queer America: A People's GLBT History of the United States.* New York: The New Press, 2008.

Echols, Alice. *Daring to be Bad: Radical Feminism in America, 1967–1975.* Minneapolis: University of Minnesota Press, 1989.

Ehrensaft, Diane, and Ruth Milkman, interview with Amber Hollibaugh. "Sexuality and the State: The Defeat of the Briggs Initiative and Beyond." *Socialist Review* 9:3 (May–June 1979): 1–11.

Elbaum, Max. *Revolution in the Air: Sixties Radicals Turn to Lenin, Mao, and Che.* New York: Verso Books, 2002.

Enke, Anne. "Smuggling Sex through the Gates: Race, Sexuality, and the Politics of Space in Second Wave Feminism." *American Quarterly* 55:4 (2003): 635–67.

———. *Finding the Movement: Sexuality, Contested Space, and Feminist Activism.* Durham, NC: Duke University Press, 2007.

Epstein, Barbara. "The Culture of Direct Action: Livermore Action Group and the Peace Movement." *Socialist Review* 15:4–5 (July 1985): 31–61.

———. *Political Protest and Cultural Revolution: Nonviolent Direct Action in the 1970s and 1980s.* Berkeley: University of California Press, 1993.

Erickson-Nepstad, Sharon. "Creating Transnational Solidarity: The Use of Narrative in the U.S.-Central America Peace Movement." *Mobilization* 6:1 (2001): 21–36.

Escoffier, Jeffrey. "The Political Economy of the Closet." In *Homo Economics: Capitalism, Community, and Gay and Lesbian Life,* 123–34. Edited by Amy Gluckman and Betsy Reed. New York: Routledge, 1997.

Esparza, Araceli. "Cherríe Moraga's Changing Consciousness of Solidarity." In *The Un/Making of Latina/o Citizenship: Culture, Politics, and Aesthetics,* 145–66. Edited by Ellie D. Hernández and Eliza Rodriguez y Gibson. New York: Palgrave Macmillan, 2014.

Faderman, Lillian, and Stuart Timmons. *Gay L.A.: A History of Sexual Outlaws, Power Politics, and Lipstick Lesbians.* Berkeley: University of California Press, 2009.

Farber, David. *The Age of Great Dreams: America in the 1960s.* New York: Hill and Wang, 1994.

Fejes, Fred. *Gay Rights and Moral Panic: The Origins of America's Debate on Homosexuality.* London: Palgrave Macmillan, 2008.

Ferguson, Roderick. *Aberrations in Black: Toward a Queer of Color Critique.* Minneapolis: University of Minnesota Press, 2004.

Ferreira, Jason. "'With the Soul of a Human Rainbow': Los Siete, Black Panthers, and Third Worldism in San Francisco." In *Ten Years That Shook the City: San Francisco, 1968–1978,* 30–47. Edited by Chris Carlsson. San Francisco: City Lights Books, 2011.

Foley, Michael Stewart. *Front Porch Politics: The Forgotten Heyday of American Activism in the 1970s and 1980s.* New York: Hill and Wang, 2013.

Ford, Tanisha C. *Liberated Threads: Black Women, Style, and the Global Politics of Soul.* Chapel Hill: University of North Carolina Press, 2015.

Frank, Miriam. *Out in the Union: A Labor History of Queer America.* Philadelphia: Temple University Press, 2014.

Franks, Lucinda. "Annals of Crime: Return of the Fugitive." *New Yorker,* June 13, 1994.

Gallo, Marcia M. *Different Daughters: A History of Daughters of Bilitis and the Rise of the Lesbian Rights Movement.* New York: Seal Press, 2006.

Garber, Linda. *Identity Poetics: Race, Class, and the Lesbian-Feminist Roots of Queer Theory.* New York: Columbia University Press, 2001.

García, Maria Cristina. *Seeking Refuge: Central American Migration to Mexico, the United States, and Canada.* Berkeley: University of California Press, 2006.

Gardiner, Judith Kegan. "What Happened to Socialist Feminist Women's Studies Programs? A Case Study and Some Speculations." *Feminist Studies* 34:3 (fall 2008): 558–84.

Gelbspan, Ross. *Break-Ins, Death Threats, and the FBI: The Covert War against the Central America Movement.* Boston: South End Press, 1991.

Ghaziani, Amin. *The Dividends of Dissent: How Conflict and Culture Work in Lesbian and Gay Marches on Washington.* Chicago: University of Chicago Press, 2008.

Gilmore, Ruth Wilson. *Golden Gulag: Prisons, Surplus, Crisis, and Opposition in Globalizing California.* Berkeley: University of California Press, 2007.

Gobat, Michel. *Confronting the American Dream: Nicaragua under U.S. Imperial Rule.* Durham, NC: Duke University Press, 2005.

Goméz-Barris, Macarena. *Where Memory Dwells: Culture and State Violence in Chile.* Berkeley: University of California Press, 2008.

Gonzáles-Rivera, Victoria. *Before the Revolution: Women's Rights and Right-Wing Politics in Nicaragua, 1821–1979.* University Park: Penn State University Press, 2012.

———. "The Alligator Woman's Tale: Remembering Nicaragua's 'First Self-Declared Lesbian.'" *Journal of Lesbian Studies* 18:1 (2014): 75–87.

Gosse, Van. "El Salvador Is Spanish for Vietnam." In *The Immigrant Left in the United States,* 302–29. Edited by Paul Buhle and Dan Georgakas. Albany: State University of New York Press, 1996.

———. "'The North American Front': Central American Solidarity in the Reagan Era." In *Reshaping the U.S. Left,* 1–43. Edited by Mike Davis and Michael Sprinkler. New York: Verso, 1988.

———. "Unpacking the Vietnam Syndrome: The Coup in Chile and the Rise of Popular Anti-interventionism." In *The World the Sixties Made: Politics and Culture in Recent America,* 100–113. Edited by Van Gosse and Richard Moser. Philadelphia: Temple University Press, 2003.

———. *Where the Boys Are: Cuba, the Cold War, and the Making of a New Left.* New York: Verso Press, 1993.

Gould, Deborah B. *Moving Politics: Emotion and ACT UP's Fight against AIDS.* Chicago: University of Chicago Press, 2009.

Graham, Gael. "Flaunting the Freak Flag: *Karr v. Schmidt* and the Great Hair Debate in American High Schools, 1965–1975." *Journal of American History* 91:2 (September 2004): 522–43.

Grandin, Greg. *Empire's Workshop: Latin America, the United States, and the Rise of the New Imperialism.* New York: Holt Paperbacks, 2007.

Green, James N., and Florence Babb. "Introduction." *Latin American Perspectives* 29:2 (March 2002): 3–23.

Guerra, Lillian. "Gender Policing, Homosexuality, and the New Patriarchy of the Cuban Revolution, 1965–70." *Social History* 35: 3 (August 2010): 268–89.

Habal, Estella. *San Francisco's International Hotel: Mobilizing the Filipino American Community in the Anti-eviction Movement*. Philadelphia: Temple University Press, 2007.

Hanhardt, Christina B. *Safe Space: Gay Neighborhood History and the Politics of Violence* (Durham, NC: Duke University Press, 2013).

Hays, Sharon. *Flat Broke with Children: Women in the Age of Welfare Reform*. New York: Oxford University Press, 2004.

Hekma, Gert, Harry Oosterhuis, and James Steakley, eds. "Leftist Sexual Politics and Homosexuality: A Historical Overview." *Journal of Homosexuality* 29:2–3 and 4 (1995): 1–40.

Herrera, Juan Felipe. "Riffs on Mission District *Raza* Writers." In *Reclaiming San Francisco: History, Politics, Culture*, 217–30. Edited by James Brook, Chris Carlsson, and Nancy J. Peters. San Francisco: City Lights Books, 1998.

Herring, Scott. "Out of the Closets, into the Woods: RFD, Country Women, and the Post-Stonewall Emergence of Queer Anti-Urbanism." *American Quarterly* 59 (2007): 341–72.

Hillman, Betty Luther. *Dressing for the Culture Wars: Style and the Politics of Self-Presentation in the 1960s and 1970s*. Lincoln: University of Nebraska Press, 2015.

———. "'The Most Profoundly Revolutionary Act a Homosexual Can Engage In': Drag and the Politics of Gender Presentation in the San Francisco Gay Liberation Movement, 1964–1972." *Journal of the History of Sexuality* 20:1 (January 2011): 153–81.

Hobson, Emily K. "Policing Gay LA: Mapping Racial Divides in the Homophile Era, 1950–1967." In *The Rising Tide of Color: Race, State Violence, and Radical Movements across the Pacific*, 189–212. Edited by Moon-Ho Jung. Seattle: University of Washington Press, 2014.

———. "'Si Nicaragua Venció': Lesbian and Gay Solidarity with the Revolution." *Journal of Transnational American Studies* 4:2 (fall 2012): 1–26.

Hogan, Kristin. *The Feminist Bookstore Movement: Lesbian Antiracism and Feminist Accountability*. Durham, NC: Duke University Press, 2016.

Holcomb, Gary. *Claude McKay, Code Name Sasha: Queer Black Marxism and the Harlem Renaissance*. Gainesville: University Press of Florida, 2009.

Hollibaugh, Amber. *My Dangerous Desires: A Queer Girl Dreaming Her Way Home*. Durham, NC: Duke University Press, 2000.

Holstrom, Nancy, ed. *The Socialist Feminist Project: A Contemporary Reader in Theory and Politics*. New York: Monthly Review Press, 2002.

HoSang, Daniel Martinez. *Racial Propositions: Ballot Initiatives and the Making of Postwar California*. Berkeley: University of California Press, 2010.

Howe, Cymene. "Gender, Sexuality, and Revolution: Making Histories and Cultural Politics in Nicaragua, 1979–2001." In *Gender, Sexuality, and Power in Latin America since Independence*, 230–60. Edited by William E. French and Katherine Elaine Bliss. Lanham, MD: Rowman & Littlefield, 2007.

———. *Intimate Activism: The Struggle for Sexual Rights in Postrevolutionary Nicaragua*. Durham, NC: Duke University Press, 2013.

———. "Undressing the Universal Queer Subject: Nicaraguan Activism and Transnational Identity." *City & Society* 14:2 (2002): 237–79.

Huhndorf, Shari M. *Going Native: Indians in the American Cultural Imagination*. Ithaca, NY: Cornell University Press, 2001.

Hunt, Andrew. *The Turning: A History of Vietnam Veterans against the War*. New York: New York University Press, 1999.

———. "'When Did the Sixties Happen?': Searching for New Directions." *Journal of Social History* 33: 1 (1999): 147–61.

Hurewitz, Daniel. *Bohemian Los Angeles and the Making of Modern Politics*. Berkeley: University of California Press, 2007.

INCITE! Women of Color Against Violence, ed. *Color of Violence: The INCITE! Anthology*. Boston: South End Press, 2006.

———. *The Revolution Will Not Be Funded: Beyond the Non-profit Industrial Complex*. Boston: South End Press, 2009.

Jacquet, Catherine O. "Responding to Rape: Contesting the Meaning of Sexual Violence in the United States, 1950–1980." PhD dissertation, University of Illinois Chicago, 2012.

Kampwirth, Karen. "Organizing the *Hombre Nuevo Gay*: LGBT Politics and the Second Sandinista Revolution." *Bulletin of Latin American Research* 33:3 (2014): 319–33.

Kampwirth, Karen, and Victoria Gonzáles-Rivera. *Radical Women in Latin America: Left and Right*. University Park: Penn State University Press, 2001.

Katsiaficas, George. "Organization and Movement: The Case of the Black Panther Party and the Revolutionary People's Constitutional Convention of 1970." In *Liberation, Imagination, and the Black Panther Party: A New Look at the Panthers and Their Legacy*, 141–55. Edited by Kathleen Cleaver and George Katsiaficas. New York: Routledge, 2001.

Keck, Margaret, and Kathryn Sikkink. *Activist beyond Borders*. Ithaca, NY: Cornell University Press, 1998.

Kelliher, Diarmaid. "Solidarity and Sexuality: Lesbians and Gays Support the Miners 1984–5." *History Workshop Journal* 77 (spring 2014): 240–62.

Kissack, Terrence. "Freaking Fag Revolutionaries: New York's Gay Liberation Front, 1969–1971." *Radical History Review* 62 (1995): 104–34.

Kornbluh, Peter. *Nicaragua: The Price of Intervention; Reagan's War against the Sandinistas*. Washington, DC: Institute for Policy Studies, 1987.

Koskovich, Gerard. "Remembering a Police Riot: The Castro Sweep of October 6, 1989." In *Out in the Castro: Desire, Promise, Activism*, 189–98. Edited by Winston Leyland. San Francisco: Leyland, 2002.

Kunzel, Regina. *Criminal Intimacy: Prison and the Uneven History of Modern American Sexuality*. Chicago: University of Chicago Press, 2008.

———. "Lessons in Being Gay: Queer Encounters in Gay and Lesbian Prison Activism." *Radical History Review*, no. 100 (winter 2008): 11–36.

LaFeber, Walter. *Inevitable Revolutions: The United States in Latin America*. 2nd ed. New York: W. W. Norton, 1993.

Lancaster, Roger. *Life Is Hard: Machismo, Danger, and the Intimacy of Power in Nicaragua.* Berkeley: University of California Press, 1992.

Lapovsky Kennedy, Elizabeth. "Socialist Feminism: What Difference Did It Make to the History of Women's Studies?" *Feminist Studies* 34:3 (fall 2008): 497–525.

Law, Victoria. "Sick of the Abuse: Feminist Responses to Sexual Assault, Battering, and Self-Defense." In *The Hidden 1970s: Histories of Radicalism*, 39–56. Edited by Dan Berger. New Brunswick, NJ: Rutgers University Press, 2010.

Le Zotte, Jennifer. *From Goodwill to Grunge: Secondhand Economies and Styles.* Chapel Hill: University of North Carolina Press, forthcoming.

Lecklider, Aaron. "Coming to Terms: Homosexuality and the Left in American Culture." *GLQ: A Journal of Lesbian and Gay Studies* 18: 1 (2012): 179–95.

Lederer, Bob. "Three Decades of Queer Solidarity and Radical Struggle: A Rich History." In *Let Freedom Ring: A Collection of Documents From the Movement to Free U.S. Political Prisoners*, 395–400. Edited by Adolfo Perez Esquivel. Montreal: Kesplebedeb, 2008.

Lekus, Ian K. "Interview with Amber Hollibaugh." *Peace & Change* 29:2 (April 2004): 266–321.

———. "Losing Our Kids: Queer Perspectives on the Chicago Seven Trial." In *The New Left Revisited*, 199–213. Edited by John McMillian and Paul Buhle. Philadelphia: Temple University Press, 2003.

———. "Queer and Present Dangers: Homosexuality and American Anti-war Activism during the Vietnam Era." PhD dissertation, Duke University, 2003.

———. *Queer and Present Dangers: Masculinity, Sexuality, and the Sixties.* Chapel Hill: University of North Carolina Press, forthcoming.

———. "Queer Harvests: Homosexuality, the U.S. New Left, and the Venceremos Brigades to Cuba." *Radical History Review* 89 (spring 2004): 57–91.

Maeda, Daryl. *Chains of Babylon: The Rise of Asian America.* Minneapolis: University of Minnesota Press, 2009.

Man, Simeon. "Radicalizing Currents: The GI Movement in the Third World." In *The Rising Tide of Color: Race, State Violence, and Radical Movements across the Pacific*, 266–97. Edited by Moon-Ho Jung. Seattle: University of Washington Press, 2014.

Marchevsky, Alejandra, and Jeanne Theoharis. *Not Working: Latina Immigrants, Low-Wage Jobs, and the Failure of Welfare Reform.* New York: New York University Press, 2006.

Martin, Bradford. *The Other Eighties: A Secret History of America in the Age of Reagan.* New York: Hill & Wang, 2012.

Matthews, Tracye. "'No One Ever Asks What a Man's Role in the Revolution Is': Gender Politics and Leadership in the Black Panther Party, 1966–1971." In *Sisters in the Struggle: African American Women in the Civil Rights-Black Power Movement*, 230–55. Edited by Bettye Collier and V.P. Franklin. New York: New York University Press, 2001.

McFeeley, Tim. "Getting It Straight: A Review of the 'Gays in the Military' Debate." In *Creating Change: Sexuality, Public Policy, and Civil Rights,*

236–50. Edited by John D'Emilio, William B. Turner, and Urvashi Vaid. New York: St. Martin's Press, 2000.

McGirr, Lisa. *Suburban Warriors: The Origins of the New American Right*. Princeton: Princeton University Press, 2002.

McGuire, Danielle. *At the Dark End of the Street: Black Women, Rape, and Resistance; A New History of the Civil Rights Movement from Rosa Parks to Black Power*. New York: Vintage Books, 2011.

McSweeney, Anne. "'Hijacking the Movement': The Saxe-Alpert Controversy, Media Politics and the Making of Radical Feminism in the U.S., 1974–1976." B.A. thesis, Wesleyan University, 2008.

Melzer, Patricia. *Death in the Shape of a Young Girl: Women's Political Violence in the Red Army Faction*. New York: New York University Press, 2015.

Meyer, Matt, and Paul Magno. "Hard to Find: Building for Nonviolent Revolution and the Pacifist Underground." In *The Hidden 1970s: Histories of Radicalism*, 250–66. Edited by Dan Berger. New Brunswick, NJ: Rutgers University Press, 2010.

Miller, James. *Democracy Is in the Streets: From Port Huron to the Siege of Chicago*. Cambridge, MA: Harvard University Press, 1987.

Mogul, Joey L., Andrea J. Ritchie, and Kay Whitlock. *Queer (In)Justice: The Criminalization of LGBT People in the United States*. Boston: Beacon Press, 2012.

Mohanty, Chandra. "Under Western Eyes: Feminist Scholarship and Colonial Discourses." *boundary* 2 (1984): 333–58.

Molyneux, Maxine. "Mobilization without Emancipation? Women's Interest, State, and Revolution in Nicaragua." *Feminist Studies* 11:2 (1985): 227–54.

Moore, Patrick. *Beyond Shame: Reclaiming the Abandoned History of Radical Gay Sexuality*. Boston: Beacon Press, 2004.

Morgensen, Scott Lauria. *Spaces Between Us: Queer Settler Colonialism and Indigenous Decolonization*. Minneapolis: University of Minnesota Press, 2011.

Morley, Morris H. *Washington, Somoza, and the Sandinistas: State and Regime in U.S. Policy toward Nicaragua, 1969–1981*. Cambridge: Cambridge University Press, 1994.

Mortimer-Sandilands, Catriona, and Bruce Erickson. *Queer Ecologies: Sex, Nature, Politics, Desire*. Bloomington: Indiana University Press, 2010.

Moser, Richard R. *The New Winter Soldiers: GI and Veteran Dissent during the Vietnam Era*. New Brunswick, NJ: Rutgers University Press, 1996.

Mumford, Kevin J. *Not Straight, Not White: Black Gay Men from the March on Washington to the AIDS Crisis*. Chapel Hill: University of North Carolina Press, 2016.

Muñoz, José Esteban. *Disidentifications: Queers of Color and the Performance of Politics*. Minneapolis: University of Minnesota Press, 1999.

Murch, Donna Jean. *Living for the City: Migration, Education, and the Rise of the Black Panther Party in Oakland, California*. Chapel Hill: University of North Carolina Press, 2010.

Murguía, Alejandro. "Poetry and Solidarity in the Mission District." In *Ten Years That Shook the City: San Francisco 1968–1978*, 61–70. Edited by

Chris Carlsson with Lisa Ruth Elliott. San Francisco: City Lights Books, 2011.

Nelson, Jennifer. *Women of Color and the Reproductive Rights Movement.* New York: New York University Press, 2003.

Ongiri, Amy Abugo. "Prisoner of Love: Affiliation, Sexuality, and the Black Panther Party." *Journal of African American History* 94:1 (winter 2009): 69–86.

Ordona, Trinity. "Coming Out Together: An Ethnohistory of the Asian and Pacific Islander Queer Women's and Transgendered People's Movement of San Francisco." PhD dissertation, University of California, Santa Cruz, 2000.

Peña, Susana. *¡Oye Loca! From the Mariel Boatlift to Gay Cuban Miami.* Minneapolis: University of Minnesota Press, 2013.

Pérez, Hiram. *A Taste for Brown Bodies: Gay Modernity and Cosmopolitan Desire.* New York: New York University Press, 2015.

Perla, Héctor, Jr. "Heirs of Sandino: the Nicaraguan Revolution and the US-Nicaragua Solidarity Movement." *Latin American Perspectives* 36:6 (November 2009): 80–100.

———. "Si Nicaragua Venció, El Salvador Vencerá: Central American Agency in the Creation of the U.S.-Central American Peace and Solidarity Movement." *Latin American Research Review* 43:2 (2008): 136–58.

Phelps, Chris. "A Neglected Document on Socialism and Sex." *Journal of the History of Sexuality* 16:1 (January 2007): 1–13.

Power, Margaret. "The U.S. Movement in Solidarity with Chile in the 1970s." *Latin American Perspectives* 36:6 (November 2009): 46–66.

Prashad, Vijay. *The Darker Nations: A People's History of the Third World.* New York: The New Press, 2007.

Puar, Jasbir. *Terrorist Assemblages: Homonationalism in Queer Times.* Durham, NC: Duke University Press, 2007.

Pulido, Laura. *Black, Brown, Yellow, and Left: Radical Activism in Los Angeles.* Berkeley: University of California Press, 2006.

Randall, Margaret. *Sandino's Daughters Revisited: Feminism in Nicaragua.* New Brunswick, NJ: Rutgers University Press, 1994.

———. *Sandino's Daughters: Testimonies of Nicaraguan Women in Struggle.* Revised ed. New Brunswick, NJ: Rutgers University Press, 1995. Original edition, London: Zed Books, 1981.

———. "To Change Our Own Reality and the World: A Conversation with Lesbians in Nicaragua." *Signs* 18: 4 (1993): 907–24.

Randolph, Sherie M. *Florynce "Flo" Kennedy: The Life of a Black Feminist Radical.* Chapel Hill: University of North Carolina Press, 2015.

Ransby, Barbara. *Ella Baker and the Black Freedom Movement: A Radical Democratic Vision.* Chapel Hill: University of North Carolina Press, 2003.

Reddy, Chandan. *Freedom with Violence: Race, Sexuality, and the U.S. State.* Durham, NC: Duke University Press, 2011.

Retter, Yolanda. "Lesbian Activism in Los Angeles, 1970–79." In *Queer Frontiers: Millennial Geographies, Genders, and Generations,* 196–221. Edited by Joseph A. Boone et al. Madison: University of Wisconsin Press, 2000.

Rich, B. Ruby, and Lourdes Arguelles. "Homosexuality, Homophobia, and Revolution: Notes toward an Understanding of the Cuban Lesbian and Gay Male Experience, Part I." *Signs* 9:4 (1984): 683–99.

———. "Homosexuality, Homophobia, and Revolution: Notes toward an Understanding of the Cuban Lesbian and Gay Male Experience, Part II." *Signs* 11:1 (1985): 120–36.

Richie, Beth E. *Arrested Justice: Black Women, Violence, and America's Prison Nation.* New York: New York University Press, 2012.

Rivers, Daniel Winunwe. *Radical Relations: Lesbian Mothers, Gay Fathers, and Their Children in the United States since World War II.* Chapel Hill: University of North Carolina Press, 2013.

Robb, Sushawn. *Mothering the Movement: The Story of the San Francisco Women's Building.* Denver: Outskirts Press, 2012.

Rodriguez, Ana Patricia. *Dividing the Isthmus: Central American Transnational Histories, Literatures, and Cultures.* Austin: University of Texas Press, 2009.

Rodriguez, Ileana. *Women, Guerrillas, and Love: Understanding War in Central America.* Minneapolis: University of Minnesota Press, 1996.

Roque Ramírez, Horacio N. "Claiming Queer Cultural Citizenship: Gay Latino (Im)Migrant Acts in San Francisco." In *Queer Migrations: Sexuality, U.S. Citizenship, and Border Crossings,* 161–88. Edited by Eithne Luibhéid and Lionel Cantú Jr. Minneapolis: University of Minnesota, 2005.

———. "Gay Latino Histories/Dying to Be Remembered: AIDS Obituaries, Public Memory, and the Queer Latino Archive." In *Beyond El Barrio: Everyday Life in Latina/o America,* 103–29. Edited by Adrian Burgos, Frank Andre Guridy, and Gina M. Perez. New York: New York University Press, 2010.

———. "My Community, My History, My Practice." *Oral History Review* 29:2 (summer–autumn 2002): 87–91.

———. "'That's My Place!': Negotiating Racial, Sexual, and Gender Politics in San Francisco's Gay Latino Alliance, 1975–1983." *Journal of the History of Sexuality* 12:2 (April 2003): 224–58.

Roseneil, Sasha. *Common Women, Uncommon Practices: The Queer Feminisms of Greenham.* London: Cassell, 2000.

Roth, Benita. *Separate Roads to Feminism: Black, Chicana, and White Feminist Movements in America's Second Wave.* Cambridge: Cambridge University Press, 2004.

Saldaña-Portillo, María Josefina. *The Revolutionary Imagination in the Americas and the Age of Development.* Durham, NC: Duke University Press, 2003.

Schoonover, Thomas D. *The United States in Central America, 1860–1911: Episodes of Social Imperialism and Imperial Rivalry in the World System.* Durham, NC: Duke University Press, 1991.

Schulman, Sarah. *Israel/Palestine and the Queer International.* Durham, NC: Duke University Press, 2012.

Sedgwick, Eve. *Epistemology of the Closet.* Berkeley: University of California Press, 1990.

Segrest, Mab. *Memoir of a Race Traitor.* Boston: South End Press, 1994.

Self, Robert O. *All in the Family: The Realignment of American Democracy since the 1960s.* New York: Hill and Wang, 2013.

———. *American Babylon: Race and the Struggle for Postwar Oakland.* Princeton: Princeton University Press, 2005.

Shepherd, Benjamin. "Play as World-Making: From the Cockettes to the Germs, Gay Liberation to DIY Community Building." In *The Hidden 1970s: Histories of Radicalism,* 177–94. Edited by Dan Berger. New Brunswick, NJ: Rutgers University Press, 2010.

Shilts, Randy. *The Mayor of Castro Street: The Life and Times of Harvey Milk.* New York: St. Martin's, 1982. Reprint, New York: St. Martin's Griffin, 2008.

Sides, Josh. *Erotic City: Sexual Revolutions and the Making of Modern San Francisco.* New York: Oxford University Press, 2010.

Singh, Nikhil Pal. *Black Is a Country: Race and the Unfinished Struggle for Democracy.* Cambridge, MA: Harvard University Press, 2004.

Smith, Christian. *Resisting Reagan: The U.S. Central America Peace Movement.* Chicago: University of Chicago Press, 1996.

Smith, Melissa, and Robert Drickey. "Education for Primary Health Care: A Report on the U.S.-Nicaragua Colloquia on Health." *Mobius* 5:3 (July 1985): 135–40.

Smith, Neil. "Contours of a Spatialized Politics." *Social Text* 33 (1992): 55–81.

Smith, Sara R. "Organizing for Social Justice: Rank and File Teachers' Activism and Social Unionism in California, 1948–1978." PhD dissertation, University of California, Santa Cruz, 2014.

Solaún, Mauricio. *U.S. Intervention and Regime Change in Nicaragua.* Lincoln: University of Nebraska Press, 2005.

Solomon, Alisa. "Trans/Migrant: Christina Madrazo's All-American Story." In *Queer Migrations: Sexuality, U.S. Citizenship, and Border Crossings,* 3–29. Edited by Eithne Luibhéid and Lionel Cantú. Minneapolis: University of Minnesota Press, 2005.

Somerville, Siobhan. "Sexual Aliens and the Racialized State: A Queer Reading of the 1952 U.S. Immigration and Nationality Act." In *Queer Migrations: Sexuality, U.S. Citizenship, and Border Crossings,* 75–91. Edited by Eithne Luibhéid and Lionel Cantú. Minneapolis: University of Minnesota Press, 2005.

Soto, Sandy. "Where in the Transnational World are Women of Color?" In *Women's Studies for the Future: Foundations, Interrogations, Politics,* 111–24. Edited by Elizabeth Lapovsky Kennedy and Agatha Beins. New Brunswick, NJ: Rutgers University Press 2005.

Spade, Dean. *Normal Life: Administrative Violence, Critical Trans Politics, and the Limits of the Law.* Boston: South End Press, 2011.

Spira, Tamara Lee. "Intimate Internationalisms: 1970s Third World Feminist and Queer Solidarity with the Chilean Revolution." *Feminist Theory* 15:2 (summer 2014): 119–40.

Spencer, Robyn C. "Engendering the Black Freedom Struggle: Revolutionary Black Womanhood and the Black Panther Party in the Bay Area, California." *Journal of Women's History* 20:1 (spring 2008): 90–113.

————.*The Revolution Has Come: Black Power, Gender, and the Black Panther Party in Oakland.* Durham, NC: Duke University Press, 2016.

Springer, Kimberly. *Living for the Revolution: Black Feminist Organizations, 1968–1980.* Durham, NC: Duke University Press, 2005.

Stanley, Eric, and Nat Smith, eds. *Captive Genders: Trans Embodiment and the Prison Industrial Complex.* Oakland, CA: AK Press, 2011.

Stein, Marc. "All the Immigrants Are Straight, All the Homosexuals Are Citizens, but Some of Us Are Queer Aliens: Genealogies of Legal Strategy in *Boutilier v. INS.*" *Journal of American Ethnic History* 29:4 (summer 2010): 45–77.

————. "'Birthplace of the Nation': Imagining Lesbian and Gay Communities in Philadelphia, 1969–70." In *Creating a Place for Ourselves*, 253–88. Edited by Brett [Genny] Beemyn. New York: Routledge, 1997.

————. "Canonizing Homophile Sexual Respectability: Archives, History, and Memory." *Radical History Review* 120 (fall 2014): 53–73.

————. *City of Sisterly and Brotherly Loves: Lesbian and Gay Philadelphia, 1945–1972.* Philadelphia: Temple University Press, 2004.

————. *Rethinking the Gay and Lesbian Movement.* New York: Routledge, 2012.

Stewart-Winter, Timothy. *Queer Clout: Chicago and the Rise of Gay Politics.* Philadelphia: University of Pennsylvania Press, 2016.

Stoltz Chinchilla, Norma. "Revolutionary Popular Feminism in Nicaragua: Articulating Class, Gender, and National Sovereignty." *Gender and Society* 4:3 (1990): 370–97.

————. "Revolutionary Popular Feminism in Transition in Nicaragua: 1979–1994." In *Women in the Latin American Development Process*, 242–71. Edited by Chris Bose and Edna Acosta-Belen. Philadelphia: Temple University Press, 1995.

Stoltz Chinchilla, Norma, Nora Hamilton, and James Loucky. "The Sanctuary Movement and Central American Activism in Los Angeles." *Latin American Perspectives* 36:6 (November 2006): 101–26.

Strub, Sean. *Body Counts: A Memoir of Politics, Sex, AIDS, and Survival.* New York: Scribner, 2014.

Stryker, Susan. "(De)Subjugated Knowledges: An Introduction to Transgender Studies." In *The Transgender Studies Reader* [I], 1–17. Edited by Susan Stryker and Stephen Whittle. New York: Routledge, 2006.

————. *Transgender History.* Berkeley, CA: Seal Press, 2008.

Stryker, Susan, and Jim Van Buskirk. *Gay by the Bay: A History of Queer Culture in the San Francisco Bay Area.* San Francisco: Chronicle Books, 1996.

Sturgeon, Noel. *Ecofeminist Natures: Race, Gender, Feminist Theory, and Political Action.* New York: Routledge, 1997.

Sturken, Marita. *Tangled Memories: The Vietnam War, the AIDS Epidemic, and the Politics of Remembering.* Berkeley: University of California Press, 1997.

Suran, Justin David. "Coming Out against the War: Antimilitarism and the Politicization of Homosexuality in the Era of Vietnam." *American Quarterly* 53:3 (2001): 452–88.

Taylor, Keeanga-Yamahtta. *From #BlackLivesMatter to Black Liberation*. Chicago: Haymarket Books, 2016.

Thayer, Millie. "Identity, Revolution, and Democracy: Lesbian Movements in Central America." *Social Problems* 44:3 (1997): 386–407.

Thompson, Becky. "Multiracial Feminism: Recasting the Chronology of Second Wave Feminism." *Feminist Studies* 28:2 (summer 2002): 336–60.

———. *A Promise and a Way of Life: White Antiracist Activism*. Minneapolis: University of Minnesota Press, 2001.

Thompson, Heather Ann. "Why Mass Incarceration Matters: Rethinking Crisis, Decline, and Transformation in Postwar American History." *Journal of American History* 97:3 (December 2010): 703–34.

Thuma, Emily. "Against the 'Prison/Psychiatric State': Anti-violence Feminisms and the Politics of Confinement in the 1970s." *Feminist Formations* 26:2 (summer 2014): 26–51.

———. "Lessons in Self-Defense: Gender Violence, Racial Criminalization, and Anti-carceral Feminism." *WSQ: Women's Studies Quarterly* 43:3–4 (fall–winter 2015): 52–71.

———. "'Not a Wedge, But a Bridge': Prisons, Feminist Activism, and the Politics of Gendered Violence, 1968–1987." PhD dissertation, New York University, 2010.

Tyson, Timothy B. *Radio Free Dixie: Robert F. Williams and the Roots of Black Power*. Chapel Hill: University of North Carolina Press, 1999.

Umoja, Akinyele Omowale. *We Will Shoot Back: Armed Resistance in the Mississippi Freedom Movement*. New York: New York University Press, 2014.

Vaid, Urvashi. *Virtual Equality: The Mainstreaming of Gay and Lesbian Liberation*. New York: Anchor Books, 1996.

Valentine, David. *Imagining Transgender: An Ethnography of a Category*. Durham, NC: Duke University Press, 2007.

Valentine, Gill. "Making Space: Lesbian Separatist Communities in the United States." In *Contested Countryside Cultures: Otherness, Marginalization, and Rurality*, 109–22. Edited by Paul Cloke and Jo Little. New York: Routledge, 1997.

Valk, Anne M. "Living a Feminist Lifestyle: The Intersection of Theory and Action in a Lesbian Feminist Collective." *Feminist Studies* 28:2 (summer 2002): 303–32.

———. *Radical Sisters: Second-Wave Feminism and Black Liberation in Washington, D.C.* Urbana: University of Illinois Press, 2008.

Vargas, Roberto. "My World Incomplete/To Complete My World." In *Ten Years That Shook the City: San Francisco 1968–1978*, 92–94. Edited by Chris Carlsson with Lisa Ruth Elliott. San Francisco: City Lights Books, 2011.

Vider, Stephen. "'The Ultimate Extension of Gay Community': Communal Living and Gay Liberation in the 1970s." *Gender & History* 27:3 (November 2015): 865–81.

Walker, Thomas W. *Reagan versus the Sandinistas: The Undeclared War on Nicaragua*. Boulder, CO: Westview Press, 1987.

Ward, Michael, and Mark Freeman. "Defending Gay Rights: The Campaign against the Briggs Initiative in California." *Radical America* 13:4 (July–August 1979): 19–30.

Warrior, Robert Allen, and Paul Chaat Smith. *Like a Hurricane: The American Indian Movement from Alcatraz to Wounded Knee.* New York: The New Press, 1996.

Weber, Clare. *Visions of Solidarity: U.S. Peace Activists in Nicaragua from War to Women's Activism and Globalization.* Boston: Lexington Books, 2006.

Williams, Raymond. *Keywords: A Vocabulary of Culture and Society.* New York: Oxford University Press, 1976.

Wilson, S. Brian. *Blood on the Tracks: The Life and Times of S. Brian Wilson.* Oakland, CA: PM Press, 2011.

Winn, Peter. "The Furies of the Andes: Violence and Terror in the Chilean Revolution and Counterrevolution." In *A Century of Revolution: Insurgent and Counter-Insurgent Violence During Latin America's Long Cold War,* 239–75. Edited by Greg Grandin and Gilbert M. Joseph. Durham, NC: Duke University Press, 2010.

Wittner, Lawrence S. *Toward Nuclear Abolition: A History of the World Nuclear Disarmament Movement, 1971 to the Present.* Palo Alto, CA: Stanford University Press, 2003.

Woolner, Cookie. "'Women Slain in Queer Love Brawl': African American Women, Same-Sex Desire, and Violence in the Urban North, 1920–1929." *Journal of African American History* 100:3 (summer 2015): 406–27.

Wu, Judy Tzu-Chun. *Radicals on the Road: Internationalism, Orientalism, and Feminism During the Vietnam War Era.* Ithaca, NY: Cornell University Press, 2013.

Youmans, Greg. *Word Is Out: A Queer Film Classic.* Vancouver: Arsenal Pulp Press, 2011.

Young, Cynthia. *Soul Power: Culture, Radicalism and the Making of a U.S. Third World Left.* Durham, NC: Duke University Press, 2006.

Zaretsky, Natasha. *No Direction Home: The American Family and the Fear of National Decline, 1968–1980.* Chapel Hill: University of North Carolina Press, 2007.

Index

Granados, Elsa, 131
Grand Jury Project, 59
grand jury resistance, 59–61, 85–86, 95–96
Green, James N. (Jim), 76–77, 223n8
Greschel, Naomi, 49
Griffith, Keith, v, 163, 164–65, 255n40,
255n67, 257n67, 258n81
Gulf War (1991), 185, 189
Gurdián, Roberto, 106–8, 112, 118, 128,
137
Gutierrez, Jennicet, 196

Haight, the/Haight-Ashbury/Haight-
Fillmore (San Francisco), 21, 50, 51, 77,
237n44. *See also* Bay Area, the (San
Francisco)
Hall, Camilla, 55, 56, 219n50
Hamilton, Joan, 57
Hamilton, Steve, 71
Hanhardt, Christina B., 20, 93, 193
Hansen, Eileen, v, xi–xii, 164–65, 167–68,
173, 260n98
Hard Times Conference (1976), 85, 229n74
Hare, Nathan, 48
Hart, Lois, 53, 211n75, 553
Harvey Milk Democratic Club, 143, 145,
230n86
Hastings, Branch, v, 258n81
Hay, Harry, 18, 205n3, 263n9
Hearst, Patty, 54–55
Helmbold, Lois, 232n105. *See also* LAPV
(San Francisco)
Hensler, Rebecca, 169, 179, 260n102
Hernandez-Polanco, Nicoll, 196
Hillman, Betty Luther, 27, 207n36, 218n38
Hinton, Charlie, 76, 80, 84, 88, 106–7
Hiraga, Martin, v, 158, 253n18
HIV/AIDS (virus/disease): AIDS related
complex (ARC), 255n36; anti-retroviral
drug therapies, 158; AZT, 158, 171–73,
258n73, 260n103; Denver Principles,
158; ELISA tests, 147, 250n125; first
reports and overview, 158; foscarnet
access, 179, 260n103; Nicaragua and,
249n110, 250n124, 250n125;
Proposition 64 and, 163–64; PWAs,
158, 185; Reagan administration and,
150, 156, 165. *See also* AIDS activism
Hollibaugh, Amber, 90, 229n75
homonationalism, 191, 193
homophile movement: anti-war organizing
and, 17–18, 205n6; gay ghetto and, 12,
18–21, 24, 26–28, 30, 34, 38–40; gay
liberation and, 17–18, 205n6; left

alliances and, 205n3; religion and, 20;
use of term, 17, 18–19
homophobia. *See* antigay oppression;
sexism
House of D/Women's House of Detention
(Greenwich Village), 46
housing/anti-gentrification activism, 51, 83,
93, 190, 193–94, 203n16, 206n14,
237n44
How to Have Sex in an Epidemic (Callen
and Berkowitz), 158
Huggins, Ericka, 39, 41

ICI: A Woman's Place (bookstore), 51,
218n30, 233n3, 245n63. *See also*
bookstores
identity politics: destabilization/radical
politicization of, 193–99; essentialist
separatism/liberal rights discourse and,
5, 192; intersectional analysis and, 5–6,
44, 202n10; relational identity politics,
191–92
immigrant rights: "English-only" initiatives
and, 163, 164, 254n30; HIV/AIDS and,
251n144; homosexual immigrant ruling,
34; I-Hotel campaign, 81–82, 228n62;
No1More campaign, 195–96; Proposition 63, 163, 254n30; Proposition
187, 190; queer immigrant organizing/
undocuqueer activism, 195–96. *See also*
barrio transnationalism; Central
American solidarity movement
INCITE! Women of Color Against Violence
(network), 194
indigenous people: anti-indigenous racism,
101, 102, 123, 246n69; indigenous
Nicaraguans, 102, 135, 246n69;
Miskitu people, 246n69. *See also* Native
American activism
Inez Garcia campaigns, 62–63, 64–67,
65fig., 67fig., 73–74, 221n72, 222n82
Instituto Familiar de la Raza, 148–49, 159
International AIDS Conference (1990),
183fig., 182–84
International Hotel (I-Hotel) campaign,
81–82, 228n62
International Lesbian and Gay Human
Rights Commission (IGLHRC), 263n9
intersectional analysis, 5–6, 44, 202n10. *See
also* Marxist thought; queer of color
critique; women of color activism

Jackson, Don, 34, 35–36, 37–38, 213n100,
226n42

Third World radicalism, 21, 23–24, 97
Third World Strike (1968–1969), 23–24,
    35, 48, 89, 103
Third World Women's Alliance/TWWA,
    105, 120, 130
This Bridge Called My Back (Anzaldúa &
    Moraga), 121, 123, 128
Thompson, Margaret Benson, 134, 134*fig.*
Thorpe, Charles, 24, 35, 36
The Tide/Lesbian Tide magazine, 59
Tillery, Linda, 218n40
Tingley, Phil (Kiowa), v, 245n62
Tometi, Opal, 196, 197
transgender identities, 21, 26, 49, 73,
    188–89, 195–96
translenguaje concept, 123–24
transnational feminism, 14–15, 121–22,
    127–29, 131–34
transnational organizing: activist travel,
    124–30; barrio transnationalism, 97–98,
    105, 130–31; brigades and, 124–30,
    162; KDP and, 81–82, 227n62, 229n74;
    lesbian and gay solidarity, 120–24,
    131–32, 152–54; Nicaraguan gay
    movement, 141–42, 145–50, 248n95,
    250n20; Palestinian solidarity
    movements, 4, 32, 194–95, 198,
    265n28; pinkwashing, 195; queer
    critiques and, 194–95; Reagan
    administration and, 120–21, 123,
    136–37; transnational feminism, 14–15,
    121–22, 127–29, 131–34, 245n57;
    universalism and, 132, 245n57. *See also*
    brigades; Central American solidarity
    movement; lesbian and gay solidarity;
    Sandinista Revolution
Treatment Action Group/Treatment and
    Data Committee (New York), 262n127
TWGC/Third World Gay Caucus, 13,
    82*fig.*, 82–84, 91, 92*fig.*, 97, 118, 163,
    232n102, 232n103
TWWA/Third World Women's Alliance,
    105, 120, 130

UC Nuclear Weapons Conversion Project,
    239n67
underground activity: Alpert, Jane, 57–58,
    60; FBI harassment, 55–56; lesbian
    feminism and, 43, 46–47, 54–62; racial
    dynamics and, 47–48; Saxe, Susan,
    55–56, 58–62; SLA, 54–55, 56. *See also*
    armed resistance; collective defense;
    Davis, Angela Y.; WUO
undocuqueer activism, 195–96, 265n31

United Fruit (Boston), 244n34
United Prisoners Union, 226n42
United States Mint protest, 174, 180
United States-Nicaragua Colloquia on
    Health, 143

Valeri, Robert, 58, 220n55
Vanguard, 20
Vargas, Roberto, 103–4, 105–6
Vázquez, Carmen: barrio transnationalism
    and, 105, 130, 131, 244n47; Central
    American solidarity movement and,
    105, 113, 120–21, 236n32; lesbian and
    gay solidarity, 120–21, 127, 129–30;
    Somos Hermanas and, 120–21, 127,
    129, 130, 245n54; transnational
    feminism of, 127, 129, 130, 131
Vector (periodical), 76
Venceremos Brigades, 8, 29, 31, 70, 71,
    108, 125, 144, 150, 209n60. *See also*
    Cuba; SDS
Veterans for Peace, 254n32
Victoria Mercado Brigade: AIDS brigades
    and, 144, LAGAI and, 118, 132–33;
    Nicaraguan gay movement and, 134–35,
    136–37, 138; overview, 14, 118, 122,
    130, 132–36, 134*fig.*, 170; racial
    dynamics of, 132–34, 135–36; sexual
    politics and, 134–35, 136–37; Somos
    Hermanas and, 244n50, 246n72;
    transnational feminism and, 134–35,
    136–37. *See also* brigades; lesbian and
    gay solidarity; Nicaraguan gay
    movement; Somos Hermanas
Vider, Stephen, 50
Vietnam Veterans Against the War (VVAW),
    39, 127, 160
Vietnam War, 4, 7, 17, 24–25, 28–29, 39,
    44, 81, 105, 160; post-Vietnam War
    anti-imperialism, 73, 74, 77. *See also*
    anti-war organizing; draft resistance
violence: gendered violence, 52–53;
    nonviolence, 44, 94, 114, 115, 161,
    165, 167, 181; self-defense as counter-
    violence, 44–46, 52–53, 62, 63–64,
    73–74, 206n17. *See also* armed
    resistance; collective defense; sexual
    violence; state repression

Waddle, David, 96
Wallace, Howard, v, 79, 83–84
Wanrow, Yvonne, 62
War Resisters League, 29, 50
Washoe people, 36–38, 211n83, 213n105

AMERICAN CROSSROADS

Edited by Earl Lewis, George Lipsitz, George Sánchez, Dana Takagi, Laura Briggs, and Nikhil Pal Singh